The Life and Thought of Orson Pratt

Portraits of Orson Pratt at various stages of his life. Top, left to right, 1850; 1856; unknown; middle, left to right, ca. 1865; 1870; 1875; bottom, left to right, ca. 1880–81. *Courtesy, Utah State Historical Society*.

THE LIFE AND THOUGHT OF ORSON PRATT

by
Breck England

Foreword by
Leonard J. Arrington

University of Utah Press
1985

Printed in the United States of America

Library of Congress Cataloging in Publication Data

England, Breck, 1952–
The life and thought of Orson Pratt.

Bibliography: p.
Includes index.
1. Pratt, Orson, 1811–1881. 2. Mormons—Biography.
I. Title.
BX8695.P69E54 1985 289.3′32′0924 [B] 85-7478
ISBN 0-87480-249-0

For Valerie

Contents

Foreword

To many Americans and Europeans in the nineteenth century, he was the best-known Mormon besides Joseph Smith and Brigham Young. He was the foremost intellectual in the Church. A convert in 1830, the year The Church of Jesus Christ of Latter-day Saints was organized, he was, at the time of his death in 1881, the oldest and most experienced general authority of the Church. He was one of the first missionaries, one of the original group of Twelve Apostles, the official Church Historian, and the leading Mormon scripturist. He was the first Mormon in the Salt Lake Valley, the leading exponent of Mormon doctrines, and for seven terms served as speaker of the territory's House of Representatives. With forty-five children, he was the father of one of America's largest families. But for a brief excommunication in 1842 he might have succeeded Brigham Young as president of the Mormon church.

At long last, more than one hundred years after his death, Orson Pratt is now the subject of a major biography. Seven years in the making, *The Life and Thought of Orson Pratt* is at once a contribution to American intellectual history, Latter-day Saint history, and the history of the American West. Breck England, who has accomplished this *tour de force*, is a native of Salt Lake City, has degrees in history and English from the University of Utah, has served as a manuscript cataloguer and researcher with the Historical Department of The Church of Jesus Christ of Latter-day Saints, has been a part-time editor with Bookcraft Publishers, and for the past seven years has taught history and English at the Bountiful, Utah, High School. He has previously published biographical essays in *The Ensign*. Married, and with three children, he has also sung in the Mormon Tabernacle Choir. As *The Life and Thought of Orson Pratt* amply demonstrates, Breck England is a thorough, imaginative, and resourceful researcher who writes with verve and insightfulness.

Orson Pratt was one of the great missionaries in Mormon history, crossing the ocean sixteen times to preach and write in Great Britain. His effectiveness is illustrated by his experience in England from 1848 to 1850, when he was in his late thirties. Appointed president of all the branches of the Church in Great Britain "and adjacent countries," Pratt was instrumental in building LDS membership from 18,000 to 31,000 and in this two-year period he chartered and fitted out twenty ships loaded with Saints for Utah. While directing the missionaries, caring for the members, delivering sermons to large audiences in the principal cities of England and Scotland, and editing the *Latter-day Saints' Millennial Star*, Pratt wrote fifteen pamphlets on Mormon doctrine that were published and circulated to thousands in Europe and America, and are still regarded as perhaps the most significant contributions to Mormon theology and metaphysics in the nineteenth century. His writings were influential in formulating the Mormons' idea of God, the religious basis of polygamy, the pre-earthly existence of spirits, the resurrection, and the doctrine of the gathering of Israel.

Pratt was more than a missionary and theologian. He was a member of that little band of two hundred Latter-day Saints who marched from eastern Ohio to western Missouri to rescue their fellow religionists in what is known as Zion's Camp. He was active in the negotiations that resulted in the selection of Brigham Young to replace Joseph Smith as Prophet of the Latter-day Saints. He was leader of the advance company of pioneers that first entered the Salt Lake Valley in July 1847 and offered the first prayer dedicating the land to the habitation of the Saints. He was the scholar chosen to make the first public announcement and defense of the practice of plural marriage in 1852; and he was selected to debate the scriptural authenticity of the doctrine with the Reverend John P. Newman, chaplain of the United States Senate, when Newman came to Salt Lake City in 1870. A surveyor, Greek and Hebrew linguist, and a philosopher, Pratt was also a mathematician and astronomer and left in manuscript an elaborate work on differential calculus. His *Key to the Universe*, published in Liverpool in 1879, was an early attempt to stretch the Latter-day Saints' gospel beyond a simple theological pattern, thus introducing a wider philosophical meaning to Church thought.

Part of the interest in Pratt's life and thought derives from the tension that inevitably existed between Pratt the philosopher and thinker and the closely bound community that he represented. A powerful speaker and persuasive writer, with a penetrating intellect and courageous heart, he occasionally presented problems for minds that were less learned and systematic than his own. Brigham Young, whose mind was also vigorous but not as academically oriented, once remarked, after one of Pratt's long disquisitions on an abstract theological concept, "When I read some of the writings of such philosophers, they make me think, 'O dear, granny, what a long tail our puss has got!'" Some Latter-day Saint leaders were inclined to discipline Pratt for public statements that had not been previously cleared by "headquarters." Brigham, who fully understood Pratt's value to the community, replied, "If you were to chop up Elder Pratt into inch-square pieces, each piece would cry out, 'Mormonism is true.'" "Brother Orson," Brigham declared, "I want you to do just as you have done in your apostleship."

We can all be grateful for Breck England's admirably detailed biography and for its fascinating insights into Mormon, Western, American, and British history.

Leonard J. Arrington

Acknowledgments

I would like to acknowledge the invaluable assistance of the friendly and cooperative staff in the Archives Section of the Historical Department of The Church of Jesus Christ of Latter-day Saints.

I am grateful to Leonard J. Arrington and James B. Allen for teaching me so much when I served as a research assistant in the Historical Department and as a fellow of the Mormon History Association.

In addition, I want to thank the editors and staff of the University of Utah Press for their consideration and friendship as well as professionalism in bringing this biography to publication. Scott Dunn, who read the manuscript, was candid and immensely helpful in his suggestions.

Finally, this project would have been impossible without the patient and wise encouragement of my wife, Valerie (Orson Pratt's great-great-granddaughter), and my parents, Jim and Afton England. Moral and financial support came also from the Pratt Family Association and from Mary and Horace Pratt Beesley and Sterling E. Beesley, two of the few living grandsons of Orson Pratt, whose interest helped sustain the work to completion.

Introduction

In his influence on the doctrine and history of the Mormon people, Apostle Orson Pratt can only be compared to Joseph Smith, Brigham Young, and his brother, Parley Parker Pratt. In fact, if he had not lost his membership briefly in the early 1840s, he might have followed these first two as head of the Church. Though he never presided, his works and his words were incalculably important to Mormon history. He was the first Mormon pioneer to enter the valley of the Great Salt Lake; he dedicated the site of the modern city of Salt Lake before Brigham Young ever saw it. He was also the first to announce the principle of plural marriage to the world and he became its chief exponent—ironically so, for his doubts about it led to a five-month excommunication in 1842. Sixteen crossings of the Atlantic made him beyond doubt the most traveled of Mormon missionaries, and his monumental series of theological pamphlets published in the 1840s–50s influenced thousands to investigate Mormon claims.

Even his contemporaries recognized the difficulties in assembling his story[2]—the overshadowing adventures of his brother, Parley; the fact that he never took absolute preeminence in the Church; the scope of his interests and enterprises. All of this was compounded by the loss of most of his journals. Furthermore, the story of Orson Pratt is very much the story of the Latter-day Saints in the nineteenth century. It is a drama of spiritual strength and determination played out against the forces of prejudice and mob violence. His friends and brother were imprisoned; ten of his children died in misery on the plains or at sea;[3] and he himself fought snowblindness and racking ague as he repeatedly walked continental distances to spread the Mormon gospel. Nevertheless, he was always an inquiring observer: his algebra book was warped from waves breaking over it in Atlantic storms. Tramping the icy mud of the Mississippi Valley among four thousand exiles, he wished for a telescope to observe the satellites of Jupiter. In the signs and systems of heaven he found the direction to a new Palestine in the vanguard of the Mormon exodus.

Scholarship was a theological imperative for Orson Pratt, and though he encountered resistance to some of his ideas among the leaders of the Mormon church, he made a lifelong effort to construct a rational theology on the revelatory foundation laid by Joseph Smith. In the currents of his mind, the Mormon world view flowed together with the scientific idealism of the nineteenth century. Like Joseph, he saw the cosmos as a "great school of experience";[4] he found in Mormonism a creed that made sense of the lessons both science and the scriptures had to teach.

1

Exiles into Canaan

> A few centuries ago, when the old world groaned under the hand of tyranny and oppression, when persecution raged against those who desired to be the humble followers of Christ, a great western continent was discovered, to which a few hardy brave pioneers sailed . . . Among these humble pilgrim fathers were my ancestors. Orson Pratt[1]

From his earliest awareness of it, the "great western continent" bore mystical significance for Orson Pratt. Reared in the hilly forests between the Hudson River and the Massachusetts border, Pratt was nurtured north of Washington Irving country in a landscape of biblical and Revolutionary place-names. Around the year 1769, Orson Pratt's grandfather Obadiah Pratt brought his fifteen-year-old bride Jemimah into these environs.[1] The French and Indian War had ended and the revolutionary impulse was already stirring in the cities. According to the Old Testament prophet Obadiah, the "exiles of Israel" would someday possess Canaan; perhaps Obadiah Pratt felt that he was fulfilling a prophecy as he moved his family into Canaan Township, Columbia County, New York. This "Canaan" in "Columbia," the promised land of the New World, became the birthplace of Obadiah's eleven children, including Orson Pratt's father Jared.[2]

The Pratts were of solid New England Puritan stock, inheriting a tradition of spiritual exile. Daniel Boorstin has noted of the Puritans that "the basic reality in their life was the analogy with the Children of Israel. They conceived that by going out into the wilderness, they were reliving the story of Exodus."[3] The Exodus pattern was repeated again and again in the history of Orson Pratt's ancestors.

Obadiah Pratt was fourth in descent from Nonconformists who had fled to the Massachusetts Bay Colony in 1633. Lt. William Pratt and his brother, John Pratt, emigrated from Stevenage, Hertfordshire, England, during the wave of civil and religious persecution by King Charles's famous Star Chamber.[4] The Pratts found brief refuge in New Towne, a three-year-old village northwest of Boston, later to become Cambridge.[5] In the same year, possibly in the same company, the Reverend Thomas Hooker arrived.[6] Hooker had fled from the Royal Court of High Commission, which had indicted him for nonconformist preaching, but soon found himself chafing against the strict theological discipline exercised by the presbyters of Massachusetts Bay—John Cotton in particular.[7] Hooker and Cotton were both products of the Puritan schools of divinity at Cambridge University, and Hooker disputed his associate's right to dictate to the churches.[8] So Hooker contemplated another move, this time deeper into the wilderness, where liberty of conscience would find fewer constraints.[9] He found ready disciples in the Pratts, who quit New Towne in 1636, leaving Cotton and Massachusetts Puritanism behind. The Bay colonies soon developed into a rigid intellectual dictatorship.

Like the Pratts, Thomas Hooker was of obscure origin, a man who had waited on tables to obtain his education. He was well known as a lecturer, which in those days connoted "agitator," with a penchant for preaching the "new gospel of free judgment in religious matters."[10] Hooker is known to have taught nonconformism throughout East Anglia, the home country of the Pratts, and it is very likely that the brothers sailed for America when Hooker did.[11] By escaping with Hooker's congregation from the oligarchic rule of the eldership of Boston, they reaffirmed the principle of religious self-determination implicit in Hooker's conception of Congregationalism: "And whereas it hath been charged upon the people, that through their ignorance and unskilfulnesse, they are not able to wield such priviledges, and therefore not fit to share in . . . power, The Lord hath promised: To take away the vail from all faces . . . the *weak* shall be as David, and David as an Angel of God . . . The church of Visible Saints confederating together to walk in the fellowship of the faith . . . is *Totum essentiale*."[12]

Hooker's rejection of priestly authority derived from his belief in a voluntary Christian confederation. Because this meant escape was justified wherever spiritual tyranny asserted itself,[13] his Connecticut community soon became an ensign of religious independence in New England. Along with Roger Williams's colony at Rhode Island,[14] Hooker's settlement of Hartford, which William Pratt helped to establish, became a fountainhead of the democratic principles that gave rise to the revolutionary spirit in America.[15]

Rooted as they were in English liberalism, the Pratt brothers belonged to the community which drew up the Fundamental Orders of Connecticut, one of the first commonwealth charters in history, promulgated in 1639. The brothers shared Hooker's belief that a confederation of the "saints" was all that was essential for church and civil government[16]—the Connecticut code agreed, thus becoming "the first written constitution of modern democracy."[17] The Pratts' role in the Connecticut experiment was significant to the intellectual and spiritual heritage of their descendants.[18]

William Pratt soon left Hartford for the Connecticut shore where he met and married Elizabeth Clark of "Saye Brooke."[19] He was awarded a hundred acres along the Connecticut River mouth for his services in the Pequot War, and for over a century the Pratt family flourished at Saybrook (as late as 1864, Pratts still made up a large part of the population of that town).[20] William served twenty-three sessions in the Connecticut Assembly between 1666 and 1678[21] and helped support the Congregational church at Saybrook.[22] Joseph Pratt, the third child of William, fathered thirteen children, one of whom, another William, married a Hannah Hough, a descendant of the famous pioneer New England preacher John Lathrop. William and Hannah Pratt were the parents of Christopher Pratt, born November 4, 1712.[23]

After four generations of settlement, the Connecticut of Christopher Pratt was no longer a refuge of religious toleration. The social order had become "relatively static," in the words of Richard L. Bushman, and church discipline was as severe here as in Massachusetts.[24] Madam Sarah Kemble Knight, a Boston traveler, noted in 1704 that the people of Connecticut were "Govern'd by the same Laws as wee in Boston, (or little differing,) thr'out this whole Colony of Connecticot, And much the same way of Church Government, and many of them good Sociable people, and I hope Religious too: but a little too much Independant in their principalls." This last was probably a reference to the colonists' chafing under the dictatorial tendencies of the ministers.[25] The controversy focused on the hometown of the Pratts when the "Saybrook Platform" was adopted in 1708. This reformation of church government established a "consociation" in each county—a presbyterian administration—that greatly strengthened the power of the ministers. Many colonists repudiated the platform and called for a return to congregationalism.[26] Bushman notes that "consociations were anathema" and to many represented "the powers of darkness."[27]

The Saybrook Platform was only one source of religious difficulty to the majority of Connecticut residents; indeed, as Milton V. Backman, Jr., has pointed out, all New England at this time was in a process of "dechristianization."[28] From the beginning, the Puritans had insisted on strict rules for church membership, including stiff interrogation and blameless conduct.[29] The solid front of the Congregational church effectively blocked conscientious dissent and excommunications were frequent. These factors, along with growing materialism and rural isolation, led to increasing disaffection with the church throughout the eighteenth century.[30] The forebears of Orson Pratt left the New England church during this period.

The reactionary church, along with limited farming opportunities in Connecticut, made the relative freedom of the territory east of the Hudson inviting.[31] When wheat farming failed in Connecticut in the 1740s,[32] Christopher Pratt, in his middle years, left the century-old homestead at Saybrook and moved on as his great-grandfather had. About this time, Obadiah Pratt, the second of his four sons, was born September 14, 1742.

Obadiah Pratt established himself in Canaan—in the foothills of the Green Mountains, where the Hudson narrows above Dutchess County—at twenty-seven. His wife, Jemima, gave birth there to Jared, the first of seven sons, November 25, 1769. The Pratts took up wheat farming during the war. No doubt attracted by tales of Hudson Valley prosperity, Obadiah Pratt and his sons nevertheless watched their fortunes sag. Although agriculture expanded during the Revolution, many individual farmers sank into difficulty. A devastating deflation forced debt-ridden farmers into the employ of more stable landowners[33]—which may have been the case with Jared Pratt as he attempted to "earn the scanty means of subsistence" by hard labor for others.[34] Jared's father apprenticed him to a weaver, probably because serious attempts at flax production were being made throughout the region.[35] But with the advent of the mechanized textile industry in the 1790s,[36] "hand looms were mostly dispensed with . . . Weavers, therefore, were thrown out of employment."[37]

Canaan, however, remained their home. In the upper stretches of the township the Shakers had established a gristmill at the foot of Mount Lebanon[38] and the cultivation of wheat remained barely profitable. Jared Pratt married early in the 1790s, just as conditions began to worsen for the small farmer and the demand for weaving dropped. Jared's first wife, Polly Carpenter, was a native of the township. There she died, too, at the birth of a daughter, Mary, in February of 1793.[39] The young, unemployed weaver took his little daughter away and decided to try farming.

The year 1799 found Jared courting Charity Dickinson of Bolton Landing, a small Lake George settlement. On July 7 he married her. With Charity another infusion of New England notables came into the line of Orson Pratt. Samuel and Huldah Dickinson,[40] her parents, were descended from the Mayflower immigrants John Howland and Elizabeth Tilley, and, through grandmother Mary Cole, from Anne Marbury Hutchinson, the brilliant rebel exile of Boston.[41] In 1637, not long after Lt. William Pratt's departure from Massachusetts Bay, Anne Hutchinson had struggled with the same forces that had exasperated the Hooker colony. Banished from Boston, she, her husband, and several of her thirteen children were massacred by Indians[42] near what is now Pelham Bay Park in New York City. Anne Hutchinson owed her isolation to her freethinking religion, her belief that faith alone, not "hard tests," was necessary for salvation,[43] and, probably more to the point, for "slighting the ministers" and defying their authority. Mistress Hutchinson had eloquently led the so-called Antinomian Schism in Boston in the 1630s, holding to the doctrine of "inner light" and disregarding what she considered "the lesser laws." That she insisted on the right of the individual conscience to guidance by direct inspiration from heaven is borne out in the document which reported her trial: "The ground work of her revelations is the immediate revelation of the spirit, and not by the ministry."[44] She and her family were cast out for these beliefs.[45] The only survivor of the 1643 massacre was Susanna Hutchinson, bride of John Cole and ancestor of Charity Dickinson Pratt.[46]

Jared and Charity Pratt shared a heritage of religious dissent and a belief in strong religious individualism. Orson Pratt testified that, though he and his brothers were taught every principle of honesty

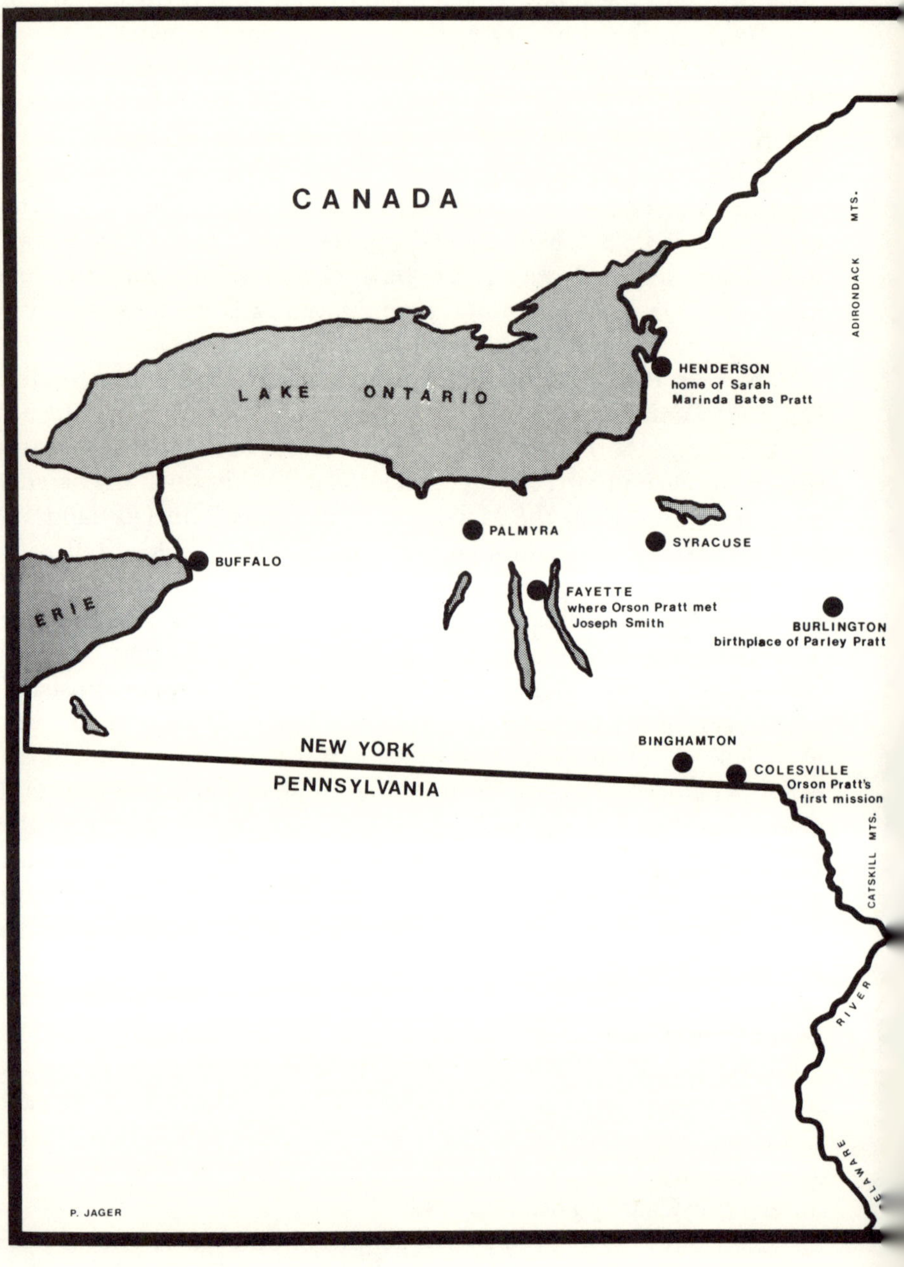

Sites connected with Orson Pratt's early life.

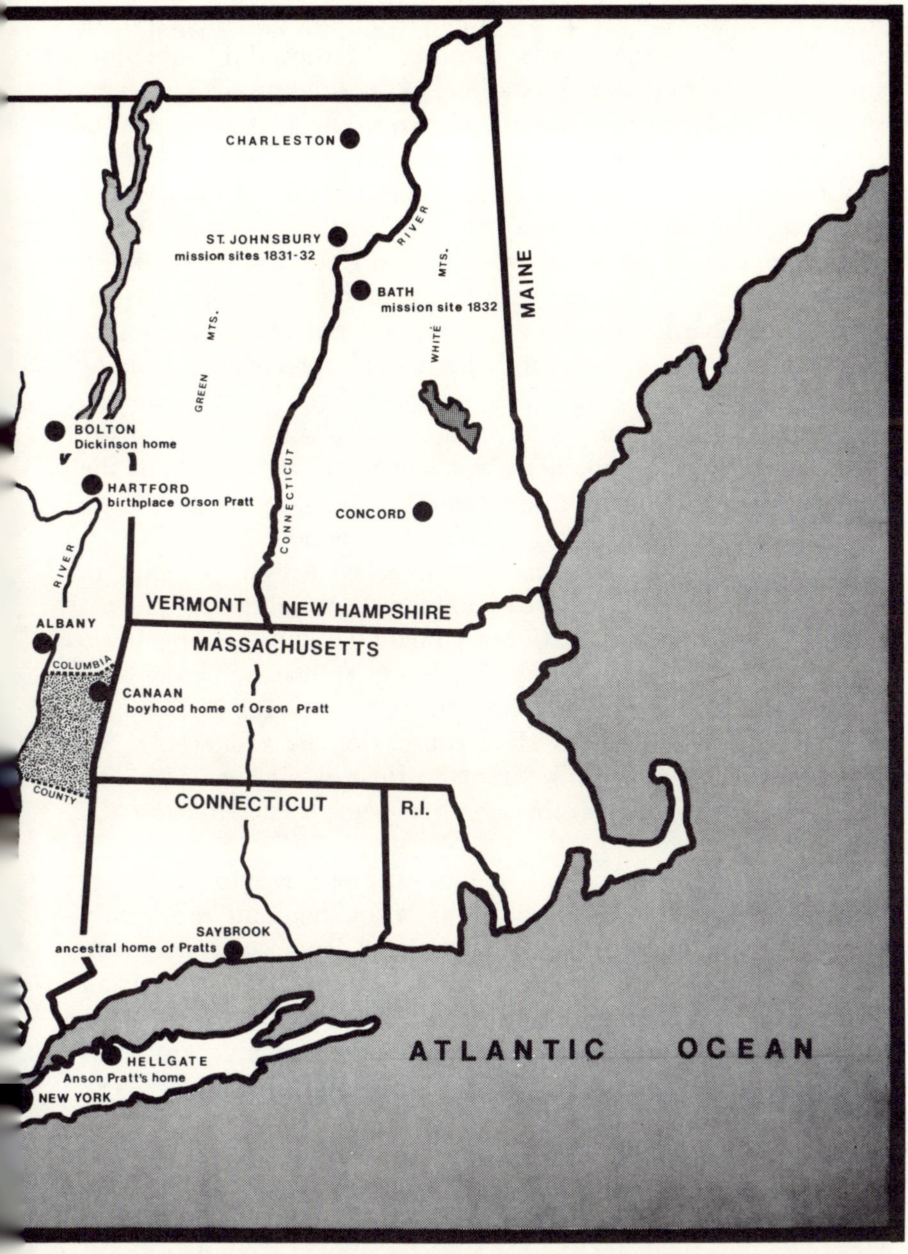
CHARLESTON
ST. JOHNSBURY
mission sites 1831-32
BATH
mission site 1832
MAINE
WHITE MTS.
GREEN MTS.
CONNECTICUT RIVER
BOLTON
Dickinson home
HARTFORD
birthplace Orson Pratt
CONCORD
RIVER
VERMONT
NEW HAMPSHIRE
ALBANY
MASSACHUSETTS
COLUMBIA COUNTY
CANAAN
boyhood home of Orson Pratt
CONNECTICUT
R.I.
SAYBROOK
ancestral home of Pratts
HELLGATE
Anson Pratt's home
NEW YORK
ATLANTIC OCEAN

and morality, his parents had "no faith in the modern sectarian principles of Christianity."[47] This is corroborated in the autobiography of Parley P. Pratt, Orson's older brother: "father did sometimes manifest a decided disapprobation of a hireling clergy, who seemed . . . to prefer the learning of man to the gifts and power of the Holy Ghost."[48] This hardworking couple, cursed with poverty in an abundant land, taught their children faith in the right of each individual to his own inner light. As exiles in Canaan, they helped nourish the culture of democracy and religious individualism in which Joseph Smith's restoration movement could take root.

Jared and Charity Pratt wandered throughout eastern New York for several years looking for land that would open up the "bright prospects of wealth" that continually eluded them.[49] Jared's travels, documented in the scattered birthplaces of his sons, ceased in the vicinity where they began, near New Lebanon, New York. In the meantime, he and his wife farmed one little patch after another in thin upland valleys similar to Jared's home ground.

Jared and Charity's first son was christened Anson (probably in honor of Columbia County state assemblyman Anson Pratt)[50] and according to Orson's record was born January 9, 1801. It seems likely that the boy was born in Canaan Township. Anson, eventually baptized into the Mormon church through Orson's efforts, was Orson's senior by ten years and his close companion in adolescence. To Anson's credit, he lodged his parents in their old age and was with them when they died, the other children being scattered across the continent.[51]

The Pratts moved sometime in 1801–2, probably into the forests near the headwaters of the Susquehanna, a land booming with nearly twenty thousand inhabitants by 1800. Jared Pratt was not among those registered in the Otsego County census for that year, but on September 3, 1802, a second son was born in the township of "Wooster" (Worcester), Otsego County, some ninety miles from Canaan. This was William Dickinson, named for the Pratts' New England progenitors.[52]

Parley Parker, the third son of Jared and Charity, was born April 12, 1807, in Burlington,[53] not far from Otsego Lake, in the hilly woods country made famous in the novels of James Fenimore Cooper. Parley, who was older than Orson by four years, eventually became the most famous of early Mormon missionaries—a candid and humorous man, renowned for his forceful, poetic defense of Mormonism and for a streak of millenarian zeal that embroiled him in adventure after mettlesome adventure.

Sometime between 1807 and the close of the decade, Jared and his family braved the Catskills and progressed up Hudson Valley in search of something new. Their destination was the town of Hartford, New York, which lay about twenty miles across Lake George from the Dickinsons' home. Hartford had been settled by numerous Connecticut Pratts in the 1790s, one of whom, Capt. Samuel Pratt, had fought in the Revolution.[54] This was to be the birthplace of Orson Pratt.

Hartford stands near the junction of the Champlain and Hudson valleys on the northwest slope of Bald Mountain.[55] Jared may have been attracted here by the fields of domestic flax, perhaps intending to farm and process some himself. Spinning the fibers represented an important industry here, and Jared's old weaver's training now proved valuable. If he could not earn his living as a weaver, he could trade in the yarn which was produced at home on foot-driven spinning wheels. In early spring the flax was swingled, or threshed, by hand and was combed for the wheel.[56] Hartford, with the Adirondacks on one side and the Vermont mountains on the other, at last seemed the home Jared was looking for.

Orson Pratt was born in this small valley September 19, 1811. The name "Orson" came from a fairy story popular in America around the turn of the nineteenth century. "Valentine and Orson" tells of a foundling prince who was reared by a family of bears, and who eventually saved the sweetheart of his twin brother Valentine from a wicked sorcerer, Agramont.[57] By his own account, Orson lived in Hartford until he was four years old and remembered on one occasion visiting his grandfather, Samuel Dickinson.[58] Bible doctrines of morality and honesty were "diligently instilled" in the young boy from the first.[59] This was one Puritan imperative that had not been abandoned by the Pratts: in Connecticut the law had required all "heads of families" to teach religion in the home, "leading in family prayer, catechizing their children . . . teaching . . . [them] to read so that they might study the Bible."[60] In addition to Bible study and the responsibilities of the farm, Jared Pratt cultivated in his sons an interest in books and music, and was, by Parley's account, occasionally singer and schoolteacher.[61]

By 1812, flax culture was profitably entrenched in Hartford.[62] Trying to break the penurious cycle of wandering, Jared Pratt farmed the silky plants for two years, while his family carded them into yarn. But mechanization brought an end to their hope in 1814 when the firm of Joel and Samuel Downs constructed a water-powered carding mill near Hartford.[63] Jared and his family were packing to leave when they learned Charity was expecting her fifth child; so they delayed their move from Hartford until after Nelson Pratt was born on May 26, 1815.

Although Orson recollects moving in his fourth year,[64] the Pratts may possibly have stayed into the summer of 1816. In that year the explosion of a volcano in the East Indies layered the earth's atmosphere with heavy dust resulting in worldwide temperature decreases. It was thought "the sun was cooling and all mankind would die."[65] Hartford suffered frosts throughout the summer, and farm failures of heavy proportions may have encouraged Jared's removal south.

Jared retreated to the familiarity of Canaan sometime in 1815–16, and it was here Orson grew to adolescence. The old Obadiah Pratt homestead was now farmed by Jared's brother, William.[66] Close by the Massachusetts border, Orson's home in the northern part of Canaan Township became known as New Lebanon after 1818. The nearby hills gushed thermal streams into the valley. Mount Lebanon, one of the Taghkanic range, gave its name to a local hot spring where a popular resort developed around 1820. Lebanon Springs and its hotel, Columbia Hall, became quite successful, attracting such visitors as Lafayette, John Quincy Adams, and Daniel Webster. Notable residents of Columbia County included Martin Van Buren of Kinderhook, a town nine miles west of Canaan, who became the eighth president of the United States (and who in later years excited the contempt of Orson Pratt), and Samuel J. Tilden, a boy three years younger than Orson, who became the governor of New York and a candidate for president. Other noted Columbia County families included the Rockefellers, the Van Rensselaers, and the artist Frederic Church. Some of these names were known to Orson; he may even have been a schoolmate of Tilden.[67]

In New Lebanon, the Pratts sent Orson to school several months each year. He apparently studied regularly from the time of the family's arrival until he was boarded out in 1822.[68] No one can be sure of the name or the location of Orson's first school, but local histories tell of "several select schools" held in an "academy" built in Lebanon Springs. These and other academies in Columbia County were part of the nation's first free public education system.[69]

Orson's education was supplemented by his parents, who taught him to read the Bible when he was very young. He seldom attended church, even though he was full of religious questions drawn from his reading. The Pratt tradition of independence in religious matters was carefully maintained by Jared Pratt, but with an attitude of openness rather than hostility toward the different parties. Parley P. Pratt, confronting his father with questions about sectarian departures from biblical patterns, found his father disinclined to judge them, reasoning that time and circumstances change religious ideas.[70] Nevertheless, Orson's parents were, in his words, "never so unfortunate as to unite themselves with any of the religious sects."[71]

The Pratts did not stand completely aloof. Parley indicates that his family "frequently attended public worship," alternating among the various denominations and "having equal respect" for them all, although Orson noted that "it was seldom that I attended."[72] Until 1820 they visited the only church in the neighborhood, a combined Presbyterian-Congregationalist meeting in an awkward building called "God's barn." Then, when Orson reached his ninth year, a little schism struck New Lebanon. The old "Church of Christ" adopted itself into the Presbyterian councils of New York state, leaving the Congregationalists among them understandably upset. The church eventually split in two, and other sects found the little township sufficiently agitated to begin proselyting. Elder Nathaniel Otis came to preach for the Baptist society in 1820 while the Methodists held services at the same time. Thus the denominational controversy burning over the state flared in microcosm in young Orson Pratt's neighborhood.[73]

This was not the first religious excitement New Lebanon had experienced. A beleaguered colony of Shakers had found refuge there in 1787. New Lebanon soon became the center of the Shaker communities,[74] a highly charismatic society that absorbed many of the local settlers. An early Baptist congregation, for example, followed their preacher into Shakerism and helped set up a commune of farms, a mill, and an arched meetinghouse (with an elliptical roof strongly resembling that of today's Mormon Tabernacle at Salt Lake City) at the foot of Mount Lebanon. Shaker influence thrived well into the

1820s under the direction first of Father Joseph Meacham, the former Baptist minister, and then of his colleague, Mother Lucy Wright.[75] The leaders were said to be prophets, gifted in visions and revelations, hollering exhortations as they led their hundreds of followers in the so-called "Square Order," worship involving singing and dancing. Distant echoes of Shakerism can be heard in later Mormon doctrine: a belief in dispensations of the gospel, degrees of heavenly reward, and the consecration of property for the common good. Shakers proselytized energetically throughout the region, and, along with the other denominations striving for converts, probably kept New Lebanon in a chronic state of religious upheaval.[76]

But New Lebanon had no corner on revolutionary religious ideas. All over New England and the northern states in the 1820s, the conflict was earnest between those who held to the strict Calvinist view that had dominated New England for two hundred years, and those influenced by the eighteenth-century religious liberalism of the Enlightenment. In Boston, William Ellery Channing was gearing up to preach the Unitarian gospel, denying the determinism of Calvin and exalting the freedom of man.[77] The wave of revivalism that engulfed New York state in 1819–20 derived partially from this controversy as well as from the tension between pragmatic frontier "free-willers" and more orthodox ministers from the eastern seminaries heading westward to "revive" the exiles in the fiery tradition of Jonathan Edwards.[78] This was an era when denominational distinctions were tightly drawn, when the zealots of the churches were energetic in mutually denying the "glory road" to each other. Orson Pratt's search for religious certainty may have originated during this time of confusion. He later wrote that his family would have embraced the "Church of Christ, if it could be found."[79]

Poverty was, however, a more immediate problem for the Pratts. A national panic hit just as they were struggling out of debt. The country's economy, becalmed since sharp breaks in 1816 and 1819, drooped into depression well into the next decade. The Bank of the United States (the central government's banking institution) initiated a policy of tight credit, making miserable the lives of petty farmers who depended on loose money in order to survive. While keeping prices down, the central bank at the same time condemned small landowners to virtually no income. By the 1820s, the self-sufficient farm was already disappearing; though many tried to live on the sale of their own produce, the depression stifled their efforts.[80]

The Pratts attempted to stretch their income in the spring of 1822 by boarding out Parley and the eleven-year-old Orson. Usually boys hired themselves to more prosperous farmers in exchange for board, room, and a few hours' schooling each day during the winter months. At eleven Orson was not considered too young to begin making his own way. Parley worked for William S. Herrick, a well-established landowner of the neighborhood, while Orson went to live with a farmer named Justin Jones. Later, presumably after harvest, Orson was boarded out to Mr. Ebenezer Church in the village of Canaan Four Corners, several miles to the south in Canaan Township, where the Pratts had relatives.[81]

As with many young Americans of his time, Orson Pratt began a quest to find a place for himself. He began humbly enough, with "three or four months" of school while residing with Mr. Church. Orson mentions becoming quite familiar with the rules in "Daball's Arithmetic," a ciphering book common to American primary schools in the nineteenth century.[82] Orson Pratt's interest in mathematics continued all his life, eventually leading to some experimental formulae for solving algebraic equations.

Although Orson did not return home to live after his eleventh year, he did not lose track of his family. Early in the spring of 1825, when Orson was thirteen, his brother Anson visited and proposed a new adventure. Anson, twenty-four and footloose, planned to set up farming on Long Island in the meadows near the Sound. After eighteen months on the Church's farm, Orson was ready for a change. He and Anson headed down the Hudson to farm for a "Mr. Greenock of Hurlgate" about six miles from New York City.[83] Since there was no village of Hurlgate on Long Island, Orson probably refers to Hellgate or "Hellegat," an old Dutch designation for the rocks just off Long Island City. Here, on the northwestern extremity of the island, lived the family of John Greenoak IV, a squire in his middle forties, who had inherited in 1821 the estate locally referred to as "Hellgate."[84] Modern New York City has long since invaded this peaceful cove, but in 1825 the island lay green and meadowed, unencumbered except for farms and peaceful villages such as Brooklyn and Flushing. Newtown, the nearest village to Hellgate, had a small academy that

Orson attended for three months where he studied arithmetic and bookkeeping. After one year on Long Island, Orson decided to seek a craftsman's career and was recommended by Greenoak as an apprentice to a New York cabinetmaking firm.[85]

New York City in 1826 sprawled up Manhattan Island with over a quarter of a million inhabitants, gradually engulfing the Old Dutch town in its bid to become America's chief port city. It was linked to the growing settlements of the Great Lakes by the Erie Canal, and, a year later, by other canals to the Ohio and Mississippi valleys. The city was jammed with poor, and many families subsisted on an average of eight cents a day. Laborers earned about a dollar and a half per week in 1831; a common practice in the 1820s was "putting out," contracting labor to widows or children at much less than the market wage for a skilled laborer. Consequently, New York City in mid-decade saw the beginnings of labor unrest and the first strikes against industry. The depression had left twenty thousand unemployed in the city with about fifteen percent of the population legally designated as paupers. Though fortunes were to be made, mostly in inland commerce, New York presented an unkind face to the newcomer.[86] In addition, the summer heat and lack of proper sanitation resulted in annual epidemics. One struck Orson Pratt the moment he arrived; he became violently sick and too weak to continue his apprenticeship. He hiked the six miles back to the relative calm of his brother's home on Long Island.[87]

Well again, Orson decided to give up on New York City and returned to Canaan Township to engage as a farmhand for a Mr. Noise, probably either John Noyes, a state assemblyman, or Nathan Noyes, former clerk of the township. About the time of his sixteenth birthday, however, Orson moved on, this time to cross the country and seek those prospects which had always eluded himself and his family.[88] He joined his brothers Parley and Nelson on a journey into the Ohio country. Parley, recently married, had resolved the previous year to escape the civilized world. He had spent an idyllic winter in Ohio's Black River wilderness, where new settlements prospered by building ships for the lake trade.[89] Now returning for his bride, he also took his two younger brothers to help improve the property he had hacked out of the forest. Together they made their way by boat along the two-year-old Erie Canal from Albany to Buffalo, boarding a schooner for passage to the mouth of Black River.[90]

Northern Ohio was the promised land of the 1820s. The young state, lopped from the Northwest Territory in 1812, lay largely untouched. The settlers lived on venison, turkey, wild-grape pudding, and ironwood bark coffee; Ohio whiskey was a form of legal tender.[91] Despite the wilderness of the country, the green and misty shores of Lake Erie and the timbered hills opened a new hope for the Pratts and thousands of other pioneering Americans. Orson spent that rainy Ohio winter of 1827 boarding with a "Captain" Eliphalet Redington, postmaster of South River (now South Amherst, Ohio) and going to a school operated by Miss Sophronia Blair.[92] Parley lived in Russia township, just south of Redington's home on the South Ridge Road.[93]

Orson did not stay to work his brother's holdings, however. When spring came, he found work fifty miles to the east at a booming village on the Chagrin River canal route to the Ohio Valley. The Ohio and Erie canal system was under construction, and Orson found employment in a hotel at Willoughby.[94] This settlement had become one of the leading towns in Ohio, far outstripping Cleveland in importance[95] until the canal traffic declined in the 1840s.[96]

The new settlers of the Western Reserve brought with them the sectarian uproar Orson Pratt had left behind in New York. Among the notable preachers of the vicinity was a disciple of Alexander Campbell's restorationist theology, Sidney Rigdon, who had established thriving congregations in nearby Kirtland and Mentor. The Campbellites advocated primitivism, a return to the simplicity of New Testament conventions. This readily caught hold among the hardheaded settlers of the Western Reserve.[97] The restorationist atmosphere certainly inspired Orson's brother Parley; in August of 1830, this exile from the civilized world became one of Rigdon's missionaries.[98] Orson, however, was not prepared to make any spiritual commitment. Instead, he broke for the East, retracing the six hundred miles to Connecticut.

By springtime 1829 Orson had completed a great circle. He reached New York by steamer and spent the winter on Long Island with Anson. Canaan Township received him again, and he settled back into his pattern of farming for other men. His seventeenth year was spent in hard work and contemplation. He hired himself out first as a hand for an established family named Haight and then to a Mr. Joshua Lord. There he managed to make enough to board at a school where he studied geography, grammar, and surveying. He grew to "a little over medium height and [was] of sinewy build." Many years later his son Milando Pratt wrote that Orson was "capable of much physical activity and endurance, and had strength far above that which is ordinary. Notwithstanding that he usually showed reserve, he occasionally threw it off, and was not always averse to a little sport with the boys."[99]

Orson's four months at the academy ended his formal education. His sporadic schooling began as a search through the philosophy and physics of his age for the terrain of truth. His desire for religious certainty had also been awakened. Orson typified what Richard Bushman has called "a recessive trait" in the New England Yankee: "a hidden yearning for union with God."[100] "From the age of ten to nineteen," Orson write, "I saw much of the world, and was tossed about without any permanent abiding place; but through the grace of God, I was kept from many of the evils to which young people are exposed; the early impressions of morality and religion, instilled into my mind by my parents, always remained with me; and I often felt a great anxiety to be prepared for a future state."[101]

Such exploration began in earnest in Orson's eighteenth year. After long hours on the Lords' farm, Orson "often retired to some secret place in the lonely fields or solitary wilderness" while others slept, bowing and praying for hours "with broken heart and contrite spirit" which was his "comfort and delight." While brother Parley was finding a measure of consolation in the Campbellite ministry, Orson remained aloof from the sectarianism his father had also skirted, exercising his devotions in solitude.[102]

Like many of his neighbors, Orson was actually seeking a revelatory conversion experience. "The greatest desire of my heart," he wrote, "was for the Lord to manifest His will concerning me." By his own account, his fervent seeking occupied a year's energies, and it often left him in uncertain health. An earnest inner quest, fueled by the fever of revivalism, was replacing the wandering of his boyhood.

In fact, New Lebanon had become the focus of a sweeping religious controversy in 1827 when the town hosted a summertime conference of evangelists. The most famous preachers of the day converged on Columbia Hall, ostensibly to create a solid bloc against both Calvinism and Unitarianism. However, the conference smoldered with confrontation and turned into perhaps the greatest revival show ever seen. Lyman Beecher, fresh from his pulpit in Boston, engaged Charles Grandison Finney in hot arguments over the liberal theology he represented. The uncompromising Finney was recognized as the first of the great cross-denominational evangelists, having made his reputation with the mass conversion that attended his 1826 revival in Buffalo. Finney's perspective of the gospel electrified the conference at New Lebanon. Whether Orson Pratt was aware that his neighborhood served briefly as the epicenter of the religious tremors of the age is unknown, but he may have gone to the meetings and heard Finney ignite the fires of conversion.[103]

In the ensuing years, Canaan and neighboring New Lebanon "got religion." Finney had popularized "the Arminianized Calvinism called evangelicalism" throughout the "burned-over district"—a theology that fit, in Klaus J. Hansen's words, "hand in glove with the individualistic rhetoric of Jacksonian America."[104] The Presbyterians, following Finney's lead, split from an indifferent union with the Congregationalists, for whom Orson's employer, Joshua Lord, served as deacon. A new Baptist meetinghouse went up in 1830 not far from Canaan Four Corners. Frequent Methodist revivals led to the construction of the Canaan Methodist Episcopal Church near Queechy on the borders of the township.[105] Between the ecstasies of the Shakers and the revivalism of the Protestants, Orson Pratt was undoubtedly affected by the controversies of the "burned-over district."

While Orson carried out his nighttime supplications through the summer of 1830, his brother Parley wrestled with "the darkness of myself."[106] Parley felt moved by the Holy Spirit to return to his native place as a Campbellite missionary and reluctantly cut himself loose from the homestead in Ohio. Nearly penniless, he shipped to Buffalo by offering to take the helm when the hands were off duty. He arrived at Rochester and felt constrained to stop in the neighborhood of Bloomfield. Here, some miles south of the canal, he began making preaching appointments. Elijah Hamlin, a deacon of the local Baptist congregation,[107] entertained the young Campbellite with the story of Joseph Smith's "golden bible," a copy of which he had just acquired. The next day Parley borrowed Hamlin's copy of the Book of Mormon (only six months in print) and immediately became excited by its message. He soon sought baptism at the hands of Hyrum Smith of Palmyra, New York, brother of the Mormon prophet-translator Joseph Smith, who was then living in Pennsylvania. After confirmation and ordination to the office of elder, he continued on his way to his original destination in Columbia County. Parley came preaching his new religion in Canaan, "a pleasant and retired mountain valley . . . consisting of farming lands and pasture . . . their summits and bosoms partially clothed with a beautiful forest of pine and chestnut." Few of these "Canaanites" responded, and his father's family chose at that time to maintain their neutral tradition—with the exception of the young seeker Orson.[108]

Joseph Smith's Book of Mormon professed to be the translation of a record written on plates of gold and concealed centuries before in a hill in the Wayne County region of New York state. It told the story of Lehi, an Israelite prophet in the Jerusalem of Jeremiah's time, who fled with his family to the American continent to escape the destruction of Jerusalem by the Babylonians. Lehi's descendants became numerous and, after a period of centuries, were visited by the resurrected Christ, who taught them the pure gospel. The result of Christ's visit was the establishment of a Christian utopia in America that soon disintegrated in apostasy and wickedness. The last faithful Christian, Moroni, sealed up the record of his people for later discovery in the "times of the Gentiles." Joseph Smith testified that this same Moroni, an angelic messenger, revealed the location of the record and prepared Joseph for its miraculous translation.

For Orson Pratt, the book represented an answer to his prayers—a check against the historical-theological intricacies that had entangled every verse of the Bible in denominational dispute. The immediate appeal of the Book of Mormon to both Parley and Orson lay in its authoritative response to the dogmatic conflicts of the day. As Orson Pratt wrote twenty years later, "Uncertainty and ambiguity have been the principal cause of all the divisions of modern Christendom. The only way to remedy this great evil, is to obtain another revelation of the gospel . . . Such a revelation is the Book of Mormon; the most infallible certainty characterizes every ordinance and every doctrinal point revealed in that book. In it there is no ambiguity—no room for controversy."[109]

The new scriptures could not fail to appeal to Orson. As he listened to his brother preach, he also became convinced of the divine authenticity of Joseph Smith's restored church. He had faithfully prayed for a year, and the teachings of Joseph Smith represented the divine revelation he had sought. He broke a long lineal tradition of religious independence when he accepted baptism at the hands of his brother Parley on his nineteenth birthday, September 19, 1830.[110] The significance of the date did not escape him: he ever afterward spoke with quiet pride of his "rebirth day."[111] In 1859 he summarized these events in a discourse at the old Tabernacle in Salt Lake City:

> For about one year before I heard of this Church, I had begun seriously in my own mind to inquire after the Lord. I had sought him diligently—perhaps more so than many others that professed to seek him. I was so earnest and intent upon the subject of seeking the Lord, when I was about eighteen years of age, and from that until I was nineteen, when I heard this Gospel and received it, that I did not give myself the necessary time to rest. Engaged in farming and laboring, too, by the month, I took the privilege, while others had retired to rest, to go out into the fields and wilderness, and there plead with the Lord, hour after hour, that he would show me what to do—that he would teach me the way of life, and inform and instruct my understanding. It is true I had attended, as many others have done, various meetings of religious societies. I had attended the Methodists, I had been to the Baptists, and had visited the Presbyterian meetings. I had heard their doctrines and had been earnestly urged by many to unite myself with them as a member of their churches; but something whispered to not do so. I remained, therefore, apart from all of them, praying continually in my heart that the Lord would show me the right way. I continued this for about one year; after which, two Elders of this Church came into the neighborhood. I heard their doctrine, and believed it to be the ancient Gospel; and as soon as the sound penetrated my ears, I knew that if the Bible was true, their doctrine was true. They taught not only the ordinances, but the gifts and blessings promised the believers, and the authority necessary in the Church in order to administer the ordinances. All these things I received with gladness . . . I rejoiced with great joy, believing that the ancient principles of the Gospel were restored to the earth—that the authority to preach it was also restored. I rejoiced that my ears were saluted with these good tidings while I was yet a youth, and in the day, too, of the early rising of the kingdom of God. I went forward and was baptized. I was the only individual baptized in that country for many years afterward.[112]

And so Orson Pratt at nineteen embarked on a life very much like that of his ancestors, a tradition of spiritual exile: he was "the only person in the country who . . . obeyed the message."[113] He had found the regeneration of the Holy Spirit which he had sought—and equally important, the certain conviction of the truth. Like many Americans of his time, such a conviction represented for him a reaction against what Klaus J. Hansen calls "the headlong retreat" of "external religious authority" in the face of individualism and the forces of "internal consciousness."[114] But even within the bounds of his adopted church, where he rose near the summit of its leadership, Orson Pratt remained isolated, curiously and assertively set apart in his independence of mind—a twofold exile from Canaan.

2

Imminent Kingdom

An early engraving of Orson Pratt reveals a congenial face, long, with arched cheekbones and a high left eyebrow; as a young man he was slender, of medium height and weight. John Henry Evans wrote of Orson, "In his early manhood his countenance was strikingly beautiful, and was not unlike Hoffman's head of Christ in its general expression." He had a "highly intellectual face," and shared the brown hair and dark blue eyes of his brother Parley.[1] The resemblance was not otherwise notable: Parley was thicker, fuller of face, and, according to one biographer, "compactly built and well muscled from hard work."[2]

The ministries of the two brothers, while equally far reaching, contrasted in style as well. Parley was an audacious preacher: he once preached the Book of Mormon to a deaf man so loudly that he attracted the attention of an entire hotel lobby.[3] And when he was brought into court for unruly conduct, he answered the charges with an offer to pray for the souls of his persecutors.[4] But the rationality of the new gospel served Orson as passion and poetry served his brother. Orson preferred calm and reasoned presentations; at the same time, he was equally courageous in his advocacy of the message. Orson was capable of heated expression of his feeling, particularly in self-defense—whether of the kingdom or his own independence of thought.

Soon after his baptism, Orson and his brother—both devoted now to the preparation of the millennial kingdom—parted for a few

An engraving of Orson Pratt, ca. 1850, by Frederick Hawkins Piercy. Courtesy, Utah State Historical Society.

days. Parley preached to the Shaker colony nearby and was discouraged by his reception. Returning by road, he had a vision of the Masonic square and compass in the sky, which he interpreted as a sign of the Lord's coming.[5] This personal assurance of the imminence of Christ's advent inspired in Parley a millennial fervor which later touched Orson. Together, they decided to join the body of the Mormon church, at the time about a hundred in number, in western New York—a two-hundred-mile walk. Here they encountered for the first time the "Seer," Joseph Smith, translator of the Book of Mormon and "first elder" of the "Church of Christ." Parley met the Prophet at the Smith farm in Manchester, describing him as tall and well built, of mild countenance and a simple, native eloquence.[6] This impression was a common one, shared by acquaintances of Joseph Smith such as Governor Thomas Ford of Illinois, who described the prophet as "full six feet high, strongly built, and uncommonly well muscled."[7] Orson's first encounter with Joseph Smith took place at Fayette, the birthplace of the Church, at the Peter Whitmer farm. Orson soon became "intimately acquainted" with Joseph, and also with the witnesses of the Book of Mormon, Oliver Cowdery, David Whitmer, and Martin Harris.[8]

The Joseph Smith whom Orson met in October 1830 had encountered much opposition in the six months since the organization of the Church. He had been tried twice in New York courts for disorderliness and had dealt with two potential schisms in the Church.[9] But, though Joseph was a beleaguered man, he was filled with visions of millennial glory. His followers had heard the ancient second-advent prophecies expounded all their lives; now here was a teacher who could provide every man a personal part in the culmination of sacred history. Many had asked the Prophet to inquire of the Lord in their behalf and were answered with calls to the ministry and warnings of tribulation to come. But the clearest theme of all in the 1830 revelations was the nearness of the kingdom.

Revelations had been directed to Parley, the Whitmer brothers, Ziba Peterson, Ezra Thayre, and Northrop Sweet.[10] Orson approached the Prophet on November 4 to request instruction for him. Accordingly, the Prophet delivered to Orson Pratt the revelation now published as section 34 of the *Doctrine and Covenants*:

> My son Orson, hearken and hear and behold what I, the Lord God, shall say unto you, even Jesus Christ your Redeemer;

> The light and the life of the world, a light which shineth in darkness and the darkness comprehendeth it not;
> Who so loved the world that he gave his own life, that as many as would believe might become the sons of God. Wherefore you are my son;
> And blessed are you because you have believed;
> And more blessed are you because you are called of me to preach my gospel—
> To lift up your voice as with the sound of a trump, both long and loud, and cry repentance unto a crooked and perverse generation, preparing the way of the Lord for his second coming.
> For behold, verily, verily, I say unto you, the time is soon at hand that I shall come in a cloud with power and great glory.
> And it shall be a great day at the time of my coming, for all nations shall tremble.
> But before that great day shall come, the sun shall be darkened, and the moon be turned into blood; and the stars shall refuse their shining, and some shall fall, and great destructions await the wicked.
> Wherefore, lift up your voice and spare not, for the Lord God hath spoken; therefore prophesy, and it shall be given by the power of the Holy Ghost.
> And if you are faithful, behold, I am with you until I come—
> And verily, verily, I say unto you, I come quickly. I am your Lord and your Redeemer. Even so. Amen.[11]

Orson studied the implications of this message throughout his life. It was an affirmation of the fatherhood of God, a theme that would later dominate many of Pratt's writings. Joseph reveals God as the outpouring of light in darkness, paraphrasing the first chapter of John, for Pratt a solemn vindication of his dark hours of prayer. Where Parley had been admonished to be "meek and lowly of heart," Orson was encouraged to shout the message with trumpet tones, for "the time is soon at hand that I shall come in a cloud." The apocalyptic theme of this revelation, drawing its imagery from the Bible (Revelation 1:7), appears to have "formed the basis of his eschatology."[12] Thereafter Orson believed that the coming of the Lord was indeed imminent. His voice was to be raised to that millennial strain "both long and loud."

For three weeks Orson stayed with the Prophet while his brother Parley headed west on the first mission to the Indian frontier where "the city (of Zion)" would be built.[13] For the Mormons the Indian mission represented the beginning of Israel's gathering, a necessary premillennial condition linked to the Book of Mormon teaching about the Hebrew origin of the native Americans. Parley passed first through the Western Reserve where he sought to convert his former Campbellite pastor, Sidney Rigdon.[14] The missionary fervor struck Orson too, but, unlike his brother, he had no preaching experience. Encouraged by the revelation, he was confirmed and ordained an elder by the Prophet Joseph Smith on December 1, 1830.[15] Orson was then sent as an authoritative minister to the environs of Colesville, Broome County, New York,[16] to serve his first mission and "help prepare the way of the Lord for his second coming."[17]

While the eyes of the Church were on the western frontier, Orson Pratt had been sent eastward. A nucleus of Church members met often in Colesville, a village near the Pennsylvania boundary with a little dam and milling enterprise on the Susquehanna River.[18] The town had been frequented by Joseph Smith as a young man, and he had friends there—the family of Joseph Knight.[19] The Knights, formerly Universalists,[20] had found Mormon doctrine congenial (one son had been healed of demon-possession by the Prophet Joseph Smith),[21] but their neighbors violently opposed the Mormons. The Knight and Hezekiah Stowell families had had their fences destroyed and their stock pillaged at the instigation of local ministers. Joseph Smith himself had been tried here before an all-night court the previous June.[22] Spurred on by their pastors, the people of Colesville showed a grim face to "Mormonites." But Orson Pratt began, perhaps somewhat hesitantly, to speak in public meetings.[23]

Pratt evidently found a few listeners. Out of Colesville, a center of a violent opposition and harassment, came the nucleus of the new Zion. The entire Mormon branch moved en masse from Colesville to Thompson, Ohio, and then, to the site of the New Jerusalem in Missouri within six months of Pratt's mission among them.[24] Fifty years later, the site of Colesville village, New York, was a ghost town.[25]

When Pratt returned to Fayette with Hyrum Smith, he found the Church busy packing up for a move to the Western Reserve.[26] A new and influential convert had been made in Sidney Rigdon, and he had persuaded the Prophet that he could find friends there.[27] Orson determined to follow the Prophet to Ohio. Falling in with Samuel Harrison Smith, the Prophet's brother, he worked for a pioneer farmer to get money for the long walk to the Lake Erie settlements.[28]

Orson was only a few days behind the Prophet when he arrived at the village of Kirtland.[29] A hill country, dense and green, Kirtland knew the distinguished-looking preacher,[30] Sidney Rigdon, from his Campbellite days at the close of the previous decade. Rigdon now renewed his proselyting for the latter-day Mormon kingdom, and converts poured in from "Rigdon's flock."[31] In consultation with Rigdon, Joseph Smith began to assess the communitarian experiments Rigdon had tried in the neighborhood.

Hand in hand with the millennial enthusiasm which swept the United States came an eagerness to try reconstituting society itself.[32] Of this era Emerson wrote, "Not a reading man but has a draft of a new community in his waistcoat pocket."[33] This impulse took many forms and emanated from a combination of sources. The earliest socialistic communities in America were formed by primitivist cults from Germany, whose traditions derived from the radicals of the Reformation. Robert Owen, a British philanthropist, had sparked with his theories an experimental community at New Harmony, Indiana, built on the principle of common ownership.[34] Founded in 1825, New Harmony had disintegrated within two years but left behind many zealots anxious to try again. Rigdon himself had read New Testament significance into such attempts and insisted that communalism was a proper expression of any restoration of the primitive church: he had stirred up "great agitation" among the Campbellites over this question.[35] As a result, a number of Rigdon's followers had formed a "family" relationship, patterned after a nearby Shaker organization, on the Mentor homestead of Isaac Morley. Influenced by the account in the fourth chapter of Acts, Rigdon was wedded to this common-property notion and solicited Joseph's approval.[36] Joseph answered with a revelation which agreed in principle with the Book of Acts account but forbade indiscriminate appropriation of common goods for private use. Joseph's vision was an orderly one and revolved around a novel concept, "stewardship," where every man retained his own property within the framework of consecration with the "residue" going to those who had no property to contribute.[37] Joseph's system of accountability bore a superficial resemblance to the associationist principles of Fourierism, according to Arthur Bestor "the most influential and . . . typical of American communitarian movements."[38] Fourier's ideas were in turn drawn from theories espoused by the ultraliberal French Jacobins.[39] Unlike Fourierism, however, Joseph Smith's communitarian theology grew from the spiritual framework he had already established[40] rather than Rousseauvian natural law.

The first attempt to incorporate this "law of the Church" proved even less successful than the New Harmony experiment had been. With the spring of 1831, the Colesville members bound themselves to the new order as they set up their colony at Thompson, some ten miles east of Kirtland. Orson Pratt had lived in this neighborhood briefly three years before and now rejoined the Colesville group, working for five or six weeks alongside the people he had befriended in December.[41] This was the entire duration of the order. It collapsed when an important participant, the former Shaker Leman Copley, quit the order and recovered some lands he had promised the colony.[42] During this time, Orson Pratt also served a brief mission with Lyman Wight,[43] a new convert who had previously headed Rigdon's experimental farm on the Morley homestead.[44] For Orson, communalism remained a permanent ideal—he always felt that the Saints "cannot be made equal in spiritual things" until they are "made one in temporal things."[45] Despite the failure of the Thompson, Ohio, community, the Church did not abandon its communitarian efforts. Indeed, such enthusiasm was just beginning.

Meanwhile news from the Indian mission fired the Mormons with a desire for a "permanent inheritance" where they could await the coming of the Lord and live the new "law of the Church." The Indian borders had theological significance for the Mormons.[46] The thirteenth chapter of First Nephi of the Book of Mormon made the redemption of the Indians a divine imperative, and in Mormon thinking the frontier of Indian territory was the "line running directly between Jew and Gentile."[47] A July 1831 revelation designated Independence the "land . . . consecrated for the gathering of the Saints"; thus, the geographical center of the continent near Missouri's western border became also the "center place" of Zion,[48] the site of the first intensive Mormon mission and the prospective capital of the millennial world the Saints looked for so anxiously. Unfortunately, Zion would not just fall into their hands, as many of them assumed.

The place the Mormons identified as their promised land was already the focal point of a major controversy. President Andrew Jackson had partitioned the territory of the United States into two enclaves, one white, one Indian, with the ninety-fifth meridian as the dividing line. Tribes indigenous to the East were being displaced to the prairie lands west of the Missouri state line. The newcomers, mostly woodland tribes, faced an inevitable struggle with the local tribes.[49] The Mormon incursion was similarly unpopular with the frontier population of Southern whites.[50]

Along with many Mormons who filtered west for the inauguration of the new Zion, Orson and Parley Pratt had been directed by revelation to make the journey to meet the Prophet in Missouri and preach by the way.[51] Parley later wrote of the heat, hunger, and thirst the two brothers suffered in this, the longest trek by far that Orson had ever made. At nineteen he was beginning to taste the hardships his commitment to Mormonism would exact of him throughout his life. Through an exhausting three months, they baptized and organized across Ohio, Indiana, and Illinois, before arriving in upper Missouri. Here they collapsed in the summer heat; first Orson, then Parley, fell ill with fever and chills, for neither one had ever been exposed to the torrid southern climate that constantly threatened cholera and other plagues. The two finally arrived at Jackson County after a thousand miles and at least fifty wayside meetings.[52]

Independence, Jackson County, Missouri, the site of the "New Jerusalem," was one of the westernmost settlements of the United States in 1831, a frontier town haunted by Indian agents and settlers mostly from Tennessee and Kentucky.[53] By the time the Pratts arrived in September, the Saints had been busy in conferences, buying land and laying the cornerstone for a temple on a prominence near the county courthouse.[54] Orson's friends of the Colesville branch had, the previous month, claimed their "inheritance" in Zion, a tract of land some twelve miles west of Independence near the southerly dip of the Missouri River that now marks the business district of Kansas City.[55] Here the little clan of Mormon pilgrims planned to await the messianic age.

Parley, incapacitated by his fever, had no choice but to remain in the care of what he called the "little church in the wilderness." In the depth of his illness, he had a dream, a vision of himself in the whiteness and glory of the New Jerusalem.[56] Meanwhile, after several weeks in bed, Orson chose to return to Ohio to rejoin the Prophet. From the time of his baptism, Orson had proved himself a self-sacrificing disciple, suffering his twentieth birthday in a sickbed on the western frontier. Still shaking from the "ague," he walked back over the same trail, once again preaching by the way, this time in the company of Asa Dodds. October and November passed, then Dodds dropped out in Indiana, but by the close of the year Orson had reached the Prophet's temporary headquarters at Hiram, Ohio.[57]

Eager for an assignment, Orson accompanied Elder Reynolds Cahoon with instructions to excommunicate followers in the neighborhood of Painesville and Kirtland who had fallen out of harmony with the Prophet. Then, at an Amherst, Ohio, conference, Orson was paired with another young convert who became a good friend and a more-or-less permanent missionary companion—Elder Lyman Eugene Johnson. Born October 24, 1811, at Pomfret, Vermont (a few miles from Joseph Smith's birthplace at Sharon), Johnson had been baptized in February 1831 by Sidney Rigdon.[58] Orson was familiar with the country around Amherst, having wintered there in 1827, and the pair got acquainted as they preached together for a week in this region.

When the conference ended, the new church had undergone some careful reorganization. So that everyone would know his place in relation to the coming kingdom, some were called to preside: Joseph Smith was acknowledged, or sustained, as president of the High Priesthood,[59] while Orson found himself designated to lead the "elders' quorum." As the first man ever called to this position in the Church, Orson now prepared for what was to be a two-year mission to the eastern states.[60] A revelation of January 25, 1832, appointed Orson Pratt and Lyman E. Johnson to travel together into the "eastern countries," with the assurance that the Lord would be "with them also, even unto the end."[61] Except for a few weeks in Kirtland on business, Orson spent the period from February 1832 until April 1834 proselytizing in the villages of New England and New York state. At Hiram, on February 2, 1832, Orson was ordained a high priest under the hands of Sidney Rigdon.[62]

Penniless and with one change of clothing each, Pratt and Johnson walked from Ohio through Pennsylvania up the Lackawanna valley (where they baptized four) through New Jersey and New York City finally reaching Long Island. Here Orson found his brother Anson (who had been baptized and confirmed near the end of March) and then stopped at Canaan to visit his parents.[63] But the little mountain states of Vermont and New Hampshire became Orson's principal mission field on this first extended mission.

This part of New England was undergoing dramatic changes in the 1830s. The settlers faced ecological disaster, the result of overharvesting and deforesting. A cholera epidemic in 1832 only added to the misery as many natives of Vermont and New Hampshire escaped to the West by the new canalways. Moreover, New Englanders were finding in President Andrew Jackson a bitter enemy. Their feeling of disenfranchisement resulted from what seemed to them a policy of deliberate sectional neglect. In consequence, Mormons and other evangelical groups brought to New England the promise of "salvation from the social and personal dilemmas of disunity" of the 1830s.[64]

Orson Pratt and Lyman Johnson spent the spring and summer of 1832 in the Connecticut River valley. They found particular success in the county of Grafton, New Hampshire, baptizing fifteen residents within a month's time,[65] among them a later apostle of Mormonism, Amasa Mason Lyman.[66] Crossing the river, the two elders made Charleston, Vermont, their base for a few days in May. Here Orson was confronted with a test of his belief in spiritual gifts.[67] Briefly separated from Johnson, he was asked by a boy named Winslow Farr, who had heard rumors of Mormon healing powers, to come and cure his mother's chronic consumption. Although the twenty-year-old Orson was "inexperienced in the ordinance of administering to the sick," he accompanied the boy to his mother's home, where he found a weak and emaciated woman "to all appearance in the last stages of human existence." Orson asked her if she believed in the Lord Jesus Christ, to which she nodded assent. After kneeling in prayer with the family members, Orson placed his hands on the woman's head and blessed her, assuring her by the Holy Spirit of Promise that "she would be healed and live until she was satisfied with life."

The woman's husband, Levi Farr, jumped from his bed the next morning to find that his wife had disappeared. After searching the house, he saw her outside carrying a small bucket of water from the spring. Weeping, she exclaimed to her husband, "I'm healed! Thank God, I'm healed!" The once-afflicted Mrs. Farr outlived Orson Pratt by several years, dying at age 97 in Utah.[68]

This incident electrified Orleans County, where Mrs. Farr and her condition were well known. The Farr family with their two sons, Winslow and Lorin, joined the Church immediately, accompanied by neighbors William and Zerubbabel Snow.[69] In later years, Orson wrote about the miracle of healing as one of the four evidences of the Restoration movement's divine authenticity.[70]

The missionaries visited each town, moved on, and then returned to ordain men to the priesthood and set the branches in order. This pattern continued throughout the summer. After holding a conference at Benson, Vermont, near the Champlain Canal, for example, the two elders made a long trek to southern Connecticut,[71] only to return to Vermont in the autumn. As winter came, they tramped from northern Vermont through the counties of Onondaga and Saratoga, New York, spending Christmas on Lake George.[72]

Millennium fever was rampant in this district. A Baptist licensee named William Miller was already spreading the word throughout upstate New York that the world would end in 1843. Miller, like Orson a native of Washington County, started his crusade at Low Hampton, New York, just a few miles from Benson, Vermont, in 1831 and was drawing widespread attention.[73] Mormonism, with all its millennial emphasis, nevertheless refused to name a date for the Second Coming. Orson Pratt made fewer converts than the Adventists did in this region—though many of Miller's followers lost interest in the movement when his predictions later failed.

At the end of winter, Orson returned with David W. Patten and Reynolds Cahoon to Kirtland, having "traveled on foot near 4,000 miles, attended 207 meetings . . . baptized 104 persons and organized several new branches of the church."[74] Among the converts were four men who would later become high-ranking leaders, or general authorities of the Church: Amasa M. Lyman, Erastus Snow, Hazen Aldrich, and Daniel S. Miles.[75] In Kirtland Orson found that the Church members were now being called upon to purify and educate themselves in preparation for the coming kingdom. A revelation to Joseph Smith had commanded the members of the priesthood to form a "solemn assembly" of "the first laborers in this last kingdom" in order to "teach one another the doctrine."[76] Apparently, the kingdom was going to come at the crumbling of the republic,[77] for Joseph Smith had announced on Christmas Day that South Carolina's threatened secession would precipitate a series of wars to be "poured out upon all nations." The key to survival and salvation was to "stand . . . in holy places";[78] a "new School of the Prophets"[79] had been organized to serve such a purpose.

Orson boarded with the Prophet and joined the new school upon its inauguration in February 1833. In keeping with the ordinance established for admission into the school, Orson washed his hands and feet "as a testimony unto the Lord that I had warned this wicked generation, and that my garments were clean of their blood."[80] In addition, members, upon entering the class, raised their hands and repeated a salutation prescribed by the revelation now found in section 88 of the *Doctrine and Covenants* and known as the "Olive Leaf." This document, longer and somewhat more abstract than many of the revelations recorded near this time, prescribed the search for truth as the highest purpose of man. The universe in its order, says the revelation, comprises a grand school of preparation for the celestial glories. But the quorums which met as an earthly counterpart to this grand school had first to become worthy.[81]

In February the council of high priests, which now included Orson, received instructions to purify themselves through abstinence from wine, strong drink, tobacco, and hot drinks. The revelation, subsequently known as the Word of Wisdom, constituted a latter-day equivalent to the Mosaic purification offering; those who remembered this commandment would be passed over by the "destroying angel." This prohibition appealed to a growing sense of exclusiveness among the Mormons and added to their feeling of enlightened and sanctified anticipation.[82]

Orson had received "much good instruction" from the Prophet during this brief retreat in Kirtland, but now it was time to resume his calling as missionary to the eastern states. On March 26, 1833, Orson and companion Lyman Johnson rejoined the corps of missionaries who were then scouring New England for converts and by June were back in their old territory near Bath Township on the Connecticut River.[83] Orson Pratt's preaching was mostly concerned with the restoration of heavenly revelation and miracles. These sermons contrasted with those of the Adventists and Universalists who were also active in the region: while one group searched for biblical clues to the millennial outcome with the technical exactitude of the numerologist,[84] and another read the scripture as a great parable, the Mormon elders, by contrast, emphasized a new light, new miracles, and a new covenant.

St. Johnsbury, Vermont, was the scene of another miraculous healing by Orson Pratt on June 15, 1833. Elder Johnson was thirty miles away in Charleston when Orson met the Harveys, a family who had shown some interest in Mormonism. Young Emily Harvey, sick three months with a malady which caused her to vomit blood, was believed to be dying. She requested Orson to pray for her and was healed the instant his hands touched her. Three days later, Orson baptized her along with three more members of the Snow family, Gardner, Willard, and Lucina, who were native to St. Johnsbury.[85] The Snow barn was used as a meetinghouse for the east village neighborhood, and in branch meetings the leaders sat along the high beams with the women sitting in the "bay" and onlookers packed in haphazardly. Hearing the Mormons preach on Sunday was considered a "regular holiday for everybody."[86] On July 20, Orson crossed the border to preach in Potten, Ontario, "the first discourse by the Saints of this dispensation delivered in the British dominions."[87]

After two thousand miles, many schoolhouse audiences, and about fifty new converts,[88] Orson returned to Kirtland, September 28, 1833, to find Church members hard at work erecting the building mandated in the December 27 "Olive Leaf" revelation. The Kirtland temple offered employment to the young missionary, so he spent about thirty days working on the limestone foundations and doing chores for his board and room at Joseph Smith's house before being ordered back to the East. For this mission he was given a pair of cowhide boots worth $3.50 from the committee supervising temple construction. Before he left, Orson preached on the gathering of the Jews and the Saints.[89]

Orson spent much of the following three months in western New York dealing with a minor rebellion among members at branches in Geneseo, Springfield, and Elk Creek. Orson clerked in Geneseo at the excommunication trial of high priest Ezra Landen, who was contemptuous of the more recent revelations of Joseph Smith. Orson's luck at proselytizing was not without hindrances. He preached near Silver Creek, New York, on February 8, 1834, "upon the first principles of the Gospel and the fourth chapter of Ephesians. There were two or three priests present, one of whom (being a Methodist) arose up after I had got through and opposed. After he had sat down I again arose in order to expose his folly, but he being ashamed and enraged would not await for me to get through; but arose up and began to speak in order to make a noise, and thus break up the meeting. On account of this I was obliged to stop before I had answered his arguments, and nearly all the people in the house appeared to be disgusted with his proceedings."[90] This was not the only unpleasant experience of this mission. Orson excommunicated twenty-four members and had to fight off fever, ague, and Methodist hecklers at his preaching appointments before returning once again to find the members at Kirtland despairing over the situation of the Missouri Saints.[91]

The wrangling in the eastern branches over points of doctrine contrasted ironically with the suffering of the Saints in "Zion." The frontier paradise had become a battleground, with hundreds of Mormons dispossessed of their land by Jackson County vigilantes. Angered by a rumored invasion of Mormon "free Negroes" and the theocratic claims the Mormons made to the land, an army of older settlers had forced the entire Mormon colony across the Missouri River in the midst of November storms.[92] The expulsion from Jackson County did not deter Joseph Smith's dream of "redeeming" Zion, however, and in February 1834 he instructed Orson Pratt to go east with Orson Hyde to solicit relief for "our suffering brethren in Zion."[93]

At the conference where Orson received this call, an interesting issue concerning the worship service was debated. Certain members were refusing to take the sacrament from the hands of an elder who disobeyed the Word of Wisdom. When the matter came before the high council, Orson argued that the members were bound to receive the administration from that elder "so long as he retained his office or license," while Lyman Johnson sided with the members who had refused the ordinance. The high council did not address the question directly, calling simply for the revocation of the man's office.[94] Nevertheless, the incident illustrates Orson's legalistic view of the holy priesthood.

Afterward, Orson went proselytizing in western New York only to have his mission interrupted again by a conference announcement calling for an expedition of young men to "go and assist in the redemption of Zion."[95] At twenty-two, Orson Pratt was a seasoned missionary. His millenarian zeal now spurred him to prepare for battle for the "Center Place." For all he knew, this might be the call to Armageddon. In contrast with the lonely foray he and his brother had made in 1831, this march to Missouri would bring together hundreds of Mormon priests, moving against modern-day Canaanites under a latter-day Joshua.

Orson referred to this small army as the "camp of Israel." Appointed to captaincy of twenty men and four wagons, he departed on May 1, 1834, inaugurating the march with a sermon upon the "second coming of Christ and Millennium, and the Saints inheriting the earth forever."[96] Orson reports the journey in biblical terms: "Behold the presence of the Lord was with us by day and by night and his Angel went before us to prepare the way. Joseph often spake unto us from the mouth of the Lord."[97] The camp, although concerned with preparations for a possible armed conflict with the Missourians, maintained their religious fervor and called down many miracles for their own preservation. Where other Christians spoke metaphorically of life as a pilgrimage, the Mormons of Zion's Camp felt themselves to be on a literal "glory road." Orson's brother, Parley, for example, heard a providential voice one morning warning him to awake.[98] Others wondered at the discovery of a "Lamanite" battleground and the skeleton of a "white Lamanite,"[99] a somber reminder that even the righteous often fall in the defense of the kingdom.

Hardship soon overcame the camp in the form of summer heat and disease. The miasmic climate that had laid Parley and Orson low three years before contributed to the misery of the cholera that overtook the camp in Missouri.[100] The spirit that had moved the men to pool all their money and supplies in the beginning now seemed to waver[101] as they toiled in want and fever across Missouri. In addition, two separate attacks on the camp were made at Fishing River. Fortunately, however, the first assault group capsized on the river, while a second was doused with rain and hail and gave up in discouragement.[102] Despite these two incidents, Zion's Camp never fired at the Missourians. Negotiations with the sheriff of Jackson County had convinced Joseph Smith that any attempt to reestablish the Saints in their new Zion would be dangerous and fruitless.[103] Moreover, the scattering had demoralized and impoverished the Saints; no effective means for recovering their lost property could be provided. With the welfare of the people in mind, Joseph established a new high council to reestablish the Church in Missouri. Among other high priests, Orson and Parley were selected to serve on the council July 3, 1834.[104] Orson accompanied Bishop Edward Partridge, head of the Missouri Mormon colony, on a mission through Clay County, instructing and assisting the displaced Saints. The pair advised the refugees to "lie low," to avoid holding public meetings,[105] and to refrain from voting in the upcoming Congressional election. Orson administered to the stricken exiles, many of whom were deeply ill with cholera and boarding with profiteers, their possessions reduced to the clothing they wore.[106] After organizing the high council, Joseph Smith returned to Kirtland. But for Orson Pratt, the epic journey of Zion's Camp was only half over. After serving the high council for six weeks, he resolved to preach his way home, although he himself had contracted cholera.[107] This fifteen-hundred-mile return trip occupied the next eight months.

Undaunted by the disappointment of the marchers, Orson saw Zion's Camp as a vindication of his faith, for "the promises of the Lord were verified . . . we were blessed and counseled from on high throughout our Journey."[108] On August 21, 1834, Orson left the Clay County settlements with his brother William Dickinson Pratt, and the two of them traveled up the north bank of the Missouri toward Illinois. Fighting the fever and convulsions brought on by "over-exertion," Orson often lay down on the wet prairie, unable to walk another step. His brother left him at Vandalia, Illinois, and Orson continued up the Kaskaskia Valley alone, reaching Terre Haute, where he baptized two converts. Here he found former companion John Murdock, a lonely widower and tireless missionary who accompanied him eastward into Indiana. Four counties later, the two elders encountered another pair of Mormon travelers near Indianapolis, Lorenzo D. Barnes and Lewis Robbins, who held meetings around Shelbyville and had baptized several new members. In December, Murdock and Robbins resolved to go directly to Kirtland; Orson remained behind with Barnes and struck southeast toward Cincinnati soon after New Year's Day 1835.[109]

At a sabbath sermon in Brookville, Indiana, sometime in January, a reporter took down his impressions of the Mormons, publishing in his *Brookville Enquirer* an evaluation of the style and impact of Orson Pratt's preaching. After a brief discourse on the compatibility of the Book of Mormon and the Bible before a "respectable" audience at the courthouse, Orson had been invited to preach again Sunday afternoon. He began with a prayer, as was his custom, "an able address to the Throne of the Most High." This was followed by an hour's treatment of the prophecies of the Bible "according to their literal meaning." Orson's literalism and manner of speech impressed the reporter as "succinct and lucid." Orson then expounded on the Book of Mormon, emphasizing its role as harbinger of the "second appearance" of Christ, "when he shall stand on the Mount of Olives . . . to reign on the Earth for the space of a thousand years." Closing on this millennial note, Orson invited debate and was challenged by a Universalist minister named Daniel St. John. The two continued the discussion for three more hours. Each of the debates was heard four times, after which "at the request of the audience, a division of the house was called for on the merits of the argument, and carried in favor of the Latter Day Saint by an overwhelming vote." Though ascribing to Orson a certain fanaticism, the reporter judged him a fluent, logical spokesman: "We have never heard . . . so much harmony in the arrangement of quotations from the sacred book. No passage could be referred to that would in the least produce discord in his arguments . . . If a man may be called eloquent who transfers his own views and feelings into the breasts of others—if a knowledge of the subject, and to speak without fear—are a part of the more elevated rules of eloquence, we have no hesitancy in saying ORSON PRATT was eloquent; and truly verified the language of Boileau: 'what we clearly conceive, we can clearly express.' "[10]

This laudatory judgment was reprinted in the *Latter Day Saints' Messenger and Advocate* (February 1835) with the observation that the reporter must have been "a Republican, and a gentleman." The account confirms the lucidity of Orson's preaching; though his premises were grounded in an uncritical conviction, the arguments he weaved from them impressed onlookers as unified and logical.

Lorenzo Dow Barnes, Orson's missionary companion, gave a detailed account of the methods and purposes of their preaching in the Ohio River country during 1835:

> We . . . proseded towards Cincinnati on Satturday and Sunday evenings being the 3d & 4th (of April, 1835) held meetings in a small village in Rush Co. called Salem We laid before the people the ancient order of things and the great work to be brought about in the Last days according to the Prophecies of the old and New Testament The people listened with great attention & much of their prejudices appeard to be remooved . . . on the 17th arived at the village of Brookville at 4 pm and held meeting in the court house in the evening and one on the next day at 2 00 pm it being the Sabath After preaching had quite a debate with a Universalian preacher by the name of St Johns Monday evening the 19th held meeting in the villedge of Harison . . . laid before them

> the ancient gosple . . . the hearts of many of the people were stired up and numbers were led to seek seriously & diligently to know whether these teachings were so or not The priests of the day used there greatest exertions to put down the Truth but all they could do was to read Newspaper stories call for signs and cry fals[e] prophet fals[e] teacher delusion imposition &c but this has but little affect on the minds of those had herd the doctrine and were honest . . . our manner of teaching the people generly was—in the first place to lay before them the first principles of the gosple faith repentance Baptism for the remission of sins & the laying on of the hands for the gift of the holy ghost these we proved from the New testament to the people were preached and practiced by the Apostles and obeyed by the people in ancient days and Paul says if we or an Angel from heaven preach any other let him be accursed and then by comparring the ancient order of things with the teachings of the preasant generation and left the people to judge who were preaching the gospel that Paul did and who wer preaching a different one Secondly shewed what the power of godliness was and who were denying it proved the nesesity of more revelations where ever the church of Christ is on the earth and then that according to the prophecies there will be more revelations given in the last days to bring about the great work that is to be accomplished And then the prophecies concerning the restoration of the hous[e] of Israel and the means that God will make us[e] of to bring about the great work The covenants made to the Fathers the Comeing of Chris[t] his kingdom and reign on the Earth &c &c.[111]

Orson and Lorenzo continued preaching to the residents of Indiana on themes of millennial light breaking in "darkness and in the dominion of death."[112] His autumn bout with cholera was now past. In Cincinnati by February, he spent the intervening weeks preaching to "large and attentive congregations" in the city and nearby villages such as Fulton and Commingsville. A brief foray up the Licking River in Kentucky resulted in seven baptisms.[113] Although Orson was never comfortable in debates,[114] he had met a few impromptu opponents. Thus, when the Campbellites of Cincinnati challenged him to debate one of the leading lights of the Disciples of Christ movement, Reverend Walter Scott, he welcomed the opportunity. The eminent Disciple apparently had second thoughts, for his agent surprised Orson with an acrimonious letter disavowing any wish to discuss "the falsehoods of Joseph Smith."[115] By contrast, while in Cincinnati Orson received a plea from the editors of the *Brookville Enquirer* to return to that village to preach again. Orson was tied to appointments in the city and so sent the invitation to be published in the *Messenger and Advocate* for the benefit of any elders who might be passing through southern Indiana.[116] After preaching along the valley of the Little Miami River, Orson and Lorenzo left the Cincinnati area on April 20 heading for Kirtland. Four days' journey brought them to Columbus, the capital of Ohio, even then a crowded city.[117] While walking the streets, Orson "caught a glimpse of the countenance of a man who passed, and whirling around instantly, I . . . inquired if he knew whether there were any people called 'Mormons' in the city of Columbus." The stranger responded that he was a Latter-day Saint himself and knew of no others in the city. This Orson saw as providential, for when they went home with him, they found an important notice in the man's March copy of the *Messenger and Advocate*.[118] Barnes recorded, "In Columbus accidentily came accross brother Rudd who lived in the city . . . found by his papers that brother Prat was requested to be in kirtland on 26 being the next Sabath."[119] Orson had been specifically called to be in Kirtland by April 26 for a special "meeting of the elders."[120]

With only two days to get to Kirtland, Orson borrowed some money and took a stagecoach posthaste for the north. Arriving Sunday morning at Willoughby, he walked the last three miles to the site of the conference.[121] At ten o'clock he arrived at the temple works, bag still in hand, to find the meeting in progress and himself greeted in amazement.[122] No one had had any word of him since he had left Missouri, but some among them had prophesied that he would arrive in time.[123] The occasion was momentous, for Orson found that he had been chosen to serve, along with his brother Parley, as one of a new priesthood quorum, the Council of the Twelve Apostles.[124]

Orson Pratt was ordained a member of the original council April 26, 1835, by Oliver Cowdery and David Whitmer.[125] Nearly six years before, a revelation to the Three Witnesses of the Book of Mormon (Cowdery, Whitmer, and Martin Harris) had outlined the calling and responsibility of the Twelve: to be special disciples who were to "go into all the world"[126] Orson and the other apostles suddenly saw their missionary responsibilities expand beyond the American republic. To fulfill the prophecy found in Matthew 24:14, the gospel should be preached in all nations, "and then shall the end come." A revelation of March 28, 1835, had given the Twelve equal authority with the First Presidency, which consisted of Joseph Smith, his father and brother Hyrum, and Oliver Cowdery.[127] Orson Pratt at twenty-three was the third youngest member of the quorum. With the appointment came a renewal of his calling to evangelize the East.

Orson considered the manner of his arrival in Kirtland to be a "miraculous manifestation of the Spirit of God,"[28] although the news that he was to stand in the stead of a modern Peter, Luke, or Paul left him with some anxiety. But it was all in fulfillment of a "great saying" Joseph Smith had made to Orson when he first joined the Church that in spite of his youth he should one day be an Apostle.[129] Of this Orson wrote: "I looked upon the Twelve Apostles who lived in ancient days with a great deal of reverence—as being almost superhuman. They were indeed, great men—not by virtue of the flesh, nor their own natural capacities, but they were great because God called them. When Joseph told me that I would be one of the Twelve, I knew all things were possible with God, but it seemed to me that I would have to be altogether changed to occupy such a great position in the Church and Kingdom of our God."[30]

These events culminated three days later when Joseph Smith, Senior, gave Orson a "patriarchal blessing" in the absence of his own father, Jared, who at the time was not strong of mind "in consequence of his infirmaties." The blessing promised the privileges of Jacob upon Orson's posterity, an assurance that his prior faithfulness would thwart Satan's power over him, and a prediction that he would go to the ends of the earth to "speak forth marvelous things." Most significant for Orson, he was to "tarry until the Savior comes."[131] This millennial assurance climaxed this period of Orson's youthful zeal as a missionary; in later years, when his preaching grew more abstract and speculative, his theories nevertheless remained undergirded by a literal eschatology and the promise of his own personal presence at the apocalypse.

3
In the Land of Middoni

It was clear from the first that the Twelve Apostles were required to dedicate the rest of their lives to preaching the restored gospel. Oliver Cowdery, in his "general charge to the Twelve," emphasized the worldwide scope of this mission: "The greatness of your commission consists in this: you are to hold the keys of this ministry; you are to go to the nations afar off—nations that sit in darkness . . . You must prepare your minds to bid a long farewell to Kirtland, even till the great day come . . . you will need the mind of Enoch or Elijah . . . all nations have a claim on you; you are bound together as the Three Witnesses were; notwithstanding you can part and meet, and meet and part again, till your heads are silvered over with age."[1] Orson Pratt was not present to hear Cowdery's charge, which Parley P. Pratt called the "oath and covenant of the apostleship,"[2] but he assented to it and took it seriously. It became, in fact, the pattern for the remainder of his life.

Orson's particular mission as an apostle was to visit foreign nations, as David Whitmer stressed in his ordination blessing: " . . . the Holy Spirit shall enlighten thy mind; thou shalt travel from nation to nation; the Lord God shall preserve thee, and return thee safe, . . . "[3] The blessing proved to be prophetic, for Orson was considered the "enlightened mind" among the apostles, and despite his many long and sometimes dangerous sea voyages, he always returned safely.

The Twelve were originally assigned to be a traveling high council, to "function officially only . . . where there were no permanent stake high councils." Their first mission was to set in order the affairs of branches scattered throughout the eastern states.[4]

The Twelve Apostles who left Kirtland at two in the morning, May 4, 1835, bound for the East[5] never again showed such unanimity of purpose. Nine of them, including Orson Pratt and his brother Parley, later faced Church discipline; three of them eventually left the Church. The oldest member of the council at age thirty-four, Thomas B. Marsh presided over the other councilors, who were assigned standing in the quorum relative to their birthdates.[6] The four youngest apostles were born in the year 1811; at twenty-three they were enthusiastic as they commenced this midnight mission. However, three of these—William Smith, John Farnham Boynton, and Lyman Eugene Johnson—later fell away from the Church in bitterness. Only Orson Pratt remained.[7]

But trials awaited the Twelve and indeed the whole Church of the Latter-day Saints before the promise of foreign missions would be realized. In the meantime the mission to the East took precedence: The purpose was the redemption of Zion. In the summer of 1835 several thousand Saints in western Missouri were living off the charity of the citizens of Clay County, a charity which was fast wearing down.[8] Joseph Smith envisioned an attempt to colonize as close to Zion (Independence) as possible, establishing a "stake" or "cornerstone" of Zion in Clay County.[9] The redemption of this spiritual Zion required a great deal of money, and the Twelve were commissioned to teach the eastern Saints their duty on this account.

For several weeks the Twelve filtered through New York state soliciting contributions for Zion. Orson preached up and down the Lake Erie shore around Westfield, then through Cattaraugus County and north to Lyons, near Palmyra. Traveling in twos, the Twelve managed to collect donations here and there ($3.50 at one meeting in Portage, New York), discoursing in taverns as well as meetinghouses and private homes.[10] But Orson Pratt was about to collect a different sort of reward for his preaching.

On June 7 Orson and John F. Boynton boarded a steamer at Oswego and sailed a little up Lake Ontario until they reached Sackets Harbor, a little Jefferson County port town not far from the Canadian border with a branch of nineteen Latter-day Saints.[11] Wandering in this neighborhood and preaching at the homes of members, the two brethren made an appointment for a meeting near the farm of Mr.

William Bates of Henderson Township. Orson gave a sermon on sectarian corruption, returning the following Wednesday to discuss the Millennium. A sober village girl, the daughter of Cyrus Bates, probably attended these lectures to hear the Mormon gospel from the two twenty-three-year-old apostles, for she applied to Orson Pratt for baptism upon his return to Sackets Harbor the next day. The evening of June 18, 1835, Orson baptized Sarah Marinda Bates, a girl of eighteen whom he courted by letter for nearly a year afterward.[12]

Orson did not remain in the neighborhood more than a week; however, upon departing for Vermont and rounding the Adirondacks and Lake Champlain, he found himself once again in the northern counties where he had enjoyed so much missionary success. Here the Twelve came together converging on the old Snow barn at St. Johnsbury. Orson continued down the Connecticut River stopping for two weeks in Hanover, New Hampshire, where he lectured to congregations including Dartmouth College students. While conducting meetings in and around Concord, the capital of New Hampshire, he received a message from Boynton asking him to return to Kirtland as soon as possible. He covered the seventy miles from Concord to Andover, Vermont, in two days and arrived in Kirtland September 25, 1835.[13]

The first mission of the Twelve had ended. Following their report Orson and his brother William took a brief trip to the source of the Ohio River with the hope of finding some interested listeners. Proselytizing a little east of Pittsburgh, they found a mixed reception; they were forced out of a schoolhouse in Fallston and Orson "washed his feet" against the village and proceeded south to Beaver and Freedom, Pennsylvania. Unlike his previous encounters with slanders and priests of "bad character," Orson was welcomed here. He was even able to establish a small branch under the direction of a former Campbellite, a physician named Sampson Avard. This talented convert, who had some experience as a preacher of restorationism, later exerted an independence of dangerous proportions.[14]

Upon Orson's return to Kirtland in November, the Lake Erie winter was blasting in. The Saints in this place were relatively comfortable, however, well established and in an increasing majority. They had finished the first story of the temple. With the arrival of heavy snows, most of the Twelve, including Parley and Orson, decided to remain in Kirtland.

Since the purchase of Egyptian manuscripts and mummies in

July, Joseph Smith had turned with renewed interest to the study of ancient languages, longing to be able to read the prophets and apostles in the original. Since for Joseph the source of God's glory was intelligence,[15] the divine imperative to "be instructed more perfectly" in geography, history, and law as well as in the doctrines of the kingdom[16] elevated intellectual development to a position of increasing theological importance. Orson Pratt concurred in this. Searching Hebrew and Egyptian the Prophet sought linguistic insights into the interpretation of scripture.

Orson Pratt began studying Hebrew alongside the Prophet in November 1835 using books procured by Oliver Cowdery. With the intermittent participation of Warren Parrish, Hyrum Smith, and Frederick G. Williams, the school of the prophets turned into a language course with only a Hebrew Bible, lexicon, and grammar for resources. The English transliterations were not always clear, and apparently Orson valued exactness so much that he engaged the Prophet in "much controversy" over the pronunciation of a Hebrew letter.[17] Three weeks later the disputes ended with the hiring of a noted Hebrew teacher, Joshua Seixas of Hudson, Ohio, to teach an eight-week course in the language. Descended from a prominent New York rabbi, Seixas was one of two men then teaching Hebrew in the Western Reserve and had written two editions of a Hebrew language manual for use in the seminary at Hudson and Oberlin colleges. He arrived in Kirtland January 26, 1836, and immediately inaugurated two hour-long sessions each weekday, drilling his students in basic grammar and vocabulary. On February 19, Seixas "graduated" a small group into a "first class" including Orson Pratt, Orson Hyde, Sidney Rigdon, and the Prophet, among others. The only one, however, who received a "certificate of proficiency" from Seixas was Orson Pratt. This rapidly acquired fluency gave him a scholarly edge thirty-four years later when he faced the United States Senate Chaplain in a debate over the correct translation of Leviticus—in front of eleven thousand people. Orson's class had specifically studied biblical translation working over each sentence of Genesis, chapters seventeen through twenty-two.[18]

Orson's enthusiasm for self-education led to a first attempt at teaching school during December 1835. While boarding at the home of his friend Lyman Johnson, Orson advertised an evening lecture on English grammar, which he delivered December 2. He was apparently well enough satisfied with his abilities to teach an evening school for about two weeks following.[19] By February Orson had received his certificate from Seixas qualifying him to teach Hebrew.[20]

Orson's spiritual and scholarly life centered about the new "House of the Lord" at Kirtland. On one level a sanctuary where sacred rituals were performed, and on another level a school, the temple came to signify that glorification of the soul was dependent upon cultivation of the mind. When the Kirtland scholars moved into the upper story in January 1836, the study of grammar, mathematics, and geography became intertwined with the dignity of the spiritual ordinances which were introduced simultaneously into the house.[21]

As the completion of the temple neared, so did the calling of the "solemn assembly,"[22] the principal spiritual purpose for the gathering at Kirtland. In preparation for this event Joseph Smith had introduced the ordinances of washing and anointing to symbolize the holy calling and purity required of the priesthood. Those who assembled in Kirtland for these ordinances sensed a revelation of higher things and anticipation of a spiritual outpouring that would "endow" the Church with the power to fulfil its destiny. According to Orson Pratt, "We were commanded to wash our bodies with pure water and to be anointed with holy oil which we accordingly did and the power of the Lord rested down upon the authorities of the church."[23] This was in keeping with the ancient practice of the priests of Israel, said Oliver Cowdery; after washing with water the brethren laved each other with "whiskey perfumed with cinnamon."[24] Joseph Smith now introduced the ordinance of washing of feet taken from the fourteenth chapter of John typifying apostolic equality and service in the priesthood. This latter ordinance was never widely practiced in the Church; as John Whitmer pointed out, it belonged to the "ordained" and not to the general membership.[25]

These spiritual exercises culminated in the dedication ceremony itself, a week-long celebration of the gifts of the spirit. As the dedication service began March 27, 1836, a "white-haired figure in robes" entered and took a seat in the chamber. In one witness's view it was the Apostle Peter come to accept the house.[26] Frederick G. Williams reported that a "Holy Angel of God came and set between him and Joseph Smith sen. while the house was being dedicated."[27] No mention of these apparitions is made by Orson Pratt; however, the dedicatory prayer of Joseph Smith greatly inspired this fervent missionary. The Prophet prayed that "thy servants may go forth from this house armed with thy power . . . unto the ends of the earth."[28]

Three days later Orson gathered with the authorities of the Church to receive the washing of feet.[29] This ceremony was accompanied by another flood of visions and prophecies. Although Orson apparently did not experience such spiritual ecstasies himself, he speaks in his journal of those who did.[30] The week's activities culminated in another eastern mission call for Orson Pratt, this time extending into Canada. He left Kirtland on April 6, 1836, accompanied by his brother Parley and Elder Freeman Nickerson. By stagecoach and on foot, the brothers made their way to Niagara Falls, as the Lake Erie passage was closed. Niagara made a "deep and awful impression" upon Parley, and he stopped briefly to compose his thoughts in verse, writing a song to the panorama of the falls resonating with millennial longings for the earth to be "restored to its original."[31] Orson records simply, "went to the falls."[32]

After crossing into Canada the three elders went separate ways—Parley to Toronto[33] and Orson and Nickerson to the vicinity of Hamilton, Ontario. Orson's message characteristically concentrated on the eschatology of Daniel and Revelation, the coming forth of the Book of Mormon, and its Bible evidences from Isaiah and Ezekiel.[34] No longer a simple curiosity, the Mormon message had begun to engender hostility so that the accustomed "preaching appointment" platform by which Orson and others had gained access to churches and schoolhouses was becoming increasingly risky. At Brantford, Ontario, near Nickerson's hometown,[35] Orson found himself on the night of April 28 in a crowded schoolhouse when suddenly a trustee of the school[36] named Lewis Burwell rose and demanded that Orson respond to a few questions before beginning to preach.

He answered the usual questions about his identity and affiliation, but balked when asked whether or not he could speak in tongues, rejecting this attempt to draw from him a "sign" of his calling. Burwell refused to be forestalled. He insisted on a simple answer, and many in the congregation began to "stamp their feet and hiss at Burwell" while others took the trustee's part. Soon the whole house was in an uproar, with some calling for a fair hearing and others crying delusion and imposture. The argument continued for two hours and finally came to blows with Orson standing calmly at the pulpit "lifting my heart in silent prayer that the Lord would deliver me out of their hands unhurt.[37] Unable to leave, he was threatened by some and defended by others; soon a delegation came forward and quietly led Orson out the pulpit doors. The crowd thronged after him, and, finding himself nearly mobbed, he ran into a nearby tavern and escaped out a rear exit, traveling back to his lodgings in the middle of the night.[38]

Orson's Brantford encounter was by no means ended, for the next day he was "sent for" by a congregation who wished to hear him and had met for that purpose in a large wagon house out of the jurisdiction of Trustee Burwell. Orson expounded the first principles of Mormonism in freedom leaving Burwell and three or four others who had heckled him in consternation. When the excitement fell off, Orson preached unmolested in this little town.[39] At Boston, Ontario, he and Nickerson requested permission from a Baptist minister to preach; they were refused and so "washed their feet" against the man, leaving an apostolic judgment in the New Testament tradition.[40]

Pratt and Nickerson soon left by steamboat for Toronto, where they found Parley flooded with work. In Parley's words the people "drank in truth like water,"[41] and their converts included such later luminaries as Church President John Taylor and Joseph Fielding.[42] In and around Toronto, however, the opposition was fierce, and the missionaries were often challenged by Methodist or Baptist preachers "calling for a miracle."[43] The early Mormon emphasis on spiritual gifts had been twisted into extravagant tales of imposture that led many Canadians to despise the very word *Mormon*.[44]

Sailing from Toronto in June, Orson left this angry but productive mission field for Oswego, New York. The evening passage found him once again in Jefferson County on an errand colored by a year-long correspondence with Miss Sarah Marinda Bates of Henderson. Upon his arrival at the Bates home, he was "very much enjoyed" to see them. The two became engaged. He writes under date of June 6, 1836, "I had previously formed an acquaintance with their daughter with whom I had held a correspondence by letter and with whom I shortly expected to enter into the sacred bonds of matrimony."[45]

His engagement did not prevent him from continuing his mission. He found Elder Luke Johnson, another young member of the Twelve and Lyman's brother, at the Bates household, and together they began laboring "with their mights, for the cause of God."[46] In fact the wedding, when it occurred, seemed almost incidental to the events of that Fourth of July 1836. Independence Day dawned with a baptism. Orson officiated for seven new members, some of whom, as Orson writes, were invited to "a wedding at Brother Bates'." Those baptized included the two brothers and sister-in-law of Sally Bates, and the entire family gathered for the afternoon ceremony that linked her with the apostle. Elder Luke S. Johnson performed the wedding, which had to be short and simple—there was still a confirmation ceremony to be held that evening, where Orson laid hands on the new members himself.[47]

Orson stayed with his bride only three days and was off again with Johnson toward the villages of Jericho, LeRayville, and Antwerp, New York, where a predominantly Quaker settlement met him with a quiet audience of two. He declined to preach.[48] Remaining in Jefferson County as a missionary until October, he took every opportunity to expound his doctrine of history—that the religious establishments were equivalent to the spiritual Babylon evoked in the Apocalypse. In September he wrote to the *Messenger & Advocate*: "I commenced lifting a warning voice . . . exposing their religious systems by contrasting them with the system of the Bible which not unfrequently produced no small stir, for the craftsmen, not of the great goddess Diana, but of great Babylon, brought no small gain unto themselves by making not silver shrines but religious systems by which . . . they could make merchandise of the people."[49]

In the meantime, his nineteen-year-old bride waited for him as she would continue to wait in later years. Orson dropped in now and then in August, but it was not until October that he acceded to the approaching winter, terminated his mission, and started with Sarah for Kirtland. The steamboat from Sackets Harbor took a little company of Saints to Fairport, then to Kirtland, around the twelfth of October.[50]

The Pratts found Kirtland changing. Prosperity and the influx of new members to the Church had created a pressured economy that reflected the optimism then prevalent throughout the Western Reserve. The completion of the Cleveland Canal and a concomitant flow of staples led to a tenfold increase in the wealth of the region between 1830 and 1836. Houses and commercial building drove Kirtland's land prices to a giddy $2,000 per acre. The city now boasted mills, a brickyard, a printing shop, a dozen factories in all, not to mention numerous little mercantiles that had sprung up in Orson's absence.[51] The young apostle soon began "trading considerably," selling stoves and ironware (possibly for the Lyman Johnson–John F. Boynton store), and he and Sarah rented an upstairs room for a dollar a month.[52]

Business left Orson with some leisure for study, and he relished the winter hours with his copy of "Day's Algebra" and his astronomy readings "without a teacher," he notes proudly.[53] The Kirtland High School, which functioned only a few months that winter, offered lectures in Greek and Latin.[54] Spurred by his mathematical exercises and his former acquaintance with surveying, he became interested in astronomy, musing on the stars with the new measuring tools made available to him in "Day's Algebra." Daniel J. Boorstin has pointed out that astronomy in America went hand in hand with the study of the surveyor's craft: "To survey small townlots and farms boundaries in long-settled Europe, arithmetic with a smattering of trigonometry sufficed, but America offered a whole continent to be measured. The property lines of extensive tracts in the wilderness could not be drawn from a large rock or the stump of a familiar tree; they had to be defined by the astronomical dimensions of latitude and longitude . . . astronomy was a surveyor's tool."[55] However, Orson's attention was soon forced earthward by misfortune—financial disaster in Mormon Kirtland.

With the cold weather came the shadow of economic collapse. Overheated business activity and an optimistic society dealing almost exclusively on credit began to threaten the temporal foundations of the Mormon kingdom. As the year closed an attempt was made to shore up the precarious economy of Kirtland by establishing a bank.[56] This cooperative venture was designed to increase the availability of cash and consequently to facilitate the liquidation of land, the principal asset upon which the credit structure was built.[57] The bank never fulfilled its purpose, partially because the anti-bank legislature of Ohio refused to charter it.[58] The bank soon became a drain on the resources of citizens who tried to save it by pouring in more capital. Orson Pratt, among others, was afraid of losing everything and plunging into debt. As a member of the "Kirtland Safety Society Anti-banking Company,"[59] he soon became disenchanted with Joseph Smith's management and, concomitantly, with the Prophet's leadership of the Church. With Sarah expecting a child and the unfamiliar necessity on him to provide for someone other than himself, Orson was very uneasy.

Mercantile failure afflicted two of the Quorum of Apostles—Orson's close friends Lyman E. Johnson and John F. Boynton. They found themselves stranded with a twenty-thousand-dollar dry goods inventory in the midst of the alarm. Orson Pratt's intimacy with both probably helped lead to his brief period of disillusionment with the Prophet. The spirits of "murmuring, complaining, and of mutiny"[60] increased generally in spring and summer 1837 as Joseph withdrew his backing from the Kirtland Safety Society and renounced its bad paper.[61] Although his troubles can in large part be attributed to the widespread bank failures that dogged the Jackson "Specie Circular" in 1837,[62] many of his followers reproached him as a false prophet and a swindler. Joseph defended himself as a victim of the "united schemes" of enemies and "apostates in our midst": "many became disaffected toward me as though I were the sole cause of those very evils I was most strenuously striving against, and which were actually brought upon us by the brethren not giving heed to my counsel. No quorum in the Church was entirely exempt from the influence of those false spirits who are striving against me for the mastery; even some of the Twelve were so far lost to their high and responsible calling, as to begin to take sides, secretly, with the enemy."[63]

Among those of the Twelve whom Joseph accused of siding with the enemy were Orson's close friend Lyman E. Johnson and his brother Parley. Parley was deeply discouraged by the inflation of land prices, "a scheme of speculation" that he attributed to Joseph Smith's "undue religious influence." In a letter to the Prophet of May 23, 1837, Parley accused him of "lying, deceiving, and taking advantage of one's neighbor." The reason for his complaint was that Joseph had sold him "three lots . . . at the extortionary price of 2000 dollars, which never cost you 100 dollars."[64] Parley's unsophisticated understanding of the market forces at work in Kirtland led him to lash out at the most conspicuous scapegoat—Joseph Smith. Possibly as a result of this letter, Parley was brought before the High Council of Kirtland only a few days later to answer charges of following a course "injurious to the Church of God."[65] Lyman Johnson came before the court on the same charge. Johnson made no response, but Parley objected to being tried by Joseph Smith or Sidney Rigdon. The trial broke up in confusion.[66] The same day, May 29, 1837, Lyman

Johnson and Orson Pratt brought an affidavit before Bishop Newel K. Whitney's court: "We prefer the following charges against Pres. Joseph Smith Jr. viz. for lying and misrepresentation—also for extortion—and for speaking disrespectfully, against his brethren behind their backs." The affidavit was signed first by Johnson, then by Orson.[67] It echoed Parley's complaints almost verbatim, which indicates that Orson's indignation resulted at least in part from his perception of Joseph's treatment of Parley.

Orson Pratt, Junior, was born July 11, 1837, nine months to the day since the Pratt's arrival in Kirtland.[68] With the end of Sarah's confinement, and the dissipation of ill feelings among the Saints, Orson escaped into the mission field. His response to the conditions in Kirtland is unclear: he may at length have realized that, as Harlan Hatcher put it, "the fiasco at Kirtland was only a part of a larger, national picture. The entire country was rocked by the Panic of 1837."[69] Orson had panicked along with a whole party in Kirtland who at first failed to understand that Joseph's troubles resulted from the depressed economy and inexperience in financial matters. In any case he moved his wife and baby back to her hometown of Henderson, New York, in August 1837.

Orson worked six weeks on the harvest, presumably for his wife's family, but left Henderson in October "with an intention of laboring in the vineyard."[70] Farm and missionary labor had apparently soothed his misgivings about Joseph Smith's leadership, as he was sustained again to the Quorum of Apostles in September. Boynton and Lyman and Luke Johnson, who had left their apostleship for "other occupations," however, were dropped.[71] Orson's crisis of belief found salving in what he called the "F.P.G.," the first principles of the gospel.[72] That fall he preached through New York on faith, repentance, baptism, and the gifts; the centrality of principle overcame his disillusionment with personalities at Kirtland. During this healing month Orson found himself under attack—boys pitched stones at him, young men jeered, cursed, and swore at his sermons. He faced the inevitable but always frustrating textual arguments, debating the "necessity" of this or that with the question of proof always foundering on the problem of interpretation. "But we passed on as though we heeded them not," Orson comments, having learned once again the serenity of holding to principle in the face of misunderstanding.[73]

After wintering in Henderson, Orson responded to a call to New York City. Parley, once again back in full fellowship, had worked for months to build up a branch in the metropolis, publishing a tract, "Voice of Warning," and preaching among the Free Thinkers of Tammany Hall.[74] Orson fell heir to Parley's presidency when Parley emigrated to Missouri in April of 1838. New York City was not the most fruitful of mission fields; as Parley wrote, "Of all the places in which the English language is spoken, I found the City of New York to be the most difficult as to access to the minds or attentions of the people."[75] A few months after Orson's arrival, however, he saw the first Saints emigrating from England. Heber C. Kimball had returned from the first mission there with a handful of converts,[76] and Orson's mind may have turned to the vast prospects which would logically ensue from this overseas beginning.

He was not to wait long for word that the entire Quorum of Apostles would be going to England. The Twelve had met in conference at Far West, Missouri, Joseph Smith's temporary headquarters,[77] and a revelation was given instructing the Twelve to labor "across the great waters." But first they were to meet and consecrate the Far West temple site. April 26, 1839, was designated for this meeting.[78]

Events moved rapidly, however, to render the prospects for the new mission not only improbable but dangerous. The conference had also featured an inflammatory speech by Sidney Rigdon which, in the minds of many Missourians, constituted a Mormon declaration of war. As the temple cornerstones were laid, Rigdon recalled the former privations of the Missouri Saints and announced that the Mormons would bear no more tramplings, that the war would be carried into the houses of the Missourians.[79] Subsequently, heat, drunkenness, and political riots set northern Missouri on fire with civil war,[80] culminating in the infamous massacre of unarmed Mormons at Haun's Mill and the arrest and court-martial of Joseph Smith and his counselors.[81] The August 1838 number of the *Elders' Journal* notified Orson of the "great mission" the Twelve were to undertake and requested his return to Zion[82] to make the spiritual preparations required by the revelation before the opportunity passed away.

The Mormon War, as it is known in Missouri annals, continued to blaze while Orson made his way down the coast and around to New Orleans on shipboard with his family. In large part ignorant of the details of the conflict, Orson must have been horrified upon arrival in St. Louis[83] at the news of Joseph Smith's and Parley's incarceration. In November, Orson and Sarah gave a melancholy welcome to a new infant daughter, Lydia,[84] while the Saints a hundred miles to the west were making foreboding preparations to leave the state en masse.[85] Iced in and without money to continue, Orson remained in the safety of St. Louis,[86] doing manual work.[87] A full year of struggle passed before the long-awaited departure for England.

As the drama of prison and trial unfolded at Liberty, Missouri, the Mormons quailed under the armed details of the state militia. Sampson Avard, a convert of Orson Pratt's, had denounced the Prophet in court and denied having led the so-called "Danites" or "Sons of Dan," a group of Mormon terrorists, in Caldwell County.[88] Joseph Smith and Parley P. Pratt languished in prison and watched helplessly as their brothers suffered with disease; once again it seemed that the Mormon community would fail. But the Saints were meeting quietly, influenced by the gathering spirit of Brigham Young, who, under Joseph's instructions[89] led a migration eastward to Illinois[90]—just beyond the grasp of Missouri law.

When the river thawed, Orson took his family up to the town of Quincy, Illinois,[91] where many of the exiles had found a temporary refuge. Brigham Young, now senior apostle, quit Far West in February 1839,[92] and the exodus was in full swing. At Quincy the Twelve met under Young's supervision to consider the purchase of sites to the north—lands in both Iowa and Illinois—for resettlement of the Saints.[93]

Another matter also weighed upon their minds: how were they to fulfil the commandment to assemble at the Far West temple site on April 26? The designated date was only weeks away, and it seemed more and more apparent that any attempt to follow the instruction would be futile. Several argued that "under our present circumstances . . . the Lord would not require the Twelve to fulfill his words to the letter . . . he would take the will for the deed."[94] But Brigham Young was now the "master spirit of the Twelve" and was "not the man to let it [the revelation] fail."[95] He did not hesitate to "obey the revelation in any case"; in order to say that prayer in Far West, they would break once again into the enemy heartland.

Orson left on April 18 with Brigham Young, John Taylor, Wilford Woodruff, George A. Smith, and Alpheus Cutler, the master workman of the temple. They ferried the river at Marion, Missouri, and encamped under the Mississippi bluffs, audaciously defying an "exterminating order" issued by the chief executive of Missouri, Lilburn W. Boggs, ordering all Mormons out of the state.[96] The travelers moved clandestinely toward Far West, keeping their mission as quiet as possible. The roads were full of emigrating Saints threading their way in the opposite direction, and soon Apostle John E. Page came into sight. While he struggled with a barrel of soap that had tumbled from his wagon, the brethren persuaded him to go back to Far West with them. Knowing their trek brought ever-increasing danger, the apostles gathered corn by night and stayed close to the woods. At length they arrived at Tenney's Grove, where Apostle Heber C. Kimball lay concealed, and passed the word that the authorities would meet on the square at Far West in the early hours of the twenty-sixth.[97] They learned that for several days the antagonists of Far West had been exultant at the prospect of defeating one of "Joe Smith's" prophecies.

The night before the sacred day, Brigham Young and the others rode into the city; though it was nearly abandoned, they found lodging at the home of an imprisoned brother. The moon still shone clear when they emerged in the public square to hold the conference commanded by the revelation of July 8, 1838. "All seemed still as death," Kimball wrote,[98] but the active threats of the locals to keep the revelations from fulfillment went unrealized. Without disturbance, they opened the council by solemnly excommunicating thirty-one apostates, among them three of their own quorum. A hymn was sung, "The Mission of the Twelve." Alpheus Cutler then helped the apostles to roll the foundation stone, a ton in weight,[99] to the sacred southeast corner of the temple site. To the five apostles present, two more were then added by ordination—Wilford Woodruff and George Albert Smith—forming thereby a majority of the Council of Twelve. Each apostle offered prayer, and then from this sacramental site, which represented to the Mormon people the land of Zion, the Twelve departed Missouri on an embattled mission to spread the Restoration around the world.[100]

A week later Orson Pratt and the others turned their backs on Missouri as the steamboat brought them into Quincy and the arms of the Saints. They had accomplished their mission "without a dog wagging his tongue" at them, in Woodruff's words.[101] To their satisfaction at having fulfilled the revelation was added word of the escape and safe arrival of the Prophet. He had been released by his guards in the course of a change of venue.[102] Nevertheless, Orson's brother Parley still lay in jail at Columbia.

Orson rode out with Brigham to visit the Prophet at his refuge near Quincy the day after their return from Far West.[103] They learned from Joseph, lean and pale from his six-month imprisonment, that a new gathering place should be established in this sanctuary by the Mississippi. Illinois Governor Thomas Carlin had offered safety to the Mormons, and within two weeks the apostles rode northward to visit a swampy promontory known as Commerce. They envisioned at this point a settlement straddling the river, inasmuch as Iowa had also offered protection to the Missouri exiles. Orson and his family thus moved into a fourteen-foot-square room at Montrose, Iowa, along with the family of Wilford Woodruff.[104] These tentative settlements clung with trepidation to the borders of three states and to the river's natural escape route. The siege-minded Mormons had lost the "center place," partially because, as Joseph Smith continually reminded them and as their own smarting retreat proved, they had claimed a righteous preeminence to which they were not fully entitled. The beatings and drivings had stunned them into an acute awareness of their vulnerability; they realized as they lay miserably in the fever swamps of the Mississippi that their inheritances would have to be redeemed against impossible odds. Cramped into an old army barracks on the river bluffs, Orson Pratt set himself to the even greater task of helping to redeem a church shattered in spirit as well as in property.

May and June of 1839 were occupied in establishing a new gathering place. Joseph Smith envisioned a city around the hamlet of Commerce. The prosaic name soon gave way to a more exalted one drawn from the lexicon of Joshua Seixas: Nauvoo.[105] This Hebrew word for "beauty" embodied Joseph Smith's emphasis on order and harmony and his theological romance with the landscape. The choice must have pleased Orson Pratt, who had taken such pride in his mastery of Hebrew. He and the others of the Twelve now dedicated themselves to the realization of its promise. The Nauvoo swamp was drained, planted, and surveyed, and all were hopeful in their quasi biblical refuge over Jordan.

At the same time, however, the legacy of Missouri continued to rankle. Orson's brother Parley was still in the Columbia jail with no prospect of release. The town of Columbia lay nearly two hundred miles from Nauvoo in the center of Missouri. Orson decided to try to deliver his brother, and as June turned to July and the miasmic fever season, Orson once again entered Missouri and set out on the long, perilous ride southwest.

The Columbia jail was a two-story wooden blockhouse[106] on the town square, shimmering in the hot sun when Orson arrived July 1 on horseback.[107] Quietly he arranged with the jailers to spend Independence Day visiting his brother, and he was lodged with the prisoners. Their story was a painful one. Along with Parley P. Pratt several others—Morris Phelps, King Follett, and Luman Gibbs—had endured the seven-month indignity of the state of Missouri without trial. Orson also met Mrs. Phelps, who had arrived for a visit along with a young Missouri Mormon, Elder Hiram Clark. Gibbs was considered a bawling apostate and was feared as an informer. Parley and the others saw in their imprisonment a trial analogous to those of the ancient prophets and apostles—complete with a set of "Gadianton robbers," for the mob reminded them of a treacherous organization that persecuted the Saints in the Book of Mormon account. The prisoners had suffered starvation and scurvy in a damp cell in Richmond for months before being transferred to this sweltering abandoned house.

Parley had spent a large part of his eight-month captivity in intimate communion with the Prophet Joseph Smith and had given much thought to some of the philosophical implications of the Prophet's teachings. He expressed these ideas in poetic form writing a number of verses on "The Millennium." In addition he had composed a "Treatise on the Regeneration and Eternal Duration of Matter." Here he first laid down some of the notions about the universe which were to characterize Mormon metaphysics, particularly in the later writings of his brother. "Matter and spirit are of equal duration; both are self-existent—they never began to exist, and they never can be annihilated." Parley advanced an explanation for what he considered the mistaken orthodox notion of creation ex nihilo (from nothing): "From the Mosaic account of the creation, many have gathered the idea that God created all things out of nonentity—that solid matter sprung from nothing. But this is for want of reflection, or an exercise of reason upon the subject." Houses and children are also *made*, he says, but not from nothing. "It is impossible for God to bring forth matter from nonentity . . . this would contradict the law of truth, and destroy himself . . . a hundred noughts added together is nothing still . . . the product is determined by unchangeable laws . . . Here then, is a mathematical demonstration that it is not in the power of any being to originate matter . . . ETERNITY is inscribed in indelible characters on every particle."[108] These ideas developed peculiar ramifications in the later philosophical work of Orson Pratt.

Parley's fasting and prayer had made his imprisonment a long vigil of humiliation, but he had not lost hope. He had had a vision of his dead first wife bringing the message that he could expect deliverance, but how soon or under what circumstances he did not know. Also not long before Orson's arrival, Parley had been startled by a dream which revealed an escape plan; with all vividness it had been repeated the following night. He saw in this the pattern of Pharaoh's dreams and anxiously waited for its fulfillment. In his brother's premonitions Orson found his own "firm impression" substantiated. He whispered his belief that deliverance was at hand and that Parley would soon see the shores of Illinois. Orson opened his copy of the Book of Mormon, and his eye fell on the words of Ammon to King Lamoni:[109] "Behold, my brother and my brethren are in prison, in the land of Middoni, and I go to deliver them!"[110] Parley later wrote: "This was indeed a similar instance to ours. Ammon, on that occasion had an own brother in prison, and also brethren in the ministry, and did deliver them. Our case was exactly similar, not in Middoni, but in Missouri. And, what was still more strange, in a book of six hundred pages, this was the only sentence which would have fitted our case."[111]

The brothers laid their plan carefully. Orson would petition the court for trial arrangements and retain "a lawyer or two" as a subterfuge. He would then procure three horses and, with Hiram Clark, would hide in a thicket a half mile from the jail.

Orson and Clark got permission to remain with the prisoners and enjoy a holiday meal with them; the fourth of July "dawned upon [them] with hope and expectation." To the sound of guns and bands playing in the public square, the little group in the jailhouse tore up a shirt and made a banner, emblazoned it with the word "Liberty," and hung it from their cell window. This brought on as much laughter as blasphemy from the frontier crowd gathered for the celebration. "Liberty! What have the Mormons to do with celebrating liberty in a damned old prison."[112]

At length, after sharing some food Orson brought, the two visiting brothers made a great show of farewells to the prisoners—all of it intended to lull the jailers. Orson then saddled the horses and went quietly off to the thicket to await darkness. As the dinner hour came on, the old jailer climbed the steps to pass his charges a pot of hot coffee through an opening in the door. The prisoners cried out that the pot was burning their fingers and that it would be more convenient to unlock the door and pass it in. The instant the key was turned, King Follett snatched the handle back and Phelps leaped on the jailer, wrestling him to the bottom of the stairs. Gibbs, the old apostate, who had not been apprised of the plan, simply laughed with amazement as the keeper and his wife struggled and screamed.

Commotion now filled the town. Columbia came alive with riflemen, boys, and dogs shouting and running in all directions, while the three escapees made rapidly for the forest. Orson bounded into the clearing to help Parley, who was nearly breathless from the sprint, and virtually shoved him onto a horse. Parley headed deep into the thicket with horsemen rushing all around him, and one of them laid a rifle nearly to Parley's head. Darkness and confusion sheltered him, however, and soon he disappeared from sight.[113]

Orson, meanwhile, was defenseless, on foot, and surrounded by the crashing and swearing of the pursuing horsemen. He fell face down into a gully and dared not move until all was dark. Several times he and Clark were nearly discovered as the crowd stamped all around them. At midnight the two men arose and began slowly picking their way through the forest. A long walk of several days brought them back to the Mississippi shore and across to Quincy, where Orson sought out Parley's wife:

"Have you seen my husband?"

"I have."

"Is he yet alive?"

"Yes."

"Is he well?"

"He is."

"O thank God for that! Is there any prospect that he will ever get free and return alive?"

At this Orson must have smiled. "Well, I hope so; for the last time I saw him he was astride a horse in the woods, and headed towards home on a gallop."[114]

Their joy was mitigated, of course, by the understanding that armed parties would await Parley at the known ferries and that he could easily be retaken within sight of the shores of Illinois. A group of Mormons took their weapons and stole across into Missouri to try to find the fugitive apostle. Orson had learned that King Follett had been recaptured, for Phelps had already achieved Quincy when he arrived. That left Parley alone in the middle of the wolves, and it is quite probable that Orson joined the clandestine search on the Missouri shore.

Exhausted and hungry, Parley had made his way directly north toward the town of Paris and then eastward along the Salt River. By good fortune he found a Mormon family who warned him away from the main ferry and encouraged him northward toward Quincy. Upon fording the Salt River he found himself on the Mississippi heath not far from Hannibal, Missouri. After a week of "living death," sleeping in snake-infested bushes by day and stumbling along half awake at night, he paid a devious little boy with a canoe to deposit him on a large island in the river. At length the same boy rescued him from the island and canoed him across to Illinois where Parley knelt and feverishly kissed the ground.[115]

Parley met Orson at Quincy, and once refreshed they went up to Commerce. The unbreakable Pratts were determined to serve their mission in England, so they spent several days buying up land and improving it to sell again at a profit. In one day Heber Kimball and Parley constructed shanties on a woodland acreage a mile from the river, and Orson moved his wife and two children into one of them. In such narrow quarters the Kimball and Pratt families were suddenly prostrated with the malarial fever that swept each summer through the Mississippi Valley. Steeling themselves against the crisis that threatened the camp of refuge, the Pratt brothers, like the Prophet Joseph Smith, shook the sickness off "by the power of God" and prepared to help their neighbors. With the Prophet they covered Nauvoo and Montrose laying hands on the malaria-inflicted Saints and watching as multiple miracles of healing quietly but forcefully tightened the Saints' faltering confidence. Among the healed was Elijah Fordham, a missionary associate of Orson's in New York City the year before.[116]

The crisis was not without its casualties; Orson Pratt's eight-month-old daughter Lydia wasted and died on August 18.[117] Her father had preached that morning upon "the order and plan of creation,"[118] but in the afternoon and evening the suffering father and the twenty-two-year-old mother stood vigil as the baby expired. The frail life of this infant girl encompassed and typified the bleakest era of the Mormon people, and with her death the epidemic ebbed. The Church of the Latter-day Saints had been brought to its nadir in the sufferings of the Pratts multiplied by thousands.

From here, Orson looked to England. Leaving his wife and little Orson in the charge of the Prophet Joseph Smith, he and Parley, along with Elder Hiram Clark, began the long overland journey to Detroit where they would engage a boat to New York City. As they traveled over the early September prairies of Illinois,[119] they rejoiced to be once again on the Lord's errand and free from the depredations of the "land of Middoni."

4

Transformation

Orson Pratt's English mission began in a two-horse carriage threading its way along the nearly six hundred miles from Nauvoo to Detroit. The weather was pleasant and the landscape picturesque, continually reminding the missionaries of the irony of their situation. The settlements teemed with the unemployed (the result of the 1837 panic), and illness was virtually pandemic; a wave of cholera, perhaps, or malaria, had closed down stores and public houses along the route. But the missionaries, who had faced forced exile, completely impoverished only months before now fared peacefully and in unaccustomed comfort on an errand that had seemed so recently unachievable.

The brothers stopped within a day from Detroit, and Orson preached to attentive congregations near the city. Here they also found their brother Anson caring for their parents Jared and Charity Pratt. Jared, nearly seventy, died from the epidemic within a few weeks. The two apostles remained with him fourteen days.

Detroit was the nearest well-developed port; from here one could travel by water all the way to London. They sold their carriage at a loss of about one hundred dollars but made enough to get to Buffalo by Lake Erie, then by canal to Albany and steamer to New York. Orson made this trip ahead of Parley, who stayed in Detroit to see through the publication of a pamphlet describing the persecutions of the Mormon people in Missouri.[1]

One of the consequences of those trials was the new notoriety that faced Mormon preachers in the East. Orson, who had preached in New York City two years before, was astounded at the crowds.[2] The western troubles did not fully account for the public interest in Mormonism; actually, lecture halls were packed on every subject. "Lyceums," lectures for self-education, were in vogue among Americans. Marshall B. Davidson has written:

> The Lyceum movement had been organized in 1826 to satisfy a swelling demand for adult education. The zeal for self-improvement amounted to a virtual crusade against ignorance during the mid-years of the century. In 1841 the elegant diarist Philip Hone observed that the theatres of New York were deserted—"flat on their backs"—while overflowing crowds stormed the several large lecture halls of the city. For Americans, wrote one astonished English visitor, "going to lectures seemed to be the next most important duty after going to church on Sundays."[3]

Men like Emerson and William Ellery Channing were already profiting from the new interest in the lecture circuit, and the Mormon preachers found a growing audience as well.

While in New York Parley published his poems and treatise on "the eternal duration of matter." It would not be long before Orson followed his brother's lead in generating a series of "Pratt's Tracts" which brought Mormonism to the attention of literally thousands on both sides of the Atlantic.[4]

The public attraction to Mormon ideas was short-lived. Orson testified that "there are hundreds believing" although few being baptized. On December 21 Orson met with the Prophet Joseph Smith at Philadelphia (after taking possibly his first rail trip from Monmouth, New Jersey to Philadelphia),[5] to hear the disappointing report of the Prophet's interview with President Martin Van Buren. The President had refused to get involved in the internal affairs of the state of Missouri when Joseph had pleaded with him for federal intervention.[6]

But in meeting with the elders, Joseph mingled his contempt for the national government with the glimmerings of new instructions and doctrine. The discussions included the "first idea of eternal family organization," as Parley called it, and involved a new concept of priesthood domination, of sealing husband and wife for time and eternity, and of offspring "as numerous as the stars of heaven, or the sands of the seashore." For Parley, this lifting of a "corner of the veil" uncovered the true teleology of earthly existence, providing a "single key" that would unlock the mystery of man's purpose in the world. The "dignity and destiny of a son of God" was for him to become a "patriarch and sovereign" in his own right; in short, a god among gods.[7]

These were Parley's thoughts; of Orson's at this point we know nothing. His mind may have been influenced by the same interviews with the Prophet. Though they had only glimpsed it before, in Philadelphia the apostolic brothers came into contact with the core of Joseph Smith's gospel, the concept of eternal marriage and progression, which they would elaborate—and suffer for—the remainder of their lives.

Orson was in New York City at the dawn of the decade of the forties. Two of the Twelve had already departed for England while the Pratts awaited the arrival of Brigham Young and Heber C. Kimball.[8] The half-year wait came to an end in March 1840 as the apostles held conference at Columbian Hall near the Bowery. They sang:

> When shall we all meet again?
> When shall we our rest obtain?
> When our pilgrimage be o'er—
> Parting sighs be known no more?
> When Mount Zion we regain.
> There may we all meet again.[9]

On March 9 Orson Pratt began the first of sixteen crossings of the Atlantic he would make in his lifetime. He bid the United States farewell from the clipper *Patrick Henry* of the Black Ball line as it was towed some distance out of New York by a steam tug. About 120 passengers, who had paid eighteen dollars each for steerage, were crowded into small compartments. The New York Saints had provided pillows, straw beds, and blankets for the missionaries.[10]

This was the second such voyage for Kimball but the first for everyone else. Brigham Young for one found himself so seasick he could not get out of bed the full four weeks of passage. Orson was prostrated with everyone else when the ship hit a gale barely twelve hours out. The vomiting, the freezing cold and ague,[11] and the storm-washed decks made the twenty-eight-day passage a miserable one. The feelings of Orson Pratt were reflected in these lines: "When we contrast the parting of Jacob and his son Benjamin . . . with our having to part with tender wives and helpless offspring, under circumstances of poverty, sickness and death, robbed, plundered and driven, houseless, and unprovided for . . . we are led to think that our sacrifice is almost as great as the old Patriarch's was."[12]

On the tenth anniversary of the founding of the Mormon church,[13] the *Patrick Henry* dropped anchor in Liverpool harbor. Brigham Young bounded out of the boat and shouted "Hosanna!"[14] The rough sea was behind them, and the apostles partook of the sacrament that night in a small room in Union Street praying that the way to success might be opened. They proceeded to call a conference of the British members at Preston, a few miles from Liverpool, where Mormonism had first been preached some three years before. During this conference, assignments were made and the country was divided up: Parley P. Pratt was to head a new periodical, the *Latter-day Saints' Millennial Star*,[15] while Orson was scheduled to open the country of Scotland to the preaching of Mormonism. After blessing and partaking of a bottle of forty-year-old wine, the Twelve separated to begin their labors.[16]

For the first time Orson Pratt found himself on the soil of the Old World. His impressions have gone largely unrecorded; however, it is possible to reconstruct the conditions he encountered upon his arrival in Great Britain. Three years into Queen Victoria's reign, the kingdom was afflicted with the mass unemployment and destitution which characterized the entire decade of the "Hungry Forties." In many parts of the industrial midlands, where the Twelve began their mission, the worldwide depression of 1837 seemed hardly to have begun; yet unemployment in Bolton and Liverpool averaged over fifty percent. The result was "bitter social cleavage and dislocation."[17] Starvation and begging were so common that the appalled elders gave all their spare change to the derelicts who crowded the streets. Describing a royal procession in London, Heber C. Kimball wrote, "You would be astonished to see the stur thare is made over a little queen at the same time thousands starving to deth fore a little bread."[18]

Along with those who sought secular reform were the "seekers" for the millennium; there was no shortage of American revivalists on the streets of England. Many of the working class yearned for a more accessible church, a simpler religion than that offered by the Church of England. As a result, many reformist religions had grown up among the common people. Indeed, the secular and spiritual reform movements were noticeably intertwined. The supporters of the 'People's Charter'' clashed with those of the Oxford Movement, who favored imposing Anglo-Catholicism on all. Although still dominant, the established church seemed, according to one historian, "more concerned with the distribution of livings than with the spiritual life of its constituency."[19] Dissenters (Methodists, Baptists, Congregationalists), though largely members of the lower class, were "numerous, particularly in the mining and manufacturing towns where families were "almost destitute of hope." There were prayer meetings and preaching services even in the "pits," or mines.[20] Little wonder so many Britons were attracted by Mormonism, which taught both temporal and spiritual salvation in a new Zion across the sea.

The attraction must have been great. Wilford Woodruff, who had preceded Pratt's arrival by a few weeks, pleaded with his fellow missionaries for help: he had baptized nearly a thousand converts on his own and cried, "I cannot do the work alone." Most converts came, as in Woodruff's case, from reformist congregations. He had baptized nearly the entire membership of a sect called the "United Brethren," which had chosen a lay ministry.[21] The Mormons were often welcome to preach in temperance halls because of their reputed emphasis on abstinence.[22]

Two young elders, Samuel Mulliner and Alexander Wright, had already established a small branch of twenty converts in the west of Scotland when Orson arrived there. He began his work with the organization of the branch at Paisley, a few miles from Glasgow. The typical British convert here had followed a checkered religious life: usually he was skeptical, but curious and easily swayed by earnestness rather than institutional rhetoric. One of the first dozen, John Leishman (or Leechman) of Johnstone, had migrated from Methodism to the "Relief Church" and after eight years of forlorn dissatisfaction had abandoned all churches. Mildly intrigued, he stopped to hear Mulliner and Wright, listened at the door while they prayed, and was immediately convinced "they were sent by God." Leishman, a cottonspinner by trade, eventually joined, traveled to Utah in the first Perpetual Emigrating Fund company, and founded a faithful Mormon family. This was the sort of humble malcontent Orson appealed to and sought to deliver from what he called the "Babylon" of Great Britain.[23] A non-Mormon British historian has written that "the Mormon converts appear for the most part to have been solid citizenry, their conduct exemplary, and their success in the new world reputable."[24]

Orson Pratt determined to do a great work in Edinburgh, the Scottish capital, where it appears no missionary had ever preached. Late in May he climbed a hill above Edinburgh Castle, dedicated the land of Scotland, and asked the Lord for two hundred souls. This heathered crag, known to natives as "Arthur's Seat," overlooks the ruins of a medieval fortress.[25] To the many thousands of Latter-day Saints converted in Scotland, it was ever after known as "Pratt's Hill."[26] From this vantage Orson looked down over a city just at the end of a period of monumental renovation along Classical lines—the "Golden Age" of Edinburgh.[27] The burgeoning city of 136,000, called "the Modern Athens," was a capital of learning and art.[28]

Pratt worked very hard for nine months,[29] preaching in the streets seven times each Sabbath[30] in association with Mulliner and an Elder Reuben Hedlock. Another helpful assistant was George D. Watt, who subsequently worked with Pratt in developing Utah's school system and who published the monumental *Journal of Discourses* (speeches of Brigham Young and other Mormon authorities during the years 1851–77).[31] By the time of Orson's departure early in 1841, the Edinburgh conference numbered exactly 226 members,[32] more than the number he had prayed for. The Mormons met the typical resistance: they were derided in pulpits and attacked by mobs who pelted them with rocks and rubbish. But the baptisms in the rivers went on nevertheless. The work in Edinburgh proceeded slowly at first; only eighteen had been baptized by August 1840, but Orson had not "given up all hope of that place."[33]

During that unproductive summer, Orson turned to writing for publication. His brother's success with tracts, combined with his desire to appeal to the more literate populace of Edinburgh, led to the first of his works. The city resounded with philosophical and scientific discussion, for the great university there was experiencing a sort of flowering—much of the important work done in physics and astronomy during the nineteenth century was then under way in Edinburgh.[34] The philosophical capital of the English-speaking world at that time, Edinburgh had contributed the great ideas of the Scottish "Enlightenment" and the "common sense" school of philosophy. Thomas Chalmers, the greatest Scottish theologian of the time and a professor in the University, was attempting to reconcile to orthodox Protestant theology the new discoveries of the scientific revolution.[35] Scottish philosophy dominated even American thinking at this time; the Scots were "empiricists who sought a science of knowledge," not "speculative metaphysicians."[36] With important differences Orson Pratt's later writings were profoundly influenced by the ideas current in Edinburgh during these days.

Hoping to arouse more interest in his message, Pratt peddled his own thirty-one-page pamphlet in the streets: *Interesting Account of Several Remarkable Visions, and of the Late Discovery of Ancient American Records Giving an Account of the Commencement of the Work of the Lord in this Generation, by Elder Orson Pratt.*[37] The work, published by the firm of Ballantyne and Hughes, and later known as *Remarkable Visions*, was distinguished as the first recounting in print of the prophet Joseph Smith's vision of the Father and Son. The prose is simple and discursive, straightforward and literate to a degree that might be unexpected of a man with Orson Pratt's education. The book breaks into two parts: the first section recounts the experiences of Joseph Smith and the history of the Book of Mormon drawn from a letter of Oliver Cowdery's published in the *Messenger and Advocate*.[38] The tale of the Angel Moroni and the revelation of the gold plates was well known among Mormons. Less familiar was the account of the vision of the Father and the Son to the fourteen-year-old Joseph. It does not differ in great detail from subsequent accounts nor from the version presumably dictated by Joseph Smith in 1838 and later incorporated into the scriptures of the Church. Yet certain illustrative details, such as Joseph's forgiveness of sins and his expectation that the sacred grove would be burned up in the divine illumination, distinguish this from other tellings.[39] Its attention to such peculiar points as the construction and dimensions of the stone box in which the Book of Mormon plates were found underscores the material reality of the incident, written here neither to allegorize nor extemporize.[40]

The second portion of the pamphlet constitutes a "sketch of the faith and doctrine of the Church" and provides an exposition of Orson Pratt's religious thought. One of the first such digests of Mormon belief (others included a work by Oliver Cowdery[41] and, of course, the "Voice of Warning" by Parley), it echoes the formulae of creeds and confessions of the major denominations. The tone is legalistic, not transcendental or mystical; the emphasis is on a proper understanding of the gospel "in great plainness." There is none of the passion and flourish of Parley P. Pratt, but Orson's individual stamp is clear—with exactness, simplicity, and a certain scholarly distance, the work expounds salvation in the tones of the mathematician. Joseph Smith drew heavily from this "sketch" to compose a list of fundamental Church beliefs that later became known as the "Articles of Faith," a document familiar to Mormons today as a part of the canonical book *The Pearl of Great Price*.[42] Orson's "articles of faith" are much more detailed than those Joseph later set down, but in many instances the wording is nearly identical.

PRATT: SKETCH OF FAITH	THE ARTICLES OF FAITH
We believe in God, the Eternal Father, and in his Son, Jesus Christ, and in the Holy Ghost.	1. We believe in God, the Eternal Father, and in His Son, Jesus Christ, and in the Holy Ghost.
We believe that all mankind . . . by the transgression of their first parents . . . not by their own sins, were brought under the curse and penalty of that transgression . . .	2. We believe that men will be punished for their own sins, and not for Adam's transgression.
We believe that through the . . . atonement of Jesus Christ, all mankind . . . are to be completely and fully redeemed, both body and spirit, from the endless banishment and curse to which they were consigned by Adam's transgression.	3. We believe that through the Atonement of Christ, all mankind may be saved, by obedience to the laws and ordinances of the Gospel.

In connection with this third fundamental belief, Orson gives a six-paragraph explication of the two basic laws of the gospel of Christ. Adam transgressed the first law given to mankind by his disobedience in the Garden of Eden. Christ's "full, complete, and universal redemption" cancels the effects of this first transgression. But now man is required to obey what Orson calls "a second law . . . against doing evil." The penalty of disobeying this second law is "a second banishment from the presence of God, both body and spirit." Even in this second law man is utterly dependent upon Christ for his deliverance from its consequences: "But, be assured, O sinner, that thou canst not devise any way of thine own to escape, nor do anything that will *atone* for thy sins . . . That same Jesus, who hath atoned for the original sin . . . offereth salvation and deliverance to thee, on certain conditions."[43] This essay on the law and atonement is summarized by Joseph Smith with the phrase "obedience to the laws and ordinances of the Gospel." Now, in both digests, comes a listing of what Orson calls the "first conditions" (first principles) necessary for salvation:

We believe that the first condition to be complied with . . . is to *believe* in God, and in the sufferings and death of his Son Jesus Christ . . .	4. We believe that the first principles and ordinances of the Gospel are: first, Faith in the Lord Jesus Christ;
that the second condition is, to repent . . .	second, Repentance;
the third condition, is to be baptized by immersion in water, . . . for the remission of sins . . .	third, Baptism by immersion for the remission of sins;
the fourth condition is, to receive the laying on of hands . . . for the gift of the Holy Ghost.	fourth, Laying on of hands for the gift of the Holy Ghost.
. . . to be administered by [those]. . . whom the Lord Jesus hath called and authorized . . . having authority from God to administer . . . ordinances . . .	5. We believe that a man must be called of God, by prophecy, and by the laying on of hands, by those who are in authority to preach the Gospel and administer in the ordinances thereof.
We believe that inspired apostles and prophets, together with all the officers as mentioned in the New Testament, are necessary to be in the Church in these days. We believe that there has been a general and awful apostacy from the religion of the New Testament [the "primitive church"].	6. We believe in the same organization that existed in the Primitive Church, viz., apostles, prophets, pastors, teachers, evangelists, etc.
It is the duty and privilege of the saints . . . to believe in . . . all the gifts, powers, and blessings which flow from the Holy Spirit . . . the gifts of revelation, prophecy, visions, . . . healing . . .	7. We believe in the gift of tongues, prophecy, revelation, visions, healing, interpretation of tongues, etc.

The gospel in the "Book of Mormon," is the same as that in the New Testament, and is revealed in great plainness, so that no one that reads it can misunderstand its principles . . .

8. We believe the Bible to be the word of God as far as it is translated correctly; we also believe the Book of Mormon to be the word of God.

Many revelations . . . have been given to this church . . . We believe that God will continue to give revelations . . .

9. We believe all that God has revealed, all that He does now reveal, and we believe that He will yet reveal many great and important things pertaining to the Kingdom of God.

We believe that God has raised up this church, in order to prepare a people for his second coming . . . and reign with him on earth a thousand years . . . We believe that in this generation a house of the Lord shall be built by the saints upon Mount Zion . . . We believe that the ten tribes of Israel, with the dispersed of Judah shall soon be restored to their own lands.

10. We believe in the literal gathering of Israel and in the restoration of the Ten Tribes; that Zion will be built upon this [the American] continent; that Christ will reign personally upon the earth; and, that the earth will be renewed and receive its paradisiacal glory.

Joseph Smith's eleventh and twelfth articles are not prefigured in Orson's "sketch," but the first ten must have resulted from a careful abridgment of the Pratt pamphlet. The two sets of articles are also laid out in roughly the same order. Orson discusses a number of issues which the Prophet chose not to include in his list of fundamentals. Among these are the problem of the salvation of infants, the apostasy of the primitive church, and the "judgments of great Babylon," which Orson equates with the "Papists and Protestants . . . the Gentiles and Jews." At the same time, the thirteenth article of faith is anticipated in a paragraph listing what might be called "secondary" principles of the gospel:

[The Saints] are then required to . . . deal justly . . . feed the hungry and clothe the naked . . . to comfort the afflicted, to bind up the broken-hearted, and to do all the good that is in their power . . . to continue faithful to the end.[44]

13. We believe in being honest, true, chaste, benevolent, virtuous, and in doing good to all men; indeed, we may say that we follow the admonition of Paul—We believe all things, we hope all things, we have endured many things, and hope to be able to en-

> dure all things. If there is anything virtuous, lovely, or of good report or praiseworthy, we seek after these things.[45]

The publication of *Remarkable Visions* came near Orson's twenty-ninth birthday, which he spent preaching in a rented Edinburgh meeting hall. He loved this city; the "romantic and sublime" spectacle[46] it presented deeply affected him, and he spent many hours in the high crags surrounding the town praying for its inhabitants.[47] An extraordinarily single-minded missionary who cared little about appearances, Orson was described at this time as "poor and shabby" by a ten-year-old girl, Marian Ross. Marian worked as a serving girl in a large house which Orson visited the day after she had prophetically dreamed his coming. Marian Ross joined the Mormon church in 1847 and became Orson's plural wife.[48]

Recognizing Orson's leadership, Brigham Young moved to elect Apostle Pratt president of the British mission conference in October 1840.[49] The motion carried and Orson helped administer the affairs of the mission for another six months. The apostles felt that one year in Britain was sufficient for their foreign mission, and they voted in an April conference to return to the United States. Orson wrote of the several thousands who had been baptized and of the "many faithful servants . . . who no doubt will thrust in their sickle and reap with great success."[50] The Twelve had accomplished much in Britain: they had organized the first European mission, printed some sixty thousand copies of various tracts and other books, begun a periodical that would continue in publication for 130 years to come, and supervised the conversion of seven to eight thousand new members, most of them general laborers, miners, and metalworkers from industrial centers.[51] This initiative would ultimately produce nearly ninety thousand European pioneer Mormons, most of whom would emigrate by means of a shipping agency established in Liverpool by the Church to assist them. Approximately ten thousand Scots would be counted in that number.[52]

The Twelve sailed for New York April 20, 1841. After a large tea party,[53] attended by several hundred Liverpool Saints, they were towed into the Mersey on board the ship *Rochester* for the return journey, facing once again heavy gales and debilitating nausea. After a week the tempest broke with full fury; Brigham Young, seeing the cargo ropes giving way between decks, shouted for the other apostles. Kimball, Willard Richards, and Orson threw themselves against the heavy mass to brace it until it could be secured by the ship hands. Wilford Woodruff was thrown headfirst across the galley, falling on and nearly killing the cook. This violent passage ended exactly one month after departure among what Brigham Young called the thieving draymen and pickpockets of New York harbor.[54]

Orson remained in New York City until the first of July arranging for republication of his pamphlet in five thousand copies, at this point entitled *History of the Coming Forth of the Book of Mormon.*[55] He then returned rapidly to Nauvoo, traveling by way of Sackets Harbor where he took his wife's sister on the journey.[56] Moving into a house "a few rods north of the Temple Block" in Nauvoo, Orson immediately advertised for sale a large stock of booklets by himself and his brother. The new pamphlet sold for twelve and a half cents, or six dollars per hundred.[57] Orson was no doubt seeking means of providing for his wife and son, whom he had not seen for nearly two years. Though the national picture was bleak and the state of Illinois was verging on bankruptcy, Nauvoo had flourished economically since the first miserable gathering in 1839. Orson shared somewhat in the prosperity acquiring title to two small narrow tracts of property, one near the temple block and another by the river. Rather than trading to support his family, he signed on to teach at the fledgling University of the City of Nauvoo, the only municipal college in America at the time.[58]

Within a few days of his return from England, Orson was installed in the chair of the "Department of English literature and mathematics" of the university. In fact he was now one of its three professors. Styled for the first time "Professor Orson Pratt" in a newspaper notice of August 10, 1841,[59] he bore this title throughout his life. He took his professorial standing among the Mormon people seriously, although the only college degree he could claim was the honorary "A.M." conferred on him September 4, 1841, by the "chancellor and board of regents."[60] Many unrealized plans circulated in Nauvoo to build a campus for the university, although in practice classes met for the most part in the Masonic Hall and the unfinished temple. Although the university was in fact a modest institution, its advertisements claimed "some of the most able men the nation affords in their respective departments." Professor Pratt, the

Times and Seasons read in December 1841, "is a self-made man, and has had to encounter great difficulties in the acquisition of an education; but he has surmounted them all. As a teacher of Mathematics and English Literature, he is equaled by few, and surpassed by none this side of the great waters; as the proficiency of the matriculates of the university now under his care abundantly testifies."[61]

According to the newspaper, Orson conducted a successful curriculum with a number of students in "a general Course of Mathematics, including Arithmetic, Algebra, Geometry, Conic Sections, Plane Trigonometry, Mensuration, Surveying, Navigation, Analytical, Plane and Spherical Trigonometry, Analytical Geometry, and the Differential and Integral Calculus; Philosophy; Astronomy; Chemistry; etc., etc."[62] Although the paper does not mention Orson's teaching any specific courses in English literature, he believed that "mental culture [should] not be passed over as a little thing."[63]

Daniel Boorstin points out that "the kind of new knowledge which life in America made possible, precisely because it was factual and miscellaneous, required no preliminary training. Men could educate themselves with the random materials of experience. They could become 'self-made' men, because they could start anytime anyplace . . . there were many . . . who 'improved' their experience to become models of learning in the American mold."[64] Orson Pratt was such a scholar, a self-educated laboring man, not an uncommon ideal in Jacksonian American.[65]

Although the broad praise Orson receives in the newspaper may have been an expression of extravagant municipal pride, later works show Orson was indeed proficient in the study of mathematics. His impact on his students sincerely impressed his neighbor, the Mormon poet Eliza R. Snow, who dedicated to "Professor O. Pratt" a lyric entitled "The Transformation":

I saw a thing of rudest form
From mountain's base brought forth
A useless gem—devoid of charm
And wrap'd in cumbrous earth . . .
That gem was chained in crudeness, till
The Sculptor lent his aid;
I wondered at the ready skill
His potent hand displayed.
But 'twas the virtue of his tool,
Of fine, transforming edge;

Which served for pencil mould and rule—
For polisher and sledge.[66]

Orson's fellow teachers at the university included Sidney Rigdon, who taught religion and "Belles Lettres," and Orson Spencer,[67] a young and earnest convert who held a degree with honors in the Arts from Union College (at that time the most prominent denominational college in America)[68] and a doctorate in divinity from Hamilton Baptist Literary and Theological Seminary, both in New York.

The university also took responsibility for the maintenance of common schools in the four wards of the city, and it is likely that Orson taught some of the town's children. Eventually this one-man math and science department also offered lessons in reading, writing, geography, and grammar—advertising a ten-dollar charge for the math, five dollars for surveying, and three dollars for the "liberal arts" under his instruction.[69] Spared the necessity of trading in hardware and following the experiences of Kirtland, he was undoubtedly far happier working through theorems and derivations and unquestionably learned a great deal side by side with his students as "mind grappled with mind in seeking after hidden treasures."[70]

Meanwhile the city of Nauvoo and the Mormon church were taking on some of the challenges of institutional growth. The city counted three thousand inhabitants early in 1841, most of them Latter-day Saints, and was rapidly absorbing hundreds more each month, many of them from Great Britain. Administrative demands on the Prophet led him to seek the help of the Twelve in conducting the affairs of the Church at home as well as in the missions.[71] Orson's business with the apostles was extensive. He met often with them to issue several "epistles" to emigrating Saints, advocating debt cancellations among the members, additional support for the construction of the temple, and contributions for the settling of converts from abroad.[72] Orson Pratt was also sworn in as a city councilor for the Nauvoo First Ward to serve under Mayor John Cook Bennett.[73] This man, an adventurer with a little-known past, had been appointed quartermaster-general of the Illinois militia when he came to greet the Mormon Prophet in the summer of 1840.[74] Apparently seeing much to further his ambitions here, Bennett was baptized a member of the Church. He ingratiated himself with Joseph Smith and boarded with Smith's family for a time during the winter of Orson

Pratt's absence. While cultivating the Prophet, he was also attracted to the Prophet's occasional boarder, Sarah Marinda Pratt, whom he considered an "amiable and accomplished woman."[75] Sarah in her impoverished condition made shirts and clothing for Bennett and did his washing, "for he could pay money."[76] By Joseph's graces Bennett advanced rapidly in civic affairs: in February 1841 he was elected mayor and justice of the municipal court.[77] As major general of the Nauvoo Legion he was second in command under Joseph Smith. Bennett also persuaded the Mormon elders to start a Masonic lodge in Nauvoo, which many of the townsmen including Joseph Smith ultimately joined. In his capacity of chancellor of the university, he became a close friend and houseguest of Orson Pratt.

With the growth of the Mormon city of Nauvoo came the introduction of new doctrines, such as baptism for the dead, sealings, endowments, and eternal marriage. Many puzzling aspects of Bible history—the polygamy of Abraham and Jacob, the importance placed on posterity, odd ritual inklings and echoes in both Testaments—came together for Joseph. In Masonry and in his papyrus treasures he saw suggestions of ancient priestly rites which may have been derived from the temple cults of the Hebrews and the Egyptians. According to Heber C. Kimball, Joseph taught that the Masonic order perpetuated a corrupted version of the order of the true priesthood of God.[78]

At the foundation of Joseph Smith's teachings was a radical concept of man and God. He taught that man is a potential god himself, coeval with his Heavenly Father, whose advancement on the evolutionary scale typifies the potential of all "intelligences" who live by eternal law. The uncreated intelligence of man is a material phenomenon, eternal and capable of infinite development. Joseph rejected Christian mysticism and the notions that characterize salvation for the orthodox. The glory of God lies in his intelligence, Joseph taught, and in the unlimited measure of his "increase," or offspring.[79] Joseph's idea of the exaltation of the individual, so foreign to traditional Christianity, struck great chords of inspired logic from Orson Pratt in years to come. But Orson was now to learn more of the corollary doctrine of "celestial marriage."

According to Orson's own account, Joseph Smith had received a revelation as early as 1831 that plural marriage was a correct principle because it added to the posterity, increase, and potential eternal glory of man. Lyman E. Johnson, Orson's missionary companion in those early days, had heard this from Joseph and had passed it on to Orson in the course of their travels together.[80] Joseph Smith had probably become interested in patriarchal marriage patterns while "translating" (revising) the Bible in Kirtland in 1831. Between February and March he had come to the passages dealing with Abraham, Isaac, and Jacob, and their many wives. Joseph often sought revelations to explain the more problematic biblical accounts.[81] Although this was his most prolific period for writing revelations, Joseph did not commit to paper the actual instruction authorizing plural marriages until 1843.[82] As one of Joseph's most intimate disciples, Orson Pratt must have been aware of the possibility that the plural marriage covenant might someday be required of the Saints.[83]

By the time Orson returned from Britain, Joseph Smith had formally taken at least one plural wife, Louisa Beaman. Joseph Bates Noble, her brother-in-law and the man who had performed the ceremony, later wrote that a heavenly messenger had commanded Joseph Smith to live the "principle." The Prophet accordingly married Louisa on April 5, 1841.[84] The doctrine of celestial marriages (for "time and eternity") and plural marriages depended upon the "sealing" power of the priesthood, following the conferral of certain spiritual "keys," or prerogatives, upon the Prophet at the time of the Kirtland temple dedication.[85] A marriage sealed by the pronouncement of one holding this authority would endure throughout eternity. Such an endless union was centrally important to Joseph Smith's theology, for he defined eternal progression in part as the increase of the family in the hereafter. The "patriarchal marriage" system, as it came to be called, did not preclude and in fact encouraged the addition of plural wives, which would redound to an increase of offspring and glory for all. Joseph viewed this revelation as a part of the restoration of the ancient priesthood order practiced by Abraham and the other patriarchs.

At this early date the controversial principle was not taught publicly, and it is difficult to ascertain how much or how little Orson knew of all this in 1841. The revelation authorizing plural marriage (now *Doctrine and Covenants* section 132) was not written down until July 12, 1843, but Joseph Smith is supposed to have taught it to the apostles upon their return from England. Whether or not he actually spoke of it to Orson, who returned somewhat later than the others, remains unclear; Joseph selected very carefully those whom he instructed in "the new and everlasting covenant of marriage," not even apprising his own brother Hyrum of it until 1843. It is difficult to imagine that Orson Pratt was kept in the dark, considering that he had known something about it since 1832. If he did hear it that summer, his reaction is unknown. He was not at that time required to enter the plural marriage covenant.

One man who was fully aware of the Prophet's polygamy doctrine was Mayor John C. Bennett. During the absence of the Twelve, Bennett had been made associate president of the Church and was very much in Joseph's confidence.[86] Bennett had led a checkered moral life, with an abandoned family somewhere in Ohio, and had been expelled from the Ohio Masons for improper behavior.[87] Upon his arrival in Nauvoo he taught free love privately to at least one impressionable Nauvoo woman, Catherine Fuller Warren. Bennett and Joseph Smith's brother William taught her in the fall of 1840 "that it was right to have free intercourse with women and that the heads of the church also taught and practiced it which things caused her to be led away."[88]

Joseph Smith's doctrine of plural marriage and Bennett's counterfeit version were thus taught simultaneously and in secret at Nauvoo. Sarah Marinda Pratt is supposed to have become a focus of both men's interest. According to Bennett's account of the ensuing scandal, Joseph Smith approached Sarah in the winter of 1840–41 with a proposal of marriage, saying that "the Lord has given you to me as one of my spiritual wives. I have the blessings of Jacob granted me, as he granted holy men of old, and I have long looked upon you with favor, and hope you will not deny me." Bennett, who said he was present at the time, recalled Sarah's response: "I have one good husband and that is enough for me." The Prophet acquiesced, then asked her not to reveal his proposal in order to protect the Mormon community. She agreed to keep the secret "if you will never insult me again."[89]

Bennett's story, with some variations, was retold forty-three years later by Sarah Pratt herself. According to this version, Joseph Smith made his proposal to her in the fall of 1840 when Orson was in Scotland. She wrote that Smith had come in Bennett's company at first; but then eventually the Prophet had told her that it was not at all "necessary" for her to be alone, that he would stay with her, and that there was no sin in it as long as she kept it to herself. In addition Bennett told her that Joseph had "invented" a revelation permitting plural marriage to "shield" his alleged attentions to numerous women around Nauvoo.[90]

Although she kept silent, Sarah was so "enraged" by Joseph's proposal "that I refused to accept any help from the tithing house or the bishop."[91] She awaited Orson's return boarding with friends (Stephen and Zeruiah Goddard and Dr. Robert D. Foster) and turning out needlework. All was apparently quiet until the spring of 1842 when Joseph, according to Bennett, renewed his appeal to Sarah and even kissed her while Orson was out. When Orson heard of this, he found himself in a rage against the man he had revered as God's mouthpiece for twelve years. He confronted Joseph and warned him never to insult his wife in that manner again.

Now Orson heard the other side of the story. Joseph professed his innocence and denied that he had made any such advances, insisting that not he but Bennett had been Sarah's lover.[92] According to a Pratt family legend, he told Orson to go home, where he would find the "mark of the beast upon Sarah."[93]

Almost overnight Orson was transformed from single-minded disciple to sullen rebel. He did not believe Joseph's denials, preferring to side with his wife and Bennett. Later, when Joseph announced that he was withdrawing Church fellowship from Bennett for claiming that the Prophet had given him "authority to hold illicit intercourse with women," Orson refused to sustain the action. From the time of this vote, May 11, 1842, Orson was "out of harmony" with his quorum.[94] All communication between Orson and Joseph broke down.[95]

Bennett left Nauvoo in disgrace a month later. Joseph Smith exposed Bennett's abandonment of his family and his expulsion from the Masonic order (he also believed Bennett planned to assassinate him).[96] Whether or not it occurred to Orson at this point to question the stories told by Bennett and Sarah it is impossible to say. Certainly he found it increasingly uncomfortable to associate with other Church members and refused to join the Masonic Lodge when the invitation was extended to him.[97] In July Bennett's account of Sarah's difficulties in Nauvoo began circulating in the *Sangamo Journal*, a western Illinois newspaper which consistently editorialized against the

Mormons. Joseph Smith then reportedly vilified Sarah as a "______ from her mother's breast."[98]

These were dark days for Orson Pratt. On July 8 a prominent non-Mormon citizen of Nauvoo, Jacob B. Backenstos, appeared before a justice of the peace and "accused Dr. John C. Bennett with having an illicit intercourse with Mrs. Orson Pratt . . . when said Bennett replied that she made a first rate go."[99] On July 13 Orson gave notice of his withdrawal as a Mormon candidate for the state legislature, explaining that there were many much better qualified than he.[100] His "cheerful" refusal of this honor ("if it may thus be called," he adds) may indicate his conflicting feelings. The next day, according to the *Sangamo Journal*, Joseph launched a public attack upon Sarah Pratt: "In a public speech in Nauvoo on the 14th, Joe spoke of this lady—a woman whose reputation had been as fair as virtue could make it until she came in contact with him—in a manner only to be fitting the lowest and most degraded vagabond in existence."[101]

On the morning of July 15 a Bennett letter appeared in the *Journal* disclosing all of Joseph Smith's alleged attentions to Sarah Pratt. Suffering intensely, Orson wandered away from town far down the riverbank—possibly intending to commit suicide. The Joseph Smith *History* reads, "It was reported early in the morning that Elder Orson Pratt was missing. I caused the Temple hands and the principal men of the city to make search for him. After which, a meeting was called at the Grove, and I gave the public a general outline of John C. Bennett's conduct . . . Elder Pratt returned in the evening."[102]

One of the temple hands, Alexander Neibaur, reported in his journal that "all of the citizens turned out in search of him."[103] Ebenezer Robinson, publisher of the *Times and Seasons*, years later attributed Orson's actions to "insanity" brought on by the "secret teachings of the spiritual wife doctrine." He relates the conflicting rumors about Sarah: "Apostle Pratt had been told Joseph Smith wanted Orson's wife as his own plural wife and John C. Bennett was accused of having committed adultery with his wife. Both men denied these charges. Under these circumstances his mind temporarily gave way, and he wandered away, no one knew where . . . He was found some five miles below Nauvoo, sitting on a rock on the bank of the Mississippi River, having lost his hat."[104] The fact that the entire town went in search of him testifies to the general consternation the people felt over Orson's situation, whether it could be ascribed to temporary insanity or not. Joseph Smith told the Saints, "Orson Pratt has attempted to destroy himself."[105] Family tradition renounces the story of attempted suicide but perpetuates a legend that Orson did cut himself with a knife in order to write a letter in blood to the Prophet Joseph Smith.[106]

The *Sangamo Journal* called upon Orson to avenge the wrongs done to his wife: "We do not know what course will be pursued by Mr. Pratt. If he sinks under the denunciations and schemes of Joe Smith—if he fails to defend the reputation of himself and of the woman he has vowed to protect . . . he will fix a stain upon his character which he can never wash out, and carry to the grave the pangs caused by the 'gnawings of the worm that never dies.' "[107]

Orson Pratt himself probably did not know what course to pursue. The matter came to a head at a July 22 meeting intended to present a public reply to Dr. Bennett's disclosures. A resolution was passed declaring Joseph Smith "to be a good, moral, virtuous, peaceable and patriotic man, and a firm supporter of law, justice and equal rights." When a vote was called, Orson Pratt registered one of a half-dozen negative votes among a thousand affirmatives. His lengthy explanation for his vote (unfortunately unrecorded) was finally terminated by a question from Joseph Smith: "Have you personally a knowledge of any immoral act in me toward the female sex, or in any other way?" Orson responded: "Personally, toward the female sex, I have not."[108]

As Orson withdrew more and more from Nauvoo society, the other apostles were determined to rescue him and called an extraordinary council for four days during August 1842 to try to convince him that he was in error about Joseph Smith. Brigham Young wrote to Parley:

> "Br Orson Pratt is in trubble in consequence of his wife, his feelings are so rought up that he dos not know whether his wife is wrong, or whether Josephs testimony and others are wrong and due Ly and he decived for 12 years or not; he is all but crazy about matters, you may aske what the matter is concirning Sister P.—it is enoph, and doct. J.C. Bennett could tell about . . . himself & hir—enoph of that—we will not let Br. Orson goe away from us he is to good a man to have a woman destroy him."[109]

Brigham Young's manuscript history relates, "I spent several days laboring with Elder Orson Pratt, whose mind became so darkened by the influence and statements of his wife, that he came out in rebellion against Joseph, refusing to believe his testimony or obey his counsel. He said he would believe his wife in preference to the Prophet. Joseph told him if he did believe his wife and follow her suggestions he would go to hell."[110] Years later, the day after Orson Pratt's funeral, John Taylor recalled his own strivings with Orson, who had "some difficulties arising out of the introduction of the Celestial Order of Marriage. It seems from remarks made in a conversation that I had with him afterwards, that he did not fully realize or comprehend the situation . . . when I saw that he was very severely tried . . . I talked with him for nearly two hours, to prevent, if possible, his apostasy . . . he was dropped from . . . the Quorum."[111]

Joseph Smith was in hiding at the time, evading extradition to Missouri to answer charges in the attempted assassination of Lilburn W. Boggs.[112] After reviewing the efforts of the apostles, Joseph assented to Orson's excommunication, which took place August 20, 1842. The trial board consisted of Brigham Young, Heber C. Kimball, and George A. Smith. Orson himself said to Brigham Young, "There is brother Amasa Lyman . . . he has been long in the ministry, go in and ordain him in my stead." And so Joseph Smith ordered it: Amasa Lyman, one of Orson's first Vermont converts, took his place as the newest member of the council.[113] Joseph Smith was hurt by the disloyalty of Orson Pratt, who he thought was "telling stories to people who would betray me, and they must believe these stories because his wife told him so!" He promised to "kick" Orson "off my heels."[114] The Twelve blamed Bennett and Sarah Pratt for Orson's difficulties, and Wilford Woodruff wrote in his journal, "John C. Bennett was the ruin of Orson Pratt."[115]

Orson Pratt had followed seven of the original Quorum of Apostles out of the Church. Now there remained only his brother Parley (away in Liverpool), Young, Kimball, and William Smith (who would one day be excluded from the Quorum).

The Mormons now turned to the defense of Joseph Smith against John C. Bennett's allegations. A flurry of affidavits came out in the Mormon papers just a few days after Orson's excommunication, testifying to Joseph's probity and Bennett's rascality. Stephen H. Goddard and his wife, Zeruiah, published a letter accusing John C. Bennett of an adulterous relationship with Sarah Pratt. Goddard testified that he wanted to have kept "forever in silence" but felt it was his duty to report what he had witnessed between Bennett and Sarah while she stayed in his house during the autumn of 1840:

I took your wife into my house because she was destitute of a house, Oct. 6, 1840, and from the first night until the last, with the exception of one night, the Dr. was there as sure as the night came . . . sometimes till after midnight; what his conversation was I could not tell, as they sat close together, he leaning on her lap, whispering continually or talking very low. One night they took their chairs out of doors and remained there as we supposed until 12 o'clock or after; at another time they went over to the house where you now live and came back after dark, or about that time. We went over several times late in the evening while she lived in the house of Dr. [Robert D.] Foster, and were most sure to find Dr. Bennett and your wife together, as it were, man and wife, lying on the floor and the bed apparently reserved for the Dr. and herself.[116]

Goddard's wife corroborated this in greater detail. Zeruiah Goddard testified that Bennett often cursed and swore at Sarah in the middle of the night. "Their conduct was anything but virtuous, and I know Mrs. Pratt is not a woman of truth, and I believe the statements which Dr. Bennett made concerning Joseph are false, and fabricated for the purpose of covering his iniquities, and enabling him to practice his base designs on the innocent." Mrs. Goddard's statement added information which must have pained Orson Pratt:

I remonstrated with the Dr. and asked him what Orson Pratt would think, if he should know that you were so fond of his wife, and holding her hand so much; the Dr. replied that he could pull the wool over Orson's eyes. Mrs. Pratt stated to me that Dr. Bennett told her, that he could cause abortion with perfect safety to the mother . . . On one occasion I came suddenly into the room where Mrs. Pratt and the Dr. were, she was lying on the bed and the Dr. was taking his hands out of her bosom; he was in the habit of sitting on the bed where Mrs. Pratt was lying, and lying down over her.[117]

Other depositions were filed, all calculated to counteract Bennett's "awful disclosures." Like Sarah Pratt, the daughter of Sidney Rigdon was also implicated in Bennett's escapades, and there was the testimony of Catherine Fuller Warren. Joseph Smith summed up his own views of the "facts relative to the conduct of our major-general, John C. Bennett" in a letter to Governor Carlin of Illinois. He denounced Bennett as an admitted adulterer:

Some time ago it having been reported to me that some of the most aggravated cases of adultery had been committed upon some previously respectable females in our city, I took proper methods to ascertain the truth . . . More than twenty months ago [October 1840] Bennett went

> to a lady in the city and began to teach her that promiscuous intercourse between the sexes was lawful and no harm in it, and requested the privilege of gratifying his passions; but she refused in the strongest terms, saying that it was very wrong to do so, and it would bring a disgrace on the Church. Finding this argument ineffectual, he told her that men in higher standing in the Church than himself not only sanctioned, but practiced the same deeds; and in order to finish that controversy, said and affirmed that I both taught and acted in the same manner, but publicly proclaimed against in consequence of the prejudice of the people, and for fear of trouble in my own house. By this means he accomplished his designs; he seduced a respectable female with lying, and subjected her to public infamy and disgrace. Not contented with what he had already done, he made the attempt on others, and by using the same language, seduced them also.[118]

The lady referred to may be Catherine Fuller Warren, although Joseph probably meant to imply that Sarah Pratt was one of the "others."

Three days after the appearance of the affidavit sheet, Orson Pratt published a surprising statement in *The Wasp*, a Mormon newspaper. He denied that he had "renounced the Church of Jesus Christ of Latter Day Saints, but believe that its doctrine which has been published extensively in both America and Europe, is pure and according to the scriptures of eternal truth . . . there is something in it which seems to whisper that 'God is there' . . . the lustre of truth cannot be dimmed by the shadows of error and falsehood. Neither will the petty difficulties existing among its votaries weaken its influence or destroy its power."[119] During September Bennett's propaganda offensive intensified, and perhaps Orson began to resent the Doctor, who now swore to "drink the heart's blood" of those who had expelled him from Nauvoo.[120] To those who allied the Pratts in the public mind with Bennett's campaign, Orson replied through the October 1 issue of *The Wasp*:

> Dear Sir: I noticed in the last week's Wasp . . . that Dr. J.C. Bennett had declared . . . that he had received a letter from me and from my wife, and that we were preparing to leave and expose Mormonism. I wish, through the medium of your paper, to say to the public, that said statements are entirely false. We have never, at any time, written any letter or letters to Dr. J. C. Bennett, on any subject whatever. Neither are we "preparing to leave and expose Mormonism:" but intend to make NAUVOO OUR RESIDENCE, AND MORMONISM OUR MOTTO.[121]

In T. Edgar Lyon's words, Orson "had no quarrel with the restored Gospel, but a personal conflict with Joseph Smith's alleged misconduct."[122]

While continuing to offer his "regular course of instruction"[123] through the university and entertaining the Nauvoo Lyceum in his home,[124] Orson contemplated what to do about his "petty difficulties" with the Prophet, who remained in hiding through the autumn of 1842. The solution came in the form of a letter from Bennett addressed to Orson Pratt and Sidney Rigdon.

Rigdon had suffered similar shocks over "disclosures" about his daughter and the Prophet, but he had also publicly disclaimed any connection with Bennett.[125] Bennett made a final attempt in January 1843 to enlist Rigdon and Orson into a conspiracy to kidnap Joseph Smith and return him for "trial" in Missouri. He addressed them as "dear friends" and announced that he was meeting with some Missouri officials who would attempt the extradition of Joseph Smith:

> Dear friends:—It is a long time since I have written to you, and I should now much desire to see you, but I leave tonight for Missouri to meet the messenger charged with the arrest of Joseph Smith . . . and others, for murder, burglary, treason, etc. . . . New proceedings have been gotten up on the old charges, and no habeas corpus can save them . . . The war goes bravely on; and, although Smith thinks he is now safe, the enemy is near, even at the door . . . nothing can save Joseph on a new requisition . . . he must go to Missouri; but he shall not be harmed if he is not guilty; but he is a murderer, and must suffer the penalty of the law . . . I hope that both your kind and amiable families are well . . . Please write me at Independence immediately.[126]

Rigdon read the letter first and passed it on to Orson, who was revolted by Bennett's presumption. Orson lost no time in presenting it to Joseph Smith.[127] This brought an end to the hard feelings between them, and five days later, on January 20, 1843, Joseph called a council of the Twelve to announce that Orson "had confessed his sins and manifested deep repentance."[128] The Prophet then remarked that "as there was not a quorum when Orson Pratt's case came up before that he was still a member—he had not legally been cut off." Orson was gratified but insisted that he would "rather die than go to preach in any other standing [than] that I had before." This was followed by some talk of sending Orson abroad to preach the gospel to Jews. Joseph said, "Let him have the same calling that Paul had. Let him have the keys to the Jews. First unto the Gentiles then unto the Jews . . . when the Gentiles have heard all they will, it shall be given to the Jews."

This idea was dropped, and Joseph raised the issue of Orson's standing in the Twelve. Referring to the ordination of Amasa Lyman to take Orson's place, he said: "Orson by transgression laid himself liable to have another ordained in his stead. And prophet Jacob and Esau were brought [up] for example." Then Brigham Young questioned whether Lyman's ordination was valid as only three apostles had participated in it. "Joseph said that was legal when no more could be had." Brigham had no objection to bringing Orson back into the Twelve, saying "all he had against Orson was when he came home he loved his wife better than David." ("David" referred to Joseph Smith in his office as a king and priest in the kingdom of God.) At this Joseph turned to Orson and said, "She lied about me—I never made the offer which she said I did. I will not advise you to break up your family—unless it were asked of me. Then I would council you to get a bill [of divorce?] from your wife and marry a virtuous woman—and raise a new family but if you do not do it [I] shall never throw it in your teeth."

Orson demurred, but the Prophet gave his blessing anyway. "I prophesy in the name of the Lord Jesus Christ that it will not be 6 months before you have things which will make you glad you have not left us . . . Orson, the latter part of your life shall be more joyful than the former." He then turned to Orson Hyde, whom he had planned to bring into the First Presidency, and said, "I can make a swap with Amasa Lyman & let him have the office we were going to give you."

At four o'clock that afternoon Orson and Sarah both stepped into the freezing river to be baptized again by Joseph Smith. (Though Orson's excommunication was voided and Sarah had never been cut off, the rebaptism was taken as a sign of renewed commitment.) They were confirmed in the "Court Room," and "Orson received the Priesthood and the same power and authority as in former days."[129]

Orson had undergone his direst test of faith to that time. Ultimately, he chose both his wife and his prophet, laying the entire blame for the scandal upon Bennett. Sometime in the fall of 1842 he settled on that interpretation, possibly after reading the barrage of affidavits printed by the Church labeling Bennett a liar. Perhaps in the light of the Backenstos and Goddard depositions he began to question Sarah's version of events. It is more likely that his long-standing personal devotion to Joseph Smith, coupled with his own deeply held religious logic, led him to reaffirm his faith in Mormonism. For twelve years he had been absorbed in the Prophet and the cause:

> I . . . became intimately acquainted with the Prophet Joseph Smith, and continued . . . until the day of his death. I had the great privilege, when I was in from my missions, of boarding the most of the time at his house, so that I not only knew him as a public teacher, but as a private citizen, as a husband and father. I witnessed his earnest and humble devotions both morning and evening in his family. I heard the words of eternal life flowing from his mouth . . . I saw his countenance lighted up as the inspiration of the Holy Ghost rested upon him, dictating the great and most precious revelations . . . I saw him translating, by inspiration, the Old and New Testaments, and the inspired book of Abraham from Egyptian papyrus. And what is now [1859] my testimony concerning that man, founded upon my own personal observations? It is the same to-day as it was when I first received the testimony that he was a Prophet. I knew that he was a man of God. It was not a matter of opinion with me, for I received a testimony from the heavens concerning that matter.[130]

For Orson that testimony was too deeply ingrained to shrug off; his commitment to what he saw as absolute truth would not admit of contradictions. He had no difficulties with doctrinal matters, and ultimately doctrine was the force that held him: "If the doctrine of polygamy were not true," he later preached, "I would not give a fig for all your other revelations that came through Joseph Smith the Prophet; I would renounce the whole lot of them, because it is utterly impossible for a man to believe a part of them to be divine—from God—and a part of them to be from the devil."[131] It was impossible for Orson to consider that truth may lie on both sides of the Sarah Pratt affair.

The tempest died with Orson's rebaptism in the ice of the Mississippi. Stories continued to circulate that he was the rival and secret enemy of Joseph Smith, but these were distortions. Orson's own journal summarizes the troubled year of 1842 without comment: "I remained in Nauvoo about one year. . . . I had the charge of a mathematical school."[132]

5
The Gauge of Philosophy

In March 1842 the Nauvoo newspaper *Times & Seasons* began a serialization of Joseph Smith's translations of the Kirtland paypri.[1] It told an apocryphal story of Abraham the philosopher, "reasoning upon the principles of astronomy" in Pharaoh's court and of Abraham the exile fleeing from the sacrificial altar of Pharaoh's temple-observatory. Burned out of his Missouri home and having passed a test of Abrahamic severity, Orson Pratt saw his own life parallel the pattern of Abraham's.

The Prophet's new Book of Abraham now defined the heavens themselves in Mormon terms: Governing from a central sphere called "Kolob,"[2] God is described as the great organizer of celestial mechanics in which time is relative. The themes of this new revelation reflected one of Orson's major interests: reconciling science and theology. "When we undertake to investigate the laws which govern the various departments of nature, we are investigating the laws of God," he said in 1875.[3]

Orson kept careful records of interesting physical phenomena, noting one icy March morning in 1843 the appearance of great "halos or circles, accompanied with parhelia or mock suns . . . these beautiful and curious phenomena, doubtless owe their origin to the refractions of the sun's rays through the minute, though differently shaped prismatic crystals of ice and snow, which float in the atmosphere."[4] The "principles and powers" of the physical world were an important subject to Orson Pratt: "When you study all these things you are learning lessons concerning God. He it is who has thus organized all these materials of nature."[5]

At the April conference of 1843 Orson Pratt spoke[6] on the "Ancient of Days," a figure who appears in the visions of the prophet Daniel. Joseph Smith had identified this personage as Adam,[7] the first patriarch, who would preside over "unnumbered millions" in the Millennium. In this address Pratt discusses the organization and preparation of worlds, the calling of grand councils for the disposition of power and dominion over the mechanisms of the universe, and the probationary war between darkness and light.

During an afternoon session of the conference that seemed to Joseph Smith a deeply spiritual meeting ("a millennium within these walls"), Pratt remarked that man's body changes completely every seven years. Joseph stood afterward and announced that he cared not "what the theories of men are. We have the testimony that God will raise us up, and he has the power to do it. If any one supposes that any part of our bodies . . . ever goes into another body, he is mistaken."[8] The exchange illustrates Orson's theological bias toward science.[9]

In civic affairs Orson had his own mind as well. When Joseph Smith suggested in council meeting that Nauvoo pass an ordinance permitting only gold and silver specie as legal tender within the city, Orson and Daniel H. Wells objected to the idea presumably because land was also a legal medium of exchange under state law. Despite Orson's objections the ordinance went into immediate effect. The Prophet, who had been nearly ruined by credit schemes in Kirtland, did not want the people of Nauvoo "in danger of being gulled by speculators."[10]

But Joseph Smith had the spiritual kingdom first in his mind. In April 1843 he ordered the Twelve to resume traveling and preaching "to save their lives." Joseph commanded them not to let "a single corner of the earth go without a mission"[11] and said, "I want Orson Pratt should go."[12] The next few weeks were occupied with preparation for another mission to the East as well as civic affairs: examining Nauvoo stock, gathering means for the construction of public buildings in Nauvoo, and helping Parley build a house for his family. On July 1 Orson Pratt and Heber C. Kimball[13] headed east to "cast up a highway for the Saints from here to Maine"[14] and smooth a path for Mormon converts both physically and financially. Funds were needed for the temple and the Nauvoo House, a hotel near the river under construction in 1843 and 1844.[15] The two missionaries preached from Cincinnati to Pittsburgh in a region well known to Orson. Here they met four others of the Twelve, among them the Apostle John E. Page, who was thunderously denouncing sectarianism in the meeting halls of the city. The first week of August the six traveled to Philadelphia where they visited Independence Hall, sat in the chair occupied by John Hancock, and inspected a painting of symbolic significance to them: Benjamin West's *Paul and Barnabas*.[16]

Orson preached in Philadelphia before heading to New York, where he gave a powerful sermon on the worldwide significance of the Book of Mormon message, laying great emphasis on its value as a history as well as a rule of faith. Proceeding to Providence and Boston, he preached on the subject of the temple: "When the temple is reared, God will manifest Himself in a peculiar manner. If we are obedient, He has told us He will make manifest to us things we are ignorant of. He has said He will reveal things which pertain to this dispensation that have been hidden and kept secret from the foundation of the world. No former age or generation of the world have had the same things revealed: all other dispensations will be swallowed up in this."[17]

In other words, the building of the temple fulfilled a sacred prophecy in providing a ritual center for the last days. Orson developed Joseph Smith's concept of the temple as a place where the Church would receive an endowment of knowledge and power. Orson went on to warn the Saints against failing in the construction of the temple under penalty of rejection by the Lord. As an example he cited "the shortcomings" of the Saints in Missouri: "Did the churches do as God commanded? No, they did not . . . the enemies of the Saints came upon them, and drove them from their houses and homes."[18]

Orson's preaching had been transformed. He now began to discourse upon the "mysteries of godliness" in order to close the widening fissure between science and religion. He believed that their unity had to be articulated and demonstrated.

In the midst of their solemn mission, the six traveling apostles consulted Mr. O. S. Fowler, a leading Boston phrenologist. Phrenology, the practice of describing individual character traits by measuring bumps and hollows on the skull, was a popular pseudoscience of the day. Orson obtained his phrenological chart from Fowler, probably with a good deal of interest although he has left no comment on the subject. Phrenology was totally unacceptable to orthodox Christians, for it "equated mental and even spiritual characteristics with cranial form and function."[19] This fact probably heightened the interest of phrenology for the Mormon materialist Orson Pratt.

In October Orson returned to Nauvoo with the other apostles to help in the temple construction and to receive endowments. Until the temple was finished the endowment ceremony was conducted on a limited scale in Joseph Smith's home. Orson Pratt first participated in this ritual there on December 23, 1843, the Prophet's thirty-eighth and last birthday. The first endowment ceremonies were introduced in May 1842 but were intended for later practice within the great temple Smith envisioned crowning the prominence of Nauvoo.[20] The ceremony consisted of washings, anointings with oil, and bestowal of certain "keys," along with explanatory initiations that would permit entrance into the celestial kingdom of God.[21] From the first it was considered an ordinance too sacred to be discussed in detail. Along with Orson came Parley and Orson Hyde, Wilford Woodruff, and Orson Spencer. For some reason Sarah did not accompany her husband on this first introduction to the mysteries of the endowment whereas most of the other wives were present.[22] A few weeks later at the home of Brigham Young, Orson received his "second anointing,"[23] an ordinance which confirmed the blessings promised in the endowment. Apparently reserved at first to the Church leaders so that the Twelve could "round up their shoulders and bear it [the Kingdom] off," the second anointing confirmed the "revealed promises of 'kingly powers' [i.e., godhood] received in the endowment's initiatory ordinances."[24] These culminating rituals became generally practiced among the Latter-day Saints as the temple grew to completion.

The importance of confidentiality in sacred things was reinforced by the need for protection from antagonists both within and without the Church. In March 1844 the Prophet initiated a number of his closest associates into a kind of inner cabinet, a "Council of Fifty," with a charge, a name, a keyword (or password), a constitution, and a penalty. An oath of secrecy underscored Joseph's determination to keep his plans for the Saints concealed from his enemies: The council dealt primarily with the problem of finding a new gathering place, and Joseph wanted these discussions hidden from the public. Although the Council of Fifty met only sporadically until its dissolution in the 1880s, it served as a vehicle for settling disagreements and articulating policy for the emigration west. Evidence indicates, however, that the council functioned primarily as a forum for airing opinions since most important decisions continued to be made by the Presidency and the Twelve. After 1851 the council was not reconvened for sixteen years, and, except for a brief period during the administration of John Taylor when it was designated "the government of the Kingdom of God," it was essentially abandoned by Church leaders. Orson Pratt was inducted into the Council of Fifty March 11, 1844, and remained a nominal member until his death.[25]

During this period of retrenchment for the Mormon church, Joseph Smith had suffered continually what he deemed harassment on the part of Missouri officials who had made attempts to force him to answer charges, among them complicity in the attempted murder of former Governor Lilburn W. Boggs, the executive of the infamous "extermination order."[26] Joseph had been forced to hide on occasion to avoid Missouri officers bent on kidnapping him. In December 1843 Joseph was angry enough to appeal directly to Congress for redress. He intended once and for all to test the hand of the federal government with a twofold petition: he demanded punishment for the officials of Jackson and Clay counties who had committed outrages on the Saints and an end to the vexatious prosecutions against him conducted by Missouri judges.[27] By this time he had been tried and acquitted three times in Illinois courts under writs of habeas corpus on the charge of complicity in shooting Boggs.[28]

The Prophet asked Orson Pratt to deliver the memorial to Congress, and Orson left Nauvoo as an "agent of the city" sometime in March 1844. They would not see each other again. For Orson's credentials, Joseph wrote "He by us is recommended . . . as a gentleman of principle and character."[29]

Orson's sojourn in Washington was pleasant but fruitless. He laid the petition before the judiciary committees of both houses, but, as he later wrote, "Our petitioners are unheeded or treated with contempt. And thousands of American citizens must linger out a life of wretched exile, deprived of the use of their own lands, and of the sacred rights of American Liberty." In May he wrote a letter to the

Senate Judiciary Committee out of a "deep sense of duty to myself, and to many thousands of sufferers who have entrusted this memorial to my charge." He argued for congressional intervention, insisting that the expense and certain outcome of litigation in Missouri courts would necessitate eventual appeal to the Supreme Court, where, even if judgment were rendered in favor of the Mormons, the army would be required to exact retribution. In addition Orson pointed out the constitutional prohibition on federal courts to judge cases of law and equity between a state and citizens of another state. His appeal, then, was to demonstrate the futility of judicial remedies; only Congress could provide redress to the much-injured Mormon people.[30]

These arguments were in vain. Once again the Judiciary Committee recommended the Mormons seek redress through the courts of the state of Missouri and emphasized the powerlessness of the federal congress in the internal affairs of any state. It was perhaps ingenuous of the Mormons to press Congress in view of the debate over states' rights then raging among the federal representatives and threatening to pull the Union apart. Congress was dominated by the strict-constructionist Democratic party, and any move that smacked of federal intervention in the affairs of individual states was quite simply out of the question.

Orson's instructions were soon to be altered, however, for in the meantime at Nauvoo Joseph Smith had encountered problems much more immediate than seeking retribution from the state of Missouri. Awareness of the practice of plural marriage was spreading both in and out of the Church, and one of Joseph's counselors, William Law, had found the doctrine too difficult to accept. Joseph Smith continued his public denunciations of "spiritual wifery" as "exposed" by John C. Bennett, but Law did not distinguish between the principles of Joseph's revelation and Bennett's system of wholesale prostitution. Among others who objected was one Francis M. Higbee, whose "slanderous and abusive language" Orson Pratt had complained of in city council meeting the previous January.[31] The Higbees were notorious for a certain irreverence toward Smith and his calling, while Law had a serious conflict of faith over the Prophet's teachings.[32] At any rate they were all charged with conspiracy against Joseph Smith before the Church and municipal courts during March of 1844.[33]

Regarding these men as "Judases in our midst," Joseph Smith feared secret violence from those who had failed to destroy him in the open. He organized an armed police force of forty members to keep careful watch on strangers and citizens alike. This along with the growing strength and independence of the Nauvoo Legion began to alarm neighboring towns; the rumors of spiritual wifery and corruption in Nauvoo served only to agitate public opinion even more against the Latter-day Saints. Inevitably Joseph Smith began once again to look for a suitable place to move. He directed Orson Pratt to present to Congress a proposal allowing the Mormons to settle and "police the inter-mountain and Pacific coast west from Oregon to Texas."[34] In April Orson Hyde left Nauvoo for Washington to deliver this message to Orson Pratt.

This was not the first Orson had heard about the Rocky Mountains. Just before leaving Nauvoo in March, he had discussed with the Prophet in council the possibility of securing "a resting place in the mountains, or some uninhabited region, where we can enjoy the liberty of conscience guaranteed to us by the Constitution."[35] The meeting had considered various measures to attain this end, but now Joseph Smith had decided. He enjoined Orson to be aggressive, to press hard the most influential men of Congress, including John Quincy Adams and Henry Clay.

Orson Hyde reported late in April that Pratt had been "indefatigable in his exertions in prosecuting the business entrusted to his charge." Apparently the Mormon proposal was met with some interest, for Pratt and Hyde had talked with Illinois Congressmen James Semple, Stephen A. Douglas, and others "who received us with every demonstration of respect that we could desire." One of the representatives thought the bill objectionable because an armed force headed for Oregon might be considered an infraction of the treaty by which the Northwest was administered jointly under British and American authority. Mormons settling in the character of emigrants, the apostles countered, could not be regarded by Britain as a deviation from the treaty provisions. Most of the gentlemen from Illinois agreed; however, Semple observed that the politicians were moving very slowly on the questions of Texas and Oregon, and he doubted the issue would be discussed before the presidential election in the fall. The Mormons concluded from this that no action was pending and that the politicians were fearful of the British and apprehensive that the election would be decided on the basis of territorial movements in the West. "Oregon is becoming a popular question,"

Hyde wrote back, and he advised against waiting for the government to take action.[36] He also added that he and Pratt had been introduced by Senator Semple to President John Tyler at the White House.[37] Hyde's impression of the president of the United States probably reflects Orson Pratt's opinion as well. They spent a very agreeable hour at the White House and found Tyler "a very plain, homespun, familiar, farmer-like man. He spoke of our troubles in Missouri, and regretted that we had met with such treatment." But it was clear that no government sanction nor protection would be extended to the Saints if they attempted to settle the West, "for you might as well drive a musket ball through a cotton bag, or the Gospel of Christ through the heart of a priest, case-hardened by sectarianism, bigotry and superstition . . . as to drive anything through Congress that will operate against the popularity of politicians."[38]

Mormon disgust with the indifference of federal authorities including a number of presidential aspirants to whom Joseph Smith had addressed pleas for help grew so strong that a May "convention" was held to nominate the Prophet himself for the presidency. Orson Pratt, then in Washington, was designated to attend the July convention of the Democratic party in order to represent the candidacy of General Joseph Smith and his running mate Sidney Rigdon.[39]

Except for his lobbying duties Orson spent his time preparing information for an almanac to be published at Washington. A twenty-four-page booklet, which sold for six and one-fourth cents, *The Prophetic Almanac for 1845*, as it was called, contained calendar information, solar and lunar eclipse predictions, and tidal tables, along with extracts from the writings and speeches of Joseph Smith and others. One intriguing aspect of the almanac is "The Mormon Creed," a list of doctrinal concepts in question-answer form. This is one of the earliest summary statements of Mormon belief: "What is man? The offspring of God . . . What is his final destiny? To be like God. What has God been? Like man . . . How many gods are there? There are Lords many, and gods many: but to us there is but one God . . . What is the kingdom of God? A theocracy; or, in other words, a kingdom governed by direct revelation from God."[40] Although these answers could not be simpler, they are very far reaching; the Mormons did not shrink from proclaiming godhood their ultimate destiny and eternal progression or evolution the basic justification for the existence of man on earth. Thus Orson's second publication, though essentially a miscellany, nevertheless contains some of the earliest exposition of Mormon cosmology.

The almanac also contained the Nauvoo council's memorial to Congress and a letter from Orson Pratt to the Senate Judiciary Committee. Brother Parley was at the same time editing a periodical at New York called *The Prophet*, intended to advance Joseph Smith's campaign for the presidency. The first week in June 1844 Orson left Washington to join him. He preached at the Marion Temperance Hall in Canal Street by appointment on June 9, "at the usual hours."[41]

But all was not "usual" in the Mormon church. The rift between Joseph Smith and William Law at Nauvoo had resulted in the formation of a rival "church," presided over by Law and a number of other malcontents. These had banded together to publish an opposition newspaper in Nauvoo, *The Expositor*. But as soon as the first issue appeared, the city council voted to "abate" the newspaper as a public nuisance.[42] The subsequent destruction of the press and the way charges brought by the outraged William Law were handled in the Nauvoo courts raised the ire of the journals and thus the citizenry of Illinois. Public petitions were brought to Governor Thomas Ford to have the Mormons "exterminated" and Joseph Smith tried for treason.[43] The Prophet responded by putting the Nauvoo Legion on alert and the city under martial law; he also called the members of the Twelve to return to Nauvoo with all urgency.[44]

Like the other traveling apostles, Orson Pratt was unaware of the fatal storm gathering at home. To show his good faith, Joseph eventually compromised with the governor by disarming the legion and promising to appear for trial at Carthage, the seat of Hancock County.[45] On June 27, 1844, the jail in which Joseph Smith was held fell to a rampaging crowd of vigilantes apparently in collusion with the prison guards.[46] Joseph tried to escape by leaping from a second-story window. Governor Ford wrote, "The fall so stunned him that he was unable to rise; and being placed in a sitting posture by the conspirators below, they despatched him with four balls shot through his body."[47]

News of the Prophet's death was slow in spreading. The Mormons of Nauvoo were too profoundly shocked to retaliate; their neighbors dug in fearfully nevertheless. No one expected the resulting peace and quiet. Nauvoo went about its business in deep melancholy, the body of the Prophet was laid in an unmarked grave to discourage curiosity, and the Twelve Apostles began to filter home one by one as they heard the tidings. Many of them including Wilford Woodruff and Brigham Young, who were sitting in the Boston railroad station that afternoon, later testified to a black depression that overcame them, a sorrowful feeling that could not be explained. Parley, sailing up the Utica Canal with his brother William, wrote that he was burdened with speechless awe and solemnity that afternoon, "as if the powers of hell were let loose . . . the spirit of murder . . . seems to pervade the whole land."[48]

Still unaware of the fate of the Prophet, Orson went from New York to Boston to help with political meetings to be directed by Brigham Young. The first reports circulated in Boston around July 9, but the apostles refused to believe them.[49] Brigham and Orson set out together to visit Lowell, Massachusetts, and Peterborough, New Hampshire; at the latter place they met with a Brother Bement and heard a letter read which gave particulars of the murder. Brigham Young wrote, "The first thing which I thought of was, whether Joseph had taken the keys of the kingdom with him from the earth; Brother Orson Pratt sat on my left; we were both leaning back on our chairs. Bringing my hand down on my knee, I said the keys of the Kingdom are right here with the Church."[50] There was no doubt for these two apostles that the Church would continue with its "keys," and this moment of inspiration led them back to Nauvoo to face the suffering Saints and to reassure them. Wilford Woodruff wrote from Boston advising that the Twelve meet to decide what to do. At the same time Parley was counseling the members of the Church at Nauvoo to await patiently the return of the Twelve to receive instructions from them.

Orson Pratt was now a member of the presiding council of the Church. That the Twelve embodied the "general authority" over the Church seems implicit in these events, but soon their predominance would be questioned. The two apostles advised the Boston branches to gather immediately at Nauvoo for a grand council of the Church, and Orson left almost at once by way of New York and the rail route west through Schenectady and Buffalo, then by steamer to Detroit and Chicago, arriving at last on August 6.[51]

The following days were taken up with preparation for a solemn assembly of all the priesthood quorums present at Nauvoo. The apostles visited and ministered to one of their number who survived the massacre at Carthage jail; John Taylor had received five bullet wounds. On August 8 the Twelve called the quorums to order around the dais of the great open-air meeting ground near the temple. They found Joseph's counselor, Sidney Rigdon, who had been "out of harmony" with Joseph for nearly a year, advancing himself as "guardian" and president of the Church by virtue of his office. Rigdon spoke to the assembly all morning, but after a forceful afternoon address by Brigham Young, the conference voted to sustain the Twelve as the presiding authorities of the Church. For most Latter-day Saints the question of leadership was resolved, although dissidents continued to arise.[52]

Orson now sat in on most decisions directing the Church. The Twelve immediately tried to put the community in order. They delegated the trusteeship of the Church to a "presiding bishop" and began to settle financial and missionary affairs as best they could while still continuing work on the temple. In September, to stem the conflicting claims still put forward by Rigdon, Brigham Young called a general meeting to vote once again. The result was the excommunication of Rigdon, who returned permanently to Pittsburgh.[53]

Orson Pratt became a valuable spokesman for the Twelve, addressing the Rigdon question (Rigdon considered Pratt an "inflammatory" speaker[54]) and the necessity of completing the temple. Brigham Young's firmness and ability won the confidence of the community, and soon Orson was looking to him as he had to Joseph Smith. For his part Brigham regarded Orson a valuable asset. He recommended to the general conference Orson's "Mormon Almanack" as a practical acquisition[55] and in the latter months of 1844 finally introduced him firsthand to the practice of plural marriage. The Bishop sisters, Charlotte and Adelia Ann, were natives of Crown Point, New York, twenty and seventeen years of age respectively. Under Brigham's direction, Orson took them by the hand and was sealed "for time and all eternity" to the sisters. (Sarah Marinda Pratt must have given her consent to the marriages, although reluctantly, as it later proved.) Charlotte, the older of the two new wives, abandoned the arrangement within a few months, while Delia remained faithful all her life to her shared husband.[56] On March 27, 1845, Orson married a fourth wife, Mary Ann Merrill, a twenty-five-year-old woman from Long Island.[57]

Brigham Young was determined to carry out Joseph Smith's vision of Nauvoo. He expanded and systematized priesthood ordinations, established a missionary training center in a two-story building called the Seventies' Hall, and put great emphasis on the completion of the temple.[58] Orson Pratt spoke at the dedication of the Seventies' Hall soon after Christmas 1844.

In this address Orson explained his nontraditional view of original sin. He announced that Adam's transgression consisted of a free choice between remaining forever alone in paradise or accompanying the fallen Eve in order to propagate the human race. "Whether Adam understood the law of redemption prior to the fall or not, I shall not decide." He spoke of the penalties connected to the laws and of the necessity of experiencing "opposites" in order to appreciate the blessings of eternal life.[59] For Orson the orthodox Christian dogma of original sin had no meaning; the concept of the inherent depravity of man was a distorted outgrowth of sectarian notions about the Bible. As Orson saw it, mankind was subject to sin not out of willfulness but rather out of necessity. This doctrine implied man's moral neutrality and the importance of wise and informed choices in order to realize his full destiny.

When the Seventies' Hall was dedicated, the Saints settled in for a quiet winter holiday. Fruit and nuts were passed out, and the Twelve held a New Year's gathering discussing the relatively serious possibility of resettling the Church community.[60]

In this interlude Orson turned once again to his mathematical and astronomical pursuits. On January 12, 1845, he spoke to an audience in the Nauvoo concert hall advancing "an idea pertaining to the magnitude of the planetary system, illustrative of the enlargement of the Saints." More and more Orson drew the connection between the visible order of the universe and the cycle of man's eternal development. The address followed one by Heber Kimball on the subject of "increase and expansion."[61]

The unspoken truce between the Mormons and their neighbors collapsed in January 1845 when recently elected legislators who resented the political power of the Mormons managed to repeal the Nauvoo charter.[62] Now without an official municipal government, Nauvoo came under the de facto administration of the priesthood leaders, who circumvented the state legislature by gaining control of the government of Hancock County. Many Latter-day Saints, alarmed by these developments, decided to get out of Nauvoo before a new conflagration began. To these Orson wrote: "Do you wish, dear brethren, to see the house of our God built up, adorned, and prepared according to the commandment . . . do you wish to enter into its sacred courts and receive your washings and anointings, and the keys of knowledge and power? Do you desire the eternal seal of the priesthood placed upon your head . . . remember that there is but one way, . . . by harkening to our counsel in all things."[63]

Orson, along with the other leaders, was determined to stay put until Joseph's temple was completed. To abandon its construction even in the face of growing hostility around them would have resulted in divine "rejection" as a church.[64] The Twelve dared not risk the spiritual consequences of failure to complete the building and the ordinances of the "keys of the holy priesthood."

Orson tried to clarify the implications of temple theology for the Saints. In April he preached upon the plurality of gods and was called upon to read to the general conference the revelation that commanded the building of the temple.[65] In June he gave a speech at the funeral of William Smith's wife on the role of the first parents and the cause of "misery and death [in] this fair creation." He was careful about speculation: "Some have imbibed the idea that the fruit of the tree which Adam was commanded not to eat, contained the properties of death, which, when eaten by Adam, diffused through his system the nature of mortality. This may be the case, and it may not; I do not pretend to say at present."[66] Also in this sermon Orson defined the destiny of the Saints who "have been ordained thereto in this life . . . What is it to be kings and priests? It is to have honor, authority and dominion, having kingdoms to preside over, and subjects to govern, and possessing the ability ever to increase their authority and glory, and extend their dominion." Orson, like the rest of the Twelve, was clearly preoccupied with bestowing upon as many as possible the "keys to eternal exaltation."

Orson's rhetorical abilities were greatly respected in Nauvoo; Brigham Young engaged him to write as well, and he helped revise the history of the Church dictated by Joseph Smith before his death.[67] Orson also assisted a Danish convert, Peter O. Hanson, in translating the new scriptures into that tongue.[68] (Presumably the assignment involved adapting the texts and clarifying for Hanson the peculiarities of the archaic English of the two books.)

In July correspondent William W. Phelps published in the *New York Sun* an article that described Church leaders: "The spiritual concerns of the Mormons are governed by a Council of Twelve, composed of the following . . . Brigham Young—'The Lion of the Lord,' Heber C. Kimball—'The Herald of Grace,' Parley P. Pratt—'The Archer of Paradise,' [and] Orson Pratt—'The Gauge of Philosophy.' "[69] Phelps, at least, considered Orson Pratt's doctrinal judgment the standard against which philosophy should be measured. Brother Parley's epithet reveals the esteem he commanded as an eloquent, piercing, and soaring speaker. The most appropriate of the nicknames was given to Young: "Lion of the Lord" exactly fit the strength and predominance of the president of the Twelve. But Orson already had the reputation of the intellectual leader—the foremost elaborator and interpreter of Mormon doctrine.

In July 1845 Orson was assigned to preside over the Church in New York and to edit a Church periodical, *The Messenger*. In addition he hoped to renew and expand an almanac for the year 1846.[70] While in the city he settled into some serious writing exploring the implications of Joseph Smith's cosmology and taking the initial steps toward a system of physics constructed from Mormon dogma.

The September numbers of the *New York Messenger* contain some of Orson's earliest and most compelling metaphysical speculations. In an article entitled "Mormon Philosophy"[71] he deals with space and time and most interesting of all with the origin and nature of matter and intellect. Although most of his thinking reflects scientific commonplaces of the day, he argues that Newton's laws of motion are ill conceived for two reasons: first, Newton does not account in his system for the presence of self-conscious entities in the universe; and second, Newton cannot offer an adequate explanation for the attractive force between atoms. Orson believed, as did most physicists, that matter consists of fundamental indivisible particles or "atoms," spherical bodies "perfectly solid, and incapable of being broken or abraded by any concussion or violence, however intense, and therefore their sizes and shapes remain unchangeably the same." Beyond this, however, he departs from conventional physics as he posits that a primal "intelligence" forms one of the basic properties of matter: "To say that some being gave this property to atoms is to admit the prior existence of a being with intelligence . . . Reason has demonstrated, that the intelligence of every atom must either be without beginning, or else be the result of contact and combination."

To Orson the presence of self-conscious beings such as men and animals demonstrated that intellect is a fundamental quality of matter, "either a property of material atoms, or a result of the combination or contact of these atoms." If the former, then intelligence must be an eternal function of the atom because underived from any other source, "for such operations would be impossible in a perfectly solid and imporous atom." If, on the other hand, intelligence results from the combination or contact of atoms, then the "capacity to receive intelligence" must be eternally present.

Orson then explains that motion results from self-propelled, intelligent atoms drawing together in combination: "Those who believe in attraction . . . assert that matter is entirely passive. . . . Now if an atom has not power to move itself, how can it move any thing external to itself? It is the very height of absurdity to suppose that a helpless passive atom can move every thing in the universe but itself . . . Every atom MOVES ITSELF towards every other atom, with a force varying inversely as the square of the distance." Pratt thus turns around Newton's theory with one of his own based on the concept of intelligent, self-moving matter.

Orson's "Mormon Philosophy" next goes on to examine the nature of these intelligent capacities: "What are these? . . . Are they not a species of intelligence self-existent and eternal? If not, how can we account for the combination or contact of atoms? Is this combination fortuitous . . . What then is the cause of atoms approaching atoms, and adhering together with such a variety of intensities according to such uniform and general laws? The only sound answer that can be given to these intricate enquiries is, that these atoms must be intelligent."[72]

Orson defines "intelligence" as the capacity to obey uniform principles while "limited to certain spheres and modes of action."[73] It is difficult to determine whether Orson is constructing here a truly metaphysical system, for his definition of the degrees of intelligence manifested by atomic particles seems restricted to the "self-motivating force." Although his terms are ambiguous, he does not necessarily apply the idea of "self-awareness" to all modes of organized matter.

In summary, Orson Pratt's "Mormon Philosophy" views the constituent particles of matter to be intelligent, self-moving, and active, and the universe as a hierarchy of intelligences varying in degrees of awareness and rational capacity in proportion to their degree of organization. Although most moderns would probably smile at Orson's system, rooted as it is in old assumptions about the atom, it continues to this day to influence Mormon thinking about these fundamental scientific questions.

Orson Pratt's notions about the materiality of intelligence probably derive more from his understanding of Joseph Smith's teachings than from readings or lectures he may have absorbed by philosophical or scientific authorities. The dominant Scottish "common sense" school of philosophy for all its de-emphasis of the "spiritual" or "metaphysical" held to a strong distinction between physical and mental phenomena.[74] Orson's assumptions echo in some respects those of Joseph Priestley, who like Leibniz before him held that matter is not solid or inert but active. For Priestley matter is dynamic, the locus of attraction *and* repulsion. Since thought occurs in conjunction with some organized material system, thought and matter are contextually inseparable.[75] Although Orson read Priestley[76] and perhaps drew from him, by far the most immediate and overwhelming influence on Orson's thought was the Prophet. Both Pratt brothers, Parley and Orson, wrote considerably upon the philosophical and scientific implications of Joseph's teachings.

Joseph had repudiated the traditional "dematerialized" notion of God and the spirit of man as early as 1833.[77] His definitive statement on this question came in 1843 in the document later known as *Doctrine and Covenants* 130: "The father has a body of flesh and bone as tangible as man's, the son also."[78] He went on to teach that "there is no such thing as immaterial matter," that what is known in scripture as "spirit" is a material substance of a refined nature generally imperceptible to our mortal senses. In the well-known "King Follett Sermon," April 7, 1844, Joseph outlined the evolution of "self-existent intelligences" from their primeval state to godhood.[79] The key to Joseph's cosmology was therefore the ubiquity of material intelligences, more or less highly organized, which were never "created or made"[80] but are eternal in duration and "susceptible of enlargement."[81] In Mormonism, as Professor Sterling M. McMurrin has pointed out, "whatever is ultimate and essential in the human soul is self-existent."[82]

The origin of Joseph Smith's cosmological views, which formed the basis for Orson's, has been a subject of sharp debate. For the faithful, these pronouncements are simply articles of faith, revealed truths from heaven. Joseph's biographer, Fawn M. Brodie, has suggested that Joseph's notion that "matter is eternal and indestructible" came directly from the writings of Scottish theologian and astronomer Thomas Dick.[83] In *Philosophy of a Future State* (1829), Dick propounds a vision of a universe peopled with "intelligences," a term which arises in Joseph's revelations now known as *Doctrine and Covenants* 88:40 and 93:29, and is used in later revelations to refer to the class of uncreated beings to which man and the gods belong.[84] Dick also suggests the possibility of eternal progression among "intelligences": "The grand aim of celestial intelligences will be, to increase in the knowledge and love of God . . . the soul of man appears to be capable of making a perpetual progress towards intellectual and moral perfection . . . without the possibility of ever arriving at a boundary to its excursions."[85] Dick thus developed a Christian theology compatible with the Baconian, empirical, scientific bias of the thinkers of his time. He extended into the hereafter Francis Bacon's popular vision of human progress: "a progressive and continuously increasing mastery over nature through the systematic and uninterrupted pursuit of knowledge."[86]

Clearly, Joseph Smith's cosmology has an affinity with the views of Thomas Dick. The contrasts, however, are equally striking. Dick is thoroughly orthodox in his views on God and creation. His perspective on the "future state" of man, like Joseph's, embraces a spiritual and material unity, with the happiness of "just men made perfect"[87] comprised in their evolving cognition of the material universe through astronomy, mathematics, and all the branches of the "natural philosophy" so highly regarded by American and British intellectuals of the time. However, Dick considers the material universe a creation *ex nihilo* in the orthodox theological tradition; and God is "infinite, both in respect of space and duration."[88] In direct contrast to Joseph Smith's theology, Dick rejected the "end product" of eternal progression which Joseph preached: the eternal exaltation to godhood. Joseph's idea that matter is self-existent and indestructible would have been blasphemous to Dick, who, although repelled at the idea of "annihilation of matter," grants that it is possible for God to will the complete cancellation of the universe. Furthermore, for Dick, the spirit of man is a created being whose immortality "depends solely on the will of its Creator."[89] By "holy intelligences," Dick intended "the angelic tribes of heaven,"[90] and had no inkling of including created man in that sphere; the dichotomy between heavenly and earthly beings still holds. On the other hand, for Joseph, the spirits of men *are* the holy, uncreated intelligences. In short, Dick's ideas were not markedly divergent from Protestant orthodoxy.

Joseph Smith never mentioned Dick or his writings, and rejected most of Dick's ideas. Edward T. Jones, who has carefully compared the works of the two men, concludes their doctrines were "radically different at vital points." Jones concedes that no foreign writer was more "generally read on this side the Atlantic . . . than Dr. Thomas Dick," but also points out that "it is impossible to determine whether the Prophet ever read" Dick.[91] Brodie bases her argument about the relationship of Smith and Dick on a quotation from *Philosophy of a Future State* which appeared in the Kirtland newspaper *Messenger and Advocate* in December 1836.[92] Her thesis is that Sidney Rigdon had read Dick and, in this way, the Prophet's theology was influenced. Her observations are inaccurate in that it was Oliver Cowdery who inserted the quotation, not Rigdon. Furthermore, the text in question, which deals with the idea of a Creator "replenishing the voids of space with new worlds and new orders of intelligent beings" appears nearly four years after Joseph's revelation (now *Doctrine and Covenants* 93) which outlined the Mormon theology of matter and evolving intelligences. It seems to have been inserted as a reasoned argument in favor of already established Mormon doctrines, as Cowdery so introduces the quotation: "We extract the following chapter from 'Dick's philosophy of a future state.' There are reasonings sufficient, we think, to commend it to the attention of the reader." (Cowdery then quotes from section ten of Dick's book.)[93]

It is clear that Joseph Smith's doctrine of the uncreated intelligences did not arise from the works of Thomas Dick, because Dick never taught such a doctrine. Joseph's disciple, Orson Pratt, was no less sparing in his criticism of the attempts of men like Dick to construct a scientific basis for their orthodox Christian understanding of the universe. Given Joseph's revelations about the unoriginated nature of intelligence and matter, Orson erected his own system to account for the organization of the physical world. As summarized by Joseph Willard Tingey, Orson's "Mormon Philosophy" affirmed that "all organizations of things and beings . . . are results of self-designs and self-combinations of these ultimate atoms. All atoms initially possessed equal capacities for knowledge and wisdom gained through experience."[94] Such a notion would have been anathema to the Scottish philosopher Thomas Dick, whatever its genealogy.

Though the *New York Messenger* was full of treatises like Orson's "Mormon Philosophy" along with solemn tirades against the "desolating ravages" of the Latter-day Saints, Pratt's humor managed to show through. He reports making a day's journey to New Jersey on the train "with the help of a little boiling water."[95] He recounts a dream in which he sees his destitute condition and the debts he has contracted "to the amount of about four hundred dollars," and a voice says to him: "Perhaps if the members and branches of the church throughout the East, knew of the poverty and unhappy circumstances in which their President was placed, they would with one accord contribute to release him from his unpleasant condition." After waking from this dream, he "fully resolved to publish my wakeful cogitations, and earnestly look for the fulfillment thereof . . . being a believer in dreams." He continued earnestly to solicit members to purchase his *Prophetic Almanac for 1846* and to tell their friends.[96]

Despite this light-hearted tone, Orson was in fact destitute. With three wives in Nauvoo, Sarah pregnant for the fifth time, and no "opportunity of entering into any kind of business"[97] on account of his mission calling, he had been forced to live on what he could borrow here and there. His families in Nauvoo still suffered. A second little daughter, Sarah Marinda, had died of the seasonal malaria while he was en route to New York.[98] Orson was weighed down night and day by the condition of his wives and two surviving children in Nauvoo.

With little time for writing except in the columns of the *Messenger*, Orson filled his second almanac primarily with excerpts from the works of his brother. Parley's tone of voice is clear throughout this collection of homiletic tidbits. There is included an important article entitled "Materiality," in which Parley argues the Mormon position that the "immaterial" God worshiped by sectarian Christianity is incomprehensible, unbelievable, and absurd and that there is no distinction between "sectarian" faith in this "nonentity" and atheism: "What is God? He is a material, organized intelligence, possessing both body and parts. He is in the form of man, and is in fact of the same species; and is a model or standard of perfection to which man is destined to attain . . . he can go, come, converse, reason, eat, drink, love, hate, rejoice, possess, and enjoy."[99]

The anthropomorphic God of the Mormons as defined here makes a sort of debut in Orson's almanac, for this is one of the first printed discussions of the subject. No doctrinal departure from orthodox Christianity made by the Mormons was so radical as this. Although a number of Protestant groups during this period renounced many of the creedal points which distinguished them from another, most theologians and philosophers in America were moving further away from anthropomorphism of any kind. In fact William Ellery Channing, whom many considered the greatest American religious thinker, publicly embraced religion as "the adoration of goodness—God is love." While Channing expounded this rarefied concept of God,[100] Ralph Waldo Emerson had just published his *Essays* conceiving that God was the soul of nature, "the universal beauty," the "eternal ONE";[101] and exalting the sufficiency and sovereignty of the individual. For Thomas Dick, God is "strictly Mind," a "purely IMMATERIAL . . . spiritual, uncompounded substance."[102] Although Mormonism embodied many contemporary ideals extolling "individuality," it directly and fervently repudiated those currents of Western religious thought which dissolved the personality of God. Parley and Orson Pratt were among the most insistent critics of the "the immaterial God they choose."[103] "Such a God," writes Professor McMurrin, paraphrasing the Mormon theologians, "can be neither living nor everlasting, for whatever is without body or does not occupy space is nonexistent."[104]

Orson Pratt's *Prophetic Almanac* acquainted the Latter-day Saints in the East with this and other doctrinal development current in the Church. It was issued in five thousand copies.

Soon Orson was preparing to leave New York. During his tenure the leaders in Nauvoo had been planning the relocation of the entire Church membership. Brigham Young favored the Great Salt Lake basin described in maps and reports by men such as Fremont and Captain Benjamin Bonneville, although he continued to investigate the advantages of Oregon, Texas, and even Vancouver Island. As early as August 1845, however, the council had laid out the projected emigration to the Salt Lake Valley and were going ahead with the construction of wagons.[105] Orson Pratt was instructed to gather as much tithing money as possible in order to bring temple building to completion and to help outfit the companies designated to leave in the spring. In addition in New York Orson managed to get several dozen "six-shooters" for the protection of the emigrants.[106]

Before leaving New York Orson entertained several times the celebrated Robert Owen, congressman from Indiana and son of the founder of the New Harmony social experiment. Owen was zealous to revive his father's communitarian ideas and wished to locate his followers at Nauvoo once the Mormons left. Orson seemed to have him persuaded; but Owen ultimately forgot about Nauvoo in the midst of his numerous advocacies (among them opposition to organized religion). Another prominent visitor was the explorer Thomas Jefferson Farnham, whose widely publicized 1839 foray into Oregon territory made him enthusiastic about the possibility of Mormon settlement there. Although he had attacked the Mormons in his writings, Farnham offered any assistance in his power. Orson was skeptical: "I thought in my heart that we have had enough of Gentile assistance & that the time had nearly arrived for us to assist ourselves."[107]

Orson also helped outfit his printer, Elder Samuel Brannan, who had been commissioned by the Twelve to lead a group of eastern Saints by sea to California. Orson wrote in the *Messenger* for November 8: "Elder S. Brannan . . . will sail about the middle of January. Those who wish to accompany are requested to give him their names as early as possible. If 150 or 200 passengers can be obtained, he can venture to charter a vessel for them . . . The voyage can be performed in four or five months. Brethren awake! Be determined to get out from this evil nation next spring. We do not want one Saint to be left in the United States after that time."[108]

In late 1845 nighttime raids had resumed against Mormon farms in Hancock County, and incendiaries had destroyed over two hundred dwellings in the region around Nauvoo; a detachment of state militia had attempted to forestall the violence with little success.[109] When Orson Pratt heard of the resolution of the nine counties surrounding Nauvoo to drive the Mormons out of Illinois by armed force if they did not evacuate voluntarily,[110] he reacted with uncharacteristic fury: "The time is at hand for me to take a long and last farewell to these Eastern countries, being included with my family, among the tens of thousands of American citizens who have the choice of DEATH or BANISHMENT beyond the Rocky Mountains. I have preferred the latter. It is with the greatest of joy that I forsake this Republic: . . . for we have received nothing but . . . the most horrid and unrelenting persecutions at their hands for the last sixteen years. If our Heavenly Father will . . . deliver us out of the hands of the blood-thirsty Christians of these United States . . . I for one shall be very thankful . . . ; we may have to suffer much in the land of our exile, but . . . there will be no Christian banditti to afflict us all the day long—no holy pious priests to murder us by scores."[111]

With this acrimonious farewell, the *New York Messenger* ceased publication, the press was to be loaded aboard the *Brooklyn*, and Orson Pratt left to join his friends at Nauvoo counting it a "privilege" to sacrifice all by being driven out of his home once again. He arrived December 11, 1845, with four hundred dollars' worth of "Allen's revolving six-shooting pistols, alias pepperboxes."[112] The Twelve were busily conducting endowment ceremonies in the temple,[113] which had been finished only days before. He found them anxious to make the fullest possible use of the building, but also eager to evacuate. Indeed, many of them looked upon their contemplated flight already as a great adventure. Parley had exhorted the Saints in October conference, "We cannot always live in one city, nor in one county . . . We want a country where we have room to expand."[114] Orson was likewise infected with a "new life and zeal . . . to gather westward ho!" The westering urge, which was noisily stirring the entire nation, had acute significance for Orson Pratt.

Meanwhile, the work in temple chambers had to be pushed rapidly to completion. Orson conducted his wife Sarah through the ordinances the day after his return from the East, and together they remained long hours in the temple assisting others.[115] Most of the authorities were restricted in their movements on account of an arrest warrant issued against them on the ludicrous charge of "counterfeiting." Orson was one of those named in the writ issued by the U.S. District Court for Illinois at its December 1845 term.[116] Orson stayed in the temple day and night, at times quite alone in the darkened courts, and Christmas Eve he spent by himself evading arrest by a United States marshal. The deputy scoured the building while Orson watched his every move from a little nook he had rigged up as an observatory. At length the officer gave up. These attempts were alarming to Brigham Young, however, and it was about this time the decision was made to abandon Nauvoo as soon as possible rather than to wait for the spring thaw to bring grass for the stock.[117]

These anxieties forced the temple to close for a few days, and the anointing ceremonies came temporarily to a halt. Orson still quietly camped inside the building taking astronomical measurements by night to prepare for the immense job of navigating the pioneers upon departure. He ascertained the latitude of Nauvoo at 40 degrees, 35 minutes, 48 seconds north on December 27. From this base he could calculate the position of the pioneer wagons on the prairies. All this time the temple was under careful watch by officers.[118]

When the authorities felt it was safe to open the temple again, they worked feverishly to bring over five thousand Saints through the full endowment sessions, and nerves began to fray. Parley's wife Mary Ann had quarreled with him and left him for good, ostensibly over something malicious reported to her by Sarah. Parley, who had long resented Sarah for her part in his brother's brief excommunication, arose in the midst of a meeting and accused Sarah of "whispering against him all over the temple" and of influencing his wife in order to break up his home. Orson then burst with indignation. Sarah was falsely accused; on the contrary, it was Parley who had been speaking against *her* for three years accusing her behind her back of apostasy. He then went on to repeat rumors he had heard in New York about Parley, the rumors Sarah was unfortunately spreading, that he had brought a young girl with him to the East and seduced her.

Orson became so distraught in Sarah's defense that the temple workers voted to bar both of them from the temple until the Twelve could pass on the matter. The next day, Orson, deeply injured in spirit, wrote a letter to Brigham Young repeating the accusations he had made against his brother and adding: "If I had, especially without the least cause, insulted any of your families in so disgraceful a manner I should have been very thankful if I escaped without getting my head broke. And I never would have voted to turn one of you out of meeting."[119]

Orson soon learned in confidence that the girl who had accompanied Parley to New York the year previous was actually Belinda, a plural wife sealed to him by Brigham Young in November 1844.[120] The dispute was rapidly settled, and Orson returned to fellowship, for by January 24 he was presiding once again in the temple and he and Parley officiating together.[121] The incident reveals perhaps nothing more than a momentary squabble between two brothers, based on a misunderstanding; however, it also demonstrates that the painful episodes involving Sarah, which Orson had attempted to put behind him, still rankled. On the eve of the departure from Nauvoo, Orson had found himself again frustrated at what he perceived as inconsistencies in those around him. He was perhaps not so much infuriated as hurt and bewildered. In his mind his family was "much injured" by events in Nauvoo, and he found it difficult not to be defensive.

The Pratts' stormy sojourn at Nauvoo ended with the birth of a son. Sarah delivered a little boy, the fifth of their children, on January 23, 1846, whom Orson blessed and named Vanson.[122] The young Mormon philosopher and scientist now prepared to leave his new brick house by the Mississippi with three wives, a boy, a girl, and an infant, to face a bitter prairie winter and a thousand-mile journey to the great American desert.

6

The Spires of the Mountains

Orson Pratt left Nauvoo the wintry morning of February 14, 1846. Three teamsters, William Higginbotham, a Mr. Simmons and a Mr. Rice, engaged to carry Orson's belongings along with their own, as Orson had no wagon. The eight members of the Pratt family crowded into a carriage and drove to the Mississippi wharf through falling snow and cold northeast wind. The ferries had not run that day because of the storm, but Orson was determined to cross. The reluctant ferrymen huddled around their fire, and the family faced nearly a mile of churning gray ice—and beyond that, a thousand miles of freezing wilderness.[1]

Despite his poverty and distress, Orson now confronted an unparalleled adventure, which would strain his navigational abilities and instruments but would also nourish his curious soul with a continent of discoveries. In his bags were the quadrant and artificial horizon of mercury with which he had "previously ascertained the latitude and longitude of the temple at Nauvoo."[2] Now the fleeing Mormons needed these tools to locate themselves along the trail.

The Saints had not planned to leave Nauvoo until spring, when grass would be available and travel more comfortable. However, rumors that the federal army might try to stop the emigration pushed the Saints into preparations all through January.[3] Crossing the frozen Mississippi, the first company had set up camp February 4 on the Iowa shore. Orson himself had worked incessantly in the temple until the very last moment, helping to dedicate the building Sunday, February

8,[4] dispensing the mysteries of the endowment to hundreds of Saints, and receiving through the sacred sealing ordinance a fifth plural wife, Sarah Louisa Chandler, a young convert twenty-four years old.[5] "Louiza," as Orson called her, was a New Hampshire woman of tender health who did not last the journey. The temple, for so many months the center of Orson's life, stood behind him now, but his experiences there had left his theology and family fundamentally and forever transformed. For these beliefs he joined hundreds of Latter-day Saints in exile.

Despite the freezing northwesterly, Orson managed to persuade the ferrymen to cross the river with his family; the boats bucked the waters, and the Pratts soon set foot in Iowa territory, leaving the states of the Union behind in search of a location "far from the abodes of what is falsely termed *civilization* and *Christianity*."[6] Once landed they found their friends mired in snow and mud and sought temporary refuge at the home of Jonathan Harrington, Sarah's uncle, some three miles from the Sugar Creek encampment. Parley P. Pratt crossed the Mississippi the same day and found shelter with his family in an abandoned cabin in the same gully.[7]

For three days the apostles met and talked. They had received a letter from Sam Brannan in New York saying certain congressmen had proposed that the Mormons occupy California and deed it over to them in exchange for "protection" from the national government. Orson and the others rejected this at once.[8] But it was clear that they would have to get moving. Brigham Young, studying the charts available in the "historian's tent" (including the Charles F. Preuss cartography produced during John C. Fremont's expeditions to the Great Basin during the early 1840s),[9] mapped out the route of "the camp of Israel."

As the cold grew more intense, the Pratts moved down to Sugar Creek to be near the main encampment. On February 26, the mercury dropped to a cruel five degrees. Meanwhile the Twelve desperately negotiated with surrounding settlers for feed corn and grain sufficient to fuel the westward migration. Orson pulled out his instruments and made the first measurements of the journey; he marked their Sugar Creek position at 40 degrees 32 minutes latitude and reflected in his journal that the quadrant's inadequacy at determining longitude could lead the company as much as thirty miles off course at any given point. Added to his worries was the possibility of misdirecting the entire encampment due to lack of a proper sextant. Orson was characteristically upset that a telescope was lacking as well, for he was unable to observe "the immersions and emmersions of Jupiter's satellites,"[10] readings of which were important in determining longitude.

By March 1 the camp had swelled into the hundreds. The Twelve had obtained "large quantities" of corn, and the time had come to start.[11] The spectacle of the exiles moving with their white-topped wagons through a vast prairie of mud and snow was not a new one for Brigham and the others of the Twelve; they had seen it before in Missouri during the winter of 1839. Now, through the country to the north of their former misfortune, they were leading a vastly increased number of Saints, not into the warm, hospitable homes of Quincy, Illinois, but toward the territory of the Sioux and onto the winter waste of the Great Plains. They made five miles the first day.[12]

After making camp that night, Orson was visited by two Iowa men who offered him three hundred dollars' worth of supplies for his new brick house on Water Street in Nauvoo.[13] The next day he inspected the supplies and eventually traded his two-thousand-dollar holdings at Nauvoo for four yoke of oxen, a wagon and harness, and eight barrels of flour. With his new acquisitions, he joined the camp on the Des Moines River, a stone's throw from the despised territory of Missouri.[14] Mud was so thick along the Des Moines that men left sucking holes as deep as their boots when they walked, and the struggling teams broke their harnesses up and down the mile-long trains. After pausing at Farmington, Iowa, for repairs, the company slowly traversed the river near the present-day town of Bonaparte.[15]

On March 5 Simmons's wagon split an axle, and Orson was forced to unload part of Higginbotham's outfit to pick up the cargo Simmons had carried. With other broken wagons strewn along the trail and a shortage of suitable camping places, the company became scattered in the Fox River wilderness. Impatient for the West, Parley headed out, while Orson struggled with his own split axle and the recalcitrant Mr. Higginbotham, who now felt queasy about going any farther. The drayman was sick and decided, despite Orson's importuning, to return to Nauvoo with his wagon. Orson now faced a pile of provisions with no means to move it; he traded several hundred pounds of flour for farm tools and a pair of shoes. The overloaded wagons, this time drawn by oxen, at length pulled out of the Fox River bottom.[16]

In the latter weeks of March, Orson struggled to catch the company of fifty which had gone ahead with Parley. The frozen nights and scarcity of corn had kept Brigham Young and the bulk of the pioneers several days' journey behind Orson.[17] Out of patience at the disorganization of the strung-out company, Brigham Young threatened to withdraw fellowship from the Pratts if they continued to follow their own course. The resulting council near the Chariton River encampment invited an airing of complaints which led to a more subdued and cheerful attitude in the camp at large: All was "made right" and "a good understanding entered into."[18] At nights they danced to the music of the Nauvoo brass bands and enjoyed the plentiful venison, wild turkey, and prairie hen. Orson himself killed some small game and a turkey.[19]

For three weeks the camp paused in the Chariton River wilderness to await drier conditions and to worship in conference on the sixth of April. Three days later the entire company began to move again, tentatively, between drenching spring rains. It became clear that the established road would remain impassable for months, and the sudden new burden of traffic could only worsen conditions. Wagon after wagon, stalled overnight in axle-deep mud, found itself encased in a rock-hard, frozen earth when morning came.[20] Despite the constant frustration and suffering, Brigham Young wrote: "I did not think there had ever been a body of people since the days of Enoch, placed under the same unpleasant circumstances that this people have been, where there was so little grumbling, and I was satisfied that the Lord was pleased with the majority of the Camp of Israel."[21]

In an April 12 council, the company decided to break away from the main road and stir up some new mud on the unsettled prairie in hope of finding better footing and a grassy, protected spot with good streams to begin a temporary settlement.[22] It was already clear to the apostles that there was no possibility of reaching the Great Basin in time to plant crops—at least not in the year 1846. Orson traveled ahead with President Young in unusually cold weather and through rattler-infested swamps until they found a reasonably dry meadow, which Brigham designated Garden Grove. Orson concurred with the choice and with the President's policy:

> I am converted to President Young's views. The idea of crossing the plains this year with our families is something I could hardly believe. It is eight years today since the Twelve parted from the Saints on the foundation of the House of the Lord at Far West, Missouri to go to the nations of the earth . . . Previous to that time Joseph had this mission in contemplation, to find a location west of the Rocky Mountains. Whenever Joseph spoke on that subject he proposed to send a company of young men as pioneers to seek a location and raise a crop previous to sending families.[23]

More and more, Orson saw the westward exile to be an integral chapter in the progress toward the Millennium. As a member of the vanguard, he felt the breath of the new prophet in the prairies and saw Joseph's visions worked out in the very processes of nature.

On April 27, the log cabins of Garden Grove were erected in the midst of a torrent.[24] The next day Orson met in a council in Brigham's dripping tent to consider provisioning a company of a hundred men for a trip to the mountains. It was also decided to sell the beloved temple at Nauvoo for the benefit of the poor Saints still in the East and unable to outfit themselves for the exile.[25] (Ironically, the Nauvoo Temple was at last dedicated in its entirety only three days later under the direction of Wilford Woodruff and Orson Hyde.[26] But the plight of those few remaining in the Mormon city required the immediate sale of the building.)[27]

There were only a comparative handful of Saints left in Illinois. As the cold spring turned into May, nearly twelve thousand Mormons now straggled along behind the advance wagons of Brigham Young, Orson Pratt, and others. It was imperative that the small temporary settlements produce as much grain as possible, and, between bouts of sickness, Orson spent the first ten days of May struggling with fencing and putting up log houses. Impatient to see more land under cultivation, Orson set off with the fifty families under his command toward the forks of Grand River, where on May 16 they encamped at "Mount Pisgah," so named by Parley, who first saw and declared it as beautiful as the promised land of the Bible.[28] The next day Orson went fishing, "which was something of a variety to us."[29] Soon thousands of acres at Mount Pisgah were cultivated.

The trains were now reaching the western extent of white settlement and the lands of the Potawatomi and the Omaha Indians. The Twelve had to decide soon whether an advance group would attempt the Great Basin that year or not. They were frustrated at the unexpectedly tedious pace of the emigration and disappointed that the people had not supplied themselves better when counseled to do so the previous autumn. Furthermore, the vote of the people was for going west as a body; thus, the Twelve gave up hope of penetrating beyond the mountains before winter.[30]

About this time peculiar rumors circulated among the stragglers. Stories were told that Apostle Orson Pratt was carrying on a vendetta against the Twelve and refusing to contribute his share to the upkeep of the trains. Orson traced these tales to the reprehensible Higginbotham, who had abandoned him on the prairie. Orson wrote a letter and dispatched it to Nauvoo denying Higginbotham's claims and protesting that he had dealt out "several hundred weight of his flour to the camp which Brother Higgin Botham knows." Orson thus was forced to continue defending his reputation even in the middle of the migration.[31]

Orson remained at the Mount Pisgah farms until June 7, but, just as his three wagons were about to start, his young wife Louisa developed a fever. A camp physician diagnosed typhus adding that the departure would not injure her and might do her good. Reassured, Orson rolled out of the fields on a Sunday afternoon. The prairies had changed completely by this time; the weather was warm and the roads well marked and dry.[32] However, Louisa did not improve. After about fifty miles Orson halted the party at the Platte River in a grove of black walnut trees.

Orson knew that Louisa could not live. Her speech failed at sundown, and by half past ten she was dead. The women laid out her body in temple robes and prepared her for burial while Orson searched out a burial place. Next day at noon one of the elders in camp spoke and prayed over her basswood coffin lying in a grave near a tree. When the mourners had gone, Orson took his knife and carved the initials of the lost young woman in the tree's bark—"L.C.P. DIED JUN.12, 1846."[33]

The Pratt carriage continued on its melancholy journey. Orson preached to the people: "We are under the Celestial Law and governed by the same God, Spirit, and Priesthood as the ancients were."[34] The celestial law, as Orson was discovering, required the sacrifice of all he possessed, and the losses weighed heavily against an already overwhelming burden of suffering: "During this journey, many have suffered extremely with exposure and the want of necessary food. Some whose constitutions being feeble, were unable to endure, and sank and died, . . . but their blood will be required at the hands of the nation who have looked on coldly."[35] At the end of this day, one of the wagons fractured its forward axletree.

However, a hiatus in the journey lay just ahead. For three days Orson's outfits bridged the swollen forks of the Nishnabotna and watched with apprehension crowds of young Potawatomi who gathered curiously, but apparently without hostility, along the route. Finally, they rolled into the main encampment of the Saints on a creek by the banks of the Missouri. An irrepressible cheer of relief swept through Orson's fifty as they gazed on the little Indian village which Brigham Young had made his headquarters. That night there was a band concert and dancing.[36]

Here the pioneers found the residence of the Indian agents and a certain Mr. Sarpee, the well-to-do representative of the American Fur Company. Sarpee passed on much information about the "Great West," and he offered the pioneers a contract for ninety thousand pounds of buffalo robes and furs in exchange for a thousand dollars.[37] The friendliness of Mr. Sarpee was not to be outdone by the Potawatomi themselves; their chief, Pied Riche "Leclerc," a literate and amiable man, offered the Mormons land and timber for their use in outfitting themselves for the westward trek. "We have both suffered," declared the chief. "We must keep one another, and the Great Spirit will keep us both."[38] This warm and reverential welcome caused no small comment among the Mormons on the irony of their reception among the "savages" compared to the cool farewell of civilization.[39] Orson went into council with the Twelve as they mulled over the possibilities now available to them.

Fully conscious of the thousands on the trail to their backs, the Twelve frantically began preparations for accommodating them. In late June, Orson crossed the Missouri into "unorganized territory" under the control of the Omaha nation and camped at Mosquito Creek, north of the present-day metropolis of Omaha.[40] Roads soon lined the Missouri on both sides, and a number of spacious settlements had been laid out and allotted. In the midst of constructing ferryboats and lean-tos, Orson packed off goods downriver to be traded for company provisions. The council ranged out into Indian territory as far as the Elkhorn River and returned to camp in late July still yearning for the mountains, knowing that the vast family of the Church must rest for the season after the tortuous traversal of Iowa.

For the first time the Saints were free of any secular government. In August Orson Pratt mounted the pulpit to comment on this new situation:

> Elder O. Pratt . . . showed that the Saints were at present, privileged to live under their own laws—that the reason why the Twelve had changed their counsel so often was, because the people did not abide the best counsel, which was given by the spirit of God. The best counsel was for the Church to fit out a company to go with the Twelve over the mountains, but as they were dilatory and failed to do this . . . we must be one . . . and when any one is told by the foreman to pick up a basket of chips and tumble them out again, then pick them up again and find no fault . . . It is unbelief that causes all our whining.[41]

The celestial law would not abide whiners, Orson insisted, stressing "the necessity of due subordination That we only had such a law given as we could stand That is the best we would recieve & so it had been with this camp. When the best way was pointed out and we recieved it not the next best would be tried and thus we were governed."[42] No one was to put in a turnip patch or cut hay without permission, as the well-being of the whole camp was at question. For now the emergency was full upon them, with thousands in the wilderness plagued with the sudden summer malaria.

Because these conditions required more spiritual and psychological courage than their individualism could provide, Orson was elected to supply it. Every Sunday Orson regaled the huge congregations who had suffered through the week from sickness and privation with visions of the glory of celestial worlds: "Elder Orson Pratt spoke first . . . on the organization of worlds & the planetary system He said that we could distinctly see with a common spy glass in the constellation of Orion . . . unorganized matter enough to make many millions of worlds as large as the sun."[43]

Orson's august conceptions thus helped the Saints muster some theological perspective against the blackleg disease and the weedy diet of the Missouri bottoms. The spring tortures of cold and wet now gave way to those of disease, heat, and mosquitoes.[44] When the Omahas began to make hostile noises about the loss of their timber to the use of the Mormon colony, Orson remonstrated with them, telling them it would not be burnt but rather used for the construction of villages which would remain for the use of the natives, if they wanted them. He then used the opportunity to introduce to them the Book of Mormon; he must have sighed when they indicated that they would like to come back and hear about it but only after their impending battle with the Sioux.[45]

Orson spent considerable time hunting in the brush, gathering venison and wild turkey, wild elderberries and grapes, in addition to cultivating green corn, cucumbers, succotash, and mushmelons.[46] Leather boats allowed quick transit up and down the river, while Orson engaged in a good deal of exploration and surveying for the new settlements. In September he submitted plats for a new city called Winter Quarters along with architectural drawings of a tabernacle for a meeting place.[47] He and Woodruff and Lyman divided Winter Quarters into wards and selected bishops for each.[48] Orson read the mail and delivered it every day, helped approve a plan for the records and histories, and gathered the police tax,[49] an important item of business due to the "devils," i.e., "rebelious wicked ungovernable men who are breeding a continual disturbance & exciting others to discontent." Orson met with the leaders to decide what to do about the alarming presence of dissidents and frontier types who threatened the peace and order of the camp: "It was unanimously decided to have the Law of God put in force on them &c. There was much said and but one feeling on the subject."[50]

Public works grew, as homes for thousands had to be built—seven hundred had been completed by December—and work started on a gristmill and a council house. Always, between sodding the roofs of neighbors, and issuing checks, and allotting "meat and tallow" to the police force,[51] Orson continued his observations, "studying the polarization of light."[52] "In relation to our journey in the Spring," Orson advised sending out "a pioneer company to get to the head waters of the Running Water [the Missouri?] by the time grass comes or before and be ready to go over the Black Hills & put in a crop of corn somewhere on this side of the mountains near the head of the Yellow Stone." Wilford Woodruff supported this plan.[53] (Orson's notion demonstrates that the Twelve were still uncertain about their destination; or perhaps it indicates an extraordinary lack of understanding of western geography.)

As the year ended under a light snow in this transplanted Nauvoo, Orson and the others began to plan the "removal in the

Spring." Brigham Young gave the word: Advance parties, three companies in all, would proceed to the Great Basin as soon as practicable to plant crops. Orson Pratt and Wilford Woodruff were appointed captains of companies on January 14, and the same day the Twelve issued a joint statement, "The Word and Will of the Lord concerning the Camp of Israel in their journeyings to the West":[54] "Let all the people of the Church of Jesus Christ of Latter-day Saints, and those who journey with them, be organized into companies, with a covenant and a promise to keep all the Commandments and Statutes of the Lord our God . . . let my servants Orson Pratt and Wilford Woodruff organize a company . . . My people must be tried in all things, that they may be prepared to receive the glory that I have prepared for them, even the glory of Zion." Orson could say amen to that. The document is now section 136 of the *Doctrine and Covenants*.

At last the course was laid. Brigham Young assigned Orson on January 25 to rush back to Garden Grove and Mount Pisgah to put the revelation into practice and organize the stragglers into companies according to the new instructions. He left immediately and read the revelation "from keg Creek to Lost Camp," returning February 12 with the report that all had been put in order.[55] The pattern of emigration set, the Saints were ready to flee the borders.

But the United States were creeping up on them. By December Iowa Territory was formally admitted into the Union, and the Saints had volunteered a battalion to help in the occupation of the boundless upper provinces of the former Mexican empire. It was the policy of the president of the United States, James Knox Polk, to "conciliate" the Latter-day Saints by "attach[ing] them to our country, and prevent[ing] them from taking part against us."[56] As the war with Mexico raged, the American blood that flowed at Buena Vista in February constituted the price for the sand and rock which the Saints had hoped to claim for an independent Zion. The night of the Buena Vista battle, Orson was meeting with the council to discuss science and the prospects for arable land in upper Mexico. While the troops of Winfield Scott marched toward the enemy capital, the imagination of Orson Pratt and the Twelve roamed the highlands soon to be wrested from Latin American grip.[57]

Oblivious to the battles in the South, the apostles watched for the first ice-free day on the Missouri. Huge flights of wild geese signaled the hour for departure, and, as the Church met in general conference on April 6, 1847, they covenanted to pray for the camp continually. Having observed the sacred anniversary of the founding of the Church, the pioneers set out. On April 7, Brigham Young, Orson Pratt, and Wilford Woodruff accompanied the vanguard ten miles onto the prairie, although the organization for the journey was stalled a few days to hear Parley P. Pratt's report on the status of the missions in England and the East. Nine days later, the pioneers said good-bye for the time to the main encampment at Winter Quarters, and "the brethren went to work with alacrity."[58]

One hundred and forty-four men, three women, and two children pushed toward the Elkhorn River—the number of men corresponding to the "twelve times twelve" spoken of in Revelation. Orson sensed the scientific as well as the theological import of the journey and obtained release from administrative duties in order to tend to the work of measuring the miles and keeping the log in order. Brigham's secretary, an English convert named William Clayton, was assigned to assist him in recording distance traveled and logging landmarks for those who were to follow. The work assigned to Orson was twofold: to keep the pioneer company on course and to maintain meticulous records for the thousands strung across the continent behind this dusty band. Orson had had precious little equipment to rely on up till now. But new instruments had arrived just in time—two sextants, one circle of reflection, two artificial horizons, two barometers, thermometers, and telescopes purchased by John Taylor in Paris and brought to Iowa by Parley.[59] As for his journal of the expedition, Wallace Stegner has fairly described it as the work of an "absent-minded scholar," mainly "latitudes, longitudes, and temperatures: he went across the plains with his eye glued to an artificial horizon and his wet fingers up to test the wind."[60]

Counted in the first ten members of the advance party, Orson began the historic journey on a day of gloom and wind. The preserve of the Omaha nation stretched in a monotonous plane to the horizon. As the wagons traversed the prairie grass, William Clayton counted each tedious turn of the wheel. Walking beside Orson, Clayton suggested after three days of counting that some mechanism be attached to the wheels to record the miles. Clayton no doubt did not look forward to a thousand miles of counting wheel revolutions, but also felt that his method was inaccurate—that distances traveled were being "over-rated," with potentially disastrous results. Brigham Young agreed. Orson puzzled a little, and he and Clayton worked out a design for a machine of wooden cogs and gears that would systematically clock each mile. They recruited Appleton Harmon, a carpenter, to construct the device, which worked by measuring the revolutions of the wheel of Philo Johnson's wagon, three hundred and sixty of which constituted one mile. Though not the first such device known, Orson's "roadometer" supplied an accurate measure of the Great Plains crossing invaluable to those who followed.[61]

Despite the assignment to keep the records, Orson did not begin his formal log of the journey until May 4,[62] partially because of the constant and harrowing demands on his strength. At the Loup River, one of those heavy, sluggish prairie streams that feed the Platte, his carriage became dangerously mired in quicksand. His was the first wagon to cross; his wheels sank and his horses thrashed helplessly in the oozing bars. Orson had to be plucked from his carriage and his load discharged before the wagon could move. Young ordered the others to ford upstream where the sand presented fewer traps. This left Orson, Wilford Woodruff, and four others alone on the far side of the Loup within the unsettling sight of a band of Pawnee, some six hundred of them, encamped not far from a smoking battleground.[63]

By the next evening they had devised a way across, and Orson spent a much more relaxed night observing the constellations through his telescope. He invited Clayton to look. The Englishman had never tried it and was amazed at the sight of the four moons of Jupiter.[64] Orson continued to take observations daily, delighted with the precision of his new instruments. Near Grand Island he found his observations differing by only a few rods from those given by Preuss in his map. In other places, however, he was convinced that his own readings were more accurate than Fremont's and so annotated his log. (Fremont was obliged to recalculate many of these observations in subsequent publications. Nevertheless, Orson's own efforts at determining longitude are also very rough.)[65] Barometric and longitudinal readings convinced Orson that the party had reached "the meridian of greatest cold," for his understanding of isothermal currents placed the Nebraska territory at the southern extremity of arctic winds.[66] His own subsequent experiences on the winter steppes showed that he had not underestimated the savage weather of this country.

Near Grand Island the pioneer camp fronted the Platte, which they called the "Nebraska," for the first time. Orson remarked that the river was very "soily," muddy, like the Missouri. A wide and stagnant effluent, treacherous with quicksands and oozing salty lime, the river nevertheless served as a convenient road west. The Oregon Trail paralleled the river on the south side, and emigrant trains were frequently seen on both sides. The Mormons stuck to the north bank to avoid fording the Platte and meeting rival emigrants, many of whom were Missourians. In fact, the Oregon Trail was not yet cold from the passing of Governor Lilburn Boggs, the Missouri chief executive who had tried to destroy the Mormon people in 1839. This Mormon nemesis, a frontiersman at heart, had scurried to California the previous year, coming very close to joining the ill-fated Donner–Reed expedition. Many other old enemies of the Saints were pushing upriver as well, and there were more than a few anxious protests to the federal authorities about the well-armed, disciplined army of Mormons moving up the Oregon Trail.[67]

Orson noted, nevertheless, that the north bank road was very good, level, somewhat sandy, but easily passable. But high winds and prairie-grass fires menaced the pioneers and feed was difficult to find in the parched and burnt prairie. The sight of tens of thousands of buffalo, at their thinnest due to the season, awed the travelers. Brigham Young strictly forbade slaughter of the buffalo, and the camp lived mostly on antelope meat. Orson came upon a feeble buffalo cow and thought about helping her but had no means; the calves had to be carried bodily out of the trail, they were so numerous. Orson writes that the buffalo's presence was in some ways convenient: "Our camp have, for the want of a better substitute, made their fires of the dry excrement of the buffalo, which burns something like dry turf."[68] But the grazing of the immense herds left the already charred plain without a blade of grass; the pioneer stock became weak from the scanty feed of the black prairie.

Signs of Indians were everywhere, and the camp kept up a strict, military discipline, firing their cannon periodically and parading for practice nearly every day. Orson speaks of finding the skull of a scalped Indian among a litter of bones.[69] The wagons at night were formed into a "circular fortification," as Orson put it, and by day a large party of outriders kept the stock on course. Straggling was forbidden, as the Indian practice of plundering smaller parties was well known.[70] Indian problems were minor, however, although a few horses were apparently stolen. Nevertheless, the pioneers remained gravely aware that they were being watched. In spite of the perceived danger, Orson's first encounter with the Sioux impressed him: "They were 35 in number, much better dressed than the Indians on the frontiers, many of them wearing broadcloth, blankets, and fur caps, ornamented with an abundance of beads . . . having bows and steel-pointed arrows . . . They were the Dacotah tribe, which, interpreted, signifies cut throat, but generally known to whites by the name of Sioux." Orson gave them "a thrill" by letting them look through his telescope.[71]

The confluence of the two forks of the Platte awakened a lyric voice in Orson:

> On the north, the surface of the country exhibited a broken succession of hills and ravines very much resembling the tumultuous confusion of ocean winds; . . . the high peaks far below were distinctly seen resembling bluish clouds just rising in the distant horizon . . . while the glistening waters of the river were here and there sweeping along its base; . . . the roily yellow waters of the north fork were making their way over and between innumerable beds of quicksand while the rich, level, green, grassy bottoms upon each side, formed a beautiful contrast.[72]

Though the weather remained cold and rainy at times with frost at night, the landscape began to afford dense grasses which greatly refreshed the stock. Orson knew that the elevation increased gradually as they continued westward. The higher land began to show outcropping rock and limestone bluffs that prefigured the foothills of the Rockies: the curiously shaped cliffs looked to Orson like "cones or pyramids . . . of remarkable picturesque beauty."[73] Fascinated by these formations, Orson filled his days with quick ascensions of the hills, examining the marl, the flowers and birds, and the eagles' nests with a naturalist's eye. He called the place "Cobble Hills," due to the huge pebbles and the bizarre petrified "bones" scattering the ground."[74] The emigrant's folk geography held this point to be the beginning of the true West—where the mean annual rainfall fell below twenty inches and the gnarled limestone bluffs resembled "the ruins of a world," as Washington Irving had described it.[75] The Mormons spoke with the same melancholy tone, christening the bluffs the "Ancient, or Bluff Ruins," for the crenelated walls and towers.[76] The

"Camp of Israel" had wandered into a New World "Wilderness of Sinai."

Orson mounted the cliffs and suspended his barometer in a small cedar. He recorded the elevation and meridian of Chimney Rock, a hazy spire in the distance.[77] He felt more and more dissatisfied with the Charles Preuss map. Certain that the accuracy of his own observations outmatched those of the published route, he resolved to develop his own map, which he and Clayton began piecing together from notes and from the readings given by the sliding wooden gears under Johnson's wagon. Clayton, however, was dissatisfied with the findings of both Preuss and Pratt and suggested waiting "until we get through the journey and take all the necessary data and then make a new one."[78] Remembering the thousands who, within two months, would cross these same badlands, the party began leaving mileage posts, the first ever installed on the Oregon Trail, along with other messages scrawled on the bleached skulls of the buffalo and left along the road.

Messages from on high were not lacking. Brigham Young stopped the train at Scottsbluff to scorch some of the more frivolous of the travelers on the subject of "light-mindedness" and enjoined them to "lay up a store of useful knowledge from everything that was seen and heard . . . instead of spending time in idleness and vanity." Orson concurred. It must have cheered him to hear his prophet speak of the importance of observing the natural world and learning from it: "If the Saints [have] leisure hours, they could spend them to much better advantage than playing cards, as there [is] a world of knowledge to be obtained and every moment should be improved in storing the mind with some good principle," Orson insisted to the fidgety Saints. Apparently they had complained of boredom and found an outlet in what their leaders considered unruly talk. Orson pointed to the books in camp and wished for twenty-three hours a day to study. But he was not the unsympathetic pedant. He told them that he knew "it is difficult to bring our minds to diligent and constant studies, in pursuit of knowledge all at once, but by steady practice and perseverance we shall become habituated to it, and it will become a pleasure to us."[79]

He also claimed that he could not understand people who had time for "nonsense." His own native curiosity occupied him constantly on the trail, with observations of the herb and insect life, the geological dream that surrounded them, and the moon and stars from Chimney Rock. He measured the river and found it to be "exactly seven hundred ninety two rods wide."[80] (Unfortunately, his longitudinal readings were much less precise; he was nearly nineteen miles off in his siting of Scottsbluff.[81]) The bugs fascinated him. The bluffs were full of "ant-hills . . . of small pebbles or gravel . . . Mingled with these were found, in different places, small Indian beads, which these insects had *collected* to beautify and adorn their habitations, I say *collected*, for it cannot be supposed that they were a home manufacture of their own ingenuity." He found a huge "mammoth bone" on the ground, but had no way to transport it.[82] And in the sky he saw wonders: a beautiful "lunar rainbow" the night of May 30 with the lowering silhouette of the Black Hills (now known as the Laramie Mountains) on the horizon.

Beyond that stood the first of the Rockies. With June came an initial glimpse of ten-thousand-foot Laramie Peak, the beginning of the granite wall that would exalt and close up Zion. Orson's interest in the peak was the way it affected the weather, for its whitened summit "act the part of a condenser upon the vapour of the atmosphere . . . we have been visited with thundershowers, which seem to originate in the vicinity of this peak."[83] Below it lay a broad meadow, whose summer appearance was described by one man as a sea of white canvas.

Laramie Peak also signaled civilization. Here at the border of the Rockies, the fur company had established its principal outpost, Fort Laramie. The Mormons approached apprehensively, but with curiosity. For his part, Orson measured the height and circumference of the adobe walls. He took six observations of the longitude and altitude and concluded that Fremont's map was three hundred and eighty feet off on the elevation of the fort. Fort Laramie was commanded by an affable Frenchman named Bordeaux (Orson writes it "Bordeau"), who welcomed the Mormon leaders and entertained them with Indian stories and information about the ascent to South Pass that lay ahead of them. He also had some edgy comments about Lilburn Boggs, who had boarded with him nearly a year before.[84] Bordeaux had nothing but praise for the Mormons, calling them "the most civil and best-behaved company that had ever passed the fort."[85]

Many other emigrants paused at this oasis before the roughest leg of the western journey. The Latter-day Saints found a few of their own among them. A sick detachment had left the Mormon Battalion near Pueblo, Colorado, some of whom had made their way north in hope of encountering their people. But many of the thousands of emigrants strung along the route were from Missouri or Illinois, and the Saints felt a little ill at ease crossing the Platte at Laramie to pick up the established Oregon road.[86]

There was little trouble, however. For days after Laramie they traveled alongside wagonloads of Gentiles who had no time to worry about Mormons, though, in Young's words, they "curse, swear, rip and tear" a great deal.[87] Traffic eased with distance from the fort, although a major Oregon-bound train flooded the trail with dust only a few hours ahead of the Mormons. Brigham Young dispatched outriders to the Platte ford over a hundred miles from Laramie with a boat brought for the crossing. When President Young's wagons pulled up to the ford, where the Oregon Trail bridged the Platte for the last time, he found his outriders ferrying the big train across—for a modest fee. On a Monday morning, the camp quit the Platte for good, but it took five days to move the whole company to the west bank. The journey from this point to the Sweetwater, a distance of forty miles, required only two days.

Here Orson was overwhelmed with the landscape. The massive granite of "Rock Independence," the violence of Devil's Gate and its chasm of water he described as "picturesque . . . serpentine." He detected five strata of scoriated rock in the cliffs and climbed Devil's Gate with his barometer and thermometer while the others amused themselves with firing guns to hear the echo and shoving rocks down the sheer cliff just to see them burst the Sweetwater cataracts. For his part, Orson fell in love with the wild sage or "artemesia" and wrote a tribute to its "clear bright flame" when burned (a welcome change from the fuel provided by the buffalo). In addition, the Wind River mountain range stood like icy bones in the northwest providing a glittering view especially to Orson, who well understood their significance. They were coming to the "divide," the boundary between the Atlantic and the Pacific worlds. Excited, he pushed ahead of the main party with Heber C. Kimball for companionship.[88]

Climbing toward the top of the continent, he reached South Pass on June 26. It was cold, and overcoats became "a necessary appendage" as Orson rode around the broad, snow-banked plain to find the exact elevation of the divide. At length he decided on two prominences separated by a half-mile-wide basin, designating this the "dividing point of land which separates the waters of the Atlantic from those of the Pacific."[89] Here, too, they crossed the nondescript border of "Oregon Territory," organized less than a year under exclusive United States hegemony. When Orson pulled his carriage over the seven-thousand-foot level, he nestled into the meadow camp of Pacific Spring at the legendary headwater of the ocean.

Now Orson encountered another legend, this time in human form. A man conducting some eastering travelers to this campground was introduced as Moses "Black" Harris, a veteran mountain man who had gone into the business of guiding wagon trains. The dusty old trapper had a great deal of advice for the Saints, along with a California newspaper printed by Sam Brannan at San Francisco. Orson shared his tent that night and heard his judgment of the Salt Lake Valley—a desolate, stagnating sink, a timberless wasteland, he was told.[90]

The next day Brigham Young came up to the pass and listened to Harris most of the day, buying furs but not counsel. His determination held for the Salt Lake Valley, and they continued on with good speed to the Little Sandy River, where they encountered another, more renowned voice in the wilderness, Jim Bridger, who was on his way to Laramie. "His information was rather more favorable than that of Major Harris," Orson writes,[91] though Bridger cautioned them about bringing a big emigration into the basin until they were sure the soil was good.[92] By this time, two thousand Saints were already coming up the Platte four hundred miles behind them.

With time closing in from both ends, the van pushed southwest for Fort Bridger, plagued by summer mosquitoes and unsettling rumors about the desert they were planning to colonize. To add to their anxieties, Sam Brannan came tottering into camp after having threaded his way eastward from California. Though they were excited to see him, the brethren palled at the tales of cannibalism he carried as an eyewitness to the tragic scene of the Donner party. He had himself examined the "skulls, bones, and carcasses" that lay strewn in the Donner Pass and had interviewed the old German Keseberg, who had personally devoured several of his fellow wanderers. Brannan was staggered at Brigham Young's idea of settling the Salt Lake Valley and tried to sell him on California. No one was listening.[93]

In the southwest corner of what is now Wyoming, the pioneer leaders sensed Zion in the distance. They encountered Ham's Fork and Black's Fork rivers, and at last the trading post of Jim Bridger, surrounded by Shoshone lodges and mosquito-infested gullies. Frost covered the ground on the eighth of July. Orson spent two days at the fort, taking astronomical observations (he was thirteen miles off on his longitudinal reading[94]) and examining the route southwest to the lake valley, while carpenters and blacksmiths were shoring up and repairing the dilapidated wagons.[95] In many ways, the journey ahead to achieve Zion was yet the most perilous.

On July 10, they left the Oregon Trail beyond Muddy Creek, where Orson calculated the so-called "Bear River Divide" at an elevation seven thousand, seven hundred feet above sea level. They had reached the Great Basin. While scouting the dividing ridge, Orson spotted smoke in the distance which came from the campfire of the only white man who could be called a permanent resident of the Basin, Mr. Miles Goodyear "a mountaineer . . . informed us that he had just established himself near the Salt Lake, between the mouths of Weber's Fork and Bear River" and that he had a small garden which was doing quite nicely—when watered.[96] The pioneers breathed both relief and anxiety: The specter of irrigating the desert clouded the future with drought and disaster.

The ice of the high country gave way to more pleasant temperatures as the pioneers descended the next day to Bear River, crossed, and climbed once again to the lacy escarpments of the Weber headwater, marking the present boundary of Utah. Passing scrub cedar and pudding-stone, Orson made his observations as he hiked the hills and waited for a new scourge to pass: the leader was prostrated. Brigham Young suffered an attack of "mountain fever" that morning. Orson's wagon moved slowly ahead and stopped at Redding's (now Cache) Cave nearly two thousand feet below the Bear River Divide. While Orson slept, leadership of the advance party of the Camp of Israel fell to him. Brigham Young was delirious throughout the night and, though lucid in the morning, couldn't "think of moving today." The vote of the brethren called for saving time and moving forty-two men down to the valley as soon as possible. Orson was elected to lead them.[97]

This was the most difficult part of the trail. Wagon ruts left by several hundred wagons the previous season were virtually untraceable, and the Donner–Reed party had wandered panic stricken in and out of the box canyons of the Wasatch for days before finally breaking through. Orson's specific charge was to find "Mr. Reid's route"[98] and guide the men (including three black slaves)[99] and twenty-three wagons through the dry, itching heat of the mountains to Great Salt Lake, clearing the road for the thousands who were coming.

"We resumed our journey," reads Orson's entry for July 14, the record of thirteen miles to the Weber River through the eerie resonance of Echo Canyon, between rock walls a thousand feet high and as red as the sun. With characteristic detachment Orson writes, "truly . . . very interesting and exceedingly picturesque."[100] Constantly taking his bearings, he led the van into the green scrub and aspen of the Wasatch, a twisting terrain delved by creeks and towering dry bluffs. He was fortunate to have chief outrider Stephen Markham with him, along with Porter Rockwell and John Brown. At the Weber River they found a fork in the road, one trail leading northward through the river canyon, another southward into the mountains. Orson and Brown rode into the canyon about six miles but determined that the river route was impassable because of high water;[101] they then struck out to look for the Donner–Reed traces in the gullies south of the Weber. Convinced he had found the trail in a cottonwood ravine, Orson returned to the camp with the cheerful news that the thickets they were about to pass through had been trampled with huge tracks and holes. The bears, he reported, "must be very numerous."[102] Two days later he came face to face with a "large grey wolf."[103]

The road took shape slowly. Orson directed a dozen men with axes through the narrowing, nearly imperceptible ruts, criss-crossing streams and hacking at willows. The discouraging prospect of "hills piled on hills and mountains on mountains" met him when he ascended a summit to look for the valley,[104] and what was worse, to discover that his road had hit one of Donner–Reed's dead ends. Sunday they rested, and Monday Orson and John Brown plunged down "Kanyon Creek" four miles to a high ridge. "On the south-west we could see an extensive level prairie, some few miles distant, which we thought must be near the Lake."[105] (Brown reports sighting "one corner of Salt Lake,"[106] although Clayton says Orson did not.[107]) Orson returned and signaled the workmen that their destination was near.

Behind them, Clayton put up a sign to prevent others from following the Weber River road: "Pratt's Pass to avoid canyon."[108] Rockwell had seen the main camp coming up within a few miles, and Orson pressed hard on the road through willows, wild rose, and poplar over the summit of Big Mountain. "From this creek to the valley," Clayton later wrote, "is decidedly the worst piece of road on the whole journey."[109]

The next morning, July 21, 1847, saw no frost but a heavy dew. Orson welcomed his brother apostle, Erastus Snow, sent up from the president's camp with instructions to head for the valley and start the seed as soon as possible. Erastus, who, along with his brothers, had been converted by Orson Pratt in Vermont fifteen years before,[110] loped up Little Mountain and then toward the valley with him, along a stream which they named "Last Creek" (today's Emigration Canyon Creek). At the summit they thought they could see it, and they charged down into the rockmaple and aspen. By afternoon, the canyon finally narrowed behind a perilous hill, where the wagon studs of the Donner party had carved a passage above the rocks. They ascended on hands and knees:

> From the top . . . a broad open valley, about 20 miles wide and 30 long, lay stretched out before us, at the north end of which the broad waters of the Great Salt Lake glistened in the sunbeams, containing high mountainous islands from 25 to 30 miles in extent. After issuing from the mountains among which we had been shut up for many days, and beholding in a moment such an extensive scenery open before us, we could not refrain from a shout of joy which almost involuntarily escaped from our lips the moment this grand and lovely scenery was within our view.[111]

"Hosanna! Hosanna! Hosanna!" they shouted at the first sight of the long-sought place of refuge. The valley of the "Utah outlet," as Snow called it, was more than an alluvial basin bounded by the glistening, monumental peaks of the Wasatch. It was Palestine turned around, geographically an uncanny echo of Israel's land of promise, with its own "Jordan" flowing from a fresh to a dead sea. Orson Pratt, like Joshua to Brigham Young's Moses, immediately clambered down the slope. "After drinking in the scene to the satisfaction of their souls, they descended to the open plain, Snow on horseback, with his coat thrown loosely upon his saddle, and Pratt on foot. They journeyed westward about three miles, when Snow missing his coat turned back, and Pratt continued alone."[112] Orson made a triumphal circle of twelve miles through the valley, a lonely figure on the plain, the first Mormon of the hundreds of thousands to follow.

Another apostle, Ezra T. Benson, and five others joined Orson and Erastus Snow as they were dispatched excitedly into the valley the next day to survey the possibilities for settlement. Skirting the gradual rise of hills on the north side of the valley, they headed in the direction of the lake and soon found one of those delightful creek mouths that watered the plain at intervals along the Wasatch. A double-forked stream spilled into the valley here, gravel on the bottom and grass burgeoning along the banks.[113] From this place, the vista of the valley sobered and delighted the brethren: John Brown remembered, "We found it covered with rich vegetation in the vicinity of the streams, and the low-lands were green and beautiful. On the benches the grass was dry and a great variety of soil . . . There were hosts of black crickets all over the valley and apparently harmless."[114] Clayton was "happily disappointed in the appearance of the valley . . . but if the land be as rich as it has the appearance of being, I have no fears but the Saints can live here and do well while we will do right."[115]

Rounding the north point of the mountains, the party found itself mired in the tepid mud of a thermal swamp. Canebrake and rushes came to their shoulders as they sniffed at the copperas and sulfur and edged their animals over peat dikes and a vast meadow awash with sand and salt. Here, nearly to the lake margins, they found a boiling spring. Erastus jumped onto a rock in the middle, judged it hot enough "for scalding hogs," and pronounced it a medical miracle. He had, he said, "little desire to remain long upon it."[116]

In this circuit of the north end, the brethren finally returned to the twin forks of City Creek. Orson moved the advance camp into the valley on July 23 and settled them on the banks of this pure cold water, which Orson judged sufficiently momentous for millsites and other machinery. Despite the urgency of planting on everyone's mind, Orson first called the company together to carry out the priestly obligation which culminated seventeen years of wandering and thousands of miles of uncertainty. It fell to Orson as company leader and chief apostle present to dedicate the land to God, to consecrate the site of a city of Saints, and to express thanksgiving for their preservation.[117] After prayer, "all went to work with a zeal characteristic of Saints."[118]

No time was lost in getting a dam started and ploughing several square rods of "exceedingly dry" soil (the legend holds that steel blades snapped like twigs against the ground).[119] But a fresh shower in the afternoon cooled the dust. Turnips and potatoes were laid in, the first permanent seed of Mormon colonization, which would within a few years flower into hundreds of cities and farms. Orson Pratt had chosen and dedicated the site of the new Nauvoo, though Brigham Young had not yet seen it.

The president of the Twelve still lay abed in his wagon, moving gingerly down the trail that Orson had graded with his advance crew, edging around the mouth of Emigration Canyon about noon Saturday, July 24. The encampment bustled some three miles below as Brigham surveyed mountain blocks and the prairie with the distant glimmer of the lake. He approved Orson's choice of a site, confirming the revelatory insights which had led the apostle here. The Saints held a sacrament meeting the next day.[120]

Within days the little settlement absorbed Indians, battalion stragglers, and Sam Brannan and his California dreams.[121] The apostles decided to explore their new Zion on Tuesday to ascertain just how much of the desert was habitable and to compare it with Fremont's descriptions. Orson rode along with Brother Brigham's carriage due west to the "Utah Outlet," the Jordan River, about six rods wide and three feet deep. They forded and cantered onto a flat range of sagebrush. About thirteen miles further they came to the looming barrenness of the mountain block that walled in the valley from the west, following the ruts left by the Donner–Reed party.

"We all bathed in the salt water," writes Orson; "its specific gravity is such as to buoy us up in a remarkable manner."[122] A small butte reared out of the water; this they recognized as the emigrant landmark Black Rock. Brigham sent Orson and two others down west to look at a valley "putting up to the southward from the lake" (Tooele Valley). They camped that night where the Oquirrh range points at the lake in a brackish little oasis.

Next morning the thermometer rose above eighty degrees as Orson clambered up the grade of the Oquirrhs to see what he could, always a few miles ahead of everyone else. From here, the whole sweep of Utah Lake, the "western Galilee," and the monumental ridge of Timpanogos came into view. Orson's were the first Mormon eyes on the Utah Valley. It looked good to him. The rest of the camp caught him, about ten miles south of the lake, standing on a mountain which would one day be ground to dust for the copper it contained. The whole party enthusiastically jumped into the Jordan for a bath to remedy the problem of the gritty skin they got from swimming in the Great Salt Lake.[123]

But the brethren were too busy founding a city to spend much time exploring. That afternoon they accompanied Brigham back to the settlement, where they walked to a level spot between the twin forks:

> On motion of Orson Pratt it was unanimously voted that the temple be built on [this] site . . . that the city lots be one and a quarter acres, and that the streets be eight rods wide. . . . We proceeded to lay out a site for the city, which we called GREAT SALT LAKE CITY. The streets were laid out eight rods wide, running at right angles, and forming the city into square blocks . . . One block of ten acres was reserved for a temple. The latitude of the northern boundary of the temple block I ascertained by meridian observation of the sun to be 40 deg. 45 min. 44 sec. The longitude . . . 7 hours 25 min. 46 sec. west of Greenwich.[124]

(It should be noted that Orson's observations were based on solar time rather than modern standard longitudinal measurements. He was accurate within five minutes. His standard reading was longitude 111 deg. 26 min. 34 sec. west, about 27 minutes in error.[125]) With the heavenly city located in time and space, the pioneers met to hear the voice of their foremost theologian on August 1, 1847. Orson had looked over the sage desert to the "utmost bounds of the everlasting hills," and a revelation formed in his soul as he spoke to the sun-blackened sons of Israel under a day-old bowery built of rushes near the place where their tabernacle of God would one day stand.

> We can build up a city to the Lord. For many years I have not read that good old book, but I remember the predictions in it and some that are now very nearly fulfilled by us. Isaiah says, speaking of the city of Zion . . . "Thou shalt be called, Sought out, a city not forsaken" . . . Isaiah and Joel both spake very plainly on this subject. "It shall come to pass in the last days that the house of the Lord shall be established in the tops of the mountains, and shall be exalted above the hills." In what part of the earth could it be established more than in this place . . . in the midst of the spires of the mountains.[126]

And so Orson located the Saints in eternity. In Orson's hymn to the heritage of Jacob the desert was transformed to a theophoric paradise, a fulfillment of prophecy, and the Saints looked around with new eyes to see what Orson saw—a great echo in the landscape of the promises given to ancient Israel. "We will circumscribe all things to the very heavens," he declared and looked up at the mountains, for him the spires of the temple the God of nature had reared for his Saints.

Salt Lake Base and Meridian, established by Orson Pratt. *Courtesy, Church Archives, Church of Jesus Christ of Latter-day Saints.*

7
The Millennial Star

Zion needed to be measured and described. Orson started out Monday morning, August 2, with another surveyor, Henry G. Sherwood, to lay out the city of the Great Salt Lake using a chain and a couple of trimmed poles from the canyon. Starting from a natural point of reference, the corner of the proposed temple block, he checkered the city into blocks ten acres square.[1] The new town was to be spacious and well ordered, as Joseph Smith would have wanted it, but it was to be compact and defensible as well; it was planned to be a world capital based on New England grids, but it was still a post in the wilderness. The Saints decided to trust in God rather than mud walls, however, when Orson pointed out the months it would take to fence in a city with a perimeter of over two thousand rods.

Orson and Sherwood directed their chain from the southeast corner of the temple block[2] along a line stretching to infinity, over mountains and lakes and deserts, to the north and the east. This was to be the fixed center of Zion, the point from which the Great Basin would be laid out in a vast square graph of section and township, and, spiritually, the whole earth would be diagrammed. The Great Salt Lake Base and Meridian, still marked by a little stone shaft at the intersection of South Temple and Main streets, remains one of only four baselines still in use in the United States. He plotted this point at 4,309 feet above sea level and at six seconds below the northern wall. From here the mountains could be measured: the expanse of "a lone peak" southeast of camp rose 6,000 feet above the valley floor; a

"Sugar Loaf Peak" capping the west range was sixteen miles away.[3] Plotting three blocks south and three blocks west, Orson lined up the main thoroughfares of Salt Lake City. All around him men dug pits for brick-making and sowed buckwheat in the valley bottom. For days Orson carefully continued staking off streets of the city that remained only a vision in Brigham Young's mind—the vision of Zion where men would be stewards rather than traffickers in land.

On Friday the Twelve met at the newly finished dam on City Creek and were baptized again by Young: "This we considered a privilege and a duty. As we had come in a glorious valley to locate and build up Zion, we felt like renewing our covenants." After the ordinance was performed, the Prophet reconfirmed and sealed the apostleship upon each just as the sun disappeared behind the lake islands.[4] The next day Brigham Young, Moses-like, took the Twelve into council to select their inheritances. Land was not to be bought or sold but to be apportioned on the basis of need and willingness to work. Brigham directed the Twelve to stake off the blocks around the temple for their own and their companies' use: the new arrivals would then have homesteads already allotted to them. Brigham Young claimed the blocks east of the temple, Heber C. Kimball the north, and Orson was assigned all the property running in a line south for four blocks.[5] The "Pratt district" today encloses everything between Main and West Temple as far as Broadway, one of the most valuable commercial zones in the West. Looking over his inheritance that day, however, Orson saw only cement-hard ground and rushes.

The toilsome and euphoric days were filled with rebaptisms as each member of the advance camp of Israel reasserted his chosen position in the sight of God. Hundred-degree heat and whirlwinds visited the camp, as did mortality. While the camp palavered with some Indians one afternoon, a three-year-old boy, Milton Therlkill, tumbled from City Creek dam and drowned.[6] The first death in the promised land cast a pall over the Saints, and Orson delivered "a beautiful and affecting prayer" at the grave. Though he could not have known it, he too had lost a little boy: After having been brought through the muddy Iowa wilderness by his mother Sarah, eighteen-month-old Vanson succumbed on July 28 at Winter Quarters to the blackleg disease.[7]

At length Orson's work of measurement was completed, and the city was staked out in the desert. Wheat and corn were showing faint

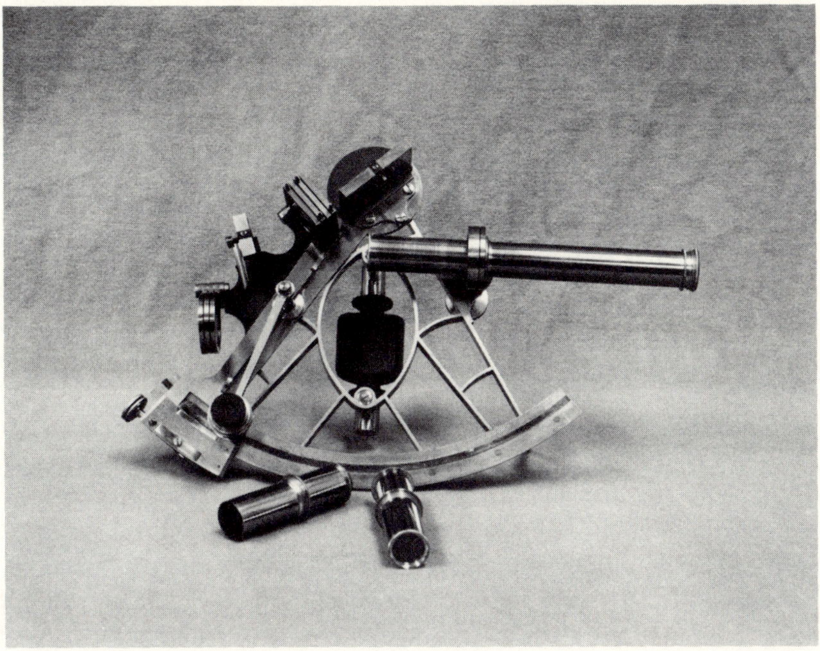

Sextant used in early survey of Salt Lake valley. This may well have been used by Orson Pratt. *Courtesy, Church Museum of History and Art, Church of Jesus Christ of Latter-day Saints.*

green heads. It was time to go back the way they had come and guide the Saints into the promised land. August 30 was gloomy and cold as Orson and a hundred sixty others took leave of a small contingent who remained in the valley. Noting the abrupt end to the summer weather, Orson's party traveled considerably faster on their return route.[8] Orson spent his time calculating and jotting while riding in the nineteenth wagon, double-checking the observations he had made for a guide that Clayton eventually published for the use of the emigrants.[9] He passed his thirty-sixth birthday at South Pass after preaching at the camp at Pacific Springs.[10]

While still several hundred miles from Winter Quarters, the returning pioneers glimpsed a vast assemblage of nearly six hundred wagons toiling up the Platte. This proved to be only the beginning of the deluge. Parley P. Pratt and John Taylor were leading thousands toward the valley. There was a good deal of celebration, though Parley found himself shrinking beneath Brigham's scolding for having a disorganized camp. Parley was humbled[11] but also carried a great deal of news to the council. Since the Saints had left Illinois, the United States had taken over upper Mexico and Oregon. The war with Mexico was winding down, though terms had not been set. (Unknown to the pioneers, Winfield Scott's occupation of Mexico City had delivered their new Zion indisputably into American hands just ten days before.) Orson now found that he had lost a son but also that Sarah had given birth to another on July 10. Parley had left Winter Quarters before a second birth in Orson's family that had taken place on September 15. A little girl had been born to Adelia Ann Bishop Pratt, one of the "young ladies" who had ridden out of Nauvoo in Orson's carriage on Valentine's Day in 1846.[12]

The two pioneering brothers embraced at the Platte on September 25, 1847,[13] and went their respective ways—Parley to suffer through the first winter in Salt Lake, where the crops so optimistically sown had proven inadequate,[14] and Orson on to the main Camp of Israel on the Missouri. They did not see each other again for seven years. By November the returning band achieved Winter Quarters without mishap, though Indians had stolen many of their horses,[15] Orson stood in the council house the first Sunday and described the lakes and valleys they had claimed, visualizing again the prophetic image of the exalted house of the Lord "in the tops of the mountains."[16] Whereas others in America talked about continental occupation and "Manifest Destiny," Orson had developed a whole theology of the West—Isaiah had seen it clearly, he reported, and the curious parallels between Mosaic history and the saga of that summer caravan did not escape him.

Orson found his three young wives settled in sod houses on the west bank of Missouri. There he met again that contemplative, thin little image of himself, Orson Junior, who was now ten; Celestia, his five-year-old; and two infants by different mothers. In a ceremony to name and bless the children, he called Sarah's little boy Laron and Delia's baby girl (less than two months old) Lucy Adelia in honor of her mother and grandmother Lucy Bishop. The infant was the first of a long list of Orson's offspring by his plural wives.[17]

Orson went to a party in February for the "citizen defenders of Nauvoo"[18] and heard a desperate tale of the Saints left behind who were suddenly forced to fight an artilleried band of "neighbors" the previous autumn. Perhaps he heard how his brother Anson had charged the Mormon cannon with the first ball and had fled across the river with aged Charity Pratt, his mother, in tow.[19]

For six months Orson rested at Winter Quarters. He watched the camp pull back across the Missouri when Indian agents protested their "stripping" the territory; observed the log tabernacle thrown up in three weeks at Kanesville, Iowa; and dedicated it before a congregation of one thousand. It was a far cry from the glories of the Nauvoo temple, but it served well for a sanctuary to reorganize the leadership of the Church. On December 27, the camp met in conference to hear Orson Pratt address them on the order of the priesthood. He concluded with a motion that Brigham Young be "elected" president of the Church and authorized to restore the quorum of the First Presidency as Joseph had established it. At first Orson had been surprised at Brigham's proposal to reorganize the Presidency. "I do consider the head . . . in the Apostleship united together . . . our Prest does not control the quorum." The New Testament, to his mind, was a sufficient model of organization—with apostles set in the Church to govern as a body. But when Brigham declared that he was motivated by revelation, Orson was satisfied, spoke in favor, and even seconded the motion.[20] Hosea Stout reported:

> O. Pratt spoke at length on the policy of electing a First President. That God had saw proper to govern the Church by the Twelve since the death of Joseph the Prophet and that he could govern it by whatever authority he saw proper even by teachers and deacons. There was a time when this Church was governed by the Lesser Priesthood But now the Lord had manifested by his Spirit that it was best to appoint a First Presidency again that the organization of the Church might be perfected and the Twelve have a chance to spread abroad again to the Nations &c. His discourse was very interesting and was received with breathless silence.[21]

Brigham was unanimously sustained and took with him from the Twelve both Heber Kimball and Willard Richards for counselors. With this action, Orson Pratt was confirmed in his calling, third now among the apostles, junior only to his own brother Parley and to Orson Hyde. Orson's relations with the new "president prophet, seer, and revelator" of Mormonism became problematic, but cordial. He continually, in his letters to the president, craves his "lenient eye";[22] he was probably well-conditioned by now to Young's exacting demands for loyalty and obedience. Young had shown considerable confidence in Orson when he appointed him navigator of the advance company and delegated the pioneering to him when he himself had been too sick to move. There had been others among the first camp who could have taken over—Woodruff, Kimball, or the experienced frontiersmen Stephen Markham and Porter Rockwell. But it was certainly because of Young's trust in Orson's abilities, as well as deference to his position in the governing quorum, that he was selected to lead the way into Zion.

The early months of the year 1848 Orson spent in study and preparation for a new mission appointed him in December. He was to preach gathering to the British Saints. Nearly seven years had passed since he had left Liverpool and in that time he had been excommunicated and rebaptized, burned out of his home, and endowed with four more wives; he had traversed the Mormon Trail in both directions and helped found a city. He would travel to Europe with a new, more radical perspective: it was time to get out of Babylon and live the celestial law.

Preparations consumed much time, however, and winter had the camp on its knees. Hundreds languished through the cold on potatoes and "corn dodger." Death came for many. Orson was, as usual, deep in his studies. On March 19, 1848, while the Omahas traded outside the tabernacle door for meal and chickens, Orson was inside shedding light for the hundreds in attendance "on the combinations of the Intelligent atoms."[23] Concerned for the books which had been brought across Iowa from the Nauvoo library, Orson arranged for several wagons to transport them to the Salt Lake settlement.

On April 22 Orson was given his commission as head of the European mission to proceed to England (now that the ice was gone) "to preach, publish, and superintend the immigration and preside over all the conferences and all affairs of the . . . Saints in the British Islands and adjacent countries . . . his family should accompany him if he chooses."[24] Sarah so chose, and on a May morning she and Orson and three children stepped aboard the Missouri steamer *Mandon* which called at Kanesville. Orson carried with him a certificate from Brigham Young: "The bearer, Elder Orson Pratt, A. M. Professor of Mathematics and member of the Quorum of Twelve Apostles, is a gentleman of sterling integrity and unblemished character, and is delegated by the authorities . . . to solicit and receive donations in money, books, and apparatus for establishing an endowment of an observatory of the first order, at the Great Salt Lake City."[25] (The observatory was eventually constructed in 1869.)

This was Sarah's first crossing of the Atlantic, and she suffered severely; she was three months from delivering her seventh child. On July 20, 1848, as they docked in Liverpool, the Saints met them and sorrowed over her condition;[26] the mission home at 15 Wilton Street provided comfortable quarters, however, and Sarah discovered the pleasures of having a serving girl for the first time in her life. A Scottish girl of nineteen, Marian Ross had worked in the office since her baptism a year before and soon became deeply attached to both Orson and Sarah. This was the little girl now grown up who had dreamed of Orson Pratt the night before she met him at the age of ten.[27]

Orson convened the Saints of Britain at the Manchester Music Hall on August 13. Hundreds of British workmen captivated by Joseph Smith's restoration now stirred inside at the message of gathering and perhaps also at the prospect of land to be had for the taking. Orson collected their tithing slowly. After a little scolding in the pages of the *Millennial Star*, the money began to trickle in. This money was to pay for the sustenance of the pioneers then making their way across the distant plains, for the temple, for the observatory (which he would finally get after two more decades), and even for "a museum for specimens of the works of nature and art" at Great Salt Lake City.[28] He also scoured the shops of Liverpool for everything necessary to build a civilization from scratch: tools for clockmaking, engineering, and copying; crockery for households on the desert; knives and forks, "white handles would be preferred, and half a gross of pocket tweezers."[29]

Orson had calculated it would take three hundred ships to move the British Saints to Zion. In spite of the enormous preparation this would require, Orson still had to contend with Babylon and call as many out as would come. His main voice was the *Millennial Star*, the periodical inaugurated by Parley nearly ten years before. It had a big circulation, and the Mormons drank in every word; Orson took over this organ with all the pent-up energy of an evangelist and announced the *Star* office would also be printing a series of pamphlets on first principles, a definitive theological statement of Mormonism to be dumped in the laps of the orthodox Christian establishment of Britain.

He was as good as his word. On September 30, the manuscript of Orson's first installment was delivered to the South Castle Street printing house of Mr. R. James. Entitled *Divine Authority*, an edition of ten thousand was circulated through the missionary system to attack the foundations of Anglicanism. Subtitled "Was Joseph Smith Sent of God?" Orson's tract was designed to "cut asunder the deeply-rooted prejudices, the iron-bound sinews of ancient error and tradition, made sacred by age and rendered popular by human wisdom."[30] Well aware of the iconoclastic nature of Mormon claims, Orson presented in his usual "practicum" voice a series of numbered arguments, the first of his forensic-style treatises. Orson's approach attempted to establish the authenticity of his own priesthood as much by a tone of sweet reasonableness as by direct persuasion.

At an afternoon tea Orson had been shown a letter that congratulated a recent convert on his accession to religious certainty and bemoaned the writer's lack of it. Orson's treatise opens as a reply to the letter noting that the question of divine authority is so critical that it bears "the savor of life or death."[31] He proceeded to show that the career of Joseph Smith conforms to a prophetic pattern discerned in Daniel, Isaiah, and John's Revelation; that the doctrine of Mormonism is "infallible" because it is so inclusive; and that its organization matches every feature of the New Testament church. Not surprisingly there was little appeal to subjective experience as a source of ministerial authority. Indeed, he denies "the infallibility of miraculous evidence, . . . abstract miracles are as likely to be false as true."[32] Orson prefers to describe the "fruits" of Joseph's labors and evaluate them against a "control," the scripture.

Divine Authority is not to be underestimated as a significant Mormon polemic. It groups together into one system the standard Mormon "proof texts" that point to the millennial mission of Joseph Smith and bridges dispensations with a certain purity of wonder at the monument of doctrine, biblical in scope, laid out by the Prophet. Throughout, Orson manifests a genuine contempt for the competition: they are stubble ready for the burning, in no way reflecting the ancient Christian pattern. In fact they are glowing in opposition to the scriptural value placed in spiritual gifts. He contrasts the priests of the Latter-day Saints with the run of sectarian divines: "While the one class are suffering martyrdom for their testimony, the other class are rolling in all the luxuries and splendours of Great Babylon, from ten to twenty to twenty-seven thousand pounds sterling per annum."[33] This swipe was surely not lost on the ears of the working-class Midlanders who crowded Mormon street meetings.

But Orson's pen had only begun warming to the cause. Orson spent most of his time crouched at a desk savoring his own clear, if not distinguished, phrasing of the eternal truths. Besides the pamphleteering he had tremendous loads of correspondence to manage. From Orson Hyde he heard the kind of political gossip that both of them had relished and clucked over in Washington four years before. The Whigs had triumphed in the American elections; Zachary Taylor was now president. In the same letter came the singular story of the weeks of the cricket plague and the seagulls, of the crop destruction—"yet . . . there will be enough for all the population."[34] From Wilford Woodruff came word of a new epidemic "raging to such an extent that the cholera is lost sight of . . . it is called the gold fever." He further learned of the Mormon soldiers who had whooped into Salt Lake with a sack of "pure virgin gold" dug from Sutter's millrace. Here, too, was a letter which no doubt started Orson from his chair: regards from Oliver Cowdery, who had recently rejoined the Church at the Kanesville, Iowa, encampment.[35]

But the most important news of all related that the world seemed to be going up in smoke. Orson arrived in England to the echoes of street-smashing riots, part of the convulsive wave of revolutionary sentiment that engulfed all of Europe in 1848. The February revolution in France had touched off insurrection almost at once everywhere else: all the German-speaking rulers were thrashing at peasant uprisings while Marx and Engels stirred the radical heart with their "Manifesto"; the battling Milanese had spread unrest all over Italy, and the conflagration had touched even the dim industrial belt of Britain. Everywhere men questioned the fabric of society and set the torch to it when they could, while others as passionately clung to the secure, propertied notions of feudal Europe.[36]

Predictably, Orson Pratt's pen advocated a clean sweep as he turned to the problem of social order. What ideal did the Mormons have to contribute? he asked with the first number of a five-part booklet entitled *The Kingdom of God*. He called this kingdom "the only legal government that can exist in any part of the universe," as his brother Parley did in the monumental pamphlet *Voice of Warning*: the kingdom was constituted of a king, officers, laws, and citizens.[37] Just as he had denounced the divines of spiritual Babylon, Orson flays its political superstructure with equal vehemence: "Any people attempting to govern themselves by laws of their own making, and by officers of their own appointment, are in direct rebellion against the kingdom of God . . . Their authority is all assumed—it originated in man . . . Their very foundations were laid in rebellion . . . a heterogeneous mass of discordant elements."[38] Whereas Parley's pamphlet fundamentally restates Mormon "first principles," Orson presents in his treatise a theocratic system founded on unescapable philosophical conclusions.

The current political upheavals were, in Orson's view, the natural consequence of rejecting legitimate authority vested only in the Almighty and his representatives. Naturally, the question of right order cannot be resolved until divine sovereignty is recognized. The perplexities of the age originated with its idolatry: "They have introduced a 'God without BODY, PARTS, or PASSIONS!' . . . Such a being could not speak, for he has no 'parts' to speak with."[39] Again echoing his brother Parley,[40] for Orson this explained the universal king's apparent "abdication" of his government of human affairs. In its five chapters he described a charter for the kingdom of God and in the process revealed some of the theocratic assumptions that undergirded the social polity of the Mormons.

The logic of Mormonism rested on the principle of revelation, as Orson made clear here. Because he was a finite being, the Father could not be present everywhere. "It is therefore impossible for [him] to attend in *person* to all the multiplied affairs of government among intelligent beings; therefore, God, in establishing a government among men has always called persons of their own number to officiate in his name."[41] The source of sovereignty is superiority of wisdom, rather than consent of the governed; ideally, knowledge is king. Orson then attempts a metaphysical justification for his concept of legitimate sovereignty: "All the innumerable phenomena of universal nature are produced in their origin by the actual presence of this intelligent, all-wise, and all-powerful material substance called the Holy Spirit. It is the most active matter in the universe, producing all its operations according to fixed and definite laws enacted by itself . . . Each atom of the Holy Spirit is intelligent."[42] The laws of nature, then, constituted the method by which intelligent, discrete, but omnipresent "spirit" operated; the source of law rested in the covenant of primal intelligences to act together in opposition to dissolution and cosmic anarchy. ("For Pratt," Sterling M. McMurrin has said, "reality is material and atomistic, each individual atom possessing powers of intelligent action and self-direction . . . Pratt's atoms constitute an intercommunicating community . . . [they] behave freely in a manner proposed but not necessitated by the divine will. Their behavior, when considered collectively, is described as natural law."[43]) Orson implied that the universe was conscious of itself, that "Holy Spirit" was its cumulative will, and that the sacramental concept of authority depended upon access to its revelatory gifts. "The Holy Spirit is the great distinguishing character between the officers of the kingdom of God and impostors."[44]

Though written as an attempt to solve the fulminating questions of right order in society, *The Kingdom of God* was in the main a brief defense of Mormon "materialism": "His kingdom . . . hath its seat in the everlasting mountains,"[45] and the ruler, himself a tangible, sentient being, derives his authority from consonance with and therefore mastery over the universal intelligences. The appeal of authoritarian Mormonism has been attributed by some to the American uneasiness with economic democracy, but this is certainly insufficient. At least in part, Mormon theocracy attracted followers thirsty for these transcendent assurances. For Orson Pratt loyalty to the hierarchy simply reflected the universal and eternally autonomous consent of the "intelligences" to defer to superior wisdom in all things.

The five pamphlets were completed in June 1849 and scattered by the thousands in Liverpool, Manchester, and Glasgow. Even before the series was finished, however, *Kingdom* began to stir up a response, a kind of clerical–academic splutter. Orson had touched a raw nerve in the "Kirk." The main thrust of the extremely influential Scottish "Common Sense" school of philosophy had been to defend Presbyterianism against the "corrosive influence of . . . necessitarian materialism (personified in . . . Joseph Priestley)."[46] Orson's insistence upon a material deity aroused the fury of a church endangered by the encroachments of demythologizing "natural philosophers." A group of Scottish clergymen banded together to oppose Orson's pamphlets, commissioning a Dunfermline minister named Joseph Paton to compose a general rebuttal. The result, *Remarks on Mormonism, with the Approbation of Clergymen of Different Demoninations,* seems a sketchy, ill-informed pastiche grouping together legends about the Saints, the Spaulding theory of the origin of the Book of

Mormon, and the standard sectarian attacks on "anthropomorphism."[47]

Orson wasted no time in replying. His contemptuous response was in print by April 1849.

> As this secret author . . . has used no arguments, therefore there are none to answer; instead of arguments he seems very much inclined to apply to the Saints and their doctrine such phrases as . . . *absurd notions—a gross, a stupid, and an unphilosophical fraud—delusion—groveling sensualism of Mormonism* . . . Very polite terms, Mr. Author! Genteel epithets! Doubtless the 'clergymen of different denominations' must feel themselves highly honoured in approbating such irresistible logic![48]

A large part of Orson's reply was devoted to correcting Paton's misreadings of *Divine Authority*. Few substantial problems were raised. For example, Paton's assertions that the "laws of optics" precluded man's visualizing God or spirits only made Orson chuckle a little. He mulled over a definition of "optics" and then called up some of the biblical prophets who conversed with God "face to face" and presumably saw him with their "mortal eyes as instruments." Nevertheless, Paton advances a rather serious criticism of Joseph Smith's vision of Father and Son when he quotes the Gospel of John to the effect that "No man hath seen God at any time." Orson interpolates "*natural* man" without much comment and with no exegetical argument, except to point out numerous examples of biblical characters who apparently "saw" God.[49]

Soon Orson's foray into "materialism" began to draw more intense fire. A "noted British theologian" residing at Liverpool,[50] Mr. T. W. P. Taylder, put out another pamphlet in reply to Orson's anthropomorphic delusions: *The Materialism of the Mormons or Latter-day Saints Examined and Exposed*. And, in this age of manifestoes and countermanifestoes, Orson dutifully rebutted with perhaps his finest essay, *Absurdities of Immaterialism, or, A Reply to T. W. P. Taylder's Pamphlet*.

Taylder's initial argument was with the rationality of "Mormon philosophy." He found it "irrational" to believe mind or spirit to be material phenomena, for, as he said, "All the qualities of matter are not comparable with the more excellent qualities of mind, such as power and intelligence . . . Mind thinks, matter cannot think."[51] For Taylder the body was merely the "medium through which the mind is manifest." In comparing the properties of matter to those of mind, Taylder found it absurd to speak of "the twentieth part of our belief, the half of a hope, the top of memory, the corner of a fear, the north side of a doubt, &c! Mind then is not matter."[52] He understood Orson to argue for a mechanistic brain that secretes affections like a gland giving off hormones. That being the case, Mormon "materialism" requires emotions to be as measurable as chemical compounds:

> If mind be matter, or matter mind, then we may have the square or cube of joy or grief, of pain or pleasure. We may divide a great joy into a number of little joys, or we may accumulate a great joy by heaping together the solid parts of several little joys. We shall then have the color and shape of a thought. It will be either white, grey, brown, crimson, purple, or it may be a mixture of two or more colors. Then we shall have a dark grey hope, a bright yellow sorrow, a round brown tall pain, and an octagonal green belief; an inch of thought, a mile of joy.[53]

Needless to say, Taylder saw this as absolutely absurd, and ridiculed Orson's notion of discrete intelligences once again on the self-evident impossibility of assigning physical mass or volume to intangibles like wisdom and intellect: "Mr. Orson Pratt calls matter into existence, of which the world knows but little. He has not only 'intelligent matter,' but 'all-wise,' and 'all-powerful' matter. This matter is capable of division into parts; for all matter has length, breadth, and thickness. Then we shall have the half of an intelligent atom of matter, the eighth of an all-wise atom . . . such are the absurdities which 'the Latter-day Saint' embraces."[54]

He went on to impute all the evils of nineteenth-century materialism to Orson's philosophy and condemned Mormonism as a dangerous force for atheism and social breakdown: "*Here is the real perfection of materialism!* It destroys man's accountability to God! There is then no such thing as praise or blame, fear or hope, reward or punishment, and consequently no religion . . . If *their God* be a material being, he must *necessarily act mechanically*."[55] Taylder compared Mormonism to the mechanistic views of Erasmus Darwin, eighteenth-century materialist, grandfather of Charles and bogeyman of orthodoxy in his own time. To Taylder the Mormon God conformed to Darwin's theory that mind was only "contractions, motions, or configuration of the fibres of the organs of sense."[56]

From the first it was apparent that Taylder and Orson Pratt were speaking different philosophical languages. When Orson asserted that God was a tangible entity in man's likeness, Taylder sprang to defend the God of the creeds by impugning Orson's "materialism," thus dragging Orson into the midst of the great philosophical controversy of the early nineteenth century. In the extreme sense materialism reduced mind to a physical process, antagonizing all believers in unembodied spirit by declaring organic mechanism sufficient to explain human consciousness. This ancient dispute between materialism and philosophical idealism goes back at least as far as Democritus and the Greek "atomists." Furthermore, questions concerning the nature of the mind have always taken on theological overtones since God has been generally considered "necessary" only by idealists. For materialists there are no necessary beings, and this undermines the whole system upon which proofs of God are traditionally predicated. It is no wonder that Taylder, an orthodox Protestant divine, bridled at the Mormon appropriation of the term *material* to describe God himself.

At the same time Taylder was mistaken about Orson's use of the vocabulary of materialism and the terms Orson employed in *Kingdom of God*. These were unfortunately imprecise, and they drew the discussion far afield. Although Orson's ideas did conform to some materialistic notions current in the 1840s, he was certainly no philosophical materialist. He purposed in his previous writings—as he does in *Absurdities*—to attack the God of the creeds as an insubstantial, amorphous "nothing." Marshaling the terms and tools of materialism, he declares it absurd to worship a being without location, extension, divisibility or magnitude—in short, "NOTHING . . . the negative of space, of duration, and of matter; it is the zero of all existence." Those who believe in this concept of God he called "Atheists, Immaterialists." That is, those who insist that God exists "nowhere" do not differ from the infidel who asserts that God "does not exist anywhere . . . the Immaterialist, whose declared belief amounts to the same thing as the Atheist's, endeavors to hide his infidelity under the shallow covering of a few words."[57] This indictment applied to Taylder and indeed all of creedal Christianity.

Although he made use of the vocabulary of materialism, Orson did not allow himself to be lumped with that school. Orson acerbically denounced the monumental question-begging presumptions of creedal "immaterialism." To quote Taylder, "Mind thinks, matter cannot . . . this thinking principle . . . clearly proves the immateriality of the mind or spirit"—an assertion that Orson understandably labels *Petitio Principii*.[58] But Orson by no means shared the skepticism of materialists about the existence of "unembodied" intelligence. In labelling spirit "material," he simply declared it possesses certain attributes of matter—extension, location, and duration.[59] He asked his readers to "endeavour to conceive of a substance which has no parts." He argued, intriguingly, that "the act of remembering" demonstrates the existence of mind or spirit as a substance that locates itself in time and therefore must occupy a position in space as well, for Orson clearly saw an interdependence between space and time: "Time is an essential ingredient to all motion . . . in our idea of motion are involved the ideas . . . of space and time."[60]

Therefore Orson was merely asking Taylder and those like him to admit the "absurdity" of this continued insistence on "immateriality" as the true mode of spiritual existence. He reduced the whole controversy to a semantic problem when he referred Taylder to the writings of the "immaterialist" Dr. Joseph Butler, Reverend Bishop of Bristol, whose *Analogy of Religion Natural and Revealed* (1736) supposes the spirit of man to be "a simple, uncompounded, indivisible, little atom of conscious substance, or, in other words an intelligent atom."[61] Orson interpreted Taylder to agree with Butler that "mind is simple not compounded":

> Where then, Mr. Taylder, is the absurdity in believing as the 'Saints' do, in the existence of immense numbers of intelligent atoms? It agrees most perfectly with the results of your own theory—the only difference is in the name. You call these indivisible substances *immaterial*, we call them *material*. You apply to them the same powers that we do. You believe them to be conscious, intelligent, and thinking atoms as well as we.[62]

Orson thus dismissed Taylder as a quibbler who was in essential agreement with him, but not before he ridiculed the divine for confusing the attributes of mind with mind itself:[63] "*Joy* is no more a *substance* than *motion*. Both are merely the *states* or *conditions* of substance." Although Orson used the term *materialism* in a nontraditional sense, he found Taylder's notion of "substance" roughly equivalent to "matter."

Later in the essay, Orson came into substantial agreement with philosophical materialism. When he posited that the only "essence" in existence was "solidity," he denied, at least in the accepted sense, the venerable Platonic tradition that the "essence" of a physical object resides in the divine mind—that the material world is somehow a reflection of God's eternal conception of the universe.[64] Orson came close to the ideas of Joseph Priestley, whom he had read and quoted by name, when he announced, "Solidity is not a property of *anything* —it is the essence itself . . . Deprive atoms of solidity, and they are deprived . . . of existence itself, and nothing remains."[65] Priestley, the foremost scientific mind of his age and a thoroughgoing determinist, believed that mind could be understood as the mechanical interaction of material substances. Orson attacked this notion as "baseless . . . Mechanism implies the incapability of a substance to act only as it is acted upon . . . But not so with an intelligent thinking substance: it can . . . act according to its own will, independently of the laws of mechanism."[66] This argument proceeded from Orson's fundamental premise that all matter is inherently active, self-moving, and therefore "intelligent in its sphere." Though he believed the universe to be "essentially" material, Orson rejected philosophical materialism as a system because he found its mechanistic arguments insufficient to account for the phenomenon of mind.

But Orson's rejection of materialism did not by any means endorse its opponents. On the contrary he considered the learned metaphysicians who had taken up David Hume's attack on empirically acquired knowledge to be victims of "wild and vague imagination."[67] Orson discussed at some length the work of Dr. Thomas Brown, light of the "Common Sense" school and disciple of Hume, who taught that mind is nonmaterial because it does not conform to material criteria of extension and resistance when touched.[68] The nature of mind was the fundamental problem for the Scottish philosophers because (like most modern philosophers) they felt that "one must begin with an understanding of the nature of human knowledge and develop an understanding of the universe as a derivative procedure."[69] Brown tried to steer a median course between materialism and immaterialism[70] but could not explain (at least to Orson's satisfaction) the contact point between mind and universe. Orson laughed off Brown's "resistance" test, using light as an example: "Has light in any way resisted his muscular efforts? Have his muscular organs ever been able to grasp a ray of light? . . . If that which produces a sensation or feeling be regarded a solid substance . . . where is the impropriety, in regarding that which receives the sensation or feeling, as a solid extended substance also?"[71] In other words, he asked, why define light as a material phenomenon and mind as immaterial? Brown's "extension" test proves mind to be material: "If mind be unextended, how can it receive any sensations from things without? It could not act upon bodily organs, for they are extended. Neither could bodily organs act upon it."[72]

However, unlike his predecessors in the school of skepticism, Brown was not hopelessly deluded,[73] because he admitted cognition of the external world to be valid. After all he helped found the school of "Common Sense" which thought it pointless to question the certainties of everyday experience. Brown taught that the contact between mind and matter produces a "change of state"—though how this happens he did not pretend to conjecture. Orson agreed with Brown's "change of state": "Now this, in our view, is really what happens. We believe that matter can only act upon mind because mind is an extended material substance. But Dr. Brown supposes there is no absurdity in matter acting upon that which is unextended."[74] This Orson found to be a strong argument in favor of the "materiality" of mind.

After disposing of conventional materialism *and* the school of skepticism, which places excessive emphasis on ideas, Orson closed his essay by answering a number of Taylder's rather typical misconceptions about Mormon doctrine. But Orson's argumentation was not without its gaps. For example, he imputed to Priestley the "absurd" assumption that mind proceeds from the operations of the brain[75]—"absurd" because it does not provide for the "separate existence of the mind or spirit" (as though the existence of spirit were somehow self-evident). Here he plainly answered assertion with assertion. But elsewhere he displayed not only cogent and original logic but a remarkable level of acquaintance with the philosophical disputes of his day. The writings of Priestley and Thomas Brown, Bishops Berkeley and Butler, Erasmus Darwin, even Dionysius Lardner, the Irish lecturer and popularizer of science are all familiar ground to him. As for the target of the pamphlet, Rev. Taylder did not try to answer Pratt, considering that his premises were not "sufficiently damaged" to "require reinforcement."[76]

In summary Orson saw Taylder's arguments as merely one more of the "numberless hypotheses" philosophers had invented to "account for the action of matter on the mind, which they have assumed to be immaterial."[77] The problem for the British philosophers was even more acute, since their acceptance of Newtonian physics implied a purely mechanistic universe. (Even the "immortal Newton" was unwilling to face up to the implications of his own system and insisted upon a theistic "first cause."[78]) The philosophers' attempt to reconcile themselves to Newtonian physics ultimately failed: "Christians found it necessary to twist and turn dexterously to avoid giving assent to its final ramifications."[79] This was of course not true of Pratt, who welcomed the Newtonian system as evidence of the "undeviating exactness" with which matter actively obeys God[80] and as an irrefutable demonstration of the "absurdity of immaterialism." For all the noise they made about "empiricism" and a new scientific Christianity, the theologians continued "essentially to do Christian metaphysics in the same way it had been done for nearly two thousand years";[81] that is, to find some tortuous way to bring the immaterial God into contact with his material creation. Thomas Dick, for example, insisted on the infinity of God, "both in respect of space and duration."[82] Like others, he persevered in the spiritualizing of the scriptures: "seeing God as he is" means "beholding the Divine glory as displayed in the physical and moral economy of the universe."[83] For Pratt this was simply an ingenious atheism "clothing an indivisible unextended NOTHING with the powers of a god."[84]

Pratt's essay laid a foundation for what Brigham H. Roberts later called "eternalism,"[85] the philosophy derived from Joseph Smith's teachings that all things are matter and all things are eternal. Pratt finds comfort in Newton's observation that "it seems probable that God, in the beginning, formed matter in *solid, massy, hard, impenetrable, moveable particles* . . . That nature may be lasting, the changes of corporeal things are to be placed only in the *various separations*, and *new associations* and *motions* of these *permanent particles*."[86] Although Orson later objected to the notion that God "formed" matter in the absolute sense,[87] he inferred here that the existence of "ultimate atoms" which cannot be subdivided points to a universe that is "intelligent in all its parts"[88] and eternally indestructible. In this last respect Orson's ideas about physical matter foreshadowed the ruminations of modern physics: twentieth-century exploration of the subatomic world has revealed particles that resist analysis and defy division. Nigel Calder has said of this research, "Maybe nature is giving us a signal that we have reached the end of the road," that the universe may not be an infinitely divisible "Chinese box."[89]

Absurdities of Immaterialism was completed July 31, 1849. This extensive effort, indicating much reading and concentration, was not produced in isolation. Orson had continued to preach in the streets of Liverpool to chattering and scandalized audiences. Once when heckled by a particularly strident bully, he merely raised his voice and matched the man's volume. When he had shouted the heckler into exhaustion, he continued his speech while the crowd laughed.[90] But the opposition sometimes took more sinister forms. Edward Tullidge records that Orson Pratt possessed "real apostolic courage" and gives proof:

> Orson Pratt with Ezra T. Benson, Edward L. Sloan, and John Kay, went on a visit to the Isle of Man. Much excitement was produced by this visit and the preaching of these elders. On the return by steamer to Liverpool, the crowd of passengers became quite as a mob arrayed against these Mormon apostles. E. T. Benson escaped below, while this mob on shipboard surrounded Orson Pratt and clamored to cast him into the sea as a Jonah who troubled the ship. They seized him to cast him into the sea. Orson calmly stood in their midst, and placing his hand on the side of the ship, "Sirs," he said, "do with me according to your threatenings. If it be God's will, I am ready." This genuine apostolic courage conquered. The mob was awed; the captain interposed, and there was peace in the ship the remainder of the passage.[91]

The missionaries in Britain idolized their president for his strength in logic and exposition as well. They "almost worshiped Orson," remembers Tullidge, who in turn delighted in the "splendid *corps* of elders under his direction . . . because of their magnificent ability as orators and logicians. Indeed, he may have been said to have been their theological father."[92] It is said that Orson's writings drew the admiration of some of the more iconoclastic British intellectuals, in particular George Jacob Holyoake, brilliant liberal gadfly of the English establishment.[93]

To the challenges of writing were added the staggering administrative demands on the European Mission president. Letters from President Young arrived requesting all kinds of machinery and beseeching him to recruit as emigrants as many artisans, mechanics, and textile workers as possible. The constant flood of emigrants, shiploads of them in 1849, required outfitting and in some cases financing. In Salt Lake the authorities had raised several thousand dollars to assist the poorer converts in migrating. This resulted in the formation of the Perpetual Emigrating Fund, of which Orson became chief agent at Liverpool, assigned to take "legal bonds" from every passenger.[94] The fund was administered only on behalf of those who could not pay their passage to Utah, and Orson himself later left England with a P.E.F. company.

As head of the Church in Europe, Orson felt a strong desire to expand missionary labors outside of England particularly onto the con tinent, which had not yet been exposed to Mormon gospel. To Denmark went his fellow pioneer, the redoutable Erastus Snow, and in July Orson sent a Welsh convert, William Howells, across the Channel to the French port city of Le Havre. Howells, the first Mormon missionary to a Latin country, reported on July 30, 1850, the baptism of his first convert, one August Saint d'Anna, in the English Channel.[95] And in Italy Lorenzo Snow canvassed the Piedmontese beginning in 1850.

In England hundreds joined the Church every month. The need for printed materials soared as Orson oversaw the publication of ten thousand hymnbooks, a whole new edition of the Book of Mormon and the other revelations of Joseph Smith, and reams of his own writings—pamphlets selling for two or three pence each.[96] Orson's were no random methods of dissemination; his strategy for spreading the Latter-day Saint gospel was plotted out for the missionaries in an article, "How to Warn the Whole British Nation in One Year"![97] Tullidge comments:

> During those periods of Orson's presidency over the British Isles, he wrote numerous tracts, and published in all, several millions, scattering them broadcast over the whole British realm. At that time the organized tract societies of the British Mormon Mission were, we believe, not equalled in all Christendom for their thorough working and missionary results. These, united with the active, comprising (we should estimate) 5,000 elders, constituted the vast missionary machinery by which Orson Pratt brought into the Church, in two years, nearly 18,000 souls.[98]

As editor of the *Star* Orson gave extensive answers to queries in its pages. In addition, an entire pamphlet, *New Jerusalem, or the Spirit of Modern Prophecy*, grew out of his response to one investigator's doubts about the designation of Missouri as the center place of Zion. The inquirer noted that the Saints were driven out of Missouri despite Joseph Smith's prophecies that Independence was to be "an everlasting inheritance" for them.[99] Orson dealt with the question by reading the relevant prophecies, laying particular emphasis on a clause in section 58 of the *Doctrine and Covenants* declaring that there would be no inheritance until after "much tribulation."[100] Orson also pointed to Joseph's prediction that the Saints would be driven "from city to city, from synagogue to synagogue" and attributed the failure to achieve Zion in Missouri to those Saints who were ill prepared spiritually to inherit the "New Jerusalem."[101] His reasoning became the stock institutional response to this question and demonstrated to his own satisfaction the validity of Joseph's predictions.

The news from home rumbled with apocalyptic possibilities, and Orson felt the New Jerusalem was not far away. Wilford Woodruff wrote to him on two occasions: "the slave question is now the great bone of contention . . . laying a firm and sure foundation for the overthrow of this government . . . All parties have now ceased ridiculing the idea of dissolving the American Union . . . Brother Pratt, the storm is coming and no mistake."[102] While Congress raged over the parity between slave and free America, Orson and his fellows piously watched for the sword of heaven to descend on the country they had tried to escape.

Utah, Parley P. Pratt wrote his brother, had become a highway for fugitives and gold seekers. "Scores or hundreds of people arrive daily to rest or refit . . . a good carriage road runs from the Weber to the Provo, great numbers of strangers attend our meetings now every Sabbath, we feel as if we were about in the middle of the world, and in as good a place to preach the gospel to all the world as can be found."[103] Parley had, of course weathered the first two years in the Salt Lake Valley, and advised Orson to get a herd of good heifers on returning, for this offered the best foundation for making a living in the wild grazing country.[104] From Orson Spencer came the undoubtedly welcome news that 560 acres had been reserved near the city for the construction of a university and that Brother Pratt was wanted to take "a leading part in these matters." A prospectus for the university solicited funds through Orson Pratt from the English Saints as of April 1850.[105]

The family of Orson Pratt in a watercolor by British artist Frederick Hawkins Piercy, ca. 1850, in Liverpool. From left to right: Orson Pratt, Jr.; Sarah Marinda Pratt; Marinthia Altheria Pratt; Laron Pratt; Orson Pratt, Sr.; and Celestia Louisa Pratt. *Courtesy, Daughters of the Utah Pioneers.*

Orson's two years in Britain were nearly completed, but he would be back in the fall. In many ways, this mission was his most productive and momentous: "Every noted town in the three kingdoms heard his voice."[106] Mormonism expanded steadily throughout England, Scotland, and Wales; missionaries pushed into the cultural ferment of the continent, and for the first time the writings of Orson Pratt began to draw the contempt (and occasionally the admiration) of the intellectual and clerical community, as well as the widespread acceptance of hundreds of the spiritually dispossessed. Clearly Orson's philosophical approach appealed to many. As one witness writes: "In your theological tenets I most cordially acquiesce . . . being conscious of your ability and believing you to be the most efficient person in this country."[107] Orson Pratt was popular with the Saints in England, and when the First Presidency called him home on April 12, 1850 Brigham Young wrote, "If the Saints should mourn his loss, we would say, be comforted and come with him, or follow him as fast as you can . . . Elder Pratt has done a great and good work in England."[108]

8

Great First Cause

Orson Pratt's second British adventure came to an end and he disembarked from the *Niagara* at Boston on March 23, 1850. Then came the slow spring voyage through the Gulf of New Orleans, then to St. Louis, where he embarked for the upper Missouri. The interior was very dry, with little rain and no snow throughout the winter; the drought at the "Camp of Israel" near Council Bluffs was making everyone uneasy. Orson arrived May 19 and immediately gathered the Saints for a meeting at the tabernacle in Kanesville. No sooner had he prayed for rain before the assembled emigrants than it began to fall copiously, the first good rainfall since the previous autumn. Here on the Iowa side he also met his two-year-old son, Milando, the offspring of Mary Ann Merrill Pratt.[1]

His chief business here was to see to the needs of his plural wives and families. He brought with him some of the money from the sale of his British mission pamphlets and distributed it as far as he could. Orson learned that Brigham Young had released him from his mission and that he was free to return to the Salt Lake Valley.[2] This news would be welcome to Sarah, left alone in England. She wrote of her homesickness and loneliness to her friend, Bathsheba Smith, who lived in Salt Lake City: "I should rejoice to be there . . . Mr. Pratt left on the 9th of March . . . perhaps you may think this is a great trial for me, but I can assure you it is no more of a trial, than if he were gone on other business, for I have long since made up my mind that it is no use to fret about those who do not fret about me."

Orson Pratt in 1856. *Courtesy, Utah State Historical Society.*

This is the long-suffering Sarah's first indication that she resented Orson's repeated abandonment, which had characterized her life with him practically from the moment of her wedding. She also complained that some of the American missionaries in England spread tales about her Nauvoo difficulties: "Instead of preaching the gospel as they were sent to do they have left nothing unsaid that they could say to make my character as black as they could." Sarah was altogether sick of England and anxious to return home.[3]

But Orson was not so anxious. Rather he enjoyed his work and his writing and arrived back in Liverpool in July 1850, stretching out his tenure until the following spring. In addition to his duties as president of the mission, he had been appointed assistant treasurer for the new Perpetual Emigration Fund company, to oversee, with Franklin D. Richards, $20,000 in paper certificates. Stock was held in deposit to redeem the paper "at any moment."[4] He and Richards then apparently allowed the borrowing to go too far, as by 1852 the P.E.F. found itself cash-depleted.[5] Orson was perhaps too generous, but the business of helping the poor to get to Zion took precedence over business considerations.[6]

The "Gauge of Philosophy" had not intended to leave England without publishing a fully developed rationale for Mormon claims, for it offered him exclusive editorship of the *Star* and unlimited opportunities for disseminating his ideas through the missionary force flung across Britain. In the closing months of the year 1850, Orson Pratt flooded the Isles with new writings, page after page of numbered theological arguments. His style was stripped for debate, at times charged with a venomous delight in turning the tables on his interlocutors, but generally spare and rational in tone.

The fall saw publication of six tracts grouped under the heading of *Divine Authenticity of the Book of Mormon*, though the tracts dealt chiefly with the indispensable nature of "new revelation" in general. In this work he found it inconceivable that the Christian churches denied even the possibility of revelation: "But we ask, what do modern Christendom know about God? They have not heard his voice, nor received a revelation from him . . . for the last seventeen centuries."[7] Orson's incredulity was aroused over the Protestant maxim that all revelation culminated in the incarnation of God himself. Therefore, goes the reasoning, no additional "messages" from heaven need appear; all is revealed in Christ. For Orson Pratt, this was a semantic dodge. It violated reason to suppose that Christ's church should be cut off from receiving additional instruction as though every spiritual principle had been defined beyond question "unto the perfecting of the Saints." Pratt denied this, pointing at the "whole of Christendom quarreling about [the] true meaning [of the scriptures]." He declared the Bible to be "an insufficient guide"—not because it is false, but because it has been "awfully corrupted" by men who deny even the possibility of inspiration.[8] In vain he searched the Bible for any justification of modern sectarian practices: "Again, what part of the Bible has established the salaries of the different officers of the church? . . . The New Testament does not tell us the amount of wages religious hirelings should have; therefore, if it be important to know, the Bible is an insufficient guide."[9]

Nor did he spare the Catholic appeals to "tradition" in helping overcome the deficiencies and silences of the Bible. Catholicism was, for Orson, a diluted and directionless system denying, as Tertullian does, even scripture as a positive standard "since these afford either no decision, or, at most, only a doubtful one."[10] Orson also found it curious that the popes, who presumably succeed St. Peter in the apostolic chair, do not profess to succeed him in his canonical role of "revelator."[11]

In nearly a hundred pages Orson detailed a defense for the Book of Mormon which remains standard in the Church today. After arguing the authenticity of its claims by material and prophetic witnesses, he asserted its indispensability as the only reliable doctrinal control: "Every point of Christ's doctrine should be again revealed in such plain, definite, and positive language, that no two persons could possibly disagree upon it."[12] He demanded that the book be given "a rigid examination" and, if it be found an "imposition," it should be extensively published to the world as such . . . exposed and silenced, not by physical force, neither by persecutions, bare assertions, nor ridicule, but by strong arguments . . . by evidences adduced from scripture and reason."[13] In favor of its genuineness Orson Pratt offered one of his few claims to a personal transcendent experience: "The Book of Mormon is a divine revelation, for the voice of the Lord hath declared it unto me."[14] Presumably he referred to his original encounter with the book that Parley brought him at the time of his nineteenth birthday. Orson said he heard the voice of the Lord but does not elaborate.

However, Orson was convinced that a sound philosophical foundation for the faith as symmetric as a mathematical proof might serve to sustain a conviction among scientists and thinkers; for Orson, self-designated apostle to the world of secular learning, sincerely believed that he could demonstrate in detail the superiority of Mormon ideas over other systems of natural theology.

As a result, on January 31, 1851, Orson presented to the world his most carefully constructed thesis yet, a compact seventeen-point excursus on "the self-moving forces of the universe," entitled *Great First Cause*. This was his most complete exposition of his "intelligent matter" theory to date, a discussion of the same problems he and Parley had toyed with five years before.

Here was Orson Pratt, the descriptive physicist and mathematician, at work. Gone was the hard edge of ridicule; what was "absurd" before was now only "erroneous." Orson employed a collected voice, the mitigating "if" clause, and drew conclusions in an impersonal tone as spare as he could make them. Once again his breadth of reading was surprising, and the smooth continuity he achieved in his arguments must have been gratifying to him. It was the only work in which he introduced himself as "Orson Pratt, A.M."

The essay began as far beyond critical objection as possible with the statement that, necessarily, "time is endless and space boundless.[15] It is not, however, necessary that space be encumbered with matter.[16] We merely perceive it to be so and, admitting that, conclude matter is eternal."[17] That is, something must have always existed in space, for something cannot be produced out of nothing. He then attacked the idea that any matter is necessarily the product of another part of matter: "the creation of one part of substance from nothing . . . cannot be established by any *necessity, experience, reason, analogy, or divine revelation* . . . it should be treated as a wild speculation, or vague conjecture."[18] Indirectly, this puts to rest the notion of a creation ex nihilo and, therefore, the necessity of a creator who is not himself a part of the created universe.[19] Orson admitted, however, that "Upon this subject, mankind are divided."[20] This he found surprising, for it was far more consistent with inductive reasoning to conclude that all substance is forever without beginning.

Orson understood the universe to be extremely old because of the illumination from stars that were inconceivably distant:[21] "When we look upon the widely extended field of existence, we are apt to imagine that we see worlds as they now exist, but this is not so . . . by the aid of light we only see the *past*, and not the present."[22] The world itself must have undergone a series of "organization and disorganizations" and was probably created from "the ruins of some more ancient world." (Not surprisingly, all of this is in accord with the nebular theory of planetary origins prevalent among astronomers of Orson's day.) Having posited the "eternal duration of the elements," Orson then delved into the nature of ageless substance.[23]

Immediately and without much comment he dismissed the notion of an immaterial God as he paused to clarify the concept of physical mass: "it is a *necessary* truth, that God and all other beings or substances which exist, *must* exist in space, and *must* occupy a constant amount of space . . . the occupied and unoccupied portions of space have been constantly the same from all eternity, and they must remain the same . . . there can be no increase or diminutions of either."[24]

The conservation of matter established, Orson introduced his seventh and pivotal argument that inasmuch as matter is in constant flux (continually changing state), then some force must be effecting the alterations. For Orson force was ineluctably tied to matter because force "cannot [exist] separate and abstract from substance." And inasmuch as inert matter cannot initiate force, it must also be as eternal as matter itself. He defined *force* as that quality of matter by which it maintains or alters its own condition. The nature of the cohesive force could be described as "pressure" rather than "attraction" (a dig at Newton)[25] because "attraction would require each part to be entirely passive, having no power whatever over itself, and yet possessing the extraordinary and impossible power of pulling every part towards itself."[26] Matter is, ipso facto, "active" rather than "passive."

In an illuminating aside here, Orson, anticipating every objection, conceded that "cohesive force" is not a necessary quality of matter; it is perfectly possible to conceive of matter which is inert, lacking any force at all. Such matter would be, however, infinitely divisible and capable of only two modes of existence: at rest or in motion "in straight lines." "Such a thing," he pointed out, "is unknown in the universe."[27]

All matter appears to be active ("self-moving"), and if inert matter exists, "it has not yet been discovered to be such by its inactivity."[28] By now Orson felt sufficiently grounded to readvance his earlier hypothesis, the reverse of Newton's law of motion,[29] that "*every particle . . . has a tendency to approach every other particle . . . with a force which varies inversely as the square of the distance*."[30] Thus, particles of "self-moving substance" must "will" not to act randomly but systematically and "intelligently."[31] Here Orson argued that obedience to law, a fundamental pattern in nature, is evidence of intelligence.[32] He calls in Sir John Herschel, "the most distinguished figure in Anglo-American science"[33] and son of astronomer William Herschel, who says in his *Preliminary Discourse on the Study of Natural Philosophy*, "To *obey* a law, to act in *compliance* with a rule, supposes an understanding and will, a power of complying or not, in the being who obeys."[34] Beyond this, however, Herschel's ideas conflict with Orson's: the scientist committed the "error" of supposing matter to be nonetheless passive carrying an impression of "spirit" from the Creator that directs it along fixed patterns of motion.[35] Orson found this contradictory and hopelessly ambiguous: "But we ask, what is this 'spirit of the law?' "[36] In other words, if particles are obedient to law, that in itself demonstrates an intellectual capacity.[37] "We consider that the *primary powers* of all material substance must be *intelligent* . . . Substances without intelligence can have no powers, no forces . . . *Unintelligent* particles, then, is only another name for *inert* particles."[38]

In concluding, Pratt borrowed from scholastic theology the term "Great First Cause," a concept as old as Aristotle[39] of an agent that initiates activity in the universe, giving "laws to blind, unconscious, unintelligent matter" and providing the force to carry them out. Pratt liked the term but redefined it according to the "self-moving" theory: "The Great First Cause . . . consist[s] of conscious, intelligent, self-moving particles, called the holy Spirit which prescribe laws for their own action . . . An unintelligent particle is incapable of understanding or obeying a law . . . It is evident that each particle must have not only perceived the utility of . . . laws, but must have mutually consented to obey them in the most strict and invariable manner."[40]

This consensus of the universe permits, as Orson proceeded to show, all intelligences to advance in a "great school of experience," continually developing increased understanding through changes in "quality" or state. That is, as one effective principle of coexistence is discerned and mastered, the intelligence may pass on to learn others.[41] "All the organization of worlds . . . of men, of angels, of spirits, and of the spiritual personages of the Father, of the Son, and of the Holy Ghost, must . . . have been the result of the self-combination of the pre-existent, intelligent, powerful, and eternal particles of substance."[42]

The famous theologian William Paley, archdeacon of Carlisle and author of *Natural Theology*, taught that design in the universe implies a designer, and the more perfect the being, the greater are the evidences of design. For Pratt, Paley's view compels belief in an ultimate "anterior designer . . . a self-moving intelligent substance . . . Parts of this most glorious substance *now* exist in the form of personages."[43]

In summary, Pratt believed that the "activity" of matter points inescapably to the "intelligence" of matter and that the primeval substance from which men and gods and worlds are formed can be defined as "Holy Spirit" (not to be confused with "Holy Ghost") which acts as the "Great First Cause" of its own painstaking evolution. He cited leading philosophical minds to illuminate his own conclusions but did not hesitate to point out where their personal orthodoxies interfere with their judgment. Although he found Herschel close to the discovery of intelligent substance, he was too much a slave to the concepts of "inert" matter and an extramaterial Creator. He criticized the famous philosopher William Whewell, master of Trinity College, Cambridge, for his insistence that matter must necessarily have weight in order to be quantifiable. It is not necessary, said Orson, for matter to be heavy in order to share the other qualities of matter, such as inertia and force: "Such a condition of things is easily conceivable, and, therefore, the assertion that all bodies must have weight is not a necessary truth."[44] (Whewell's a priori reasoning was rejected by other, more conventional philosophers of science as well.)[45] Even Paley, who provided Pratt a tidy argument for the evolution of higher minds, clearly did not go far enough for Orson. Newton suffered the most. To Orson, Newton's idea of gravitational attraction was a logical absurdity; it was more reasonable to think of atoms as intelligently and obediently moving toward the harmony of structure.

Any attempt to locate Orson Pratt within an established school of philosophy will falter. His premises include not only the activity but also the divinity of primal "intelligent matter." This in turn seems to be based on the observation that some inner force binds the atom and that there is no conceivable activity in nature that is not somehow a manifestation of intellect. Nevertheless, Orson's system corresponds quite closely to the philosophical tradition of "panpsychism," which views matter as intrinsically "active" rather than "passive" and, after a fashion, "alive." Orson agrees substantially with the panpsychists, a formidable company in the history of philosophy: Empedocles, many of the Stoics, Francis Bacon, Leibniz, Schopenhauer, and in the twentieth century Alfred North Whitehead and Monseigneur Teilhard can all be considered "panpsychists." Bacon, for example, believed in a limited sense that all matter has perception. Panpsychist proofs bear a resemblance to Orson's arguments. They maintain that continuous motion in the universe demonstrates inner psychic processes, that the idea of inert matter is untenable in the face of modern physics, and that any exertion of energy requires an agent that wills it.[46]

Many philosophers question the intelligibility of panpsychism. They point out that to insist that an atom "wills" its own motions in the same sense that a human being "wills" himself to move an arm or a leg is to commit the logical error of arguing from analogy. Furthermore, such an analogy ignores the observable differences between intellectual man and atomic particles. For example, man's capacity for making random choices clearly differs from the atomic capacity only to obey. It is interesting to note that analogical reasoning was widely accepted among Victorian thinkers (particularly the Scottish philosophers) as an effective tool for understanding the world.[47] They tended to downplay the limitations of analogy as a logical device, namely, the danger of assuming that if two things seem similar in one respect that they are similar in other respects as well. In this case, the analogical trap consists of using inappropriate terms—activity and passivity—in discussing physical processes.

Mormon philosopher Sterling M. McMurrin criticizes Orson's logic as deficient: Orson reasons "axiomatically"; that is, he appeals to self-evident truths to generate his premises. For example, he considers the existence of the "Great First Cause" inescapably true, since there is no effect without a cause.[48] (This generalizing from experience is another manifestation of Orson's Baconian approach to reasoning. Orson has never observed causeless phenomena; therefore his experience requires that there be no causeless phenomena.) Such axiomatic reasoning, according to McMurrin, is "fundamentally in error."[49] In partial explanation, if not justification, of Orson's reliance upon this system is the accepted British attitude toward logic: as Berkeley and Hume insisted, "a statement has no meaning unless it has an absolutely clear-cut reference to experience."[50]

Orson's contemporary, French writer Jules Remy, criticized Orson's philosophy as old hat. In his book *A Journey to Great-Salt-Lake City*, Remy writes: "The metaphysical system of Mormonism is not an invention peculiar to itself . . . it is the old materialism of Epicurus and Lucretius, of D'Holbach and of Lamettrie, . . . with a considerable dash of pantheism . . . It is in fact, the philosophy most in favour in America, and Orson Pratt, who has constituted himself its teacher amongst the Mormons, is hardly anything more than an echo of many a philosophical school in Boston and Philadelphia."[51] Remy is nevertheless surprised at the erudition of the "Mormon doctor," reporting his astonishment to hear from the mouths of the Mormons "language which reminds us of that of the eclectics of the Sorbonne."[52] Actually, Remy need not have been so surprised since the "philosophy most in favour in America" was the same Scottish Realism[53] which had produced French eclecticism in the early nineteenth century. Both philosophical movements attempted to combine spiritual and epistemological approaches to truth.[54] (This blend of religious idealism with scientific rationalism has been called "Protestant Scholasticism."[55]) Remy is describing the contemporaneous movement to "integrate natural and Biblical philosophies . . . to arrive at a religion free from doubt . . . a scientific theology."[56]

Of course, Orson was not above this effort and indeed contributed to it. He spoke of his respect for "the views entertained by philosophers generally at the present day."[57] Remy fails to realize, however, that Orson eschews the mechanistic view of the Scottish Realists and the French eclectics, that his is a materialism with a difference. Remy compares Orson's philosophy with that of Julien O. De Lamettrie, French materialist and author of *L'Homme Machine* (The Mechanical Man, 1747), who posited that the mind is indeed a material phenomenon but who also "failed to commit himself definitively to the materiality of the soul."[58] Nevertheless, the anti-Christian De Lamettrie is not at all radical in comparison to Orson, who teaches that the soul is not only material but also subject to a set of physical laws appropriate to its own sphere.[59] The whole problem with nineteenth-century philosophy as Orson saw it was its unwillingness to give up its "innumerable conjectures" or attempts to connect a nonexistent, "imaginary," immaterial substance with the material world.[60] Although Remy recognizes that Orson Pratt is a "thorough materialist,"[61] he errs in describing Orson as nothing more than "an echo of many a philosophical school in Boston and Philadelphia." (Orson seems far more concerned in any case with the work of British natural philosophers than with that of any American thinkers of his own time.) As Joseph Willard Tingey points out, Orson Pratt's theories were "not so much the products of metaphysical speculation as extensions of his interpretation of scripture and revelation" given by Joseph Smith.[62]

In a way, Pratt's philosophy can be seen as a reaction against the "Protestant Scholasticism" of the nineteenth century. His ideas bear an affinity with those of the great French positivist, Auguste Comte, who at the time Orson was writing issued his brilliant attacks on the same occult metaphysics of Christian orthodoxy (though for different reasons than Orson). For Comte, the attempt to connect the material world with some mysterious, immaterial, transcendent otherworld was evidence of immature thinking. Comte felt that it was useless to explore the problem of why events occur; it was enough to discover the relatively constant relations between self-existent objects and material events. The contrasts, of course, are just as great: where Orson's active materialism proceeded from revelatory premises, Comte's positivism was derived from pure scientism and ended in a godless universe. Furthermore, Comte would have considered Orson's theory of "intelligent atoms" quite simply a throwback to a primitive stage of reasoning.[63]

One critic has called Mormon metaphysics "apocalyptic nonsense."[64] The difficulties in Orson Pratt's reasoning, however, should not obscure the contributions he makes. The notion of "active matter" finds at least partial vindication in the philosophy of Joseph Priestley, who also considers it the answer to the "mind vs. matter" dilemma facing nineteenth-century thought: "Once matter is taken as active the incompatibility between mind and body simply disappears."[65] Though Orson criticized Priestley for not going far enough,[66] it is interesting that both share a view of matter as dynamic rather than passive. Orson's inventive application of the term "Great First Cause" to self-moving substance serves to render more intelligible his own definition as well as to show the contrast with the established one. In addition certain key terms in Mormon revelation—"intelligence," for example—assume substance and definition from his conjectural pen. The result is a new theological vocabulary which is uniquely "Mormon." *Great First Cause* provides Mormon philosophy with the beginning of a genuine metaphysics.[67]

Furthermore, Orson's cosmology apparently accords with the doctrines of the Latter-day Saint prophets. The panpsychist Deity seems to be echoed in the pronouncements of President Brigham Young: "We are created for the express purpose of increase . . . What is there that is not ordained after an eternal law of existence? It is the Deity within us that causes increase . . . He is in every person upon the face of the earth. The elements that every individual is made of and lives in, possess the Godhead. This you cannot now understand . . . The Deity within us is the great principle that causes us to increase, and to grow in grace and truth."[68] This notion implies more than the orthodox doctrine of "indwelling Holy Spirit." It describes the very elements as "possessing" the Godhead in a normative and natural way. Though a Protestant would agree that God is omnipresent, he would never hold that the nature (intelligence?) of the Godhead is somehow "possessed" by the elements of a fallen world.

The treatise, along with the fifteen other pamphlets Orson had written during this mission, was bound for distribution just as he prepared to depart. A title page and table of contents were composed, and for the first time the bulk of Orson's theological writings appeared in one volume under the title *A Series of Pamphlets*, published at Liverpool by Orson's successor, Apostle Franklin D. Richards.

Early in 1851 Orson finally gave up his position as president of the British Mission. His voice and his writings had brought thousands into the Mormon church. Thomas Brown Holmes Stenhouse, one of those converted to Mormonism partially by Orson's persuasive pamphleteering and a man of considerable journalistic skill, wrote this tribute to Orson's presidency over the British Mission:

> The greatest dispensation of spiritual power experienced in the Mormon Church fell upon the British Saints during the Presidency of the apostle Orson Pratt, from 1848 to 1851 . . . [due to] his better education and eminent ability . . . his pen furnished the first logical arguments in favour of Mormonism, and his influence spread like a con-

> suming fire among the Saints of the Old World . . . armed with his arguments . . . Mormonism in England, Scotland, and Wales, was a grand triumph, and was fast ripening for a vigorous campaign in continental Europe.[69]

This time Orson was really going home, back to Utah, back to his three families, back to the hardship of the desert. The release became official when Richards took over, and Orson arrived at Kanesville aboard the St. Louis steamer *Statesman* on May 20, 1851, a year and a day since his last landfall there.

The passage was not made without difficulty. Sarah had lost one baby, Marlon, in Liverpool and another little girl, born in England, did not survive the sea: "Marintha Althera Pratt, my daughter, died March 24, 1851, at sea, a few miles northeast of the island of St. Domingo. She was brought on shore and buried in the Kansas burying ground, Jackson County, Missouri."[70] Such memories had to be left behind; it was time to move everyone west.

By now there were three boys and five girls. Orson, the eldest, was nearly fourteen; Celestia, nine, was the oldest of the girls. Two infant girls had been born in Orson's absence. Delia's baby received the name Elsina and Mary Ann's was christened Vianna. And the family now included another wife—the devoted Marian Ross, the Liverpool serving girl who was to become Orson's sixth on February 19, 1852, under the hand of Brigham Young. After a month of outfitting Orson crossed the Missouri with the company of John Brown, which included Orson's brother William Dickinson Pratt and his family and the George D. Watt group (Watt had been one of the earliest British converts and was an old friend of Orson's). After camping at the site of Winter Quarters, Orson realized his horses were missing and supposed them stolen by the Omahas.[71] Otherwise the crossing was uneventful. The pioneers who traveled with Orson made up one of the innumerable poor companies. Most of them were emigrants from Britain traveling on promises of payment to the Perpetual Emigration Fund. The journey consumed a little over three months, and on October 4, 1851, Orson came with his three families through the mouth of Emigration Canyon giving them their first look at the promised land they had waited four years on the Missouri to see.[72]

In the autumn of 1851 Great Salt Lake City was no longer merely an adobe outpost clinging to the edge of the greasewood desert; fortune-hunters had made Salt Lake prosperous as they refitted on their way to the Sierra gold fields,[73] and ditches flowing with City Creek water fed stark saplings along the streets. Orson's first home stood on the east corner of West Temple and First South Streets and was built of adobe—no floor at first, though it boasted lintels of red cedar.[74] A huge bowery roofed with brush sprawled over the temple block; Orson preached in conference there the day after his arrival.[75] The vast Great Basin empire envisioned by Brigham Young had already been mapped and divided by Congress into territories with unnatural boundaries tying lines of latitude to the dry ground. Utah Territory was a hemisphere away from the soot and damp air of England and its philosophical controversies. Here Orson could turn again to the observable and measurable and leave polemics behind him.

From England he had brought a new telescope, a microscope, and apparatus for chemical experiments.[76] The new Deseret University's department of science had arrived,[77] but the polymath of Mormonism did not have much time for contemplation and experimentation. Within two weeks he was on his way with a committee of commissioners (including Albert Carrington, Jesse W. Fox, and William C. Staines) to locate a new capital city of the territory more central to its vast stretch. In deference to the new president of the United States, the settlement would be named Fillmore.[78]

In 1851 Utah Territory stretched across the map from the Continental Divide as far as the present western limit of Nevada. In the middle of the 1851 map lies a stretch of lava rock and alkali tortured by towering dust storms, a country where creeks disappear from sight; this was the Pauvan (Pahvant) Valley.[79] It took Brigham Young and his party six days to reach this valley from Salt Lake, and on October 28 they began laying out the new territorial capital on a site that hugged a small stream from the eastern mountains (Chalk Creek) and overlooked desolate cinder cones to the west. Orson, however, was rhapsodic about the landscape: "bold and rocky precipices . . . crests . . . sweeping gracefully . . . richly mellowed by the blue haze."[80] Only a few days later, on November 15, Orson Pratt was elected a member of the first territorial legislature of Utah, a representative from Salt Lake City to the capital city that was still only a mirage in the desert.[81]

Orson wintered for the first time in Salt Lake City that year. In his absence he had been made a regent of the new University of Deseret[82]

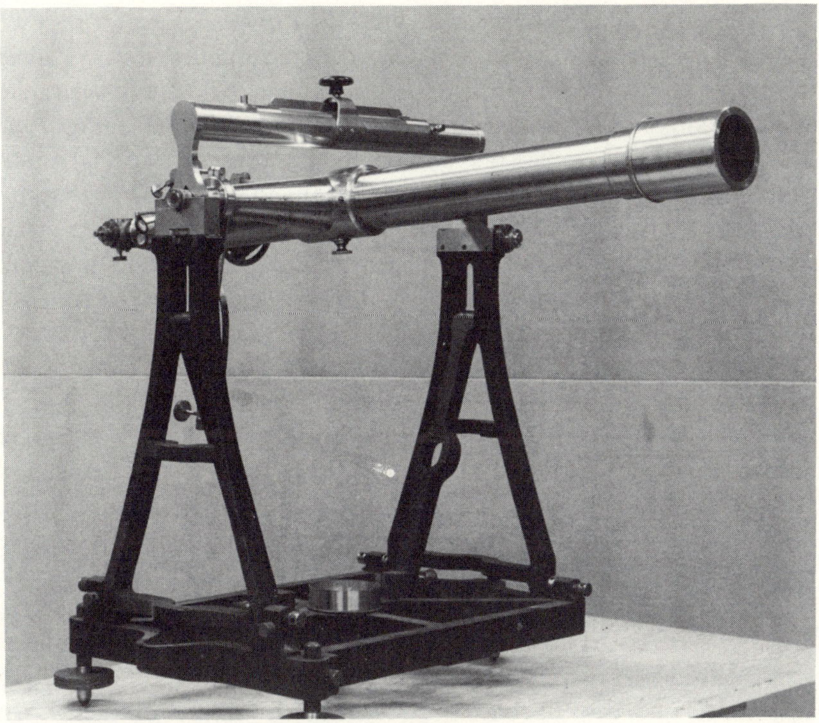

One of Orson Pratt's telescopes. *Courtesy, Church Museum of History and Art, Church of Jesus Christ of Latter-day Saints.*

and soon threw himself into teaching. He advertised astronomy lectures to begin in December in the lower room of the sandstone Council House on Fourth South Street.[83] To his gratification, the house was full. Not accustomed to speaking of his secular interests in public, he apparently showed a little diffidence, for the *Deseret News* gave his performance a mixed "review": "Professor Pratt's lecture on astronomy on the 15th instant was as numerously attended, as the Representatives Hall would permit; and we are pleased that he has consented . . . to the publication of the same in this paper. Though this was the Professor's first attempt at lecturing, on this subject; the lovers of truth will require no more apology for its awkwardness, than the work itself does for its praise;—it speaks for itself."[84] Orson's friend, George D. Watt, took up lecturing on phonology, and together they conducted the series through the winter. Unfortunately, this helped very little to relieve Orson's penury.

To compound the problem, he had little time to work for his own support. While the astronomy lectures continued, Orson worked through the day on census papers that had to be forwarded to Washington,[85] mapped out proposed county boundaries on latitude lines,[86] and served as ad hoc adviser to the authorities on technical problems. This included anything from theorizing on the composition of salt air to speculating on the possibility of "inhabitants living inside the earth."[87] The Twelve had quietly resumed endowment ceremonies in the newspaper offices and elsewhere, often leaving Orson in charge as chief officiator.[88] In April Orson was appointed "topographical engineer" to the Nauvoo Legion, which had been reorganized,[89] and Brigham was proposing a second exploratory trip south. He and Orson combed the country near the settlement of Parowan at the Little Salt Lake, visiting with the Indians and evaluating the land for the cultivation of cotton and grapes. They also inspected bits of iron ore from the western hill deposits, which gave the new county its name.[90]

When the apostles returned to Salt Lake City, they found disturbing reports from the East awaiting them. The previous autumn a group of federal officials appointed by President Fillmore to Utah had absconded with the entire treasury of the territorial government.[91] In Washington the three men were now spreading stories about lawlessness and open immorality practiced in Utah under the guise of "celestial marriage."[92] Brigham Young apparently felt it was no longer feasible to live this principle without a public defense of the doctrine. Orson Pratt and Orson Spencer were assigned to draft a memorandum to President Fillmore outlining conditions in Utah from the Mormons' point of view.[93] But the thirty-page memorial dispatched that summer was only part of Brigham Young's strategy. He determined that it would be best to make the doctrine public and then immediately petition Congress for admission to the Union as a state, stifling federal interference in Utah's internal affairs. He also depended on Orson Pratt's qualities of persuasion to effect all of this.

General conference met the last week in August so that mission calls could be given out before the snows fell. Brigham was determined to spread the Mormon network literally worldwide and announced missions for India, China, South America, and the islands of the sea. Orson stood afterwards and said, "When I see so many of my brethren . . . going forth to the different nations, I almost feel as though I wanted to go to all these different places at the same time myself."[94] He had not long to wait for satisfaction. The next morning Heber C. Kimball called the crowded conference to order in the new rectangular Tabernacle with the overflow attenders under a canopy of rushes and promptly moved that Orson Pratt "take a mission to Washington to preach and preside over the Saints in the United States, Upper and Lower Canada, and the British Provinces in North America."[95]

Orson Pratt was then asked to speak. He made no recorded reference to the mission call but proceeded directly to his text, "Marriage." The Saints soon found that this discourse would mark a fateful turning point for the entire Church. Orson began to talk about the ancient biblical patriarchs Abraham, Isaac, and Jacob and the privileges and blessings they enjoyed. He asked the congregation why the Lord had permitted these former worthies to take more than one wife. The answer, according to Orson, was that this was the most efficient way for the Lord to raise up a righteous and numerous people thereby hastening the glory to be poured out upon those who committed themselves to "eternal increase."[96] Orson did not go deeply into his theological justification for this view—that there are innumerable intelligences awaiting opportunities afforded only in this mode of existence—but stuck to his biblical texts. After all this discourse was meant not only for Latter-day Saint ears but for the contemplation of a world which would be hostile to such a practice. It was a discourse that would be heard in Washington and, if the Mormons were fortunate, might at least serve to clarify the rumors of indiscriminate lechery in Utah. Orson certainly had his non-Mormon hearers in mind when he employed what Kimball Young has called the "then current argumentative style." Outlining the polity of Mormon plural marriage, Orson gave four reasons for the Mormon people to live the principle of plural marriage: (1) God's grand design for the human race required a more efficient system for peopling the world; (2) the historical acceptance and even prevalence of the plural marriage system; (3) the social advantages of polygamy over monogamy; and (4) the requirement of all Latter-day Saints to obey the counsel of God.[97] When Orson sat down, Brigham Young took the floor and spoke on the doctrines and ordinances of "the last dispensation," after which the "great revelation on celestial marriage given to Joseph Smith the Prophet in Nauvoo, Illinois, July 12, 1843, was read."[98]

This official announcement was received affirmatively by many Latter-day Saints—Hosea Stout recorded that "we have looked forward so long and so anxiously for the time to come when we could publickly declare the true and greatest principles of our holy religion."[99] The first public acknowledgment of Mormon plural marriage thus came at least ten years after the practice began in Nauvoo. It had also been ten years since Orson Pratt had been excommunicated partly because of his confusion over the doctrine of "celestial marriage." Perhaps there was some measure of requital in the assignment to Orson to make the first public discourse advocating the plural marriage revelation. In any case it is ironic that Orson, who had nearly apostatized in 1842 over what he had considered an assault on his family, should become a chief defender of the "principle." At the time of his death he had ten living wives and had been "sealed" in marriage to some two hundred dead women.[100]

Almost immediately Orson left Salt Lake City for Washington, D.C., to interpret to the world the intricacies of the geographically and philosophically distant Mormon culture. His license was to "preside and also to write and publish . . . illustrative of the principles and doctrines of the Church."[101] Orson required three weeks to prepare for the eastward journey and on September 21, 1852, was already on his way through Echo Canyon with Orson Spencer and William Clayton.[102] As chief apostle, Orson was elected leader of the eastering camp at Black's Fork. They traveled repeatedly through muddy roads, rain and snow, but were "full of the spirit of their missions." Clayton noted, "I think it would be difficult to find a company of men . . . who ever journeyed together with a better spirit; or a set of missionaries who ever went with a more settled determination, and firm ambition to do good . . . to gain intelligence—to treasure up doctrine—to learn truth, and be prepared to do good." Orson passed his time writing a "lengthy piece on the pre-existence of man," which, according to Clayton, "will evidently be one of the best works ever published by this Church. It bears truth on its face throughout, and his arguments are beyond refutation. It will be an invaluable document to the Elders abroad."[103]

Once the camp was secured, the elders would gather in the evenings for preaching services. With Spencer and Pratt, two leading Mormon intellectuals, participating, there was no lack of doctrinal discussion. Two of the subjects they debated were the resurrection of infants and the origin of Adam. Wrote Clayton, "The baby resurrection finds in [Pratt] an unflinching opponent. If sound reason, coupled with revelation would convince a man of the error of such a doctrine, one discourse from brother Pratt would settle the question, but it appears some are hard to convince."[104] Much of their time they spent trying to settle a controversy which had grown up since Brigham Young had announced in the previous April conference that "our Father Adam came into the garden of Eden . . . with a celestial body, and brought Eve, one of his wives, with him . . . He is our Father and our God, and the only God with whom we have to do."[105] At the August conference Brigham had again preached that celestial beings colonize worlds and become fallen by ingesting "gross matter."[106] Orson had listened to this discourse apparently with some skepticism. He felt this notion was repugnant to the scriptures but refrained from any public expression; instead, he dickered over it with Spencer and Clayton on the trail. Clayton reported to Young:

> Another subject which has occupied much of the time, and in which the difference in opinion seems to be wider, and more firmly established than the baby resurrection; and that is in regard to Adam's coming on this earth; whether he came here with a resurrected body and became mortal by eating the fruits of the earth which are earthy, or he was created direct (that is his mortal tabernacle) from the dust of the earth, according to the popular opinion of the world. on this subject brother Pratt and myself, have rather locked horns, he holding to the latter opinion, and I firmly believing the former, but there can be no difflculty between us, as he is my superior and I shall not argue against him; but if, it were an equal I should be apt to speak my feelings in full. There are difficulties on both sides, take it which way we will, and he is unwilling to express anything more than *his opinion* on the subject . . . it will be wise to let such subjects alone when we get amongst the benighted nations.[107]

Despite the disagreement Clayton had the highest respect for Pratt and the equanimity he showed: "Brother Pratt has given some very interesting discourses . . . and both by precept and example, has shed a salutary influence on the minds of the brethren. His course is steady, mild, and evidently full of sympathy."[108] Pratt was unflinching in his opinion (though he stressed the word *opinion*) that Adam was not the God he prayed to.[109] This controversy put the apostle at odds with his president for years to come.

By November 1852 the party was on the Missouri en route to St.

Louis, where Orson paused to lecture on plural marriage at the Concert Hall.[110] Within the month Orson had arrived in Washington and established a printing office. To the *Millennial Star* he wrote: "We expect to establish a book Agency. We shall publish a monthly periodical which will be entitled THE SEER . . . In this advanced state of the Church, there are many doctrines, highly important, but partially understood, which we hope more fully to develop; among which may be mentioned the doctrine of patriarchal or celestial marriage . . . the sealing of the marriage covenant for time and for all eternity . . . We also . . . have in manuscript . . . a treatise entitled CELESTIAL MARRIAGE or the PEOPLING OF WORLDS."[111]

The capital city flurried with change. Though the president had lost the recent election, Orson paid a courtesy call on Millard Fillmore and found him an amiable man.[112] The Democrats had won, and an ephemeral hero of the Mexican War named Franklin Pierce was about to be sworn in as chief executive. Utah's delegate to Congress, Dr. John Bernhisel, invited Orson to the inaugural ceremonies, which took place March 4, 1853, and to an afternoon "levee" at the White House (described as a "muddy-footed throng" pressing into the mansion),[113] where, presumably, Orson for the third time shook the hand of a president of the United States.[114] Pierce, they discovered, was not deeply interested in the Mormon question, but despite some of his regrettable appointments to Utah (notably W. W. Drummond and Almon W. Babbitt), the Mormons were to have little real friction with him.

Washington did not rise to Orson's challenges. A sleepy southern city preoccupied with parties and protocol, the capital yielded no conversions. Orson was discouraged by the worldliness of Washington and wrote Brigham Young that the whole nation was "going after the beast." Orson preached twenty lectures at the Temperance Hall in the shadow of the half-finished Capitol, but few attended: "Not one soul have I found in Washington."[115]

As a result, Orson withdrew to the office of *The Seer*. Once again he was free to publish, and the copious articles he produced demonstrate his joy at expounding the logic of Mormon revelation. Soon after his arrival, Orson received a letter from Brigham Young encouraging this inclination: "We feel assured that ere this you have accomplished the desert trip and before this reaches you, you will be at your destination snugly ensconced in some office or room, busily engaged in forcibly illustrating, elucidating, and demonstrating to the understanding of the children of men, the principles of our Holy Religion . . . the excavation for your house is completed and some lumber is on hand . . . I remain truly and sincerely, your friend and brother."[116]

The first number of *The Seer* appeared January 1, 1853, under a cabalistic seal with an open eye staring out of a radiant heart. Its pages advocated gathering to the mountains and described "celestial marriage" as no different from the polygamous pattern of life practiced in Old Testament times. The famous 1842 revelation was printed verbatim in the first issue to dispel any doubt that the "patriarchal order" was a bona fide religious tenet and not a mere expedient to rationalize indulgence.[117]

Twelve numbers of *The Seer* were devoted to a continuing discussion of preexistence and to the treatise on polygamy, "Celestial Marriage." Searching the stories of the patriarchs and their wives, Orson marshaled every polygynous detail of Bible history in support of the doctrine but did not stop there. He argued from cultural history as well, pointing to the widespread practice of plural marriage among most populations of the earth. Many so-called heathen nations considered plural relations the norm.[118] In this Mormons began to see a peculiar affinity with the Moslems reflected in sermons by Parley P. Pratt and George A. Smith on "Mahometanism"[119] that speculate whether Mohammed had been to some extent an inspired prophet.

Orson also developed a theological history of "Christian polygamy" deducing that the "Romish priesthood" was to blame for its proscription in the early church. Concluding his series, he served up a letter bearing the signatures of Martin Luther and Philip Melanchthon advising the Landgrave of Hesse to go ahead and marry his concubine, "For the gospel hath neither recalled nor forbid what was permitted in the law of Moses with respect to marriage." He points out the irony that the practice of polygamy should be approbated by the Reformers and yet condemned by outraged Protestant divines in the nineteenth century.[120]

To the question, "Cannot Gen. Pierce do something to stop this dreadful evil?"[121] Orson replies that laws forbidding plural marriage "are founded wholly on custom . . . the American nation . . . are only free in part," because European traditions still bind, and there is nothing inherently reprobate in the practice of plurality: "We wish some of our wise statesmen . . . would take up the subject of plurality and show wherein it is immoral, or unscriptural, or criminal. Upon this subject the people want arguments, not denunciations; reason, not sophistry."[122]

The Seer did well for subscribers at first; counted among them were several "old apostates . . . William McLellin is a subscriber." They also stimulated considerable correspondence. Some fifty letters a week issued from Orson's desk. In March, to supply the demand in Utah, he forwarded three thousand copies of the periodical to Sarah with instructions to pay one-tenth of them as tithing.[123] Sarah put the magazine on sale from her front door charging a dollar "per annum in advance."[124]

Washington was not disposed to make much of polygamy, however. A rancorous national debate over popular sovereignty and abolitionism held Congress virtually paralyzed while the Whig party collapsed in ruins. Though it cast a cold glance at "peculiar institutions," Congress was obsessed with other, more sanguinary questions. Even among the Saints, subscriptions were renewed with decreasing frequency, and by April 1854 *The Seer* was losing money. Orson finished out the July and August numbers that year and ceased publication after twenty issues and 320 pages, almost exclusively his own writing. In its pages he had indulged most of his intellectual interests with articles on the formation of the universe, the nature of preexistent intelligences, speculations about the "Millennial map" of the earth. But its importance lay in the magazine's systematic theology-rationale favoring polygamy not only as a religious principle to be left unhindered by constitutional law but also as a practice which, if adopted, would prove salutary to the human race.

Behind his desk in Washington, Orson had enough time to interest himself in his own family background. Spurred by his belief in Mormon doctrine concerning salvation for the dead, he began putting out feelers to learn more about his own lineage. The job of reconstruction would not be easy. Both his parents were now dead —Charity had succumbed to cholera in 1849 on her way to Utah along with Orson's oldest brother Anson[125]—but his surviving brothers might have more information than he already had. He decided to get off a letter to Parley to see what could be discovered, along with a list of their "fathers" as far as he could ascertain it.

This was apparently his first contact with Parley in several years.

The latter had been en route from South America when Orson had last visited Salt Lake, and Parley quite clearly felt neglected:

> Read your letter . . . with great joy. I will be compelled to pardon your former neglect for so many years, although it was strange indeed, and appears to me unnatural and unkind in a brother. As I could never obtain a line from you, or even an acknowledgement of the Receipt of any of my letters, I had ceased to correspond with you . . . How great then was my joy on the Receipt of your kind letter not only containing renewal of your brotherly recognition and friendship, but also the good news of the genealogy of our Fathers."

It appears that Parley had little to add to Orson's genealogy, but took the opportunity to bargain a little on sympathy for some financial help:

> I am weary all the day long and cannot find time to rest . . . I have never been able to possess in these valleys, sufficient of cows to do us much service . . . I have thought sometimes that while my brother had abundant oppertunity to purchase young Stock and have them driven here and was verry careful to pay a tenth of them for Tithing, if he should happen to remember a brother who has toiled till nearly worn out, and lend him half a dozen cows it would not be a miss and could probably be paid in two or three years. But, however, I presume that Brother has enough to do to attend to his own necessities.[126]

Apparently, Orson had negligently or wilfully failed to answer a number of letters from Parley. Perhaps Orson had not forgotten the incident in the Nauvoo temple when Parley accused Sarah Pratt of slander. Whatever the reason, the two brothers had maintained a strange coolness. In August 1853 Parley wrote again explaining in a wounded voice that on the instructions of Brigham Young he had appropriated some of the land allotted to Orson. Now it appeared that Brigham denied giving any such orders:

> Verrily believing that these lots were free . . . I took them in my own name, and paid the surveying and Recording. Intending to keep the choisest corner Lot for you. Now you may judge my surprise, when after toiling with my wives and children for so many years, and going hungry and destitute, even selling our clothes, to make improvements . . . President Young informed on last sunday that I had entirely misunderstood him . . . His decision was: That if you and I could agree and be satisfied it would satisfy him . . . Well now, Bro Orson, we can certainly do that with all ease. Because, whatever you wish of me in regard to the matter I will do, if in my power. I want you perfectly satisfied.[127]

Clearly Parley had no intention of getting into Orson's debt. They settled on the corner lots, and Parley did not have to sell any more clothes to make improvements.

Parley was not the only neglected brother of the family. Apparently, none of them had had contact with the youngest, Nelson, since his youth. Orson wrote to Nelson's homestead in Huron County, south of Sandusky, Ohio. Nelson responded immediately to Orson's letter and tracts. This youngest of the otherwise Mormon Pratts had never joined the Church. But Orson's letter "caused a thrill of joy through my soul even to know that I have a Brother in the United States . . . I have received and read with interest the seer although its doctrines are new and novel to me."[128] A small farmer with ten children, he was to remain on his plot the rest of his life.

To realize his project of publishing a family genealogy, Orson needed more information than his brothers could give him. He reached into the past for names of distant relations and wrote letters aimlessly, always sending tracts. From Asenath Pratt Gorsline, a cousin of Jared Pratt, he received a deferential testimony to the "revelation of the Lord" she received in the Free Communion Baptists—and forwarded a pamphlet of her own to him. She took a sly swipe at Orson in her response: "It was with some diffidence I resumed my pen knowing your dignity . . . The Seer as far as we can judge is an able and well written work . . . I am really sorry that there are such diversity of opinions . . . My husband has a brother . . . a firm believer in the seventh day advent doctrine . . . to follow some lights would be to follow a jack lantern."[129]

Seth Pratt, Orson's first cousin, was a little more candid: "I have perused your works somewhat . . . I cannot but think that you are in error . . . you would do well perhaps to examine well, the subject for your soul's welfare is at stake . . . Your ideas of Pre-existence I cannot gainsay but is it not a fruitless speculation? Polygamy, I consider to be impolitic if not unscriptural."[130]

Orson received a little information from Seth about the family of Obadiah Pratt, but Seth's indifference to Mormonism contrasted with the careless cheer of cousin David Pratt of Augusta Center, New York: "Rev. and Dear Friend, I received your Epistle and also the Books and Seer . . . as respects the faith and practice of your denomination . . . I do not object . . . Please send me a M——n Bible mark the price and I will remit the money I should be glad to accompany you to Utah to preach the gospel."[131]

Orson's great genealogical breakthrough came with the chance discovery of a little item in an exchange newspaper. A Protestant minister in South Glastonbury, Connecticut, had advertised for information concerning the descendants of Lieutenant William Pratt, who had colonized Massachusetts in the 1620s. Orson immediately wrote to Rev. Frederick W. Chapman, who was able to supply him with "the connecting links between . . . grandfather, Obadiah Pratt, and the first settler, William Pratt." Upon receipt of this letter Orson wept with joy at the miraculous turn of luck. He wrote later to Parley, "There are none among all the descendants of our ancestor, Lieutenant William Pratt, who have so deep an interest in searching out his descendants as ourselves . . . we might stand as saviors upon Mount Zion, in behalf of our ancestors . . . Let us, my dear brother Parley, take hold of this matter in earnest."[132]

Chapman had already collected the names of some two thousand Pratt descendants in the United States. Orson excitedly forwarded him every name he could think of and promised Chapman he would personally scour the parish records of England to carry William Pratt's family line back as far as he could. This was the beginning of an active correspondence that led ultimately to a wonderfully definitive book on the Pratt family in America published in 1864.[133] By this providential stroke, Orson Pratt also became the first Mormon to research his own lineage on a systematic basis, fully four decades before the small beginnings of the Genealogical Society of Utah.

During the summer of 1853 Orson made a brief crossing to Liverpool[134] hoping to fulfill in part his promise to Chapman. He also disseminated copies of *The Seer* and was greeted with a new, second edition of his mission tracts. From America he carried a remarkable manuscript he had obtained from Almon W. Babbitt, a disaffected Mormon attorney—a biography of Joseph Smith written by his mother, Lucy Mack Smith, who was then only three years from death. An energetic, conversational work, the book delighted Orson, who arranged to have it edited and published in Liverpool by Church printer Samuel W. Richards at a cost of "two or three thousand." The book never brought him any renumeration, though he purchased the copyright from Mother Smith in a moving letter he wrote from Washington that fall:

> I send you $100 as a present, keep it whether you send me the copyright or not. I wish I was able to give you still more; but I am poor & my circumstances will not admit of it at present. Perhaps I may, at

> some future time, have it in my power to help you still more . . . the great work of the Lord which your son was the honored instrument in bringing forth, is spreading rapidly into the four quarters of the globe. Oh, mother Smith, how often do I think of those happy days, when I first had the joyful privilege of coming under your roof in Waterloo, N.Y. I have been your true friend from that day to this, although, I am sorry to say that I have not been as faithful in all things as I might have been; I greatly appreciated the society of the prophet while living; but I ought to have appreciated him still more: and could I have my life to live over again in his precious society, I think, with the experience that I now have, that I never could do enough for his happiness & welfare . . . P.S. Please remember my kind love to all your dear children that are now living, and to your grand children; and also to sister Emma. May God remember his promises to them and bless them all.[135]

Clearly the old wounds from Kirtland and Nauvoo still hurt Orson; his devotion to Joseph Smith had nevertheless increased over the years, and though many of the Smith family were disaffected, he expressed nothing but warmth for them. The book, printed under the title *Biographical Sketches of Joseph Smith the Prophet, and His Progenitors for many Generations*, was to give him no end of trouble in the future.

Orson stayed only a few weeks in England stopping in Birmingham long enough to wed convert Sarah Louise Lewis—wife number seven, Sarah number two.[136] Upon his return to Washington he found he had been appointed to head up the entire program of emigration for the coming season. This meant endless preparations along with the duties of editing *The Seer* and arranging for housing accommodations, agents, tons of meat and flour, steamboats for the Mississippi passage, and mechanics to work on the wagons in far-off Missouri. He himself joined the emigrants at St. Louis in May 1854. Finding the companies in the usual state of disarray, he warned them sternly not to attempt the passage to the valley after June 25.[137] He accompanied the Kesler group with his new wife, making a smooth nineteen miles per day all through midsummer.

But the good fortune did not last. On August 5 for some unknown reason, their hundreds of oxen and cattle broke away with a terrific rush and roar and stampeded into the desert southward. For days the distraught company combed sandhills and poked through buffalo herds, scaring out their cattle and horses. Those that were brought back had been terribly broken down, and the loss required many of the wagons to "double team" making it difficult to travel more than six or eight miles a day for fear of exhausting the stock. This was worse than tedious, for the pioneers depended on the stock as much for food as for transportation. With meat and meal running out and his carriage horses weakened, Orson decided to leave Erastus Snow and Ezra T. Benson in charge of the company while he rode ahead for help. Travelling as fast as they could he and Horace Eldredge arrived in Salt Lake in nineteen days. The assistance they sent—horses and mules—saved the company from disastrous isolation in the Wyoming desert.[138]

Orson visited his six households one by one. Far from his wives for nearly two years, he was glad to find Sarah and the oldest children in good health. They were living in the small adobe home on the corner of West Temple and First South Streets.[139] At length turning toward another, even humbler adobe cottage where Third North Street met Third West, he embraced his Scottish Marian undoubtedly in tears, for she had lost during the winter her infant Marian Agnes, a daughter Orson never saw. Perhaps she showed her husband some verses on parchment, composed by her friend Eliza R. Snow:

Lines for Mrs. Marian R. Pratt on the Death of her little child

A precious jewel has withdrawn
A jewel richly dear
A royal gem from Earth has gone
And left the casket hear
A fondly cherished tender flower
Most delicetely fair
Has gone to grace a holier bow'r
And bloom in purer air
That lovely babe so sweet and fair
So sinless and so pure
Has gone where holy angels are
Where happiness is sure
That child is not within the tomb
It is not wrapt in sleep
Such loveliness Death's icy gloom
Holds not the power to keep
Dust unto dust the Earth received
And treasures up its own
But yet that darling baby lives
In paradise she's known
Her Noble spirit daigned to come

But could not long remain
Ere she recalled to her high home
Rejoined the blest again

Great Salt Lake City, December, 1853
E R Snow

(exquise this Martha as it is lat
and I cannot see very well to write
at Night my eyes are week)[140]

9

The Appearance of Fire

Looking over the Mormon kingdom upon his return in the fall of 1854, Orson Pratt could see flowers in the dust. The city now counted its inhabitants in the thousands, and Orson recognized among them hundreds he himself had dispatched, and even helped to convert, from Britain. His tracts had brought into the Church a number of intellectuals bred in the hardy discipline of English schools. Among them were the writer Edward Tullidge and the scholarly Elias L. T. Harrison, who later became a firebrand of apostasy. Among his own people Orson was the philosopher of the Church, Mormonism's unofficial apologist against whose authority the feeble sophistries of sectarianism evaporated. Now that the harrowing passage of the summer was over, Orson once again dreamed of the academy in the wilderness, the great school of progress"[1] which would be built here. His October addresses in the Tabernacle dwelt on "The increased powers and faculties of the mind in a future state" and "On Language, or the medium of communication in the future state and on the increased powers of locomotion."[2] "What is the body compared with the mind?" he asks. "Just nothing at all comparatively speaking," he answered, proposing that the system of arbitrary sounds and symbols we call language would in the eternities give way to the "process and power" of the Holy Ghost.

Orson set himself immediately to teaching, writing, and promoting educational interests throughout the territory. A reelected member of the legislative council, he spent the month of December in committee meetings on printing, appropriations, and expenditures for schools.[3] From England came a load of newly published copies of *Biographical Sketches of Joseph Smith the Prophet* by Lucy Mack Smith, edited by Orson and containing a preface he composed. These were advertised and offered for sale for the first time in Salt Lake.[4] Just before New Year's Orson proposed through the newspapers to open

> An Evening School in Great Salt Lake City, wherein the following branches will be taught: Natural Philosophy, Electricity and Electro-Magnetism, Chemistry, Astronomy . . . Algebra, Surveying, Analytical, Descriptive and Common Geometry, Plane and Spherical Trigonometry, Conic Sections, Analytical and Celestial Mechanics, Differential and integral Calculus . . . Professor Pratt can furnish students with some twenty copies of Day's Algebra, open six till nine weekday evenings except Friday, $15 per quarter . . . school to commence when twenty scholars have subscribed.[5]

Orson's personal efforts to stimulate the intellectual life of Salt Lake were supplemented by the formation at April conference 1855 of the "Deseret Theological Institute," an organization patterned after Joseph Smith's "school of the prophets." Orson Pratt was appointed a director of the institute with a charge from Brigham Young that "this society . . . will be nothing more than a schoolhouse, an academy, a seminary to teach the brethren all that is good, and then try to get more." Orson met with the other directors to draft a constitution for the institute, declaring that the "science of Theology embraces a knowledge of all intelligence, whether in heaven or on the earth, moral, scientific, literary, or religious."[6]

The "science of theology" led to a certain amount of theorizing, and this was a period of vigorous doctrinal debate, even dispute. Brigham Young, for example, was concerned about Orson Pratt's doctrinal teachings. With his ruminant mind Brigham had digested the philosophical corpus of *The Seer* and had admired its style. But some of Orson's propositions struck him as heretical.

Differences of opinion between Orson and Brigham were nothing new. Orson had seven years before challenged the President's right to impose his will upon the Church. In a meeting of the apostles at Kanesville, Iowa, before Brigham had been sustained President of the Church, Orson suggested that Brigham's authority was not superior to a majority vote of the Twelve. "I consider the decision of 7 men as superior to the Pres." he said. Brigham shot back, "Do you O. P. hold the Sealing Keys of the Priesthood?" Orson conceded that Brigham had the right to preside but pressed him further: "This Quo[rum] has to sit in judgmen[t] on every revelation—if we get a rev[elation] the Quo[rum] has to say whither it is right or wrong." Brigham's opinion was that God would disown the president if he made "absolutely wrong" decisions. "Has 11 men the right to say—If I receive the Will, mind of the Lord—that it is wrong—[?]" Then Brigham put the question to the eight apostles present. Seven voted with Brigham, and Orson cast the lone dissenting vote. "I have unburdened my mind," he said. "I am perfectly submissive, receive all chastisments either private or public, when I am wrong I want you to right me."[7] Brigham remembered those words as he began his long struggle with Orson Pratt over Mormon theology.

The preeminence of Brigham Young in matters of doctrine was only part of Orson's personal religious commitment. At the same time he saw the gospel as something to be apprehended rationally as well as spiritually; the universal intelligence who reveals secrets will not, must not, contradict himself nor violate the laws of reason. For Brigham Young, revelation overwhelmed and transformed all man's petty logical constructs: the gospel was the immediate practical course he must discern to save a desperate people in the wilderness. Indeed, the definitive gospel sermon was the living of life itself: "To commence, continue, and finish this Gospel sermon, will require all the time that is allotted to man. . . . No man is able to set before a congregation all the items of the Gospel . . . for this mortal life is too short . . . I do not even commence at the beginning of it; I only catch at it, where it comes to me, in the 19th century."[8]

Brigham had to "catch at" revelation and resented the idea that boundaries could be set to revealed truth. Some of Orson's speculations in *The Seer*, no matter how innocently intended, sounded to him like the precepts of men which Joseph testified had deadened the primitive church. Above all Brigham was uneasy with Orson's view that God had progressed to the limit of knowledge and wisdom. He believed that God increased eternally in both understanding and power. Although he later confessed uncertainty on this question,[9] he was offended at the closed universe implied in Orson's writings. Therefore, he had written to Orson in the summer of 1853, "There are many points in the Seer that are not Sound Doctrine."[10]

Orson Pratt replied to this objection deferentially. He had heard Heber C. Kimball preach that the gods progress in knowledge, but thought the idea had been "thrown out" and was "mere conjecture." Orson was anxious to learn if this were the "settled" opinion of the president, and if so he would not teach otherwise. From Orson's letter it is also apparent that Young rejected Pratt's doctrine summarized in *The Seer* that the One God of the Bible was really a complex of attributes shared by many individuals who had achieved exaltation: "All . . . Gods are equal in power, in glory, in dominion . . . each possesses a fulness of truth, of knowledge, of wisdom, of light, of intelligence . . . The fulness of all these attributes is what constitutes God . . . Persons are only tabernacles or temples, and TRUTH is the God, that dwells in them . . . when we speak of only one God . . . let it be distinctly remembered, that we have no reference to any particular person or substance, but to *truth* dwelling in a vast variety of substances."[11] For Orson this was the only way to reconcile Joseph's revelation on the plurality of gods with the insistent monotheism of the Bible. He made a courteous attempt to persuade Young to his point of view: "without these arguments I could not stand one moment before arguments brought by our opponents . . . I could only bear my testimony that there was but one God as clearly declared in our revelations, & that there were many Gods as asserted in the same revelations." However, though *The Seer* was already in print, Orson offered to retract anything Young disapproved: "I do most earnestly hope that the Saints throughout the world will reject every unsound doctrine which they may discover in the 'Seer' or in any of my writings. Whatever may come in contact with the *settled & permanent* views of our president should be laid aside as emanations of erring human wisdom."[12] The September 1853 issue of *The Seer* repeated the notion that Young had objected to defining God as "the FULNESS OF TRUTH.")[13]

To complicate matters Orson found himself unable to reconcile Brigham Young's teachings about Adam with his understanding of the scriptures. Young had preached that Adam was a celestial being who had brought Eve with him from another world and had fallen to an earthly state. Orson believed it was impossible for resurrected personages to "fall" and become mortal again. He felt more comfortable with the scriptural account "that Adam was made of the dust of the Earth" and insisted to Young that it was inconceivable that "minds accustomed to severe thought and meditation as yours have been these many years, can, after due reflection . . . still believe in a doctrine which appears to be so contrary to what is revealed."[14] Nevertheless, Brigham reaffirmed his theory in a conversation with Orson in autumn 1854.[15]

Many of the other authorities supported Young in his teachings. Even Parley subscribed to them when he wrote in his 1856 doctrinal book *Key to the Science of Theology*:

> Earth, its mineral, vegetable and animal wealth, its Paradise prepared, down comes from yonder world on high a son of God, with his beloved spouse. And thus a colony from heaven, it may be from the sun, is transplanted on our soil. The blessings of their Father are upon them, and the first great law of heaven and earth is again repeated, "Be fruitful and multiply." Hence the nations which have swarmed our earth . . . when heaven was veiled from view, and, with few exceptions, man was no longer counted worthy to retain the knowledge of his heavenly origin . . . at length a Moses came, who knew his God, and would fain have led mankind to know Him too, and see Him face to face. But they could not receive His heavenly laws or bide His presence. Thus the holy man was forced again to veil the past in mystery, and in the beginning of his history assign to man an earthly origin. Man, moulded from the earth, as a brick! Woman, manufactured from a rib![16]

Although Orson could and later did agree that in a sense Adam was indeed a "god," he was not as quick as Parley to renounce the Genesis account of Adam's creation. Orson preached fifteen years later that "some angels are Gods, . . . Adam is called an Archangel, yet he is a God."[17] When Brigham Young discussed his beliefs about Adam in a Deseret Theological Institute meeting, he made the disclaimer that they were "for you to believe or disbelieve as you please."[18] The statement was possibly prompted by Orson's skepticism, which sometimes led to a sharp division of opinion with Young, as an 1856 record reveals: "The subject was brought up concerning Adam being made of the dust of the earth and Elder Orson Pratt pursued a course of stubborness & unbelief in what President Young said that will destroy him if he does not repent & turn from his evil way For when any man crosses the track of a leader in Israel & tryes to lead the prophet—he is no longer lead by him but in danger of falling."[19] The controversy continued.

Another conflict arose over Orson's edition of *Biographical*

Sketches of Joseph Smith primarily because of its defense of now-dissident William Smith. On January 31, 1955, Brigham published a notice:

> There are many mistakes in the work entitled "Biographical Sketch of Joseph Smith the Prophet" . . . by Lucy Smith . . . and published at Liverpool for Orson Pratt . . . A monthly periodical called the "Seer," published by Elder Orson Pratt at Washington City, D.C., contains beautifully written articles; but notwithstanding the general beauty of the style, and the apparent candour and minuteness of the reasoning, the "Seer" has many items of erroneous doctrine. As it would be a lengthy and laborious operation to enter minutely into their disapproval, I prefer to let the Saints have the opportunity to exercise their faith and discernment in discriminating between the true and erronious; and simply request them, while reading the 'Seer,' to ask themselves what spirit they are of, and whether the Holy Ghost bears testimony to the truth of all the doctrines therein advocated.[20]

And so began the public campaign to tighten the reins on the philosopher of Mormonism. Although Orson cared little for the prestige his office accorded him, he was clearly embarrassed by the growing tension between himself and his prophet. While he acknowledged Brigham's right to enunciate Church doctrine, he still could not reconcile his concept of God with Brigham's views. However, he published an advertisement a few weeks later which confessed with diffidence that Brigham was right about the Smith history: "I procured the manuscripts while on my last mission in the United States, and was informed, at the time, that most of the work was written under the inspection of the Prophet; but from evidences since received, it is believed that the greater part of the manuscript did not pass under his review, as there are items which are ascertained to be incorrect . . . In future editions the work will be carefully revised and corrected." (He goes on to recommend it, nevertheless, as "interesting to the people" and as a first reader for schoolchildren.)[21]

Debate and dispute were not the only activities of the Deseret Theological Institute. The institute's inaugural meeting featured a benediction by Orson Pratt, a "catch," or song, by Orson Junior, and a discourse on useful knowledge by Ezra T. Benson. The Pratts and their friends took a delighted interest in the new forum. For example, young Orson, now eighteen, found there an ideal audience for his art. A musician, he tried out a composition on the institute choir entitled "Although the Fig Tree Shall Not Blossom." The school listened to professor as well as prophet: George D. Watt acquainted them with the principles of phonography and the foundations for the new "Deseret Alphabet," a script developed by Parley P. Pratt and himself to assist the large number of European converts in Utah in learning the English language phonetically. But in the summer Brigham Young suspended the institute meetings "until the evenings became more lengthy." The institute did not meet again.[22]

Brigham was careful to maintain cordial relations with Orson Pratt and took opportunity to elevate him in the eyes of the members without implying sanction of his doctrinal speculations. In a hot July conference Orson roused the Saints with a sermon on the "Kingdom of God" and the right of the Church to establish its own ecclesiastical polity within the United States protected by the Constitution, which Orson faintly praises as "well suited" to the "present condition" of the American people. Brigham stood immediately and announced, "I would not disagree in the least with . . . brother Pratt" on the subject of the kingdom of God.[23]

Nevertheless, Brigham made October conference 1855 an occasion to denounce Orson's reservations about the inspiration of the Bible. When he felt Orson the ideologue was taking over, Brigham did not hesitate to check him and on this point the president was at his spiciest: "People must be chastened; we believe in this principle . . . why I make this peculiar remark is because this congregation heard brother O. Pratt scan the validity of the Bible, and I thought by the time he got through, that you would scarcely think a Bible worth picking up and carrying home, should you find one in the streets . . . the Bible is good enough just as it is . . . it used to answer . . . very well when I was preaching in the world." After this little dig over the pulpit, the president attempted to appease Orson by assuring the congregation that "the Lord loveth whom he chasteneth." Brigham announced, "It always takes something besides chastisement . . . to bring tears from me."[24]

Orson continued to calculate and write on his own time despite the public attention given his errors. For some time he had been studying the problem of planetary motion, particularly the irregularities and inconstancies he had both observed and read about. This inner impulse to discern order and meaning in the universe had preoccupied him since youth, as he himself testifies. For a year he struggled with a formula that would predict planetary movements based on the observable density of the bodies:

> Firmly believing, from my early youth, that the diurnal periods of the planets were the results of some hidden law, I have endeavored . . . to discover the same . . . to determine the periods . . . by calculation instead of observation . . . I was led . . . to seek for the law of rotation connected with the masses and diameters of the planets . . . with their densities. These investigations resulted in the development of the following beautiful law: THE CUBE ROOTS OF THE DENSITIES OF THE PLANETS ARE AS THE SQUARE ROOTS OF THEIR PERIODS OF ROTATION.[25]

One modern critic has written that Pratt's law "to obtain laws of rotation" for the planets is "erroneous." He provides "no experimental evidence and little observation."[26] Nevertheless, in the words of another historian of science, Orson's formula "does give better than order-of-magnitude agreement with modern observations for the superior planets then known."[27] Though all heavenly bodies do not conform to Orson's theory, still it is significant. To his satisfaction he had found one more astronomical proof for his ideology of perfect order in the universe. His philosophy of Mormonism implied a strict correspondence between mass and motion, for movement was proof of intelligent substance at work. The formula was announced in the columns of the *Deseret News*: "Professor Orson Pratt, by whom the LAW OF PLANETARY ROTATION was discovered on the eleventh day of November, 1854, will lecture before the "Universal Scientific Society" at the Social Hall . . . Admission free."[28]

Orson spent the summer working and lecturing on the formation of the solar system and building a new two-story house for a part of his family. School teaching went on, but without much financial reward. He advertised: "Come gentlemen, hand in your names to brother Pratt, secure for yourselves a suitable room, and prepare to be governors, statesmen, philosophers."[29] The days were long and hot, and Orson celebrated Independence Day with ice cream and ice water, bursting melons on the edge of the canal. This was as leisurely as things could get for him. His impulse was always to measure and expand Zion and to interpret and rationalize the very motions of the planets on a Mormon scale.

The boundaries of the "Promised Land" had never really been

fixed, so Orson drove north with President Young on a surveying expedition to the Oregon territorial border. They traveled through the burgeoning settlements of Kaysville, Bingham's Fort (now Ogden) and went as far as the "Malade," a small stream near the present Idaho state line. This was the northern limit of Zion, and when Orson took a sight on Polaris, he could point to the spot on the Fort Hall road where gentile territory began. They wrestled into place a large stone slab and carved "U" for Utah on one side and "O" on the other.[30]

Having fixed the northernmost limits of Utah, the brethren next assigned Orson to delineate the eastern frontier. On September 11 he and Jesse Fox left for Green River. Their mule train straggled over the emigration trail for nine days, and on September 19, Orson's forty-fourth birthday, they encamped exactly at the forty-second parallel. Here Congress had decreed the division between Utah and the unorganized Wyoming badlands. From then on, Orson's marker signaled to emigrant trains of Saints that they had reached at last their Zion in the mountains.[31]

Coming down the rugged trail he had crossed so many times, Orson encountered his brother Parley. The two had crisscrossed in their assignments for seven years with one arriving home from a mission after the other had just left. After years of silences, resentments, and pleading for favors, the two were thrown together again for a brief time. Brigham Young assigned them to work as "Home Missionaries," setting in order the Mormon settlements and holding instructional meetings among the stakes. The brothers were appointed first to visit Davis Stake in Farmington, Utah. They wandered over Utah Territory, to Provo, Ogden, Kaysville, Bountiful, and other outlying settlements discussing all they had seen and been through in seven years.[32] Finding a certain comfort in this middle-aged brotherly closeness after so long, they shared a carriage to the legislative assembly meeting in snowbound Fillmore, where a new sandstone capitol building had been erected. Here Orson had arranged his most unusual match yet: an Indiana widow's sixteen-year-old daughter was given to him in a private ceremony at her home. Juliaet (Juliet) Ann Phelps became wife number eight on December 14, 1855.[33]

The town that Orson had helped lay out three years before had been settled by a handful of stalwarts willing to face the black rock and dusty winds. Now, despite the serenity of the snow, another storm was about to begin. The peace of Utah Territory was going to be ruffled from this day on.

On December 11 Orson met with President Young and others to consecrate the new statehouse, but were afterwards assailed by a melodramatic and insulting speech by the new territorial secretary. Almon W. Babbitt, now the highest federal appointee in Utah other than Young himself, was a disgruntled Mormon who had wandered in and out of the Church for years. His speech elicited both outrage and fear: Babbitt's reports to Washington, if distorted as in the case of earlier federal officials, could mean serious trouble for the Mormons. After grumbling over the situation, the brethren realized that they must work with Babbitt or risk disturbing their peaceful relationship with the Pierce administration. No one was happy with Babbitt, and the fears were eventually justified. Partly on the strength of Babbitt's representations, the first legislative proposals aimed at Mormon practices came before Congress the following summer.[34]

These discouraging developments compounded a difficult year for Orson. With his families now scattered from Salt Lake to Fillmore and his trustworthiness seriously questioned by the president of the Church, he was further oppressed by the news of Orson Spencer's death from cholera during his mission to the Cherokees. This man, who had shared not only Orson's given name but also his inquiring mind, had been one of his intimate friends: "It pained my heart," he wrote. "I love him, he was a man of God."[35]

In April 1856 Brigham decided it was time to send Orson out again. The British Mission needed a new presiding authority, and Orson needed the stimulation of another venture into the climate of the Old World. His final words to the general conference echo with disappointment at the attitude of his colleagues who devalued his "philosophical" strivings: "There are those around me here who are better qualified to teach you in relation to your every day duties."[36] Within two weeks he said good-bye to seven wives and brother Parley, who was very ill when he left. The two must have parted in some pain—Parley himself felt that his end was imminent—but it was appropriate, for although Parley recovered and lived another year, the two brothers did not meet again.[37]

Winter did not end that year. The hills blazed with snow as Orson's eastering company broke through the passes under the high Rocky skies of flat blue. It was impossible to keep warm, and the stock had to snuffle through drifts for the scanty spring grass. Never had the overland journey taken such a toll on the brethren. In their poverty they faced Indian country with two Colt revolvers and fifteen rounds among them. Just beyond Fort Bridger they girded themselves with buffalo robes and harnessed themselves to the teams, for the snow blasted the plains with a fury none of them had ever experienced. Orson Pratt shouted encouragement to the others as they fought their way through this gale until the blue of the sky showed again on the morning of May 6.

When they awoke, everything was white. The badlands stretched before them a deadly blank with the sun flaming overhead—pure light but no heat to relieve the excruciating cold. As the brethren breasted the snow, treading it down to make a path for the teams, they felt gritty torture in every blink of the eye. The next morning Orson was quite snow blind. The severe brilliance had inflamed his eyes all through the preceding day as he led out, and now three apostles laid hands on him to administer in the name of the holy priesthood.

But the searing whiteness continued. Buried in their robes, encrusted with ice, the brethren clutched frozen handkerchiefs to their faces to blot out the glare. Maddened, they began to shelter by day under the wagons and to travel by night when the light subsided into moon glare.[38]

Nearly iced through and with eyes festering, Orson arrived at Florence, Nebraska, the old site of Winter Quarters, and boarded the steamer *Polar Star* for St. Louis. The long voyage by Boston to Liverpool gave him time to heal, however, and upon his landing in England he had projected an entire book on the doctrines of Mormonism.[39] Though in trouble at home for his writings, he was certain that with a more systematic format he could logically develop the full implications of Mormon belief from first principles to the most complex universal truths. Although the Pratt pamphlets read smoothly and are clearly the works of a man of a persuasive and at times sophisticated pen, the process of composition was never easy for Orson. He wrote to his brother Parley:

> Writing has always been tedious to me, but seeing the good that may be accomplished, I have whipped my mind to it, till I am nearly baldheaded, and grey-bearded, through constant application. I almost envy the hours as they steal away. I find myself so fast hastening to old age. A few short years, if we live, will find us among the ranks of the old

> men of the earth; and how can I bear to have it so without doing more in this great cause? I wish to accomplish something ere I die, that shall not only be esteemed great by good and holy men, but that shall be considered great in the sight of God. You would no doubt counsel me to be patient, but I would remark, that I sometimes fear that while I am waiting with *patience* that the day of my probation will be past and that I may be called away before I have prevaled with God as did the ancients. I will try, my dear brother, to be patient, but sometimes my anxieties are so great that it is hard to wait.[40]

Pratt's urgent sense of mortality forced him to overcome the "tedium" of his self-defined mission, and with a spurt of energy he went to work on the last of his theological writings.

The chapters of this book came out piecemeal—one per month, beginning in August 1856—under Church contract in Liverpool. The first installment, entitled *True Faith*, is notable for its simplicity. This is not the florid philosopher at work, but a man who sees subtleties as obfuscation. In keeping with his *Seer* format, each point is numbered and logically builds on the preceding premises. In the next chapter, *True Repentance*, Orson constructs a brief for "the Divine Law of Plurality" as a panacea for all "criminal connexions, and they will soon be cleansed from the stench and filth of those cursed dens of pollution which have so publicly infested their cities for ages." Polygamy is thus prescribed as the remedy for urban evil. The chapter offers an insight into Orson's personal views on sin and social suffering. Decrying the thousands of prostitutes in Britain, he advocates the death penalty for adultery tossing this severe challenge into the teeth of the established church: "Repentance is not to ascend into a finely cushioned pulpit and there whine over the wickedness of the people, without taking any effectual means to suppress that wickedness."[41]

In November Orson brought out the fourth chapter of his doctrinal summa: *The Holy Spirit*. This tract largely repeated Orson's notion of an immanent intelligence, present in all substance, compound in nature and yet unified in purpose. "The Holy Ghost exists, not only as a person, but as a diffused fluid substance."[42] This is necessarily so because "one personage of the Holy Spirit could not be in two or more places at the same instant; for such a condition is absolutely impossible . . . Therefore, one personage, called the Holy Ghost, could not dwell at the same instant in two or more Saints. If he were in one, He would most certainly be absent from all others."[43]

He goes on to demonstrate that this spirit is divisible and yet "infinite in quantity," a spiritual substance capable of softening, animating, and teaching the heart. This fluid is like fire: "When the . . . disciples were waiting, on the day of Pentecost, for the 'Baptism of the Holy Ghost,' . . . there appeared unto them cloven tongues, like as of fire . . . The whole house was filled with the Spirit; hence, these disciples were baptized or immersed in it . . . On this occasion, portions of this Holy Fluid . . . transform[ed] its parts into one hundred and twenty tongues, having the appearance of fire.[44]

Orson thus saw the Holy Spirit as a living, intelligent, self-moving "fluid," a nineteenth-century scientific catch-term used to describe any motive phenomenon such as electricity or the "ether" medium through which light waves were thought to move. *Holy Spirit* implies that this living "universal fluid" existed even prior to the gods. "This boundless ocean of Spirit possesses in every part, however minute, a will, a self-moving power, knowledge, wisdom, love, goodness, holiness, justice, mercy, and every intellectual and moral attribute possessed by the Father and Son." In other words, the attributes of godliness exist separate from any personality (though they may be ascribed to certain personalities): "Man has been accustomed to associate wisdom, knowledge, love, joy, and all the other faculties and passions, with an organized being or personality. Therefore, when he is informed that the Holy Spirit possesses all these attributes, he, from habit, supposes it to be a person; but there is no necessary connection between these attributes and a personality. Indeed, there is no reason why these attributes may not also belong to a Fluid Substance."[45]

Pratt's "Holy Spirit" is not exactly the panpsychic deity proposed by Spinoza, nor does it duplicate Emerson's notion of an "Oversoul" that infuses nature with life.[46] These philosophers taught that the "world soul" was a *plenum*, that is, undifferentiated and immaterial substance. For Pratt "an infinite number of particles" makes up the Holy Spirit moving "universal nature, as if by the will of one Being." He uses the spirit of man as an analogue to make the concept clearer: "This may be represented by the human spirit which is in the image of the human tabernacle, and dwells throughout the body . . . The myriads of particles in the human spirit, move the human body by one united will."[47] Though the other tracts of 1856 were orthodox enough (and even a little narrow), the propositions of *Holy Spirit* were to haunt Orson at home.

Even during the composition of this worrisome piece, Orson was under attack by the firebrand assistant prophet, President Jedediah M. Grant, in the Salt Lake Tabernacle. Protesting Orson's teaching that God does "not progress in knowledge," he accused the apostle of "lariatting out the Gods in his theory; his circle is as far as the string extends. My God is not lariatted out."[48] Grant's fiery campaign against what he saw as Orson's limitation of God's progression helped make up part of the "great Reformation" among the Saints in Utah:

> I know brother Orson Pratt says we shall at some time come to a dead stand, but that time is a long way off . . . I never want it to come, or to believe that it ever will come. When a man . . . wants no new principles, no new revelation, but desires a dead stand, saying I have got enough, and I want no more, he is pretty sure to apostatize . . . I do not know but brother Orson Pratt is right in his conjecture; he is a philosopher, and a great reasoner; but . . . I cannot see that we shall ever come to a dead stand. I have an idea that progression is eternal . . . That which is limited is not Mormonism![49]

For Orson it was philosophically impossible for an absolutely perfect being to progress or increase in perfection. Grant, in turn, was faithful to that tenet of Joseph Smith that "all intelligent beings are susceptible of enlargement"[50] seeing no reason to exclude God from the picture of eternal progression.

But the question of what is or is not Mormonism soon took a back seat to the question of political survival. That autumn, bad news had come from Washington. The newborn Republican party had resolved to fight the contracting of plural marriages in any of the territories of the United States, and no one knew quite what to expect from the incoming Democratic administration of President James Buchanan. As it turned out they could expect the worst. The Mormons girded up with a new austerity, and apostles were dispatched to brand the Saints with hot moral irons, to rebaptize the whole Church and eliminate any creeping evils in the community of Zion. Franklin D. Richards wrote to Orson and enjoined him to spread the "spirit of Reformation" in England[51] and vigorously admonish the huge shiploads of incoming converts so that they would not be lax and troublesome on their arrival.

Orson was glad to hear of the Reformation,[52] not imagining that he was one of its targets. In Victorian England such Mosaic severity seemed far distant indeed, and Orson was already preoccupied with distilling the rudeness of Mormon rhetoric into effective and rational argumentation. He wrote to his teenaged bride Juliaet (as he called her) encouraging her to develop an interest in things of the mind, to go to school, and to write him more often.[53] And in disseminating hundreds of thousands of his tracts, he found time to make a trip to London to visit the British Museum. Entry into that formidable cultural treasurehouse required from foreigners a letter of introduction, and consequently Orson paid a call on the United States Consul in Liverpool the day before New Year's. The official who received him was tall, with a towering forehead and a silver bush of hair. A crony of the outgoing President Pierce, this man was Nathaniel Hawthorne. It is not recorded whether Orson knew he was in the presence of America's premier novelist, but Hawthorne, then serving out the last year of his political appointment, left his own record of the meeting in his *English Notebooks*:

> O() P(), the famous Mormonite, called on me a little while ago—a short, black-haired, dark-complexioned man, somewhere about forty years of age; a shrewd, intelligent, but unrefined countenance, exceedingly unprepossessing; an uncouth gait and deportment—the aspect of a person in comfortable circumstances, and decently behaved, but of a vulgar nature and destitute of early culture. I think I should have taken him for a shoemaker, accustomed to reflect, in a rude, strong, evil-disposed way, on matters of this world and the next, as he sat on his bench . . . he said he had been in Liverpool about six months.[54]

Unfortunately, there was little discussion between them; Hawthorne referred Orson to the consulate secretary, a Mr. Dallas, and Orson's encounter with the author of *The Scarlet Letter* occasioned nothing more than the offhand description Hawthorne jotted in his journal.

While Orson examined the delights of the British Museum, Utah debated the doctrinal merits of his writings. Brigham Young did not mince words anymore, whether in public or in private, lighting into Orson's theories over the pulpit. He appears to have been irritated that the apostle had returned (in *The Holy Spirit*) to the teachings of a "universal spirit," a "Great First Cause" that he had promised in 1853 to put aside.[55] "Orson Pratt puts his feet in it," the President stormed echoing the disdain of Counselor Grant. "With all the knowledge and wisdom that are combined in the person of brother Orson Pratt, still he does not yet know enough to keep his foot out of it, but drowns himself in his own philosophy, every time he undertakes to treat upon principles that he does not understand."[56] And to Orson he wrote words of measured warning: "I feel again to say . . . labour with all your might, rightly dividing your word of truth, with much wisdom in all meekness and patience."[57] Brigham was clearly concerned about the potential impact of Orson's speculations upon the Saints; nevertheless, the mountain of tracts Orson was spreading over Europe played an important role in the conversion of thousands to Mormonism. As Hawthorne noted, Orson Pratt had become "the famous Mormonite," a widely recognized spokesman for the cause. About this time disaffected Thomas B. Marsh returned to the fold crediting Pratt's writings for his change of heart. "The doctrine of plurality was a great bugbear to me," Marsh told the Bowery congregation at Salt Lake, "till I got to Florence and read the works of brother Orson Pratt, and now I see that it is heaven's own doctrine."[58] Senior Apostle Orson Hyde, who had always been friendly with Orson, assigned him a "masterly technique". "The last Eastern mail . . . brought me a pamphlet or tract written by Elder Orson Pratt, of Liverpool . . . The whole matter is handled in a masterly way, free from blind obscurity, unchecked and unrestrained by fear, and untramelled by the religious or political dogmas of the age. It is the product of a clear head, of a strong heart, and of an unflinching hand. In short, it is *Heaven's eternal truth*."[59] Brigham Young was not slow to compliment Orson whenever possible; it was important to maintain the credibility of one of his chief spokesmen regardless of the errors. In response to Marsh's comments he praised Orson's defense of polygamy as "beautiful, consistent, and exalting."[60]

Quite unaware of the little storms he caused at home, Orson continued writing. By April he had completed eight chapters of his book outlining Mormon doctrine with *Holy Spirit* raising the most comment at home. His final installment, *Latter Day Kingdom*, extolled as Zion the western kingdom established in the mountains. By now Orson was personally supervising the departure of whole shiploads of Europeans bound for Utah—not only British, but Danish and Norwegian converts by the hundreds. The sight swept him away, like Isaiah, "enrapt in prophetic vision":

> The poor trust in Zion for a place of deliverance, see them come from the islands and from the nations afar off! See mighty ships spread forth their sails to the winds of heaven, filled with Zion's children! hear their cheerul songs, as they are swiftly carried up the rolling current of the broad majestic rivers of Zion's land . . . These are the pastures of the Lord . . . bespangled with the flowers of Eden! . . . Here they gradually ascend the great highway of the redeemed, til they gain the mountaintops . . . the lovely vales of Ephraim.[61]

On this exalted note Orson closed his English mission tracts. Whether or not he intended to continue is not clear. He assigned the tracts successive page numbers intending a unified volume of commentary or perhaps just an open-ended series which could be picked up again in the future. At any rate the last tract was published near the first of April 1857.

At forty-five Orson was well into middle age for a man of his time. While Hawthorne described him in 1856 as short, dark, and "uncouth," Orson saw himself as "fleshy." The enormous weight of business and the responsibility for the safe passage of hundreds of emigrants began to tell on him. He wrote to his wife, "I am in good health, at present, with the exception of being somewhat afflicted with dizziness."[62] His eyes were still bright, his smile still peculiarly childlike, but his increased girth and light-headedness possibly foreshadowed the onset of a slow, malevolent killer: diabetes. A sad and dark-hued message from Parley in St. Louis brought home the inevitable fact of mortality: "You ask me how long I will stay in the States. I answer till spring. I will then go home if God will, if I have to go with a handcart. This country is no place for me, the darkness is so thick I can litterally feel it . . . Now dear Br. Orson be of good courage, our pilgrimage will soon be over & our personal history in this world will naturally come to the word:—Finis."[63]

The year 1857 was to prove him wrenchingly prophetic. On a June morning Orson fumbled through the mass of correspondence that settled over the Liverpool office every week to find a letter from Eleanor McLean Pratt, whom he had met in Salt Lake only the year before and who was the latest plural wife of his brother. She explained that Parley was dead, murdered in Arkansas by her own former husband. Hector McLean had pursued Parley in insane anger, stabbed him twice, and shot him in the neck near the town of Van Buren. Reportedly, he had lain dying in the road for hours before some diffident locals came upon him. Pleading for water, he paused and in a weak voice offered a dying testimony: "I die a firm believer in the Gospel of Jesus Christ as revealed through the Prophet Joseph Smith . . . I am dying a martyr to the faith."[64] From Brigham Young came a melancholy letter to Orson. "May God comfort and strengthen you in your afflictions, brother Orson."[65]

He had little time for grief. The news from the States echoed ominous rumors that Washington had determined to crush Mormonism and the rule of the priesthood in Utah. Nothing definite was known until Orson received a dispatch—grave, almost frantic in tone—instructing him that it was time to decamp. All American elders were to return to the valley immediately, and Orson was specifically ordered to dismantle the Mormon trail and to see that all roadside notices were taken down and all Mormon stations between the Missouri and Utah were broken up. The United States was at war with the Saints. It was July 24, 1857, Orson's ninth wedding day, to Eliza Crooks, when Mormon Utah was informed that an army had been sent against them.[66]

Brigham Young's letter of August 12, 1857, explained to Orson that 2,500 federal troops were even then on the plains and about to march on the Mormon settlements. James Buchanan, the new president of the United States, mistakenly believed that the Saints were being kept in bondage, that enforced prostitution was rampant in Utah, and that Brigham Young had established an obscene dictatorship in his mountain fortress. Most of these representations came from the hazy mind of one W. W. Drummond, a Gentile official who had suffered Mormon coolness for two years.[67] Buchanan responded by appointing a new governor, Alfred Cumming, accompanied by an infantry division.[68]

Orson tried to wind up all pending business as soon as possible, but there were delays in closing up such a detailed operation as the LDS emigration offices and the printing and missionary efforts. On October 14 he locked the Islington Street office and departed aboard the *Baltic* in the company of Ezra T. Benson.[69] With the overland route closed for the winter and occupied by the soldiers of General Albert Sidney Johnston,[70] the two apostles made the seven-week voyage to California by ship. Eleven days out of New York Orson found himself in the tropics for the first time in his life. Catching the railhead on the northern coast of the isthmus, the apostles chugged the fifty miles south to Panama and the Pacific Coast.

On this torpid side of the world, the Mexican steamer *Sonora* dragged its interminable way along the shore for two weeks finally depositing Orson and Benson at San Francisco. The two apostles hurried southward to San Bernardino and the only passable access into the Great Basin at that season. The little town on the Santa Ana was a Mormon outpost shaking with the tremors of war when Orson arrived. He found the Saints following orders to sell out as fast as possible,[71] while many of the less faithful jeered them. "San Bernardino is full of apostates and wicked men," the apostles reported,[72] for they were fleeced in the panic of the largest part of their money to get a span of mules for crossing the desert. In addition the settlement rang with the news of martial law in Utah and rumors that Gentiles had already been slaughtered in the ranching country near Cedar City.

Orson and Benson faced the freezing Mohave Desert with a crowd of Saints who for all they knew were heading into an apocalyptic massacre. Over the Cajon Pass and into Las Vegas they found a settlement of Saints virtually deserted; thence to the Colorado and Rio Virgen, they reached Cedar City not long after the first day of the year 1858. Here they heard the local version of the slaughter of a group of Arkansas emigrants at nearby "Mountain Meadows." At that time the incident seemed only a minor aspect of the crisis which had the entire territory in an uproar. Between Santa Clara and Cedar, Orson may even have crossed the mass grave of the murdered emigrants who continued to haunt Mormon legend forever after.[73]

Orson staggered into Salt Lake City in mid-January after a three-month journey from England through two oceans and the forbidding deserts of the Southwest. After he had rested for a day Apostle George A. Smith, a heavy-jowled man with a voice husky from consumption, visited him to explain the latest developments in the crisis. The authorities had already parleyed with an army representative buying enough time to prepare for the occupation sure to come in the spring. From the first Brigham Young's policy had been to treat the federal troops as invaders; the Latter-day Saints had had enough of such treatment and would burn their own cities rather than be driven out of them. To this foreboding report Elder Smith also related to Orson once again the incidents of his brother's death.

Orson mounted the podium that Sabbath day clearly tired and not a little bitter:

> I begin to be almost weary in trying to carry salvation to the wicked nations of the Gentiles; and because of the many years that I have spent on missions, I find myself almost a stranger in the midst of the Saints at home. There are now but very few that I can recognize . . . If any one should ask me where my home has been for the last quarter-of-a-century, I should answer—Among the nations; for that has been my . . . abiding place ever since the year 1830.

But despite his fatigue and confessed loneliness, there was no despondence; he felt stronger in the work than ever and confident that the Saints had nothing to fear from the threatened conflagration:

> When we were . . . tried, we went forth and whipped out the religious world spiritually . . . I must say to the Latter-day Saints . . . that the same God who has strengthened them to overcome their enemies spiritually will be their defence . . . Wherefore the righteous need not fear, for thus saith the Prophet, they shall be saved, even if it so be as by fire . . . 'You need not fear.' Do you hear it, Latter-day Saints? You need not fear.[74]

Orson's words of encouragement seemed too optimistic though, and when a "council of war" was called among the apostles, Brigham unveiled his plan: to go into the desert after burning everything and to leave the armies with no means of sustenance.[75]

The winter of 1858 was made even more bitter for Orson as Brigham Young resumed his doctrinal disputes with the apostle. Despite the invasion crisis Orson asked for a formal hearing before the authorities of the Church to resolve the controversies over "Holy Spirit" that had arisen during his mission. Wilford Woodruff represented Orson in the council, exploring the possibility that the President had treated Orson unjustly in his absence.[76] After a lengthy discussion, the brethren decided to uphold Young's contention that the Pratt "philosophy" was "no criterion or guide for the Saints in doctrine."[77] Afterwards Orson "confessed his faults and said that he would never teach those principles again or speak them to any person on the earth."[78] With a reaffirmation of their fellowship with Apostle Pratt, the authorities turned once again to the external conflict that faced them.

When general conference convened in late March, the word went out: Everyone was to prepare to burn all that stood upright or grew in the ground of Utah. Plans for the destruction of the city were laid before the people, and Orson was specifically directed to begin moving his families and herds to Fillmore. It looked like the beginning of a new exile with no end in sight this time.[79] The brethren considered various places of refuge, and some foreign agents arrived among the Saints with overseas colonization offers. In Provo Orson and the others met in council with a man named Cooper who was promoting development of the Mosquito Coast of Panama. Almost nihilistic in his frustration, Brigham Young saw no reason why the contemptible United States government should not one day annex Central America just to harass the Saints: "If you were to sell me all the land for nothing, I would not go there. It sounds unhealthy," he said, and turned the discussion back to the propriety of burning Great Salt Lake City.[80]

Orson waited in Fillmore for the issue of the crisis. His optimistic words of the previous January were borne out, for the federal commissioners entered Salt Lake peacefully in June, the troops were quartered forty miles from the city, and the new governor turned out to be an affable gentleman sympathetic to the Saints.[81] The torches were put out.

Tensions continued, naturally, and Orson tried to unruffle the people with the observation that it was necessary "for the iniquitous to be in our midst" in order to purify the Saints,[82] although he himself wore weapons when escorting Brigham Young to sittings of the federal court.[83]

Orson clearly hoped to be able to rest awhile[84] and took simple delight in his families and in the everyday tasks assigned to him. He preached in the old Tabernacle almost every week drawing most of his texts from Daniel and Isaiah, his favorite apocalyptic prophets. With all the interest in agriculture and manufacturing, he admonished the people not to neglect "the interests of our future state" and to devote an appropriate amount of time to study.[85] Orson invariably appealed to the reason of his hearers, often serving to dispel prejudice in visitors to the Mormon capital. One morning he preached for two hours drawing solely on Bible texts. "Many transient persons were present, and were heard to say that they thought less of the Bible than ever, but that they were the most sensible discourses they had ever heard."[86]

The most celebrated transient of the decade, Horace Greeley, came to Salt Lake in July 1859 expressly to learn about the true condition of the Mormon people and to hear the famous Orson Pratt. Greeley, the most influential editor in America and later a Democratic candidate for president, was not favorably impressed with Mormon homiletics, as he reported in his book *Overland Journey*:

> Their religious services [in the Tabernacle] are much like those that may be . . . witnessed in the churches of most of our popular sects; the music rather better . . . the prayers pertinent and full of unction; the sermons . . . rambling, dogmatic, and ill-digested; in fact, Elder Orson Pratt, who preached last Sunday morning, prefaced his harangue by a statement that he had been hard at work on his farm throughout the week, and labored under consequent physical exhaustion . . . Now, I believe that every preacher should be also a worker; I like to see one mowing or pitching hay in his shirt-sleeves . . . but when a preacher is to address a congregation of one to three thousand persons . . . I insist that . . . he should prepare himself . . . to speak directly to the point . . . life is too short to be wasted in listing to rambling, loose-jointed harangues . . . I am not edified by this sort of preaching.[87]

Greeley may not have enjoyed it, but most Mormons did, and Orson Pratt was one of the most popular preachers in the Church.

At home Orson scratched the soil with the best of them—the quality Greeley admired. But he was no longer young and depended more on his growing sons for help. When one of them broke his arm, Orson knelt to pray for the boy and felt a forcible inspiration to go look after him. He shook off the impression, but within two hours the boy had broken his other arm. Orson Junior, now twenty-two, had married and become quite independent of the father he had known so little. Although he clearly shared his father's intellectual bent, the younger man was more detached and poetical, given to music and to writing for its own sake rather than for the purpose of persuasion. He was often heard to lecture others on "the culture of the mind."[88]

Educational and technical matters occupied the older Orson in the councils of the Church. When Orson's advice was sought on the correctness of a pirated version of the Book of Mormon published in New York, he pronounced it accurate enough. Brigham was gratified, for he hoped to pull the royalties away from its printers. Also engaged in writing books, Orson and his friend George D. Watt produced a speller for the territorial schools by transcribing Webster's Dictionary and casting it into the "Deseret Alphabet" as well. As chancellor of the University of Utah in 1859 and 1860, Orson nominally headed the school system of the territory, but there was little money or material to work with. He estimated it would cost a million dollars to furnish books and educate all the children in Utah.[89]

Despite his contributions to the territory's development, Orson continued to have trouble in both family and quorum. As contrary as ever, Sarah Marinda was provoking Orson's other wives and had even argued property claims with Brigham Young himself. As Young recorded in his diary, "One of O Pratts wives called at Tithing office and rehearsed to me her many wrongs, by Sarah Os first wife. I told her either to Leave Orson or Stop talking about it. and spent some time in conversation on principles of Orsons philisiphy—many are incorect."[90]

"Orsons philisiphy" unsettled Brigham Young more and more as the apostle's speculations became increasingly esoteric. In discourses late in 1859, for example, Orson made his subject "the inexhaustibility of the fountain of light from which the Saints draw their intelligence." When the authorities met to consider a successor for Parley P. Pratt in the Quorum of Twelve, Orson speculated that perhaps offices in the priesthood ought to be hereditary and that Parley P. Pratt, Junior, should therefore fill his father's place. The meeting closed abruptly when Brigham Young nominated George Q. Cannon to fill the vacancy.[91]

Then, in December 1859, Orson drew the wrath of the president of the Church with a public sermon in which he once again professed devotion to "the attributes of God and not the person & that he worshiped those attributes." This declaration, to Brigham's mind skirting heresy, had to be resolved formally. On January 27, 1860, Orson attended a meeting of the First Presidency, the Twelve, and the First Council of Seventy to find himself the subject of the discussion. George D. Watt's stenographic report of Orson's sermon was produced, and Brigham accused Orson of worshiping the attributes of God instead of God Himself.[92] Offending portions of *The Seer* were read demonstrating Orson's view that ultimately God (as distinguished from "the gods") is not a personality:

> "God is Light." "God is Love." "God is Truth." The Gods are one in the qualities and attributes . . . It is truth, light and love that we worship and adore . . . these constitute God . . . when we speak of a plurality of Gods, let it be distinctly understood, that we have reference

> alone to a plurality of temples wherein the same truth or God dwells . . . Wherever you find a fulness of wisdom, knowledge, truth, goodness, love, and such like qualities, there you find God . . . therefore, if you worship these adorable perfections you worship God.[93]

> [The] endless existence of Christ has reference to the fulness of Truth, and Light, and Knowledge which now dwell in His person. These attributes are personified and called God: these had no beginning, while His *person* did have a beginning in its organized capacity . . . the fulness of Truth . . . is called by various names, such as, God the Great I AM, the Father, the Son, Jesus Christ, &c. All these names, as well as the personal pronouns He, His, and Him, are applied to the FULNESS OF TRUTH, wherever it or He may dwell, whether in one tabernacle or in unnumbered millions. This Great God—the FULNESS OF TRUTH, can dwell in all worlds at the same instant . . . He is in the personage of the Father; He is in the personage of the Son; He will be in the personages of all His Saints when they receive of His fulness; and in fine, He is the only living and true God, and besides Him there is no God: He is the only God worshipped by the righteous of all worlds; for He exists in all worlds, and dwells in all his fulness in countless millions of tabernacles. He has no beginning, neither have His works a beginning, but each of His organized tabernacles had a beginning . . . Light and Truth is God.[94]

Orson defended these statements until midnight: "Now the reason I worship the Father is because in him is combined the attributes if he had not those attributes I would not worship him anymore than I do this chair. I cannot see any difference between myself and Prest. Young . . . I am not going to crawl to Brigham and act the Hypocrite and confess what I do not Believe . . . it may cost me my fellowship But I will stick to it."[95]

"You have been like a mad stubborn mule," retorted the president. Forcefully, he cited passages from *The Seer* and *Great First Cause* as false doctrine. He specifically objected to the latter's sixteenth and seventeenth concluding points, where Orson discusses the "most glorious substance" he defines as "Holy Spirit."[96] In Brigham's mind this was just a variation on the old trinitarian mystery he thought he had left behind with the Protestants. He was not impressed with Orson's philosophical arguments about necessary modes of existence.

Young then turned to a passage in *The Seer* regarding the intelligence of the gods. Orson had proposed that once the Saints had acceded to exaltation the grand school of the universe would close and they would stand on a perfectly equal footing with the Father: "Then there will be no Being or Beings in existence that will know more than what we know . . . It has been most generally believed that the Saints will progress in knowledge to all eternity; But when they become one with the Father and Son, and receive a fulness of their glory, that will be the end of all progression in knowledge, because there will be nothing more to be learned."[97] Points 95 through 97 of "Pre-existence of Man" argue the notion that God's knowledge "cannot . . . be increased or expanded in the least degree."[98] Here President Young disagreed. It was one thing to believe in orderly progression to comparative godhood, but quite another to postulate an arbitrary end to the eternal progression of the Father. He cared not for Orson's semantics; Brigham Young did not understand the God of Heaven to be at the end of his increase.

The Twelve now remonstrated with Orson. The revelations would certainly not back him up, they declared. Wilford Woodruff was painfully candid, dredging up the mortifications of 1842:

> Every man in this room who has a particle of the spirit of God knows that President Young is a Prophet of God . . . and his doctrines are true . . . he has explained everything so plain this evening that a child can understand it, and yet it is no evidence to you . . . But Brother Orson, I have seen the day when you were in sorrow. It was when you were cast out of your quorum and out of the Church, and that too in consequence of pursuing the same course you are this evening. Then you could . . . see, feel, and understand . . . when you saw your glory and crown departing from you. I beg of you to repent and not let your will carry you too far in these things.[99]

That midnight convocation devastated Orson Pratt, and he wrestled all the next day with this repudiation by the only man on earth whose opinion he revered as untainted truth. *Great First Cause* was his definitive statement of an authentic Mormon cosmology. It had been in print nine years, read by thousands, and clucked over by leading divines of the Old and New Worlds. Once again the specter of apostasy shadowed him as he contemplated having to renounce the philosophical system which he felt followed inescapably on the premises revealed by Joseph Smith. To tear down this structure would not only hurt his prestige among the Saints—to him a minor consideration—but violate what he saw as heaven's own truth. As in 1842, he grappled once again with irreconcilable creeds: his faith in his own reasoned systems against his reliance on the incontestable oracle from which he drew his premises. Sometime on that lonely Saturday he decided that Young had the primary claim on his loyalties. He visited the President's office and apologized for being "excited" the previous evening promising that he would "confine himself to . . . first principles" in future. "Reasoning men" were to blame, for in England Orson had felt constrained to answer their arguments with reasoning of his own. Brigham Young told him such men "who did not want to hear the simple Gospel message" did not deserve to be answered.[100]

Voluntarily, but still unsure where he had erred, Orson confessed before a massive congregation the next morning "a few things wherein I have done wrong":

> I have, no doubt, grieved the feelings of my brethren; and inasmuch as I have done this, no doubt I have also brought at many times darkness upon my own mind. I want to make a confession . . . There are a few things which have been a source of sorrow to myself, at different times, for many years . . . There are some points of doctrine which I have unfortunately thrown out before the people. At the time I expressed those views, I did most sincerely believe that they were in accordance with the word of God . . . But I have since learned from my brethren that some of the doctrines I had advanced in the *Seer* at Washington, were incorrect . . . I did not feel to yield to the judgment of my brethren, but believed they were in error. Now, was this right? No, it was not. Why? Because the Priesthood is the highest and only legitimate authority in the Church in these matters.

Of *Great First Cause* he said nothing and avoided any detailed statement of "false doctrines" he had published in *The Seer*; moreover, he dwelt at much greater length on the binding authority of President Young than on his own transgressions, making his confession a discourse on priesthood order:

> God placed Joseph Smith at the head of this Church; God has likewise placed Brigham Young at the head of this Church . . . We are commanded to . . . receive their words as from the mouth of God . . . I am going to do it. I am going to repent . . . When I say I am going to repent . . . I mean that I am going from this time henceforth . . . to try and show . . . that I shall be able to carry out those views; but these are my present determinations . . . I feel exceedingly weak in regard to these matters.[101]

He felt weak indeed, for it was not pride nor prestige he was being asked to surrender, but the system of universal order which gave rational sustenance to his yearning soul. "We get into darkness," he confessed.

Brigham rose on Orson's heels to command a reading of the offending texts: "*The Seer*, pages 24 and 25; page 117, paragraphs 95, 96, and 97; *Great First Cause*, points 16 and 17 . . . all of it not true."[102]

After Pratt's heresies had been recited verbatim over the rostrum of the old Tabernacle and the fires had cooled, Brigham apparently felt a twinge of sympathy for Orson. He called him in some days later for a private talk and insisted that "he never had had any personal feelings, but he was anxious that correct doctrine should be taught for the benefit of the Church and the Nations." The president went on to approve Orson's proposed lectures on "Natural Philosophy," arts, and sciences, planned for the Tabernacle and social hall and then asked him directly about his family's financial circumstances. They were of course destitute. Though Brigham looked askance at any who could not acquire and maintain property, he cast about for something remunerative for Orson to do. In February he hired him personally to superintend a free high school at Union Academy in Salt Lake.[103] The public lectures on the laws of motion, hydraulics, and philosophy began well, and Orson was innocently glad of it: "There is quite a spirit prevalent for education in this city," commented the *Deseret News* after one of Orson's night classes.[104]

But when Brigham Young reviewed the text of Orson's "confession" for publication, the flames began to smolder again. Brigham brooded over it deciding it was not so much a confession as a concession to his rights of presidency; he could not allow it to pass. At the last minute he stopped the press (but not before a portion of the speech had already been printed and distributed). For Orson's own good and to preserve the doctrinal purity of the Church, Orson himself would have to recant in detail and in the proper spirit. Informally, Brigham confided to friends that Orson Pratt's heresy ought to be explicated in general conference, but that he was afraid of hurting Orson's feelings. At another meeting on March 4, 1860, Brigham tried to persuade Orson to yield by conceding his own uncertainty: "I corrected O Pratt to day I did not say to him that God would increase to all Eternity. But I said the moment that we say that God knows all things comprehends all things and has a fulness of all that He ever will obtain that moment Eternity seases you put bounds to Eternity & Space & matter and you make a stopping place."[105]

Again a month later on April 4, 1860, the Twelve met in the historian's office to work out this volatile problem. Hewn by the frontier, the Twelve were candid but not insensitive men; many of them had had their own problems with the leadership, including Orson Hyde and Amasa Lyman. But they too were suspicious of Orson's ideas. Having recently opposed the reading of novels,[106] they did not take lightly Orson's semantic experiments with the revelations of Joseph Smith. Brigham Young turned everyone's attention to Orson: "It is my duty to see that correct doctrine is taught and to guard the church from error it is my calling."[107]

> Brother Orson, your late sermon came near to being published . . . before I had an opportunity of reading it. I am not satisfied with it as a confession; it does not present me in a true light; it makes me appear to be a tyrant, and because I am the president . . . every man's will and judgment must bend to mine. I want to get an understanding of your views and see if we see things aright; perhaps if I could see it as you do, it would be all that I could ask, but if not, we want to have the matter laid before the conference in a manner that will injure Brother Orson's influence as little as possible.[108]

Everyone must have recognized the danger of disturbing Orson too much; his reputation throughout America and Europe as the epistolary of Mormonism had to be jarred as little as possible. "I want to save bro Orson," said Brigham Young. "I want a confession that . . . will cover the church and preserve bro. Orson a whole Apostle." Orson saw the conflict as a matter of "judgment" (interpretation) of the revelations. Furthermore, he declared that "certain points taught by Bro. Y" disputed the revelations of Joseph Smith—foremost among them the idea that "Adam is the . . . father of Spirit & father of our bodies." Brigham maintained that Joseph Smith had taught the doctrine himself, but refocused on Orson. If the revised confession were not forthcoming, "you will be voted a false teacher [before the conference] & your false doctrines discarded."[109]

But Orson, tight-lipped, demurred. He would not again be paraded as some sort of heretic. He told the Twelve he thought President Young had been perfectly satisfied with the confession and was quite astonished at this renewal of the controversy. As for publishing to the world that the doctrines he had been preaching and publishing were false, he could not do it because he would prove himself a hypocrite. His writings, he insisted, were predicated on the revelations of Joseph Smith, and to his mind renouncing the obvious conclusions that reason drew from the inspired works would be tantamount to denying the Spirit itself. Once again he decried Brigham's own notion that "Adam is our Father and our God . . . I have no confidence in it . . . I have never intended to advance new ideas, but to keep within revelation!" Clearly, Orson thought the speculations of Brigham Young far more outlandish than his own ideas. "I have heard brother Brigham say that Adam is the Father of our Spirits, and he came here with his resurrected body, to fall . . . that is revolting to my feelings."

At that point Orson Hyde forestalled the discussion of Young's theory, called on Pratt to "modify his confession," and directed a prayer circle. Soon Orson humbled himself. After several hours, the confrontation ended with a sermon draft to be read the next day in conference. It was the eve of the Church's thirtieth anniversary.

Once read, the revised confession mollified Brigham Young, but Orson kept wiser eyes open in the future. "I want you to do just as you have done in your Apostleship," said Brigham, "but when you want to teach new doctrine, to write those ideas, and submit them to me, and if they are correct I will tell you."[110] In the ensuing years Brigham continued to correct Orson's preachments, and Brigham's apparent distrust of Orson's intellectual leanings persisted. From Sir Richard F. Burton, world traveler and journalist who visited Salt Lake City in the fall of 1860, we have a pithy, if somewhat condescending, insight into this conflict:

> There had been a little miff between Mr. President and the "Gauge of Philosophy," Mr. O. Pratt. The latter gentleman, who is also an apostle, is a highly though probably self-educated man, not, as is stated in an English work, a graduate of Trinity College, Dublin. The Usman of the New Faith, writer, preacher, theologian, missionary, astronomer, philosopher and mathematician,—especially in the higher branches,—he has thrust thought into a faith of ceremony which is supposed to dispense with the trouble of thinking; and has intruded human learning into a scheme whose essence is the utter abrogation of the individual will. He is consequently suspected of too much learning, of relying, in fact, rather upon books and mortal paper, than that royal road to all knowledge, inspiration from on high, and his tendencies to let loose these pernicious doctrines often bring him into trouble and place him

> below his position. In his excellent discourse delivered today, he had declared the poverty of the Mormons and was speedily put down by Mr. Brigham Young, who boasted the Saints to be the wealthiest (i.e. in good works and post-obit prospects) people in the world. I had tried my best to have the pleasure of half an hour's conversation with the Gauge, who, however, for reasons unknown to me, declined.[111]

Orson's refusal to meet with Burton can possibly be explained by the defensiveness brought on by his brush with the other authorities and his unwillingness to air these internal conflicts in public. It perhaps seemed safer not to speak at all. Consequently, later years heard less and less of his philosophy as he turned to the more abstract and less controversial method of describing his Mormon cosmology in mathematical terms.

Ironically, the twentieth-century Mormon church leans in its dogma much in Orson's direction. The view propounded by Brigham Young that God continues to "progress" has been modified in Orson Pratt's favor: "It should be realized that God is not progressing in knowledge . . . or any of the attributes of godliness," notes Apostle Bruce R. McConkie.[112] And the notion that "Adam is our Father and our God," which Orson found so confusing and repugnant, has been re-interpreted by pronouncements of Church presidents.[113]

However, Orson's speculations on the "Great First Cause" and the nature of the holy spirit remain unsanctioned. The Mormons certainly do not profess to worship the attributes rather than the person of God, as Orson advocated at one time; nor has the Church officially rendered judgment on Orson's notions of "intelligent matter" or the so-called "sacred fluid" which makes up "Holy Spirit." Ironically, Brigham Young himself also taught that "there is not a particle or element which is not filled with life, and all space is filled with element . . . There is life in all matter, throughout the vast extent of all the eternities; it is in the rock, the sand, the dust, in water, air, the gasses, and in short, in every description and organization of matter."[114] The differences between Brigham and Orson, however subtly shaded, have ceased to be an active controversy within the Church and are generally passed over. As Professor McMurrin observes, "The Mormon pioneers for whom Pratt wrote, while delighting in intellectual adventure, were not especially partial to the doctrine that sticks and stones are composed of little living souls."[115]

In addition, the Young–Pratt dispute over the origin of Adam seems to have been addressed at least in part in an editorial of the First Presidency (of Joseph F. Smith) in the April 1910 *Improvement Era*: "Whether the mortal bodies of men evolved in natural processes . . . whether the first parents of our generation, Adam and Eve, were transplanted from another sphere, with immortal tabernacles, which became corrupted . . . whether they were born here in mortality, as other mortals have been, are questions not fully answered in the revealed word of God."[116]

The controversies between Brigham Young and Orson Pratt helped Mormon leaders to come to grips with the far-reaching philosophical implications of Joseph Smith's revolutionary doctrines. Although Orson's views did not then prevail, he remained loyal to Brigham. And when the president heard the exceptionally orthodox "ride down" this troubled apostle, he dismissed the remarks with a tribute: "If Brother Orson were chopped up in inch pieces, each piece would cry out Mormonism was true."[117]

10

Cities of the East

"If the bishops wish to do their duty, let them raise means enough to help the poor Saints who are going away. Orson Pratt and Erastus Snow are poor," Brigham Young announced on a September morning in 1860.[1] Two weeks later these two apostles cleared Parley's Canyon on a grave mission: they were to evacuate all the emigrants in the East, for it appeared that the hour of judgment had come down hard on the United States. Armed and ready not just for snow and Indians but also for the rebellion that could explode any time, they got to Florence, Nebraska, the same day the voters chose Abraham Lincoln to preside in defiance of southern threats to secede from the Union. The two apostles passed election day poking through weeds in the old Winter Quarters cemetery "yearning to see any trace of our little departed ones there laid away."[2] But the winds of the Missouri bluffs had beaten the epitaphs into blank boards.

Picking up new rail connections, the apostles could now bypass the fever swamps of the Mississippi valley and steam directly east by Chicago to New York. They found the city in financial panic over the secession crisis; martial talk was turning to reality as armies marched the streets of Boston and Philadelphia. Orson wrote home, "For the great American republic, her death-struggles have come, and they will be long and terrible."[3] No surprise to Orson, the outbreak of civil war seemed a natural consequence of America's abuse of the Latter-day Saints. Moreover, Orson himself had published in *The Seer* six years before Joseph Smith's prophecy that "the Southern States shall be divided against the Northern States . . . beginning at the rebellion of South Carolina."[4] When in April 1861 the Carolina artillery fired on Fort Sumter, Orson felt he had been documenting history in reverse: "War between the Southern and Northern States commenced on the 12th of this month: the first battle was fought in South Carolina; great armies are volunteering on both sides; and soon we may expect to hear of dreadful times."[5]

For months Orson combed the ports, guiding recent converts from Europe up the railways to Zion and steering them away from the Mississippi route, now under federal blockade. Many refused to "clear out of Babylon," particularly the complacent older Church members still living in Pennsylvania whom Orson called "fossil Mormons."[6] He had no idea when he would be allowed to return to the valleys; dreaming nights of his youngest bride, he wrote poignantly of the children he had in Utah whose names he did not even know. And a slight edge can be heard in his voice: "I have no intimations from Pres't Young when to return; it may be this year; it may be next; it may be never."[7] Nevertheless, Orson finally received word and picked his way home by September 1861 and his half-century birthday.

Brigham Young, now sixty years old, determined not to allow Orson to sit for long in Salt Lake. Only a few days after the exhausting overland trip, Orson headed south under orders of the general conference to help start a "cotton mission." Since the staple cotton supply had been cut off by war, Brigham thought it might be profitable to give the Old South some competition while the going was easy. He instructed Erastus Snow to relocate and try growing cotton in the sandy warm country of the Rio Virgen and to take the fatigued Orson with him. (Orson Hyde and two other general authorities, Jacob Gates and Henry Harriman, came too; Hyde soon returned to Sanpete Valley.)[8] A resident of the "sunny south" as of December, Orson Pratt found the climate anything but pleasant. In fact, Orson walked into the middle of a natural disaster.

Several towns, including St. George, Rockville, and Grafton, had been laid out in a morass of red mud and gravel. On Christmas Day, 1861, the blizzards began and the rain fell for forty days without a break. Within a month floods ripped through the towns of Rockville and Grafton causing adobe houses to collapse from sheer saturation. The prolonged rain did not let up until late February.[9] Orson, who had settled at Rockville, gave up in discouragement and moved south to St. George March 1, 1862.[10]

Orson apparently complained to Brigham Young that the mission might prove too much of a hardship. Brigham responded, "You have passed a winter there, and of course are able to form some estimate as to how your present mission pleased you . . . should you conclude that you had rather return to this City, with your family and effects, you are hereby given liberty to do so. And should you so conclude, you are welcome to the property in this city I purchased of you at the time of your departure."[11] The dutiful Orson sent a hangdog response: "I have no choice in this matter other than to do your will, and the will of Him whose servants we are. Wherever the Spirit in you suggests that I can be the most useful, it is there I desire to be sent—it is there I can be the most happy, untill recalled or another feild of labor is assigned to me."[12]

With spring the cotton planting proceeded and the colony began to thrive. But it soon became clear that Pratt and Erastus Snow would not make a workable partnership. Erastus was the practical spirit; Orson more interested in the inspirational needs of the people. When Orson reacted to a local theft by offering a curse on the thief and a cow as a reward to the discoverer, Snow responded with ridicule.[13] While Snow built the cities, Orson made his melancholy circuit of the settlements, plotting and surveying. He lived in a tent near Grafton for over a year although he had built a home in St. George and even brought an organ down from Salt Lake.[14] Orson Pratt, Junior, who had moved south with his father, observed all this with some resentment.

The rift between Pratt and Snow probably arose over the location of the main settlement in the Rio Virgen country.[15] Orson had expressed reservations about the bottomland location because of "chills and fever" said to be common to the region,[16] which was why he chose to settle at Rockville. It is also possible that Orson resented Snow's aggressive direction of the colony at St. George.[17]

Utah's "Dixie" returned Orson to a new state constituent assembly in December 1862 providing him with an escape from the hardscrabble existence of the desert. Once in Salt Lake, Orson was elected speaker of the assembly. He had only to hear Governor Stephen Harding's insulting speeches a few times before personally signing a House resolution to Lincoln requesting Harding's removal.[18] Lincoln, otherwise preoccupied, complied without any trouble. The president was less tractable when it came to sponsoring Utah's statehood, and the new constituent assembly remained only a "shadow" state government for many sessions to come.

While presiding "with much ability"[19] over the legislature, Orson strained his aging frame to plant some spring vegetables in his Salt Lake garden. On an uncharacteristic April morning with the apricots and peaches in bloom, he threw off his flannels to sweat over the earth a few hours. The overexertion and briskness of the air took a heavy toll on his weakened condition, and he fell "very sick indeed." Wilford Woodruff and others came to his house in the nineteenth ward to find him desperately aching from pleurisy. Following a priesthood anointing, Orson felt much better but soon fell ill again. For one whole wasted year he lay in bed, preaching faintly only twice in the Tabernacle when winter brought a slow recovery.

In the early months of 1864 Orson roused himself enough to participate in the evening lectures of the expanded free high school. Others had enlarged its scope, and the new program featured Elias L. T. Harrison lecturing on "modern" writers, Edward Tullidge on "The Universality of Mormonism," T. B. H. Stenhouse on the New York press, and Orson once again on principles of electromagnetism.[20] His associates, all British converts originally swayed into Mormonism partially by Orson's pamphlets, formed a coterie of well-educated, promising men of affairs in the growing business community of Salt Lake. Harrison, who had served Orson as a district president in England, soon enlisted Tullidge and the others to write for a publication he envisioned. Designed as a general interest magazine, the *Peep-o-Day* served primarily as an outlet for Salt Lake intellectuals. Its pages gave attention to some of the serious scienticfic and philosophical issues of the day.

Another liberal-toned biweekly came out of St. George under the editorship of one "Veritas," in real life Orson Pratt, Junior. In his late twenties Orson had come home lukewarm from a mission; unlike his father he could not reconcile the occasional un-Christian behavior of his St. George neighbors with their pretensions to sainthood. In a newspaper which he founded, *Veprecula*, the younger Orson displayed the polished style of a philosopher and scientist. His skepticism was rooted in what Andrew Karl Larson calls his belief in "facts observed and pondered upon—facts tested, classified and arranged so as to form a consistent whole."[21] He was a schoolteacher, postmaster, musician, debater, and even actor;[22] and his humanism clearly guided the tone of *Veprecula*. Its columns defiantly echoed Apostle Pratt's heterodox views and reflected young Orson's objections to what he saw as Mormon attempts to circumscribe God. Utah's "Dixie" boasted some of the most exalted zealots in Mormondom, he well knew, but their ostracism of his father and their peculiar touchiness on the subject of the massacre at Mountain Meadows set his teeth on edge. For years he had doubted the singular claims of the Mormon gospel and confessed to his high priests' quorum that, though he had been a believer in his youth, he did not now feel that Joseph Smith was especially sent of God. Summoned to a Church court, Orson Junior denounced his neighbors in turn. They knew he bore a good character, he said, and he could not see why they would withdraw fellowship from him but not from those "guilty of ever so heinous a crime"—a veiled reference to suspected participants in the Mountain Meadows Massacre still in good standing in the Church. Then, pointing at the presiding authorities in Dixie, he spat out what no one had spoken in public: "Father had not been down here long, when he found there was a secret influence working against him . . . and he sought for another mission . . . The individual is Erastus Snow."[23] With that, "Veritas" left the Mormon church and receded into a quiet existence with his family, his books, and music, teaching organ and piano at the University of Utah. His fellow journalists in the *Veprecula* enterprise eulogized his departure with a satirical obituary: "Sacred to the Memory of OP A. M. . . . He leaves three compositors and a Devil to mourn his death."[24]

Sarah Pratt in later years maintained that she had taught her son Orson and the rest of her children to reject Mormonism. From the mid-1850s she endeavored "to rear my children so that they should never espouse the Mormon faith, and, at the same time, to conceal from my neighbors and from the Church authorities the fact that I was thus rearing them. Fortunately my husband was almost constantly absent on foreign missions . . . Many a night, when my children were young and also when they had grown up so as to be companions to me, I have . . . locked the door, pulled down the window curtains, put out all but one candle on the table . . . and talked to them in whispers for fear that what I said would be overheard."[25]

The excommunication of her son probably gave Sarah Marinda Pratt the courage she needed to break with her husband and the polygamous system once and for all. Since Nauvoo days she had nursed the wounds of a degraded reputation among leading Mormon families, for the John C. Bennett affair was not easily forgotten. On top of this Orson had out of conviction proposed to live on a more equal footing with all his wives, and this she could never accept. The polity of plural marriage in Utah generally accorded the first wife a certain precedence, in Orson's case strictly observed until 1864. His wives maintained their households in Salt Lake or outlying Tooele or Fillmore, supporting themselves as far as possible. Marian, for example, provided for her three children by preparing linens for the Endowment House[26] (a kind of temporary temple where marriages for time and eternity were performed), while Juliaet and her mother lived on a skimpy government pension.[27] But now Orson felt he should share his time more equally among the nine of them. For Sarah, this was the crowning blow. She had acquiesced in Orson's marriage to these women and had watched them bear him children while six of her twelve expired around her. But when he proposed "to commence living [with the others] upon principles of greater equality," she balked angrily. She would stand no more and would never live with him "in time, nor in eternity" if he persisted.[28]

In 1877 Sarah spoke of her feelings to a *New York Herald* reporter:

> I believed, when he decided to enter upon practice of polygamy, that he did so not from any violence of individual passion, but from sheer fanaticism. He told me that he believed it was his duty to take other women besides myself to wife, and at first he said that this would make no difference in his affections for me . . . By and by he told me that he intended to put these five women on an exact equality with me; that he should spend a week with one, a week with another . . . and that I should have the sixth week! Then patience forsook me . . . It was a crisis. It brought out all that was bad in my husband's nature. He said to me fiercely, "If you don't choose to live with me I don't know that I'm obliged to support you. You have my permission to go to hell. Stick to it or to starvation."[29]

The comments sound very much out of character for Orson Pratt but serve to emphasize the poignancy of Sarah Pratt's suffering.

Thus in one year Orson lost a wife and a son to unbelief and bitterness. The estranged mother and son continued to live quietly among their former coreligionists. Though Sarah never sought divorce nor excommunication from the Church, she remained no less deeply embittered against her husband than against the institution he represented. Later, after Orson's death, she dictated a short account of the conduct of Joseph Smith towards her in the 1840s. Called "The Workings of Mormonism related by Mrs. Orson Pratt," the statement contained essentially the story she had first told Orson in Nauvoo. "Workings" eventually became stock evidence in the case against Mormon polygamy.[30]

Sarah grew into a prime source for anti-Mormon propagandists: she told the anti-Mormon writer Wilhelm Wyl (Wymetal) that the "Danite Band" had been revived in 1868 with fifty new members sworn to wreak murder and mayhem among the influx of Gentiles. (It is true that the ostensibly "secret" Council of Fifty was revived about that time, but records show it was concerned primarily with the establishment of ZCMI and other cooperative efforts to combat Gentile economic influence.[31] Other outside reporters equally familiar with Mormon affairs dismissed the "Danites" as created "out of air and foolscap.")[32]

Sarah's bitterness once more forced Orson to make the melancholy choice between his family and his Church. He was perhaps used to it by now, but he wrote, "This was a hard and grievous trial to me: but . . . I firmly concluded to follow my convictions, though it should be at the sacrifice of life itself."[33]

Physically, Orson was gaining ground, and Brigham Young had a mission in mind for him—this time to central Europe, which had not been exposed to Mormon preaching. Orson leaped at the chance and was set apart on April 24, 1864. With the overland routes cut off by the commerce of war, Orson left on the new stagecoach line that now linked Salt Lake City with San Francisco. Taking passage for the isthmus he once again endured the four-hour ride over a jungle railroad from Panama to the British port of Aspinwall and then by steamship to Liverpool.[34]

Back in St. George Sarah Marinda Pratt lugged into her back lot a huge pile of diaries, notebooks, journals and sermon jottings—thirty years of her husband's accumulated memoirs—and with a match and a little kindling made a bonfire of his life's record.[35]

Orson's journey of 9,000 miles to preside in Europe left these troubles behind. Rejuvenated by the voyage, his health, by his own account, had never been better: "I feel well in mind, and believe that the Lord is with me to prosper and open the way before me." On a New York stopover he encountered a Salt Lake merchant, William S. Godbe, who slipped him $200 (in the new "greenbacks" which flooded the post–Civil War economy) for his mission and the support of his families at home. Godbe, an affable, bearded, smiling gentleman, was in New York buying warehouse stock for his large outlet in Zion and offered Orson several hundred dollars in dry goods for his wives to sell in their homes. Godbe's generosity so excited Orson that he wrote instructions to the family on setting up a mercantile cooperative among themselves. Putting Marian in charge, he shipped on Godbe's train to Utah bales of shoes, laces, soaps and perfumes, combs, hoopskirts and "Fancy Head dresses" to be sold at the "lowest Salt Lake prices."[36]

With the confidence of the tyro businessman, Orson donned his new broadcloth coat—another gift from a Salt Lake merchant—and lectured the London conference on Tottenham Court Road on the wars that could now be expected with the conclusion of the conflict in America. He told them he had been sent personally to call the righteous out of the heart of spiritual Babylon, the popish empires of the continent. In his exhilaration he informed Juliaet that he had let a few Lincoln-esque whiskers grow: "I am more fleshy than when I was in Utah. I am also letting my beard grow, and as all the front portions of it are white, it gives me quite a venerable and patriarchal appearance. My cheeks are a little more plump with flesh than they were, which somewhat adds to my good looks; upon the whole, I think you would fall in love with me if you could see me. Don't you think so?"[37]

Crossing into the continent for the first time, Orson traveled through the German states, which had closed their borders to Orson Spencer's proselytism in 1852, and went on toward Austria. This huge polyglot empire, welded together by the chains of the "apostolic monarchy" of the Hapsburgs, had never heard of the revelations of backwoods farmer Joseph Smith and entertained no desire to do so. The white-bearded apostle who now shambled from one customs office to another received worse than a hostile reception—he got no attention at all. The government in Vienna eventually gave him a shrug, refused him a visa, and turned him back to the

German authorities. Forced to accept the greatest of his few missionary reversals, he returned to Britain with high spirits deflated. To Juliaet he wrote:

> No one is permitted to teach any religion but the Catholic, either publicly or privately, under heavy penalties. No one is permitted to give away or circulate pamphlets or books under a penalty. No stranger can visit the country without passports. The whole country swarms with police officers whose duty it is to put about one hundred and one questions to all travelers, among which you must inform them where you are from, where you are going, what your business is, how much money you have, what hotel you put up at, how long you intend stopping. You cannot visit from place to place without informing the police.[38]

In the *Millennial Star* he raged against his banishment and called down tides of heavenly fire on the Christians of the Austrian Empire:

> O Austria! the stronghold of Catholicism! Why have you so framed your unholy laws, that the light of truth cannot penetrate your country? Why have you effectually shut out all religious liberty . . . ? Why do you imprison those who meet together to read the Bible? Why do you banish the servants of the Most High from your dominions . . . Do you vainly flatter yourselves that God will not call you to an account . . . That you can forever revel in your filth, and glory in the abundance of your whoredoms? . . . Woes, fearful desolations, and raging pestilences, will sweep over your guilty provinces, and the end thereof shall be with consuming fire.[39]

Nevertheless, Orson loved the Old World and knew that Brigham would call for him when the news of Austrian recalcitrance reached home. In Edinburgh he noted sadly that this might be his last visit to the city that had rewarded him so richly twenty-five years before; and at a conference in Kent he told of an old vision, a dream he had had when he was just a new member of the Church: "[I] had a dream of a high wall . . . upon reaching the top [I] saw the cities of the east, and was told to fly over them with a trumpet. The missions which I have filled have all been in fulfillment of that dream, having always been eastward."[40]

To discourage him even further, worse news awaited him in Liverpool than he had left behind in Austria. Brigham Young had once again taken up the crusade against his writings.

Four apostles, distressed at the continued currency of some of Orson's pamphlets, had met in Brigham's office June 13, 1865, to read over once again the essays *Great First Cause* and *Holy Spirit*, which, though many years in print, struck them anew on this collective reading as false doctrine. The president asked the others what should be done "with these works written by Orson Pratt"—the consensus: to destroy the works.[41] Although Orson's public acknowledgement of his errors was available in the printed discourses, the offending works could still be found in many Latter-day Saint libraries and in the hands of many missionaries sworn to dispense only gospel truth to their hearers. Brigham immediately began the work of suppression.

To over six thousand people gathered in the Tabernacle, Brigham Young began once again a detailed denunciation of the doctrinal speculations of Apostle Orson Pratt. The congregation included prominent Republicans visiting from the East in the party of Mr. Schuyler Colfax, Speaker of the House and future vice-president of the United States. Brigham lashed out against his own without hesitation, however: "Orson Pratt has written extensively . . . when he writes . . . upon subjects which he understands, he is a very sound reasoner; but when he has written upon matters of which he knows nothing, his own philosophy, which I call vain . . . he is wild, uncertain and contradictory."[42]

A few days later George Q. Cannon wrote up an encyclical under Brigham's eye giving exact references from Orson's works that were held unsound and heterodox in spirit. This document went with Brigham as he preached against *Holy Spirit* and *Great First Cause* in stakes and wards from Nephi to Salt Lake. His zeal reached its heights when he thundered "concerning O. Pratt & his publications . . . Orson Pratt would go to Hell . . . He would sell this people for Gold. What would I give for such an apostle, not much and yet we hold him in Fellowship in the Church."[43] To those Saints he could not reach personally he published the following notice in the *Deseret News*:

> Doctrines which have been extensively published and widely received as the standard and authoritative doctrines of the Church, but which are unsound . . . have been published by Elder Orson Pratt. We had expressed our disapproval of some of these doctrines through the columns of the *Millennial Star*, . . . there are others, however, of a kindred character, which have not been alluded to in public print, that also require comment.

There followed a paragraph-by-paragraph denunciation of parts of *The Seer* and the other tracts "as most prominently objectionable and self-confounding" along with advice to the Saints to cut up the essays and destroy all copies of *Biographical Sketches of Joseph Smith the Prophet*:

> [These writings] would convey the idea that the physical and spiritual organization of a human being conferred no additional powers or benefits on the creature thus organized, but that any single atom of the 'spiritual fluid,' however minute, possessed every attribute that an organized being could possess . . . the expounder of these points of doctrine acknowledges that he has not had any revelation . . . in relation to them. The last half of the tract entitled 'Holy Spirit' contains excellent and conclusive arguments . . . the first half . . . contains doctrines which we cannot sanction . . . Where these works are bound in volumes, they should be cut out and destroyed; with proper care this can be done without much, if any, injury to the volumes.[44]

Brigham's objections to Lucy Mack Smith's *Biographical Sketches* focused on the sympathetic treatment of William Smith by his mother. Brigham's aversion to the Prophet's recreant brother was well known.

In England Orson soon learned of the suppression of his works through the columns of the *Star*. By now accustomed to these spasmodic attacks, Orson wrote resignedly home to his president the news of a chest cold, and, almost incidentally, of his total acquiescence in the sacred holocaust of his works:

> Now in Liverpool, resting my lungs . . . I have had the last ten weeks severe cough and cold . . . I learn that many of my writings are not approbated. Anything that I have written that is erroneous, the sooner it is destroyed the better, both for me and the people; for truth is our motto, and eternal truth alone will stand . . . most sincere regrets, in having put you and the highest authorities of this Church to so much trouble and expense . . . [I] most sincerely hope . . . to live near enough to the Lord to avoid all error, and cleave most steadfastly to the light. In the meantime, let me humbly crave forgiveness . . . as touching anything which may have come from my pen, either erroneous or unwise. In relation to doctrine, or prophecy, or philosophy, or science, *truth, and truth alone* is all that I desire. Let my name be recorded among the righteous; let me enjoy the society of my brethren; let me bear a humble part with them in bringing forth and establishing Zion, and my soul will be satisfied—this only is the height of my ambition; this is the great joy of my life—my hope—my salvation—my all. Please present my kind love to the Council, and may God bless you and them forever, is the humble sincere prayer of your brother in Christ.[45]

Orson also published in the *Millennial Star* a renunciation of his own teachings, asking the members of the Church to dispose of any of his work "which meets with the disapprobation of the highest authorities of the Church."[46] For Brigham's part, the *Deseret News* announced that "whoever publishes any new doctrines will be liable to lose his priesthood."[47]

With this firm warning in mind Orson took over the presidency of Britain from Brigham Young, Junior, and genially set about an innocuous series of articles published weekly in *Millennial Star*. Most of his writings were brief homilies rehearsing principles well known among the Saints. However, he did not refrain from subjects as diverse as "Discovery of an American Mastodon" (which he considered a confirmation of the Book of Mormon "elephants")[48] and "Con-sanguineous Marriages." Reporters of Orson's sermons were generally complimentary, impressed with his "lucid, impressive and interesting manner, . . . which appeared to make a deep and very favorable impression on both Saints and strangers."[49]

Accessibility to the printing press in the *Star* office made possible at this time Orson's only published work on mathematics. In June 1866 he offered for sale *A New and Easy Method of Solution of the Cubic and Biquadratic Equations*, a pamphlet which drew sporadic interest in the states and in England, mostly among hobbyists and a few teachers. A safe outlet for his abstruse spirit, the symmetry and economy of numbers drew his attention more and more as a shorthand substitute for describing the universal balance he felt demonstrated the existence of all-pervasive intelligence.

The booklet actually offered little fresh insight into the problems of higher algebra; only a handful of copies ever came off the press, and Orson himself was later dissatisfied with his "discovery." His suggested "equation of differences" was no different from that developed by Lagrange, and his solution of biquadratic equations "is the same as that given by Descartes." A critic has written that Pratt's "method of arrangement of figures in solving a problem may be somewhat easier to use, but that is a matter of personal fancy."[50] Essentially, he had proposed a system that differed only slightly from recognized procedures, although one mathematician later agreed that his ideas had merit: "I have no recollection of ever having seen a general equation representing the differences of the roots of Algebraic Equations, and have no doubt your discovery . . . is new. And you seem to have applied it very profitably in the solution of equations."[51]

For years Orson had corresponded with *Analyst*, an Iowa-based journal for scholars both serious and amateur interested in the solutions of technical problems. In its pages readers were invited to submit their own original math problems. For Orson, working through the periodical was a kind of hobby, and in the 1870s he contributed a number of equations of his own design. But he was not a simple dabbler. For many years he labored over a calculus text, never published, designed for use in the fledgling University of Deseret; over two hundred pages of recastings and derivations from the well-known principles of elementary calculus issued from his pen, and when the work was completed he envisioned a sequel.

Mathematicians who have examined Orson's original proofs in manuscript pronounce him to have possessed "an impressive breadth of mathematical knowledge."[52] Legends have arisen that Orson's *New and Easy Method* was once hailed by scholars worldwide for its revolutionary contributions and "was used in some of the English and French universities";[53] but no evidence exists that this was so, nor do modern historians of science see any justification for such an attitude. Says one, "No new discoveries, new theorems, nor new formulae are given . . . no simple methods which were not already in existence were advanced."[54] His theorems, basically derivative in character, show only that he was indeed conversant with the rudiments of higher mathematics.

After Orson's death a congenial scientist celebrated in his time "gave it as his opinion that there were but four real mathematicians in the world, and Orson Pratt was one of them."[55] Richard Anthony Proctor, himself more a popularizer of scientific "wonders" than a creative contributor, made this extravagant comment before a Salt Lake lecture audience in 1884; the Mormons, drinking in this praise for their revered polymath from such a widely known observer, must have gasped with satisfaction. Proctor had made his own reputation as an astronomer with intriguing publications on the Pyramids of Egypt and other "mysteries" related to the heavens.[56] Coincidentally, although Orson never encountered the famous Proctor, he too was tantalized by the ancient monuments of Egypt. In his later years, he proposed that they had been constructed under divine direction. With his literalistic imagination, Orson began more and more to look to mathematics rather than philosophy. Though his mathematics were not of the highest quality, he nevertheless broke ground as the first theoretician of the West; no one else in the region approached his level of accomplishment in the physical and abstract sciences.[57]

As the Civil War came to an end, Orson Pratt was in the midst of his sixth tour of duty in England. There is some indication that his anti-American sentiment had softened, for he attended a victory celebration at the United States embassy in London after General Sherman took Savannah in January 1865. He encountered here the American minister, Charles Francis Adams, and his secretary, Benjamin Moran. In his journal Moran recorded his impressions. "There have been a good many persons here this morning. I always observe that victories produce friends. The most noted were M. R. Ryan . . . U. S. Consular Agent at Limerick . . . and Orson Pratt, the Mormon leader. This last man is a cool character. He speaks very deliberately and is evidently a shrewd person. His age is 53, he is about 5 feet 6½ in. high—has bluish eyes, mixed grey hair, and a firmly knit figure. He looks like a man who would fight, if need be."[58]

After a final epistle "To the Saints in Great Britain," Orson left Liverpool on April 26, 1867, not to return for a decade. The old emigration office had become more a home to him than the eight households he had left in Utah more than three years before. Upon arrival in New York he was forcefully reminded of the strict discipline Brigham Young maintained over the priesthood; a document withdrawing fellowship from Apostle Amasa Lyman awaited his signature in the mission offices.[59] As each member of the quorum had to give assent to such an action, Orson examined the case carefully. He himself had baptized Lyman over thirty-five years before in New Hampshire and watched Lyman take his own vacated seat in the Council of Twelve at the orders of Joseph Smith. Now Apostle Lyman, it was found, renounced Mormon teachings.[60] When Orson had first encountered him, Lyman was a practicing Universalist openly preaching that salvation was an inevitable gift to every man. Lyman had apparently reverted to his old faith. To Brigham Young and the Twelve, "Universalism" meant denial of the efficacy of Christ's atonement.[61] Given the evidence, Orson had no choice but to sign and reflect on his own brush with excommunication.

Although anxious to return to Utah after such a long absence, Orson was forced to remain in New York a few weeks. Indian depredations on the plains and the still unfinished overland railroad made it imprudent to cross to Utah without adequate protection. He threw in his lot with the same group of Salt Lake merchants who had helped him so generously upon his departure; once again William S. Godbe and one of the Walker brothers along with his old friend George D. Watt took him in and promised him a place in their "merchandise train." The news of Lyman's excommunication troubled them, for the merchants considered Lyman along with Orson Pratt the most intellectual and progressive of the Mormon hierarchy, which they felt was growing more and more oppressive.

All was not well in Zion in the opinion of the merchants, for Brigham's careful control of spiritual matters was no less tight over Utah's economy; the official policy discouraged importing anything from outside that the Saints "could do without." But in the view of these men of commerce, business in Utah could never expand without trade. As Orson wended westward he became an offender himself, for he was packing some dry goods of his own, purchased on credit from Godbe, which he thought "ought to be worth at the retail prices in Utah, about one thousand dollars."[62]

Godbe, Watt, and Orson Pratt arrived in Salt Lake on August 6, 1867, dragging behind them a huge stock of millinery, wholesale textiles, and even sewing machines for Orson's wives. His dream was to "work ourselves, in a few years, into a small capital, that will furnish an annual income . . . for my time is so much occupied in my calling, that I fear that I shall not be able to engage in any occupation which will materially benefit [you] temporally," he wrote Juliaet. The western terminus of the Union Pacific with its promise of a Gentile influx was running perilously close to Utah and Orson found the authorities brooding over the opening of the murderous wounds the people had suffered at the hands of their disagreeable neighbors in Missouri and Illinois. With this in view Brigham established soon after Orson's arrival a new "School of the Prophets" to be conducted in every settlement, composed of leading brethren. The revived "schools" would serve two purposes: first, to draw the elders into close communion on doctrinal points, fencing out the risk of Gentile contamination; and second, to combine economically in a permanent boycott of Gentile and dissident business interests. Orson attended a convention of the school on December 2, where he was appointed to the regency board of the revived University of Deseret.[63]

Brigham Young kept Orson by his side for a few weeks after his return from the extended mission. The two went on tour together apparently somewhat to Orson's chagrin, for he had family he sorely missed scattered from Fillmore to Tooele:

> The President . . . requested me to accompany him on a preaching expedition throughout Utah County, which I did. Before starting I procured a free ticket to go from Pason to Fillmore, . . . but the President hearing of my intentions, requested me to accompany him . . . on a tour to Cashe and Bear Lake vallies . . . This frustrated my contemplated visit to Fillmore. I hope you will not blame me . . . You must begin to think, that you have no husband. Come and see, before I cut off my beard; you will perhaps recognize the voice, if not the countenance.[64]

Orson's work was by no means confined to roaming the territory with President Young. Too busy and too late to do any farming, he once again tried his hand at running his own school. He was still very enthusiastic about his mathematical "discoveries" and proposed through the *Deseret News* to open a mathematics school: "First course, algebra, geometry, trigonometry, surveying, and 'Pratt's Cubic and Biquadratic Equations.' Second course, Analytical geometry and trigonometry, quaternions, conic sections, differential and integral calculus, physics . . . need twenty students, . . . $5 a month, or $6 in merchandise, produce, or wood."[65]

Each week Orson instructed some two to three hundred elders in theology class of the "School of the Prophets" without remuneration—in addition to his general instruction to the Saints nearly every Sabbath. At general conference Orson was assigned a detailed explication of the doctrine of atonement, possibly to combat the dissident influence of Amasa Lyman, and also preached a new emphasis on an old revelation: the 89th section of the *Doctrine and Covenants*, better known as the "Word of Wisdom." Orson himself was an inveterate coffee drinker, his wives sold coffee through their starveling little mercantiles, and considerable tobacco was being imported into Utah Territory. The Twelve themselves only avoided it when they were fasting.[66] Nevertheless Orson lectured the Saints in favor of vegetarianism and against the wanton slaughter of animals. He was also moved to dwell on "home manufactures," the bugbear of Salt Lake's merchant class with which he had such close ties.[67]

Orson undoubtedly had great faith in Brigham's cooperative

"home manufacture" program to relieve "the general scarcity" in Utah Territory. But his own family, deeply in debt to Godbe's mercantile accounts, continued to suffer "in serious straits for breadstuff." Apparently Orson's wives had received only scanty assistance from the tithing office during his absence, but this was immediately discontinued with his return to the valley. One of his wives, Delia, was literally without shelter, living off charity in the dusty little town of Tooele: "Adelia Ann writes: they have lived several weeks by borrowing. Adelia and family have no house to reside in, and the time is about up, when she will have to leave the little bed-room where she has been staying during the winter . . . It is expected that [she] will remain in Tooele city, if they do not perish with starvation."

Delia had only a twelve-year-old son, Lorus, to assist her; but Orson could not come to her aid, for his families in Salt Lake were no better off. "I have taken up from day to day, diligently applying the spade, and digging in the ground to procure a scanty morsel . . . I shall occupy myself in trying to *raise Potatoes*."[68] (The emphasis may indicate his disgust at his plight.) "I have not yet received the first thing for my labors in the office. I do not know but they think that my family and I, have learned to live on nothing, and keep fat."[69] Orson was a painstaking gardener, however; he had a pleasant dooryard garden "expressive of his fine temperament and education." His home on West Temple boasted a beautiful ornamental tree called the "Paradise Tree" that according to family tradition stood undisturbed until 1940, "erect, impressive, and useful."[70]

On the promise of payment he still spent most of his time on office projects. Holed up by a little stove, he wrote day and night behind a partition in Marian's house. After six months his family's lot had improved little by all this labor: "While I have been straining every nerve to pay these debts, my family at Tooele have been almost starving. Adelia Ann has . . . been living with her family out of doors, eating and cooking out of doors, and part of the children sleeping out of doors. She has a very small bed room large enough for her own bed."[71]

To add to his burdens Orson was assigned the immense task, as regent of the university, to transcribe a case of schoolbooks, a speller, Latter-day Saint catechism, and the Book of Mormon into the "Deseret Alphabet," the phonetic script devised years before by

Parley and George D. Watt. The Deseret schoolbooks went slowly, and transcribing the scripture was the labor of a year or more; when it was finally completed, the *Deseret News* called it "the greatest stride yet made in the world toward phonetic reform."[72] Unfortunately, none of the transcriptions was ever used for its intended purpose. The books (which cost $20,000 to produce[73]) rest today in library collections and museum cases, curious relics of Mormon attempts to reform even the spelling of the English language. For Orson, however, this job meant the welcome sum of one thousand dollars, which came close to settling his debts. (This was only partial payment—by 1870, the University of Utah owed Orson, with interest, some six thousand dollars. There is no indication this amount was ever paid.[74])

In the midst of this moribund project, Orson once again faced criticism of his philosophical works during a meeting of the "School of the Prophets" on the afternoon of Independence Day, 1868. As before he confessed his error in opposing revealed doctrine whenever he had done so and "excused himself because of what was written, his mind became darkened and he felt bad." After the apostle had asked forgiveness of the Twelve and of the whole school, President Young pronounced himself satisfied with Orson's confession.[75] Everyone felt spirited and happy at Orson's position, and he was himself considerably relieved. Throughout the summer, Brigham's envoy, young Joseph F. Smith, traveled the territory gathering "items pertaining to Orson Pratt's mission in 1853" probably for the purpose of destroying what publications remained in the libraries of the Saints.[76] Orson was by no means discouraged, however. He continued to preach and read copiously: fascinated by the new translation of Joseph Smith's "Inspired Version" of the Bible published by the Reorganized Church of Jesus Christ of Latter Day Saints, he stayed up nights comparing the remarkable book with the King James Version.[77]

In the fall of 1867 the Reverend Daniel S. Tuttle, who was to become the first Episcopal Bishop of Utah, paid a visit to the LDS general conference and left an account which demonstrates that Orson was still apologizing for those publications. Tuttle describes Orson as "a fine looking, stout man, with a very intelligent forehead, a long flowing white beard, and a pleasant and well-managed voice." As Tuttle entered the Tabernacle, Orson was speaking: "He spoke fluently and well. His ideas were absurd and his theology wild, but rhetorically, oratorically, grammatically, he did admirably well."[78]

Tuttle did not explain how in his view so obviously intelligent and skillful a speaker could be so "absurd" in his ideas, but he left an interesting synopsis of Orson's remarks and Brigham Young's response: "We are to be Gods. Ay, we are to be God . . . brethren we will all be, one day, in one sense, one God; and in another sense we will be, each of us, millions of gods." Orson then apologized for advancing "the idea that an attribute can exist without a person for it to be tabernacled in. I have not meant to teach such doctrine."[79] Orson sat down, Tuttle reports, and President Young stood to deliver, "in a businesslike, almost nonchalant way," what was now a customary injunction to the Saints to beware of some of the teachings of the "Gauge of Philosophy":

> I approve in the main of what Brother Pratt has preached to you. There are one or two exceptions. I take the liberty to point them out. Brother Pratt keeps telling you what the Latter Day Saints believe; that they believe this and they believe that. Now he has no business to preach anything like this . . . Brother Pratt philosophizes too much . . . the elders . . . when they read what he writes or hear what he speaks . . . find themselves in the swamp, in the fog . . . Speculations are ruinous . . . I warn him not to get up to talk more unless he knows what he talks about, . . . and not enswamp us with speculations about what would have been if Christ had not died . . . if Eve had not eaten . . . if man had not fallen . . . if Joseph Smith had not been killed, and what would have been if it hadn't have been, and what would have been if it had have been. If Brother Pratt will stick to the truth and come out of the swamp, I will be thoroughly satisfied with him.[80]

Orson was soon enough called upon to combat the heterodoxies of others in the bosom of Zion. When the railroad finally came through, the Church shepherded its business community into "cooperatives" designed to resist, as Brigham made clear, the inroads of Gentile commerce.[81] But the Main Street merchants balked. Conspiring under the progressive zeal of Elias L. T. Harrison, they announced a "new movement" that they hoped would galvanize Utah into rebellion against the economic and spiritual dictates of Brigham Young. The "liberators," almost to a man converted in Britain under Orson Pratt's written influence, banded together as "the Church of Zion" late in 1869,[82] inaugurating their church with an account of revelations received through spiritualist "mediums" they had consulted when visiting New York's wholesale warehouses. The group included Harrison, Edward Tullidge, T. B. H. Stenhouse, and, to Orson's alarm, his benefactors and friends Godbe and Watt. Their ideology mixed curiously elements of Mormonism (they had all talked with Joseph Smith in a New York séance) with the liberal social gospels of universalism and spiritualism, then thought to be a sort of parascientific substitute for religion. But their motivating force was at least partially their pocketbooks, for ZCMI and other cooperative Church ventures had thinned out Godbe's clientele to a disturbing degree.

The "new movers" were immediately dubbed "Godbeites," and Orson was in the fight from the first. Brigham Young believed that they would listen to Orson Pratt more willingly than to other authorities; Woodruff and Cannon went with him, but Orson fasted and labored with his old friends in vain. They had appealed to Amasa Lyman, now growing old and addled on his farm near Fillmore, to come up and lead them against economic theocracy and the "dictatorship" of the priesthood; Lyman demurred at first but joined them years later, never really taking an active part.[83] Orson told them candidly that he thought they were fools: "No man, when he is commanded by the voice of the priesthood . . . [is] to be his own judge . . . That is not the way of Heaven . . . Now these spirits have taught [you] directly contrary to this."[84]

The eastern newspapers, imagining the Godbeites the beginning of a major schism in the polygamous cult they so firmly and editorially detested, picked up Orson Pratt's replies to the heretics and gave great amounts of space to the debate going on in Utah. Thus Orson got his first nationwide exposure. Though Orson did not prevail with his recalcitrant friends at first, most of them eventually wandered back into the Church or lost interest in their own movement.

Defending the kingdom against eastern pressures became almost as worrisome for Orson as reclaiming the rebels within. With increasing frequency he took the pulpit and the legislative floor in his capacity of chief unofficial apologist for Mormon society. When the East visualized the face of Mormonism, it saw Brigham Young's rigorous countenance; but the voice it heard was Orson Pratt's—placid, stoical, but uncompromising in its own logic. He was always looking for an empirical rationale for Mormonism's peculiar claims. While on a quick trip to New York—his first ride east on the new overland railroad—he had the Deseret Book of Mormon published, and he also

Orson Pratt, fourth from left, and other missionaries in New York City in 1868. *Courtesy, Utah State Historical Society*.

took the opportunity to visit a famous Ethnological Society exhibit that included a stone found near Newark, Ohio, ostensibly carved with Hebrew figures of ancient origin. Whether or not the glyphs were genuine, this provided him with matter for an extensive discourse on "Scientific Dating of the Book of Mormon."[85] When eleven Pullman Palace cars rolled into Salt Lake bearing over a hundred rich members of the Boston Board of Trade, it was Orson who was sent to greet them and to regale them in the Tabernacle with a lecture on the "physiological grounds" favoring the practice of polygamy.

Orson also fought for "the principle" in the territorial legislature, where he served several terms as Speaker. Over his signature an official protest went to Washington concerning the Cullom Bill, an act enabling the federal courts to crush polygamy in Utah. And, while men should be permitted to have plural wives, Orson could see no reason why women should not be permitted to vote. On February 12, 1870, he sent up to the territorial governor legislation giving the franchise to women.[86] Woman suffrage thus found in Orson Pratt's signature one of its earliest legislative imprimaturs in America. When in 1871 Elizabeth Cady Stanton and Susan B. Anthony gratefully attended an Independence Day celebration in Salt Lake City, it was Orson Pratt who gave a "fervent and patriotic prayer, invoking blessings upon the Union and President Grant."[87]

When the Cullom Bill passed the House of Representatives in Washington, three thousand of Utah's just-enfranchised women marched into the Tabernacle to try their new powers. The huge mass meeting, in which Orson served as "vice president," sent the sharp message east that Utah's women sustained the principle of celestial marriage and would not yield on this or any other question of religious conscience.[88] Still, most of the federal congressmen were radical crusaders who had succeeded in dismantling the "barbaric" southern culture and firmly believed Mormon women to be in some kind of bondage with Brigham Young maintaining women as chattels by a system of terror.

Actually, polygamy never involved more than fifteen to twenty percent of all Mormon households even in those days when it was stringently defended by the Church.[89] Mormon men who sustained even two families were rare enough; those with more than two amounted to only a handful of leaders. Some have suggested that the privileges of polygyny were restricted to the prosperous, but Orson's case clearly shows otherwise. Most felt it their duty to set an example by living the principle as far as they could, and Orson, who married his tenth and last wife, Margaret Graham, in 1868,[90] was no exception. In regard to this, Orson wrote in sober terms:

> Believing my proposition to be, not only right, but a duty, I firmly concluded to follow my convictions . . . I have done so, with all the faith and sincerity that I ever had in receiving any religious principle . . . I have done my duty to other branches of my family, and have thus fulfilled the obligations, entered into with them, under the law of the marriage covenant for eternity, which I esteem as equally sacred with all other divine laws and covenants.[91]

The liberals in Utah and the righteous Republicans of the East were not dealing with promiscuity, but, ironically, with a rock-hard, almost Puritan determination to guard the divine sanctuary of conscience.

The Mormons won a temporary reprieve when the Cullom Bill

died in Congress. But the crusaders who had "liberated" the South were by no means discouraged—they would liberate Utah even against her will. In so doing they had the nearly universal support of public opinion in the East. The Senate chaplain, for one, had boiled with evangelical fury while listening to the arguments advanced by Utah's delegate to Congress and determined to reply to the Mormon arguments in favor of polygamy with all the vigor of Protestant certitude.

The Reverend John Philip Newman, chaplain of the United States Senate and pastor of the Metropolitan Church of Washington, D.C., controlled the most prestigious pulpit in the land. He counted among his congregation presidents and ambassadors, justices and congressmen, and in all the splendor of his primacy announced that he would once and for all devastate the Mormon claims that God had any hand in such a system of wholesale licentiousness as the "patriarchal order of marriage." His sermon, advertised two weeks in advance, drew such notables as President Ulysses S. Grant, Vice President Schuyler Colfax, and Chief Justice of the Supreme Court Salmon P. Chase.

The Salt Lake newspapers soon picked up Newman's tirade, which had been published in the *New York Herald*, and everyone immediately turned to Orson Pratt for a reply. Protestant theology had trained its sights on Mormonism, and so it was up to Orson to return the volley. His response dealt mainly with the biblical foundations for the patriarchal order of marriage and, as he pointed to Abraham, Jacob, and Moses, inquired rhetorically of the distinguished chaplain whether such openly polygynous worthies had enjoyed God's approbation or his condemnation. Both points of view were printed in a pamphlet that circulated in Utah; when the enterprising editor of the Mormon-leaning *Salt Lake Telegraph* read it, he offered to sponsor a public debate between Newman and some spokesman for the Church position: "Orson Pratt, for example."

When Newman heard of the challenge, he declared that he would go to Utah to face the enemy in person. The war against the revolting polygamists was no less important than the recently concluded conflict over human bondage, and he drew the theological battle line, with himself as the attacking general. He and his second, a Reverend Sunderland, arrived on the Utah Central from Ogden on August 6, 1870, with the cheers of the nation's leaders still ringing in their heads. Immediately the chaplain announced to Brigham Young that he had arrived "to accept the challenge given in your journal."[92] But the president refused to pick it up.

Brigham had never issued any challenge to debate Newman, came the official word from the Beehive House; if Newman wanted to argue, he could take the matter up with the *Telegraph*. Edward Sloan, the *Telegraph* editor who had suggested the exchange, felt somewhat abashed and offered to take full responsibility in an apology to Newman and the Church leaders. It appeared there would be no debate.

But Brigham may simply have been maneuvering himself out of the way. Perhaps he was secretly pleased that the eastern establishment had come for a dialogue on home ground. With all the publicity accorded Newman, such a debate could possibly turn to the advantage of the Saints. To accomplish this Brigham employed his secret weapon, Orson Pratt. If Orson, better equipped than anyone else in the art of argumentation, could make any points at all against Newman, the image of the Church would immediately improve. On the other hand, if Orson were bested, Brigham could stand aloof and treat the debate as mere contumely between two theologizing hotheads. Accordingly, Brigham suggested through the *Deseret News* that the "discreditable" and "ungentlemanly" Newman take up his argument with Orson Pratt, "whose name [was suggested] in the article."[93]

And so Orson went up against the chaplain to defend Joseph Smith's patriarchal order. Curiously, the disputants had much more in common than an interest in marital practices. Newman to some extent shared Orson's backwoods New York upbringing; he had "started as a rustic." Like Orson he had experienced conversion in his adolescence and devoted his life thereafter to preaching. He had studied Methodist divinity at Cazenovia, New York, when Orson was tramping that very region on one of his early missions. Newman had only recently received a largely honorary degree from Rochester University. Celebrated for his imaginative homiletics, he had gone on to pack churches in Albany and Washington Square, New York, before taking a mission to conquered New Orleans where he built up nine congregations for free blacks. A trip to Palestine resulted in an exhortatory book entitled *From Dan to Beersheba*, which made him famous and brought him to Washington with the incoming Grant administration. There Newman's brilliance provided one of the most corrupt political machines in United States history with weekly harangues on the uprightness of American institutions, to the gratification of his high-placed listeners.

"I know Reverend Dr. Newman very well . . . a splendid man, and as a political preacher he is unsurpassed . . . but we have enough politicians in the Senate already." So ran the opinion of Richard Yates, one Illinois senator known for his candor, when Newman's name was brought up for confirmation as Senate chaplain. For years Newman spoke soothing words to a cabinet and Congress whose members were often secretly and shamefully profiteering in partnership with the railroad interests.[94] As a reward he was later designated "inspector of U.S. consulates." The appointment was a comfortable one, permitting him a leisurely cruise around the world, attending one elegant embassy banquet after another. Although his appointment occasioned some criticism, he was responsible enough in his duties. When the Grant crowd fell into disgrace, Newman followed his general into retirement at New York, secure in his own pious rectitude. A contemporary described Newman in knowing terms: "Fine-spirited . . . a rather grandiose style with rehearsed gestures and pose and a wealth of allusion and illustration drawn from literature and foreign travel . . . his musical and sonorous voice made his audience uncritical of his thought, which was not analytical or profound. In the public mind, he was 'Grant's pastor.' "[95]

No doubt Newman felt self-assured as he entered the Tabernacle on a Friday afternoon to meet his opponent. Both debaters were represented by seconds who had arranged the terms, and a U.S. marshal had been selected to umpire the proceedings. One of the arbitrators raised a titter from the three thousand Saints in attendance when he stood to introduce the first speaker, Professor Orson Pratt—the audience found it amusing to hear a federal judge "introducing" their own apostle to them.[96]

The debaters had agreed to discuss a question rather than an affirmation: "Does the Bible sanction polygamy?" Without wasting words, Orson turned directly to Deuteronomy, chapter 21, verses 15 through 17: "If a man have two wives, one beloved, and another hated, and they have borne him children, both the beloved and the hated; and if the first-born be hers that was hated: Then it shall be when, he maketh his sons to inherit that which he hath, that he may not make the son of the beloved first-born before the son of the hated."

The passage actually deals with the problem of primogeniture, but Orson's implication was clear: not only did the laws of God contain no proscription of polygamy, but they regulated the practice as a matter of course.[97] Orson thus set the pattern for the debate. For three days, each spoke for one hour each day, amicably contesting the proper contextual interpretations of numerous Bible passages. The men became engrossed in the technical problems of translation, but Orson soon felt he had stymied the chaplain on a critical verse, Leviticus 18:18: "Neither shalt thou take a wife to her sister, to vex her."

To Orson this verse implied that plural marriage was sanctioned in ancient Israel so long as the relationship did not involve sisters who would "vex" each other. Newman asserted a marginal reading of the verse; he maintained that the King James Version was in error, that the verse actually implied a flat prohibition of polygamy. The debate narrowed to this question; all else became secondary, for Newman emphatically hinged his whole case on his marginal understanding of Leviticus 18:18:

> Now I propose to produce a law this afternoon, simple, direct and positive, that polygamy is forbidden in God's holy word. In Leviticus xviii and 18 it is written: "Neither shalt thou take one wife to another, to vex her, to uncover her nakedness, besides the other in her life time." There is a law in condemnation of polygamy . . . what I have read is as it reads in the margin . . . He [Pratt] says—"inasmuch as polygamy is nowhere condemned in the law of God, we are entitled to construe this law as applying to polygamists." But I have shown already that Leviticus xviii. 18. is a positive prohibition of this law . . . "Neither shall a man take one wife unto another:" and I will try every passage by this law.[98]

The next and final day of the debate, Orson offered his refutation of Newman's proposed "law" against polygamy. Pulling out his Hebrew Bible, Orson read the original clause, in the original tongue, to his audience: *veishah el ahotah lo tikkah*. The grammatical relationships among the words, Orson calmly explained, could by no stretch of the imagination imply a prohibition of taking more than one wife:

> Somebody, I know not whom, some unauthorized person, has inserted in the margin another interpretation: recollect, in the margin and

> not in the text. It is argued that this interpretation in the margin must be correct, while King James' translators must have been mistaken . . . The gentleman reads the passage "Thou shalt not take one wife to another," . . . But does the language forbid, as the margin expresses it, the taking of one wife to another? No; we have the privilege . . . to apply to the original Hebrew. What are the Hebrew words—the original—that are used? *Veishah el ahotah lo tikkah*: this, when literally translated and transposed is, "neither shalt thou take a wife to her sister," *veishah* being translated by King James' translators "wife," *el-ahotah* being translated "to her sister;" *lo* is translated "neither;" while *tikkah* is translated . . . "shalt thou take." . . . The phrase will then read: . . . *Neither shalt thou take one sister to another* . . . It will be seen that the latter form of translation gives precisely the same idea as that given by the English translators in the text . . . the passage from the margin was quoted by Dr. Newman as a great fundamental law by which all the other passages were to be overturned. But it has failed.[99]

Reverend Newman was now in a very uncomfortable position: he was disputing the wording of the King James Version, the standard text both had agreed upon. Newman was calling in question his own Bible.

The deferential parrying ended as Newman flailed around for some substantiation of his reading. But at least from the Mormon perspective, he had missed the point: historical and exegetical disputes over the Bible merely underscored the need for inspired prophets to give out correct interpretations.

Despite the technical character of the debate, the rapt audience increased dramatically. By the third day, more than eleven thousand listeners had packed the new Tabernacle for the two-hour final exchange.[100] Verbatim reports of the proceedings, printed in the *Deseret Evening News*, came stuttering over the wires to the eastern newspapers, and the *New York Herald* reserved them front-page space. The debate had taken on the proportions of "an international drama."[101]

When Newman returned to Washington, he was greeted with plaudits. He had devastated the Mormons and gained a great rhetorical victory in the fight for enlightened Christianity in Utah. His followers ignored the fact that no standard commentary, Jewish or Christian, would back up his reading of Leviticus. Those who did know quietly conceded that Newman's tortured assertions had been hopeless in the face of Orson Pratt's competence in Hebrew. The

Church newspaper *Banner of Light* cackled, "Someone carrying more guns than Dr. Newman will have to be sent out missionarying among the Mormons."[102] A Catholic writer later recalled, "Newman, whatever his qualifications as chaplain of the Senate or his merits as an orator, proved neither a scripture scholar nor an apt debater, and his anthropology was both strange and wonderful . . . Pratt, a clever, though equally shallow, polemist, scored heavily . . . The debate showed a tendency to wander off into Hebrew roots, about which it is extremely doubtful whether either contestant had more knowledge than he could bone up the night before."[103]

From the Mormon perspective, Orson had scored a genuine triumph over the "wise and learned of the world," and, if the outcome of the debate was unclear, there was no question that Orson Pratt had shown himself more than equal to the president's spiritual adviser.[104] The world's sunken opinion of Mormonism now had to account for this carefully reasoned defense of an "indefensible" system. More important, the Pratt–Newman debate lent a certain legitimacy to the spiritual claims of Mormonism. Indeed, the very fact of the debate alone had this effect.

One modern non-Mormon professor of Hebrew gives the victory to Orson Pratt, who had proved by logical analysis and "massive" comparison of all the syntactic parallels in the Old Testament that Newman's reading was an imposition unjustified by the original grammar. The Revised Standard Version of the Bible along with several important Bible commentaries agree with Orson Pratt on the sense of the Hebrew in Leviticus leaving polygamy permissible if not sanctioned.[105]

Orson observed his fortieth anniversary as a member of the Church not long afterwards. Although among his people he had been viewed as a visionary, an advocate of impractical and dangerous philosophies, perhaps even heterodox, his apostolic courage and the value of his erudition had at last been publicly recognized. *Millennial Star* in England printed the word-for-word account of the great debate only a few weeks later with an evaluation of Orson's performance: the piece was entitled "Plucky."[106] But his able defense of the Latter-day Saints was earning him a more noble nickname, one more fitting the pilgrimage of this epistolary and philosopher: they called him "The Saint Paul of Mormondom."[107]

11

Key to the Universe

Temple Block in Salt Lake City had been the center of the Mormon world since Orson Pratt traversed the spot on July 21, 1847. It was also the center of his personal world. By 1870, the six towers of the temple had risen only five feet above the solid shafts of the foundation. Hundreds of ox teams snorted in and out of the adobe gates each week dragging granite slabs that were then hoisted into place by sagging pine derricks. In the northwest corner of the square stood a mysterious little building. This was the Endowment House—like Moses' tabernacle in the wilderness, a temporary temple for the sacred ordinances of the Latter-day Saints. Here the ceremonies of the endowment and sealing of eternal marriages could be performed until the completion of the sacred grey fortress a few rods away. Orson Pratt, with a number of sons, daughters, and wives, came here several times that summer to be baptized for their dead.

In cooperation with Reverend Frederick Chapman of Connecticut, Orson had obtained and helped publish the names of thousands of his relatives, descendants of the first settler, Lieutenant William Pratt. By the end of the summer every individual known on those records had been baptized by proxy. Baptism and other ordinances for the dead were rarely performed in the Endowment House—it was thought best to serve only the living there until the temple could be finished. However, Orson and his family were baptized over twenty-six hundred times that summer; Orson interrupted the sessions only to prepare for his debate with Newman.[1] To that time no one in the

Orson Pratt's observatory on the southeast corner of Temple Square. *Courtesy, Church Archives, Church of Jesus Christ of Latter-day Saints.*

church of the Latter-day Saints had done as much of the genealogy and proxy ordinances mandated in Joseph Smith's revelations as had Orson Pratt.

In the opposite corner of Temple Block was another little cabin, much smaller than the Endowment House. Erected in 1869, the one-room shanty stood very near the spot where Orson had two decades before located Salt Lake City in relation to the rest of the world. This building was the Salt Lake observatory, one of a chain of observatories constructed from Cambridge, Massachusetts, to San Francisco under the direction of George W. Dean of the United States Coastal Survey.[2] A first-class astronomical clock rested on one table along with a "Bond's chronographic register," a machine capable of recording time to the hundredths of a second. On another stand Orson Pratt was allowed to keep his prize English telescope; when a row of slats in the roof was opened, two full transits of the night sky could be observed through its three-inch lens. The primary purpose of the observatory was to obtain meridian solar readings every day at noon to

Temple Square with observatory. *Courtesy, Church Archives, Church of Jesus Christ of Latter-day Saints.*

ascertain the correct time for the community's clocks and watches, but Orson spent many long night hours in the little house taking astronomical observations for his own purposes. And in the corner of the room a squat stone obelisk marked the exact intersection of the Salt Lake Base and Meridian, the points established by Orson Pratt from which the entire Great Basin had been surveyed into sections and townships.[3]

The buildings on opposite sides of the Temple Block thus symbolized the two great forces in Orson's life: his science and his faith in the supreme intelligence revealed by Joseph Smith. Both allowed him to take his bearings on the cosmos.

Astronomy possessed him increasingly as he grew older. Part of his interest grew out of natural curiosity, but he also saw in the behavior of distant worlds and nebulous stars the "grand key" described by Joseph Smith[4] which would explain the purpose of creation. Orson spent much effort trying to communicate this to the Saints:

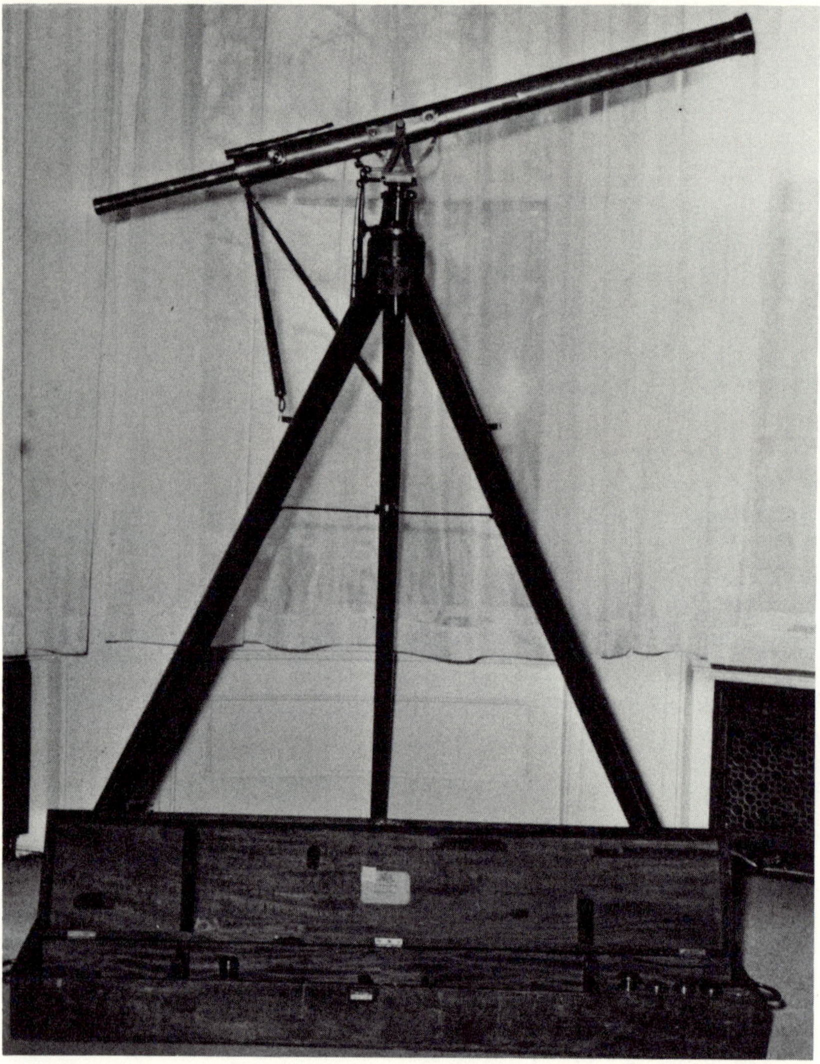

The telescope that Orson Pratt used in his Temple Square observatory. *Courtesy, Utah State Historical Society.*

> Professor O. Pratt is to deliver a series of astronomical lectures under the auspices of the University of Deseret, every Tuesday and Friday evening until the course is completed . . . as the rooms of the university are not sufficiently spacious, it has been decided to throw open the Tabernacle, and to extend, free of charge, the privilege of hearing the lectures to all . . . Professor Pratt has given a great share of the time at his disposal, when not engaged in the ministry, to the subject of Astronomy, and its kindred science mathematics, and in both he is acknowledged to have few superiors.[5]

Still popular because of the plural marriage debates, Orson drew audiences of three thousand and more to his lectures. He discussed planetary motion and formation, denounced the "nebular theory" of LaPlace as insufficient, and speculated on the sun's origin and possible character as a "glorified world." Orson's "astrotheology" must have fascinated the Mormons; his lectures were reproduced in full in the *Deseret News Weekly*, which also commented with surprise on the size and animation of the audiences: "The learned professor must feel highly gratified at the great interest manifested by the public."[6]

One of Orson's listeners was Brigham Henry Roberts, a young man destined to take Orson's place as the foremost Mormon intellectual of his time. Roberts was fascinated with Pratt's lectures on astronomy and mathematics, which, as he later wrote, "had structure and symmetry, like a column of Roman soldiers marching by in stately, regular fashion, or it was more nearly like the unfolding of a scroll which you followed chained to the reading of it as it was unfolded, its stately treatment of the facts, and of which you never tired."[7] Roberts's later career paralleled Orson's in striking ways: he too would become a general authority of the church and he would also find himself at the center of serious doctrinal controversies in the next century.

Pratt continued to promote better organization and funding for the University of Utah (known as the "Parent School") and the lesser schools throughout the territory. He disputed "the dominant group of so-called practical men . . . who questioned the desirability or propriety of more than minor or supplementary Territorial support for colleges."[8] As professor of mathematics, astronomy, and "Moral Science,"[9] Orson was usually paid with "wheat, potatoes, flour . . . the teachers' salaries, instead of being drawn on a bank, were drawn on wheel-barrows," in the words of Levi Edgar Young.[10] To help advance the cause of teachers like himself, he attended the organizational meeting of the "Territorial Teachers' Association" at the University in October, 1873.[11]

As an educator Orson valued above all a thorough study of mathematics. In 1860 he said, "There is no study which is so well calculated to give a concentration of mind as that of geometry or mathematics. If a person follows these studies, he . . . obtains power to abstract his mind from surrounding objects . . . He reasons from known relations to those which are unknown."

Orson believed that man does not reach his fulfillment until he possesses the power of God, and the only way to obtain this power is by "concentration of mind" upon the principles of faith. The trained mind, inspired by the "spirit of revelation," can open "the hidden mysteries of the works of God . . . of astronomy, chemistry, geology, and ten thousand mysteries." The concentration which brings us to a knowledge of "the great system of universal truth" must not be neglected: "There are many hours that run to waste which might be profitably employed in training the mind, when the body is not fatigued, which are spent in idleness or foolishness . . . hours and hours which might be profitably spent in disciplining the mind and treasuring up both spiritual and natural knowledge, that often run to waste."

Like most natural theologians of his time, Orson emphasized that reason and revelation go hand in hand, but the great tragedy of the human race is the waste of mental and spiritual energy, the lack of concentration on learning the eternal truths: "The study of science is the study of something eternal . . . let all classes of citizens and people endeavor to improve their time more than heretofore—to train their minds . . . it is not only necessary to have a single eye to the glory of God in searching for religious truths, but also in acquiring scientific truths, and in all our researches for truth we should seek the aid of the Spirit of God."[12]

Whatever conflicts Orson had experienced because of his equal commitments to reason and revelation did not seem to trouble him now. He could speak of both on alternating Sabbaths. One week his subject might be "Zion"; the next week he might delve into "The Nature of Light." He was not affected by the intense rush of religious doubt that flooded the scientific community in the mid-nineteenth century; his contempt for sectarianism came from a "revealed" perspective rather than a scientific or philosophical one.

The world of knowledge was open for the Saints to explore because, as Orson believed, very little was really understood about the gospel, let alone of the complexities of the physical universe.

His Mormon convictions remained absolute: "I received a testimony . . . that gave knowledge that the work was of God; it was not through the administration of angels, or open vision, but through the Holy Ghost."[13] His firm, yet tolerant, sense of commitment and his long proximity to the prophets made him a natural counselor to many who were troubled. Because the aging Brigham Young had to deal with the temporal needs of a Church under siege, doctrinal questions increasingly flowed to Orson instead. He commented on the relative powers of the priesthood offices, on baptism for deceased children (unnecessary, he deemed), and on the promises made to the "Lamanites." Letters came in frequently from Saints who trusted him asking him questions about Brigham's statements, some of which seemed to equate God the Father with Adam. Orson simply refuted the idea from the Bible. One question troubled many elders: were those who did not take plural wives living God's law? Orson responded: "Celestial marriage is a law of the Church, and plural marriage, when it is commanded, is likewise a law unto the individual so commanded." (This distinction no doubt caused at least a few sighs of relief.)[14]

There was little relief for Orson Pratt and his own polygamous families. The alienation between Orson and Sarah became more public and more bitter. She complained that Orson had gradually become estranged from her children: "He spoke harshly to them. He had and has no interest in their careers. But as for me, these children are my only pride; if they were not living, and if they did not love me, as I know they do, I should not wish to live another hour."

Sarah's objection to the polygamy doctrine became rejection of all the tenets of Mormonism, and she was grateful that of her six living children "not one of them is a Mormon."[15] (This was not entirely true, as her deaf son Laron remained a practicing Mormon all his life. The other children were indifferent or hostile to the Church.) Sarah herself apparently became involved in the spiritualist movement among the "Godbeites": Amasa Lyman recorded that he "visited Sister Sarah Pratt and family held Seance with them" on March 9, 1871. Another guest, someone named Lorenzo, "was controlled for writing [practiced automatic writing] for the first time."[16]

Sarah also became embittered against Brigham Young at this time. After her return from St. George in 1865, she had accepted Brigham's offer of her old home back (he had purchased it for $4,000 upon Orson's departure for the Dixie mission). Now, apparently because he felt Sarah was disloyal to her husband and to the Church, he asked for the return of the property, located on the northwest corner of the block south of Temple Square. Sarah fought him before the Probate Court, which ruled that "Sarah M. Pratt is not the legal and rightful owner and occupant of the property therein in controversy, but that the said Brigham Young, senior, is the rightful owner and occupant thereof and entitled to a deed in fee simple thereto." Sarah fought the decision in higher courts, remaining in the house for nearly three years. She was excommunicated for "apostacy" (*sic*) on October 4, 1874, and her son, United States Deputy Marshal Arthur Pratt, followed her the next day,[17] Unfortunately, she found no sympathy from her estranged husband, who wrote to the *Deseret News*: "It is with extreme regret, and deep sorrow, that I witness the attempt of my wife Sarah to procure through the technicalities of the law the property which rightfully and justly belongs to another."[18] The courts wavered, the District Court awarding the rights to Sarah, but the Supreme Court finally ruled for Brigham Young in the summer of 1876.[19]

The following spring Sarah lashed out at her husband and the polygamous system in an interview with the *New York Herald*. The document contains many errors, reporting that Sarah had known Brigham Young as a "vulgar illiterate boy" and that she had married Orson before his introduction to Mormonism. The journalists of the day were often unscrupulous in coloring their reports, particularly about Mormonism, but the tenor of Sarah's remarks is probably genuine and reflects her understandable grief:

> I doubt . . . whether any tongue could describe the sufferings I endured . . . I was a witness to the change in my husband's manner and disposition which always accompanied polygamy as it is practised in Utah . . . Here was my husband, for example, gray headed, taking to his bed young girls in mockery of marriage.
>
> Of course there could be no joy for him in such an intercourse except the indulgence of his fanaticism . . . The inevitable result came about at last . . . he lost his former feeling for his legal wife, forgot whatever affections he may have had for other so-called wives, and came to look upon and treat his women as if they were cattle. I clung to him as long

as God and duty to my children would let me. It was with a pang that I separated from him at last. But the pang is over."[20]

The evidence of Orson's letters to his wives suggests quite a different picture from the one Sarah paints. He often wrote of his tender feelings and sympathy for their hardships. However, Sarah does not exaggerate Orson's "fanaticism": to him it was merely single-minded performance of his duty to God.

Orson's loyalty exacted unremitting travel and office work as well. Assigned to revise the scriptures of the Church, he spent many hours poring over the revelations and the Book of Mormon drawing detailed cross-references, breaking up illogical or amorphous paragraphs into shorter verses, and rearranging the texts in modest ways. Misspellings were corrected—"wrecked" becomes "racked" in Alma 27:29—and modifying phrases and referent pronouns moved around to make better sense. All in all, Orson Pratt was responsible for about three percent of the differences between the original Book of Mormon and present-day editions. Orson also arranged the *Doctrine and Covenants* chronologically; his was the first edition to contain 136 sections in the order given by revelation.[21] Another project was the revision of the *Pearl of Great Price*, a singular book of scripture containing writings of Joseph Smith including the intriguing Book of Abraham and passages from Smith's reworking of Genesis. Orson drew the text for the 1878 "Book of Moses" from the "New Translation" of the Bible published in 1867 by the Reorganized Church of Jesus Christ of Latter Day Saints.[22]

Book work and legislative duties as Speaker occupied Orson in Salt Lake while most of his brethren had been assigned to preside in outlying areas—Orson Hyde in Sanpete County, Charles Rich at Bear Lake, and Lorenzo Snow at Brigham City. Of the older apostles, John Taylor and Wilford Woodruff kept Orson company in the capital. They frequently traveled together as Brigham Young's emissaries. Given the success of the "cooperatives" and a national economy depressed by the Panic of 1873,[23] Brigham felt the time was right to reestablish the "Order of Enoch." Joseph Smith's vision of a millenarian community in which all things would be held in common had lapsed over the years particularly since the financial disasters at Kirtland. But at the April conference of 1874 Orson Pratt and John Taylor received a directive to organize the stakes into cooperative economic ventures.

The two apostles carried a list of officers for a "United Order"[24] in the St. George Stake but proceeded to organize the intervening communities as well. At Ephraim they demonstrated for the people the rules of conducting the order, appointed a new stake presidency, and set in order the government of Sanpete County as well. Upon returning from the southern settlements, Orson presided over the formation of small United Order projects in the individual wards of Salt Lake City. In Bountiful he organized a large cooperative mercantile and manufacturing institution with over $12,000; the "BCMI" was soon thriving.[25] These economic experiments heartened Orson, for it meant that the order of Zion might be in sight. He preached often and radiantly these days about the coming Millennium. The day he offered the dedicatory prayer for the huge new ZCMI building on Main Street,[26] he could look out over one of the largest warehouses in America and see nothing but the "City of Enoch."

The "United Order of Enoch" (so named for Enoch's Zion described in the Book of Moses)[27] Orson considered a necessary condition for the celestial society described in the revelations of Joseph Smith. He had waited long for its realization. "Forty-three years ago we were commanded to become one in regard to our property. Forty-three years we have been in disobedience. Forty-three years have rolled over our heads, and we are far from oneness still."[28] In *The Seer* he had described the "Zion of Enoch" as a society " 'of one heart and one mind, and there were no poor among them,' a perfect union of sentiment and feeling . . . no person seeking to aggrandize himself by heaping up riches while others were poor."[29] "The Saints are not only one in doctrine, but they are to be made one in temporal things . . . The same order of things existed in the Zion of Enoch: there were no poor among them. And the same order of things must exist in the Zion of the Latter-days . . . Anything short of a perfect equality in temporal things is a sin: hence, the Lord says, '*It is not given that one man should possess that which is above another, wherefore, the world lieth in sin.*' "[30] Twenty years before the institution of the United Order, Orson foresaw it in his essay "The Equality and Oneness of the Saints": "We want to see the time come, that when the Saints arrive in Utah, all their surplus property shall be consecrated . . . And when the Saints have learned to keep this inferior law of consecration, it will prepare them to keep the more perfect one, when they shall return to build up Zion according to the celestial order; when all the riches and wealth of Zion shall be common property."[31]

Orson's perpetual financial difficulties may have influenced his emphatic repetition in many writings and discourses that "it is not given that one man should possess that which is above another."[32] At times he keenly felt his own poverty and resented all his life the arrogance of the rich and powerful. But the United Order also represented a logical part of his theological system, an indispensable step forward to the "celestial order" which was to prevail in the Millennium. "I rejoice exceedingly to hear, that the President has been moved upon . . . to alter the order of things that has existed for many years here in these mountains, among the Latter-day Saints. In what respect? To bring about a united order of things in regard to their property and labor . . . a different order of things that will strike the axe at the root of this pride and distinction of classes. I am glad; I rejoice in it."[33] He attributed the Saints' sad history of persecution and drivings to their failure to conform to the "united order of things"—"Now, why is it, Latter-day Saints, that we have been tossed to and fro and smitten and persecuted for these many years? It is because we have disobeyed the law of heaven, we have not kept the commandments of the Most High God, we have not fulfilled his law."[34]

He also expected the United Order to clear away the chief obstacle to an earthly Zion society: "An inequality in riches lays a foundation for pride . . . while those who are poor labour and toil from morning until evening to procure a scanty subsistence; . . . their children are not so highly educated . . . it produces great inequality in education . . . It is the great barrier erected by the devil to prevent that unity and oneness which the Gospel requires."[35] Riches or their lack stand as a wall between man and his fundamental purpose in life—"to grasp the fulness of all knowledge."[36] This wall must be taken down: "It is true, there may be obstacles in the way by which [a] being is prevented from acquiring . . . truth; but remove all obstacles and place the being in a favorable condition . . . We can see no possible hindrance to its advancement in knowledge . . . wherever a being exists that has any knowledge, . . . that being has infinite capacities, capable of perceiving all things past, present, and to come, just as soon as the intervening barriers are removed."[37] Inequality in riches must not be allowed to distract man from the serious business of the "grand school of experience" wherein he progresses toward a fulness of knowledge. In this respect Orson's Zion society resembles the transcendentalist vision of Utopia, a community with every man going to "tinker upon our *lives* to improve *them*," as Thoreau expresses it, rather than amassing wealth.[38] Nineteenth-century American philosophers with their Baconian leanings dreamed of realizing Bacon's "New Atlantis," a paradise of learning, "a utopian society guided by a community of scholars who devoted themselves entirely to research, to the organization of knowledge, and to the pursuit of wisdom."[39] Surely Orson Pratt's conception of a celestial order on earth was similar to Bacon's; but this philosopher's paradise required that men sacrifice the pursuit of wealth: "As it regards earthly things, temporal things, the riches of this world, or the honors of this world, I will not say they are of a secondary nature to me, but they are far beneath this [the things God has revealed], which belong to our peace, happiness, and welfare, both here and hereafter."[40]

But to the more practical minds among the Church authorities, the United Order was less a fulfillment of principle than a quick solution to the hardships imposed by the depression of the mid-1870s. Brigham Young made it quite clear that this was no "new system, order or doctrine." He compared it to measures taken by other communities to save themselves from economic ruin. "There are numbers of organizations of a similar character, as far as they go, in our own country and in other countries. Our object is to labor for the benefit of the whole, to retrench in our expenditures; to be prudent and economical; to study well the necessities of the community, and to pass by its many useless wants; to study to secure life, health, wealth, and union."[41] In other words, the United Order was good economics in a time of panic and scarcity. Others were invited to speak freely on the merits of the proposal; Erastus Snow for one saw it as a kind of "mutual insurance institution" to "afford security and protection."[42] These remarks reveal a view that the Order was necessary to get the community through hard times. It is not surprising, then, that most of the Orders were dissolved as the economy began to improve.[43] The grand step forward to the earthly Zion envisioned by Orson Pratt did not materialize as he had anticipated.

The Millennium was to be long in coming, and the fight between federal government and Church over polygamy was intensifying. The

Mormons had little wherewithal to carry on the battle. A few Church leaders hoped for a political solution. Utah tended to be anti-Republican, a result of the offensive crusades against the Saints carried on by the Radicals. A Democratic government might permit Utah to join the Union and gain her sovereignty. As expected, the 1876 Democratic platform of Samuel Tilden preached forbearance toward the Mormons, and the Utahns dared to hope for statehood once again. But Tilden was barred from the White House by a shameful bargain falsifying the election results of three southern states.[44] The Saints despaired another four years under the pharisaical eyes of the Republican Stalwarts.

Congress began finding ways to enforce the polygamy statutes, moving the religious controversy into the courtrooms of Utah. As the defender of "the principle," Orson was interrogated several times by a grand jury but stayed laconically within the bounds of the questions put to him. When asked if he knew anything about the marriages of George Q. Cannon, he replied that he would not know the Cannon family if he met them on the street. Another time the prosecution questioned him about his advocacy of "theocracy" in the pamphlet *Kingdom of God*. Here was an inquisition of a different sort. Orson had written that the kingdom of God is "the only legal government that can exist in the world,"[45] and the federal lawyers interpreted the statement as subversive; "Perhaps no other statement by a Mormon leader gained as much notoriety in anti-Mormon literature," observed Klaus J. Hansen.[46] Orson answered the prosecutor that he had spoken in purely ecclesiastical terms with no disobedience to civil government implied or intended.[47]

Over the pulpit, however, Orson continued his flaming vindication of plural marriage contrasting it with the tawdriness of being "joined together by a justice of the peace."[48] He reiterated the biblical grounding for polygamy that the gates of the New Jerusalem "will be inscribed with the names of twelve polygamous children"—the tribes of Israel—and that Deuteronomy clearly sustains the practice.[49]

Along with the other authorities of the Church, Orson settled in for a lengthy siege while the courts reviewed the antipolygamy laws. The Church leaders were clearly tired of the fight but kept quiet and refused to say more than was necessary. Orson published a brisk denial of rumors that his own son, Marshal Arthur Pratt, had arrested him on polygamy charges[50] but was careful to say nothing about the circumstances of anyone else. He looked around now and saw his aging brethren struggling to maintain their families and covenants in the face of legal persecution.

Now over sixty, Orson inevitably began to reflect on his life's work. Looking back with both anxiety and satisfaction, he took up the historian's pen. Orson's discourses increasingly turned into reminiscences. He wished wistfully that someone "with a good memory" would write a small, plain history of Joseph Smith[51] and smiled to recall what a "slow and awkward writer" was the man who produced the Book of Mormon.[52] One winter morning in the new Tabernacle, Orson reflected for a few moments on the revelation he had received when nineteen years old from the Prophet's mouth:

> I wonder if I have fulfilled that commandment as I ought to have done . . . felt sometimes to condemn myself for my slothfulness and little progress . . . to prophesy out of my own heart is something perfectly disagreeable to my feelings . . . I have oftentimes avoided . . . when a thing would come before my mind pretty plain, uttering or declaring it for fear that I might get something out . . . that was wrong. I have endeavored . . . to inform my mind as far as I could by reading what God has revealed . . . I have derived great advantage and . . . edification from reading and studying that which God has revealed to others.[53]

Here emerges an almost indefinable lack of confidence; clearly, he suspects his own inspirations and fears he has relied too much on "pretty plain" reasoning to the detriment of his own and others' progression. He now finds his former speculations distasteful, "perfectly disagreeable to my feelings." He nevertheless considers his reading and study to be the saving factor of his life.

Although Orson looked with some dismay at his own past, he was delighted in 1874 to receive an appointment to serve as historian of the Church. He had always seen a providential thread in every trial, every exile, and every mission and felt that the rise of the Mormon church simply culminated the evolution of human events toward the Apocalypse. The records of these sacred events would write more than mere history—he would literally be compiling a new Chronicles for a new chosen people, and Orson threw all his energy into the new assignment.

He now had a large office, a two-story building facing Brigham

Young's Beehive House, crammed with old library volumes and mountains of manuscripts and letterbooks. From this he was determined to create an orderly account of God's people. He assigned himself the duty of recording every day's events, clipping relevant items from newspapers, and putting the whole together in a "journal history" of the diurnal drama of Mormonism. In two years, he compiled and copied over ten thousand pages.

While he wrote the history, he was also part of it—a fact that came home forcefully when he was invited to join the first "Old Folks' Excursion" in honor of Brigham Young's seventy-fifth birthday. With reverence for the aging pioneers, Salt Lake City nearly closed down on June 8, 1876, while 800 people over 65 boarded a festooned train for a day's outing in Utah Valley. The three oldest apostles, Orson Pratt, Wilford Woodruff, and John Taylor, spoke to the gathering and blessed them all.[54]

Few had publicly contemplated Brigham's passing, or what would become of the Church the day its leader was no longer there. Many thought of Orson Pratt as the second man in the Church and expected him to succeed if the president were to die. Others were confident that the senior apostle, Orson Hyde, would be the logical successor. In October 1861 Brigham had declared that seniority in the Twelve determined succession and that this seniority was based on date of ordination. At that time Orson Pratt had been sustained as second apostle after Hyde, and Brigham had been very careful to call for the sustaining vote of the general conference every six months on each apostle in order.[55] But suddenly in June 1875, Brigham announced that he had reconsidered the entire matter; henceforth, seniority would be a matter of continuous service in the quorum.

Again the shadows of 1842 arose and blighted any possibility that Orson Pratt would succeed to the Presidency of the Church. There was little ambition in his character in any case, but a tinge of humiliation must have accompanied this reshuffling of rank, particularly in view of his long service in both quorum and Church. Hyde fell with him, for he also had suffered a brief period of disaffection in the 1830s, and Pratt found himself now ranked fifth in the council, after Taylor, Woodruff, George A. Smith, and Orson Hyde.

President John Taylor explained the events leading up to this change in a discourse the day after Orson Pratt's funeral in Salt Lake City. Apparently George A. Smith had brought up the "impropriety" of permitting Pratt and Hyde to return to their standings in the Twelve after having been dropped from the quorum. Smith had told Taylor of his feeling that Taylor "stood before them in the quorum." Taylor responded:

> I told him that I was aware of that . . . but that I did not choose to agitate or bring up a question of that kind. Furthermore, I stated that, personally, I cared nothing about the matter, and, moreover, I entertained a very high esteem for both the parties named; while at the same time, I could not help but see, with him, that complications might hereafter arise, unless the matters were adjusted. Some time after, in Sanpete, in June, 1875, President Young brought up the subject of seniority, and stated that John Taylor was the man that stood next to him; . . . He also made the statement, that Brother Hyde and Brother Pratt were not in their right positions in the Quorum. Upon this statement, I assumed the position indicated.[56]

Some have suggested that Brigham's memory was even longer than the 1842 excommunication: Orson Pratt's 1837 affidavit accusing Joseph of "lying" and "extortion" was probably not easily forgotten.[57]

In the spring of 1877 Orson and Marian Ross Pratt boarded the Utah Western for St. George to attend the dedication of the temple there. The elderly president of the Church had established residence there and called the general conference to convene in the southern settlement which Orson had helped pioneer. The arrival of the authorities in St. George compounded the excitement begun by the execution only days before of one John D. Lee for his part in the Mountain Meadows Massacre. The new temple with its walls of white stucco, so like the battlements of the house of the Lord at Nauvoo, struck Orson. He preached the first day in the new assembly room, invoking the ardent romance of the Kirtland dedications and the greater blessings of Nauvoo with its washing, anointings, and endowments.[58] He then listened to the sermons given by Brigham Young in the avuncular voice of age; the president once again made his text the divine fatherhood of Adam.[59]

The house at St. George signified for Orson the reopening of the celestial school of progress begun so many years before in Kirtland. Another such edifice rose far to the north where a few weeks later Orson knelt on a muddy hill in Logan to sanctify the broken ground for a third Utah temple.[60] On July 18, 1877, Orson left Utah for the first time in eight years.

Although burdened by the scriptural revision project and the work of the historian's office, Orson had enjoyed an unusually long respite between missions. He had passed eighteen of his sixty-five years as a wanderer for the cause of the new dispensation among the hostile nations of Europe and America. Now Brigham Young was anxious that the revised canon of the Church be published, and Orson was once again on his way to Liverpool. But a comfortable transformation had taken place, for the hardship of previous thousand-mile treks was now a thing of the past. Whereas Orson had once figured his journeys in months, he could now make the transit to Britain by rail and steamship in the same number of weeks.

After six days of travel Orson arrived in New York accompanied by four young missionaries. Here he encountered his two sons, Milando and Lorus, both of whom were serving missions in the area. With his boys, as Milando later wrote, he toured some of the scenes of his youth:

> Father pointed out to us scenes of his boyhood, one of which was "Herald Gate" [*sic*], now called 'Astoria', where once resided his eldest brother, Anson Pratt, who then kept a butcher shop. My father . . . used to get into a rowboat and row down the East River to New York City and do trading for his brother, and he remembered that once the tide caught him, which he had to row against and made it very difficult for him to get back home . . . pointed out some of the very points of land and also houses which he remembered well, which were connected with his boyhood days.[61]

Orson and his sons spent two days together strolling the ground of the Battery Park enjoying the sea breeze. Orson told them an incident in the life of his father, Jared Pratt, who had once served on Governor's Island in New York harbor as a soldier in the Revolutionary War. Jared had escaped from Governor's Island "in consequence of ill treatment . . . rather than run the risk of death by deserting, than suffer the ill treatment . . . he resolved to have 'Liberty or death'!" Together, father and sons sat on the beach and read the "Proverbs of Solomon" in "Pittman's Phonetic." Orson explained the different characters and sound correspondences, "which we could almost read off soon after first looking at them."[62]

On Sunday July 29, 1877, the missionaries went with their father to hear the great Henry Ward Beecher preach: He used "all the eloquence characteristic of his notable abilities, but rather overdone

. . . at one point of his discourse by an overexertion, which caused the blood to gush a little from his left ear and trickle down onto his collar and shirt bosom." A great mimic, Beecher did an imitation of a bulldog: Milando wrote, "He reminded me very much of President Brigham Young in person, voice and action. I have seen Prest. Young . . . assume an attitude portraying the different dispositions and characters of men and animals." After listening to the most noted preacher of the day, they went to sacrament meeting in the Williamsburg (Brooklyn) Mormon branch, where Orson delivered "a powerful discourse on the restoration . . . also spoke on the subject of Divine Marriage, which caused the reporters present to sit up and take notice and write a little faster . . . the next day . . . the leading newspapers were very sparing with favorable comments . . . the Herald and the World were quite bitter and perverted the very excellent discourse given by my father."[63]

By August 27 Orson landed in Liverpool aboard S.S. *Montana* to the cheers of the Saints—many of them old friends who greeted with reverence their "able and indefatigable" president and his son, Lorus. Milando had completed his mission and returned to Salt Lake.[64]

Two days later, Orson was preparing a quick tour of the mission before setting in to the work of publishing nearly a thousand pages of revised and cross-referenced scripture. He would travel first to Leeds, to exhort the Saints there in the gospel and the learning of phonetic shorthand (he was preparing a "Pitman" edition of the Book of Mormon on his office desk).

On August 29, 1877, a wire arrived from the First Presidency headquarters in Salt Lake City. Brigham Young had died of fulminating "cholera morbus" in his bed at the Beehive House. For the second time Orson had lost his prophet. This time, however, he had the news the very same day. As he eulogized Brigham in Leeds a few days later,[65] nothing but reverence showed in his words. People knew of the hurt Brigham had caused him, of the supplanting, of the ripping of books. But Orson now exhibited no rancor at all.

The "thirty-years' war" that smoldered between Brigham and Orson was over.[66] Their relations had been characterized by bitter flare-ups and years of sullen submissiveness on Orson's part and the conflict was a complicated one. One biographer of Brigham Young declared that the president "hated" Orson Pratt with a profound suspicion dating from the troubles of 1842.[67] Hatred is a strong word. That animosity should arise between two such strong-minded "oxen in the yoke" was perhaps inevitable, and Brigham Young was the kind of leader who demanded loyalty and obedience. There is no question that he distrusted Orson Pratt's ideas and motivations. He and Heber C. Kimball were the only members of the original Quorum of Twelve to remain steadfastly loyal to Joseph Smith; Brigham felt a certain distaste for those who did not (such as Orson Hyde and Orson Pratt), despite their repentance and subsequent devotion to the cause. His long memory extended beyond the troubles of Nauvoo to Orson Pratt's attack on the beleaguered Prophet Joseph in Kirtland. He also recalled Orson's attempt to limit his authority in the crucial Kanesville meetings of the winter of 1847–48, when Orson suggested that the Twelve should govern as a body. Some have interpreted Orson's numerous and prolonged missions as Brigham's method for disciplining the troublesome apostle and keeping him subjugated and poor. In the *New York Herald* one of Orson Pratt's sons gave this anonymous assessment:

> Orson Pratt, . . . one of the most talented men among the Mormon priests, has been held by Brigham Young in a state of almost disgraceful bondage. He has been repeatedly banished as a missionary to various countries of Europe and the East, and was nearly always, as he is now, in a condition next door to penury . . . He [Brigham] avails himself of Pratt's talents, but keeps him a dependent at his feet. The latter uncomplainingly occupies the position, sustained in it as he is alike by religious zeal and an almost unexampled indifference to the opinion of men.[68]

On the other hand Orson was one of the ablest spokesmen for Mormonism and, besides the mission to St. George, his missions put him in an independent and very public light. Brigham was too competent an administrator to waste the persuasive talents of Orson Pratt. He knew Orson was not a "kingdom-builder" like Erastus Snow or a maverick like Amasa Lyman or Orson Hyde. But Brigham had a use for him and he used him hard—to write, to edit, to publish, to preach, and to argue for Mormonism. Brigham was harsh with many of his followers when he sensed disloyalty or even simple incompetence—he once slapped Ezra T. Benson for no apparent reason. Brigham was jealous, too, particularly of his prerogatives as the mouthpiece of the Lord to the Mormon people.

When Orson tried to lead out in matters of doctrine, Brigham corrected him emphatically and publicly; however, nearly every remonstrance was tempered with admiring concessions to Orson's style and the lucidity of his reasoning. In addition Brigham showed occasional generosity toward Orson. On one occasion Marian Ross Pratt opened her door to a messenger from the Beehive House carrying an envelope packed with enough money to pay off her home.[69] After Orson's 1871 lectures on astronomy, he refused $5,000 in compensation. But Brigham received the money and purchased with it two houses for Orson's families.[70]

Orson's eulogy in Leeds reflected nothing of this—only his respect for the office and accomplishments of the late Brigham. Orson was not demonstrative in public; and whether he felt pained, indifferent, or just reflective at the president's death is impossible to know. One thing seems significant. Orson devoted only a part of his speech to memorializing Brigham. He then went on with his dispassionate lecture on the prearranged subject: Pitman's shorthand.

Upon Orson's return to Liverpool, a transatlantic cable summoned him to return at once to Salt Lake City. Dropping the publication work, he and Joseph F. Smith took a rough passage home. Orson's arrival in Salt Lake was met with some apprehensiveness; the twelve had issued, without concurrence from their missioning members, an epistle declaring senior apostle John Taylor head of the Church. Many feared the possibility of a contest. Everyone knew that Orson Hyde and Orson Pratt had served much longer than Taylor and that the 1875 shuffle had overturned expectations of long standing. In addition while Hyde was old and sick, Orson Pratt bore an international reputation as the leading doctrinal authority of Mormonism.

Orson could have been the perfect schismatic: if he had chosen to exploit his legendary position, Taylor's dignity might not have sufficed to hold the Church together. Orson dismissed this possibility immediately. After only two days home he published a pointed affidavit in the *Deseret News*: "I unreservedly endorse John Taylor."[71] When the general conference convened, Orson described the rationale of succession in the Mormon church; he explained the nature of the apostolic priesthood and how under Joseph Smith the apostles were ranked equally with the oldest appointed to preside. The First Presidency was now dissolved, the Twelve were the rightful leaders of the Church, and the only business before the conference was to sustain them in a solemn assembly.[72] The quorums did so without reservation.[73]

The question of accession was resolved. Orson would not become the third president of the Mormon church, and he turned to his beloved observatory and the work of the historian's office. Reading and composing tables of planetary motion for months, he contemplated the "ether" and puzzled over the geometric possibilities that might crack the code of the universe and open up a system of celestial mechanics that would meet Joseph Smith's tantalizing challenge: "If the world can find out these numbers, so let it be."[74] The patriarchal apostle became a familiar sight as he shuffled the streets of the busy city mumbling theorems and derivations under his breath, his head crowned by a ragged straw hat. Once, when a daughter asked him why he continued wearing the straw hat in winter, he replied, "To keep my head warm." "But is a straw hat warm in the winter?" "Better than no hat at all, my daughter."[75]

One of Sarah's sons, possibly Orson, Jr., or Arthur, described Orson in this period.

> Orson Pratt is employed as church historian on no specified salary but gets a little money once in a while from the Tithing office. He has frequently been without a decent suit of clothes. The Salt Lake City police force once presented him with habiliments, and Brigham Young has had once or twice to remind him of his seedy appearance and to give him garments suitable to appear in at the Tabernacle.[76]

In his age and poverty Orson was indifferent to such things, although he had never been a vain man. Marian Ross Pratt, who was devoted to him, nonetheless thought he looked like a common tramp when she met him in Scotland. His photographs show him decently but not extravagantly dressed—his one point of pride was his seven-inch-long white beard.

Orson's beard shone as he preached in the assembly rooms of Salt Lake or presided with honor among the fresh and reverential missionaries in their instructional meetings. Forty years had passed since he had crossed the Mississippi by night for fear of marauders. Such days were not gone forever, though. One spring morning Orson set apart a young missionary named Joseph Standing who was bound for the southern states. Within a year this elder's corpse was abandoned in a Georgia thicket, his face brutally gun-shot by anti-Mormon vigilantes.[77]

The memories of Missouri and Illinois were dying rapidly, however. As church historian Orson grew more and more concerned that the majority of Latter-day Saints knew nothing of those days but what they heard in the stories of old men, and he proposed to Taylor a new project: to reconstruct the past, to take affidavits, and to evaluate the remains of Mormonism's bloody trail, recording that story before the witnesses to it disappeared forever. Taylor approved and assigned as Orson's companion the young apostle Joseph F. Smith, nephew of the Prophet, who had been born on the run forty years before during the Missouri period. Together they planned an itinerary intersecting the pathways of Mormon exile; afterwards Orson went to Britain on a final mission to complete the publication of the scriptures. In reverent preparation for this pilgrimage, he renounced tea and coffee for the duration of the journey.[78]

On September 6, 1878, Orson descended at the railway station in Kansas City not far from the spot where decades before he and Parley had gone hungry together in a cabin on the frontier of Zion. Orson looked about him. The revelations still stood, now annotated and cross-referenced; this was still to be the New Jerusalem, the site of Christ's millennial capital. But Kansas City and its suburb, Independence, buzzed with stockyards and the grimy steam of locomotives; the Missouri festered from the sewage and drought that afflicted the city. The arbored wilderness of five decades before had given way to tiny ramshackle plots and gardens in every direction. The two apostles strolled to the site of the millennial temple, once a beautiful grove. There was now not even a stump in sight among the little dwellings which sat insouciantly on the very spot where Christ's earthly kingdom would one day be headquartered.

Upon inquiry Orson learned that the land belonged by tax deed to the Reorganized Church of Jesus Christ of Latter Day Saints, a schismatic group under the leadership of the Prophet's oldest son, Joseph Smith III. About seventy "Josephite" families lived in the vicinity awaiting the redemption of Zion among their thousands of unsuspecting neighbors. Orson found with them the widow of Apostle John E. Page, whom he knew well. She greeted him kindly enough—though there was little love among "Josephites" for "Brighamites"—and offered the two emissaries from Salt Lake a bunch of "grapes grown in Zion."

Orson found that most of the persecutors were long dead with the exception of one Colonel Pitcher, who considered himself a good-hearted man (naturally) "acting under orders" in that long-ago episode. Orson was surprised to encounter William E. McLellin, once a member of the Quorum of Twelve, still living in Independence. To Orson the old man was dreadfully confused, believing in the apostleship but denying the priesthood, revering the Book of Mormon but rejecting the other revelations; in one breath he would extol Joseph Smith and in the next slander him. McLellin clung to his visitors with wistful relish and only let them alone grudgingly when they insisted on departing for Richmond.

In this village across the Missouri Orson found the only living "witness" to the Book of Mormon. David Whitmer, a well-preserved seventy-three, was a "good-sized man . . . close-shaven, hair perfectly white and thin . . . has a large head and a very pleasant, manly countenance." Whitmer, though dissident for many years, seemed wonderfully surprised and pleased to see Orson Pratt and said he would not have known him, he had grown so stout; he remembered Orson as a "slender, bashful, timid boy." Despite his pleasant conversation Whitmer seemed curiously inaccessible—the two apostles could not get him alone to ask some vital questions. he met them in barrooms and restaurants, always with others present; finally, he assented to talk to them in their hotel room. A shrewd man who had been plagued by misrepresentations and attacks on his character all his life, Whitmer had learned not to discuss his "witness" experiences without witnesses of his own, and so he brought with him a journalist acquaintance from Chicago and several other friends. Despite this Orson launched into his questions. Whitmer did not know the date of the restoration of the Melchizedek Priesthood but remembered seeing the golden plates, the brass plates, the sword of Laban, and many other "Nephite" relics on a table. "I saw them plain as I see this bed," he exclaimed, striking the bed with his hand, "and I heard the voice of the Lord as distinctly as anything I have ever heard in this life." Whitmer also regaled them with the story that a "Nephite" had plowed his land one night so that he might be free to help Joseph. The Nephite had been a heavy man wearing brown woolens, with hair and beard white "like Brother Pratt's."

Traveling north from Richmond Orson took Joseph F. Smith to the place of his birth at Far West. The melancholy apostles found the once-flourishing town a ghostly litter of bleached foundations overgrown with hay. One house still stood nearby, which, upon inspection, turned out to be the farm of a Whitmer nephew. This person turned them and their questions away abruptly and made it clear that he wanted them off the land. Elder Smith supported his aged companion back to the road. They surveyed once again the temple lot where Orson had met his brethren one night forty years before to fulfill the word of the Lord. From here the great foreign missions had begun, and a hundred thousand souls been claimed for the Restoration.

A day or so later a ferry debarked the two Mormons at Quincy, Illinois, where Orson reminisced over the bloody scenes of exile in 1839. By train they journeyed to Plano, a town not far from Chicago where the Reorganized Church maintained headquarters. They had hoped to meet with Joseph Smith III and obtain an interview; more especially, they sought an examination of the manuscript of Joseph Smith's "New Translation" of the Bible. To their chagrin Smith was absent in Iowa conducting a conference, and his printers did not know where the manuscript was kept. Orson and Smith were received with surprising warmth among these old-time Mormons, who even requested them to preach at a prayer meeting. They declined at first, but when the leaders insisted, Orson stood to speak.

Orson well knew polygamy had largely engendered the schism between Josephites and the Utah Saints. Nevertheless he addressed the topic frankly and from a personal perspective:

> Lyman Johnson, who was very familiar with Joseph at this early date—Joseph living at his father's house, and . . . we having traveled on several missions together—told me himself that Joseph had made known to him as early as 1831, that plural marriage was a correct principle. Joseph declared to Lyman that God had revealed it to him, but that the time had not come to teach or practise it in the Church; but that the time would come.

Knowing the Josephites disputed the Prophet's involvement in the origin of the polygamy doctrine, Orson went on to detail sealings he had seen performed by the Prophet Joseph Smith, one as early as April 5, 1843. Surprisingly, he then referred to his own trial "in regard to this matter in Nauvoo." In one of his few public statements on his excommunication, he said he had got his information "from a wicked source, from those disaffected," but as soon as he learned the "truth" he was satisfied.

From Plano the two men proceeded east through Kirtland, where the Josephites owned the temple and used it as a meetinghouse. Nearing Rochester, they decided to visit Cumorah, which Orson had never seen. With the support of Joseph Smith's nephew, Orson climbed the hill where the Book of Mormon plates had been unearthed. He prayed and enjoyed a quiet spiritual "blessing," an event never explained in his report.[79]

Riding the Hudson River Railway south from Albany to New York City provided Orson with a last look at the scenes of his youthful wanderings. Still thick with forest, though much more populated than in the days when Orson hiked them, these green hills seemed a world away from the valleys of stark stone he had wrestled with for thirty years. In the great city he enjoyed staying in a pleasant hotel attended by stewards and waiters, "all of which amounted to some $40 or $50."[80] This was another far cry from his first visit to the diseased island of Manhattan to start his apprenticeship five decades before. A visit to the mission headquarters produced little correspondence, but none so surprising as a letter from Sarah Marinda Pratt. She was thinking of him and wanted him to write to her. Dutifully, after many troubled years of separation, he responded:

> As you requested me to write to you, I do so, addresing you, as formerly, under the affectionate title of *wife*. You once were one with me in the new and everlasting covenant. You once, professedly, believed in the sealing ordinances, according to the revelation on Marriage for eternity. You, at several times, did put the hands of others into my hand, and did give them to me as *wives* . . . after several years had elapsed, I proposed to you, to commence living upon principles of greater equality [with them] . . . this proposition you positively rejected . . . You, doubtless, looked upon the trial as one too great for you . . . and accordingly separated yourself from me, as far as some of the conjugal duties of a wife were concerned . . . How long I shall live to contribute my mite to you, is unknown to me.

There was never to be full reconciliation between the two; even in their advanced age, Sarah's resentment of the plural marriages stood between them. But he believed he had done his best for his families: "My trials, though hard to endure, have been somewhat lightened, by the constant knowledge that I have done my duty to other branches of my family."[81]

In New York City Orson completed drafts for the revised version of the Book of Mormon that was to be printed at Liverpool and spent much of his time poring over algebraic demonstrations of his new work on the physics of motion. In December he finally cleared New York harbor on the steamship *Wyoming* with the carefully crafted foolscap in his satchel. Rough water did not disturb him; he was accustomed to it, for this was his fifteenth Atlantic crossing. In Liverpool the portly apostle heartily embraced the missionaries.[82] Among them was office printer Joseph Bull, who looked over Orson's "New Theory of the Universe" and generously offered to issue it at no charge for his services. With free labor and printing press, Orson still had to struggle for the "60 or 70 dollars" it would cost to provide paper and a few mathematical type.[83]

While Orson negotiated around Liverpool and London to have electroplates made of the revised scripture, he watched with anxiety as his "New Theory" came off the rollers. He had no illusions of upsetting the scientific world with his proposals, but the little pamphlet symbolized for him a final demonstration of the Mormon hypothesis of creation:

> I shall try to raise enough means, so that I can accept bro. Bull's kind and generous offer, and thus be enabled to distribute a few hundred copies among the Universities, Colleges, Acadymies, and the great mathematicians of both Europe and America. I do not expect that such a work would sell, excepting now and then a copy. But my object is not speculation, but to preserve the mathematical propositions which cost me so much time and labor to discover, from falling into oblivions. O. Pratt Sen.[84]

The three or four hundred copies of this work did go essentially unnoticed, although it dealt with questions of general scientific interest in his day and showed beyond doubt great competence in the analytical geometry necessary to describe spatial relationships. *Key to the Universe or a New Theory of its Mechanism* speaks rarely of Mormon doctrines. It tries to be a purely scientific treatise suggesting a solution to the fundamental problem facing nineteenth-century physics, namely, how to explain the nature of the dynamic forces so recently put to work electrifying the cities of the civilized world. A single Mormon reference faces the title page: "Planetary and Stellar

Worlds 'roll upon their wings in their glory, in the midst of the power of God.' "[85] Those words are drawn from section 88, the "Olive Leaf" revelation of the *Doctrine and Covenants*, which lyrically describes the motion of the spheres in a paean to God's creative majesty. Adorning the jacket of the second edition is a golden key set in a schematic of spheres and lines suggesting the arcane imagery of the Masons.

Here Orson clearly searches for a principle that will adequately account for all interactions of active matter with the passivity of space. Like most physical theorists of his day, he postulated the existence of a substance, "ether," which fills all space and provides a medium for all observable dynamic forces such as electricity, magnetism, and gravitation. Scientists considered light, for example, to be a disturbance of this "ether," like the waves of a pond rippling around a fallen stone. But at the same time they were unable to explain the relationship of "ether" to observable matter. Orson wanted to resolve this fundamental question: "The aim of the author . . . is to vindicate the UNIVERSALITY of the law . . . A new theory of celestial mechanism is, at first, startling to those who . . . have unhappily formed an idea, that all the varied phenomena of the universe can be accounted for, by the grand discoveries already made."[86] This notion is erroneous, Orson explains, for the movements of planetary bodies show up many weaknesses in the standard hypotheses of celestial physics. For example, Mercury's orbital path does not follow the pattern predicted by Newton's theory of universal gravitation. "Indeed, a new theory is imperatively called for . . . we may consider the great science of astronomy but imperfectly developed."[87]

Since the days of Newton, scientists had considered gravity to be "an instantaneous force." Orson thought this notion absurd. "How can force . . . pass through space without occupying time? Time and space are essential characteristics of all motion."[88] (Orson was not alone in his rejection of Newton's "instantaneous force." Cartesian physicists "regarded Newton unscientific in that he brought back onto the stage . . . the idea of an influence which could operate across space between bodies that did not touch each other.")[89] For the theistic Newtonians gravity represented a mystic proof of God, a hedge against the "necessitarian materialism" of men like Priestley.[90] Newton himself believed that "this gravitation of his represented an effect that had to be produced by God throughout the whole of space—something that made the existence of God logically necessary."[91] In Orson Pratt's mind, however, Newton had to be wrong—in his theology as well as his physics.

Pratt theorizes that gravitation waves disturb the ether just as light does and reduces all dynamics to two forces: an apparent or "aberrating" force and the resisting force of ether. The time lapse between the emanation and the reception of gravitation waves produces an "abberation" and the body falls toward an illusory point in space. This effect, combined with "ethereal resistance," Orson pictures as an "iron-wire" dragging the planets along spinning and revolving one step behind the sun. Ether, Orson explains, governs by virtue of its rarefied, or refined, immanence—present everywhere. This substance, thoroughly porous and yet dense in the extreme, acts like a tidal undertow on the stars. He envisioned the universe to be oceanlike with great bodies dancing through it in suspension, resisted and set in motion at the same time by the whirling ether.[92]

Believing that the ethereal sea governs modes of activity everywhere, Orson presented mathematical postulates demonstrating an inverse relationship between density and motion. The vast maelstrom brings new worlds into being by "sweeping" randomly floating "cometary" bodies together into planet systems like ours:

> Thus the process of organization or the creation of a new world is accomplished by the word of God, or which is the same thing, by his unchangeable laws . . . by law, materials move from distant space in regular cometary orbits . . . by law, they are compelled into invariable orbits . . . until the new creation becomes perfected, and fully prepared for higher and more God-like purposes, than merely to traverse the wilds of space . . . it is studded with vegetation, and filled with animal life, and peopled with moral and intelligent beings, who also by law may attain to immortality and endless life. All these laws came from the Great Supreme Architect of the universe.[93]

Orson was thus able to construct a physics in conformity to the revelations. The *Key* reflects Orson's "strong materialistic, commonsensible disposition."[94] He had no more need of philosophy, with its numerous semantic traps that had caused him so much difficulty. Now he felt he had used the inarguable language of mathematics to show that a rarefied form of matter, analogous to the "spirit matter" described in the revelations of Joseph Smith,[95] flows in immense currents throughout space, accounting for gravitation and other oblique forces. In addition at the vortices can be found "great solar centers" or "glorified worlds."[96] These cosmic whorls are in turn set in motion by greater ones until the first creation is reached: "Kolob, nearest to the celestial . . . First in government, the last pertaining to the measurement of time . . . holding the key of power also, pertaining to other planets."[97]

In the light of modern physics, Orson's theories are intriguing but clearly based on outmoded science. "Ether drag" was indeed the subject of vital controversy at the time of Orson's writing, with many propositions afloat similar to Orson's concept of ethereal resistance. Fizeau's formula for ether-drift was considered confirmed by an 1851 experiment.[98] Only two years after Orson published *Key to the Universe*, however, the famous Michelson–Morley experiment established that light travels in all directions at equal velocity, striking the first blow at the whole idea of resistant ether. Eventually, the very existence of the ether was called into question, and, after the publication of Einstein's *General Theory of Relativity* in 1905, most scientists concluded that the qualities attributed to ether could just as easily apply to Einstein's "space-time continuum." When Einstein solved the problem of Mercury's unusual orbital path, the ethereal hypothesis was almost universally abandoned. It is important to note, nevertheless, that the present conception of "dynamic space–time" is rooted in the old "ether" idea. And in a few striking ways Orson Pratt's theory foreshadowed the attempts by Einstein to construct a so-called "unified field theory" in which matter could be interpreted as "disturbance" in the cycle of time and space.

In *Key to the Universe* Orson's criticism of the old Newtonian system was well founded: according to one twentieth-century scientific observer, Orson "set forth the surprisingly modern idea that the force of gravity must be transmitted by waves traveling at the speed of light since the concept of gravity acting at a distance was unthinkable to him."[99] Another historian of science has written that Orson's statement, "Gravity is not propagated instantaneously, but with the velocity of light,"[100] is "remarkably modern, and is today accepted as a consequence of the general theory of relativity."[101] In addition Orson asserted that gravity affects light waves;[102] Einstein's relativity theory was considered virtually proven when in 1919 light from a distant star was observed to bend around the sun during an eclipse, exactly as Einstein—and Orson Pratt—had predicted. Coincidentally, just as *Key to the Universe* rolled off the press in England, Albert Einstein was born in Ulm, Germany, March 14, 1879.

Orson's ideas about planetary formation—that jetties in the ether bring worlds together by accretion—conformed quite readily to the "planetesimal theory" of the origin of the solar system, a theory only recently advanced in Orson's time. During the 1870s LaPlace's nebular hypothesis of the origin of the solar system, which Orson attacked[103] in the *Key* and which had enjoyed almost universal acceptance among American scientists, began to lose ground;[104] similar theories have nevertheless gained wider acceptance once again in our own day.

In *Key to the Universe* Pratt achieved a kind of synthesis of the opposing Cartesian and Newtonian views of the universe. In the seventeenth century Descartes had theorized that space was dense with ether, agitated by invisible whirlpools and tides; Newton mocked this idea, primarily because "ether" could not be directly observed and also because he believed that "in its whirlings, the strength of so strong a resisting-medium would have the effect of slowing down all the movements in the universe."[105] For Orson the ether has to exist as a medium for the transmission of gravitational waves. Too, it must be a *resisting* medium, for all matter in the universe necessarily shares this property. (This was as much a part of his theology as of his science.) Orson overcomes Newton's objections with the idea of the "aberrational force" which equalizes ethereal resistance and provides "orbital propulsion." A modern scientific writer has categorized this idea as "ingenious, but wrong,"[106] and offers this critique:

> Energy is never mentioned in the *Key*. Pratt seems conversant enough with linear and angular momenta and their conservation, but he betrays no concern for the energy principle. Here indeed is the most glaring defect in his theory: It does not conserve energy; and in a region void of gross matter it allows perpetual motion, since work is continually done on the planet by the aberrant force without an external energy source.[107]

Orson's unfamiliarity with electrodynamic field physics as well as his neglect of the techniques of integral calculus and the mechanics of fluids add up to "some unwarranted simplifying assumptions."[108] Another critic finds Orson's "aberrational force" a totally unwarranted conclusion: "No proof is given that the velocity will be great enough to maintain a circular or elliptic orbit."[109] To the modern scientist, "The harvest of Pratt's effort is bountiful, if occasionally untoward; someone more thoroughly trained would have sensed trouble."[110]

All of Orson's analytical geometry is sound; though his concepts may be out of fashion, they resemble in curious ways some of the most advanced theories of our own time. As an exposition of Joseph Smith's astronomical revelations in the Book of Abraham, Orson's hypothesis provides a methodology for the priesthood, "the governing power, which governs . . . fixed planets or stars."[111] In his own way Orson had met the cryptic challenge of the Prophet, who had seen in the hieroglyphics of Egypt a "grand Key" to the heavens.

Orson's preoccupation with Abrahamic astronomy was increased by a wave of interest among Europeans in the pyramids of Egypt. Scotland's "Astronomer Royal," Charles Piazzi Smyth, had published in 1864 a theory that the construction of the Great Pyramid provided a key to sacred history. He had conceived of a "pyramid inch," a unit of measurement corresponding to one year, and believed that the internal passageways of the structure constituted a monumental calendar describing the key events of the Bible account —the Flood, the Exodus, and the advent of Christ. By extending his reasoning, Smyth had determined that the corridor's end signified Christ's second coming and calculated it for the year 1881.[112]

Orson read all of this with fascination. Applying Smyth's formula to the same diagrams, he came up with his own results and published them in *Millennial Star* under the title "The Great Prophetic Pyramid: An Important Discovery by Professor O. Pratt, Senior."[113] The Pyramid of Cheops, he wrote, was built under divine direction, typifying the economy of God in relation to this planet. He saw the various dispensations of the gospel clearly indicated in the passages, galleries, and chambers when measured according to Smyth's "pyramid inch": "The incline of the entrance passage marks the Exodus, where the portcullis signifies the separation of Israel of a distinct and peculiar people . . . the 'Hebrew passage.'" Extending the line "from the upper frontal edge of the step perpendicular with the inclined floor of the grand gallery" gives the pyramid date of April 6, 1830, the Mormon holy day of Restoration. From there to the upper edge of the court provides the spring of the year 1891. Here, at the top of the Pharaonic Chamber, Orson found another possible correspondence with Mormon revelation, for Joseph Smith had tentatively foretold Christ's Second Advent for his own eighty-fifth year.[114] Entranced by these findings, Orson speculated in the *Star* that the Great Pyramid could be "the altar of the Lord in the midst of the land of Egypt" mentioned in Isaiah 19:20. Orson's theory that the structure served as a type of celestial calendar might also suggest connections with the astronomical activities of Abraham in Egypt as recounted in the *Pearl of Great Price*.[115]

Orson's speculations show an increasing preoccupation with the "winding-up scene" (the last days). His Egyptian "discoveries" merely coincided with the prophetic pattern he had embraced in 1830: "this is the later times near the dawn of the millennium; in the morning of the seventh thousand years, great events will transpire."[116] "At that time," Orson's son Milando later wrote, "he was greatly exercised in his mind respecting the subject of the redemption of Zion, and he prayed much concerning her deliverance. he repeatedly asked the Lord whether he would live to behold it. He told the writer that the Lord would not give him any satisfaction upon that point, and he doubted whether he would live to see what he desired." At Liverpool he went out for a daily walk methodically and invariably "along the same streets . . . never changing his route, and it almost appeared as if his feet were planted on the same spots each time upon the flagged sidewalks." His spiritual anxiety was no doubt increased by a sudden awareness of his mortality, for it was in Liverpool that he began to show "symptoms of the complaint which carried him off"—diabetes.[117]

Orson preached a farewell discourse to the Saints of Great Britain, an hour and a quarter in a sweltering Liverpool hall. Perspiration drizzled from the old man's face as he expounded on the higher priesthood, the sealing power, eternal marriage, and the ordinances for the dead. "If a vote had been taken, the congregation would have desired him to continue another hour."[118] Afterwards he found it impossible to get away as so many crowded around to shake his hand. He left Liverpool for the last time with their prayers in his ears: "Many fervent prayers will go up for his preservation and comfort across the great deep, and for his safe arrival in his mountain home, long to live upon the earth to be a blessing and comfort to the people."[119]

Arriving in New York aboard the S.S. *Nevada*, Orson telegraphed that the precious electroplates for the printing of the scripture had been finished and the presses had begun to roll. In Utah he resumed his rounds among the stakes, spoke first among all the authorities in general conference, and went to ward socials in his own block. As he looked about him, he saw hundreds of youth preoccupied with a far different world from his own: "The programme varied with music, songs and recitations; no round-dances were held in deference to the older people, because they are 'offensive to modesty and true happiness.' " The young people were exhorted not "to crowd out the old folks who built the halls they are using."[120]

Orson, one of those who "built the halls," began to lapse. Diabetes closed on him as winter set in, but the symptoms occurred only sporadically, so that he was able to welcome the Saints to the great "Jubilee Conference" which convened on April 6, 1880, under the massive dome of the Tabernacle. Though the Church was still beleaguered with juridical processes and the less subtle campaigns of the anti-Mormon press, still Orson could pray thankfully for the fortunes of the gospel, praising the fulfillment of Daniel's prophecies, the jubilee, and the great gathering to Zion.[121]

His homilies revealed that he still held to the fundamental philosophical principles he had advanced in *The Seer* and the British mission pamphlets. He was pleased with the reception among the astute of Salt Lake of his *Key to the Universe*, so much so that he brought out a second edition. And in his discourses he tied astronomical law to his notion that all substance was intelligent:

> The earth seems to take one continued course. It has an orbit. It does not deviate from this orbit . . . Some, in reflecting on this, might say that the earth is obliged to follow this course. I do not know about this. I am not so sure. I think if we could see a little further, we would understand that, connected with the materials of the earth is a living principle . . . that acts according to certain laws, intelligently, not blindly . . . It is not a law of blind materials which have no knowledge or life connected with them . . . "the earth abideth the law of a celestial kingdom, for it filleth the measure of its creation."[122]

Citing the "Olive Leaf" revelation, which elucidated the patterns of celestial law and government, Orson found that the principle which sustains the universe is "intelligence." Everything is alive—and intelligent. Though he did not speak with the unequivocal certitude of the 1850s pamphlets, he still invoked the principle that godliness and glorification depend upon the acquiring of wisdom.

Orson began his greatest sermon, "The Majesty of God," by reading a large portion of the "Olive Leaf" to an intimate congregation in the sixteenth ward assembly rooms. To him these words of Joseph Smith contained knowledge "far beyond that which you will find recorded in the writings of the learned," for they clearly exhibited the nature of "that Being whom we worship." He pointed to the emphasis on celestial bodies, that God is "in" them as they move shining through space, and that we reverence him precisely because he governs the heavenly luminaries: "We are also told that we are his sons and his daughters, that we were begotten by him, before the foundation of this world; that we are his offspring . . . but can we form an idea of the intelligence that he possesses?"[123]

Scoffing at the idea that "these are mysteries . . . the Lord never intended us to understand," he chastised his fellow religionists for their passivity in thinking mere compliance with first principles will make them gods. "If there be knowledge . . . let us seek it . . . by using our reasoning powers, by reading books, or by human wisdom . . . let us seek to a higher source—to that Being who is filled with knowledge."[124] All truth he sees as indistinguishably divine. The laws of Newton were "a revelation . . . concerning the forces of the universe"; the elasticity of the ether, the velocity of light, and the motions of the planets are all equally holy manifestations of the grand progress of the "intelligences" towards perfection.

The lord of the fields "shows the light of his countenance" to each of his kingdoms in succession, runs a parable of the "Olive Leaf" symbolizing to Orson an evolutionary process of achieving divinity. As the Creator strives with each of his innumerable creations in turn, "in our hour and in our season," the "veils" are gradually removed: "By and by, when each of these creations has fulfilled the measure and bounds set and the times given . . . it and its inhabitants who are worthy will be made celestial . . . Then . . . there will be no intervening veil between God and his people . . . They will be able to see him at all times."[125] For Orson, the "majesty of God" meant that "all things are before him"; he knows all because nothing is veiled from his sight, and the same potential lies dormant and undeveloped in man. Orson saw the gaining of knowledge as the prime sacred imperative, without which man has no purpose. The astronomical keys he had found describe the workings of divinization in both man and matter, for God "quickeneth all things."[126]

On September 19, 1880, Orson Pratt stood to speak to a Sunday morning Tabernacle audience under the direction of his immediate superior in the Quorum of Twelve Apostles, Wilford Woodruff. All those who had come ahead of him were dead—Brigham, Heber, Orson Hyde—and he had known Mormonism even before any of them. Orson announced quietly that it was fifty years to the day since he had joined the Church of Jesus Christ in Canaan, New York; to him, it was a double birthday, his sixty-ninth, and a year of jubilee for him personally as well as for the entire Church. When the meeting concluded, Woodruff rose and apologized for keeping the congregation a moment:

> We are not in the habit of flattering any man, but I want to say a few words concerning Brother Pratt. If there is any man, dead or alive, who has dwelt longer in this church and kingdom than he has I do not know him. If there is any man that has travelled more miles in preaching the Gospel of Christ, in bearing testimony of the kingdom of God on the earth, I do not know who he is. When Brother Pratt embraced this Gospel, he was a boy, in one sense of the word illiterate and unlearned, the same as Joseph Smith . . . I never saw a man in my life that I know of that has spent as few moments idly as he has. I have never seen a storm at sea so heavy, even when shipping seas over the bow, side, and stern, but what he would read his book . . . He has improved his time . . . Brother Pratt was one of the earliest men who shouldered his knapsack and travelled through the American continent to preach the Gospel of Christ to this nation. Frequently he would suffer from ague all day and go along and preach his sermons at night . . . I feel to thank God that we can still hear his voice.[127]

Everyone dispersed and at four o'clock there was a happy gathering at Juliaet's residence in the seventeenth ward. Nearly seventy of his children and grandchildren surrounded him. His son Laron, "the oldest of the children in the Church," read the birthday tribute. Laron's tribute ranked his father with the patriarchs and prophets of old, lauded the purity of his well-spent life, and led the others in a resounding "GOD BLESS YOU, FATHER!" Orson's daughter Ruby, who was only six years old, joined another sister in a piano recital; there was violin music and a vaulting hymn from the voice of the president of the twelve, John Taylor. Milando Pratt presented his father with a large family record of six hundred folio pages recording the names of the living and the dead. The patriarch then arose thanking his family. He had one wish left, he said—to see the "winding-up scene," but the infirmities of age weakened his faith, and he "sometimes thought he would not realize his desire to the fullest extent." If he should pass on he wanted his children to continue and fill up the record. "Altogether, it was a rare and pleasant gathering."[128]

As historian, Orson tended the records of the Church as well as his own, but as he became more feeble, the work fell increasingly upon his assistant, Elder Woodruff. During the general conference in autumn of 1880, Orson rose to present John Taylor, George Q. Cannon, and Joseph F. Smith as a new First Presidency over the Church and went on to discourse upon the "history of the priesthood" from Abel's sacrifice through Melchizedek and Abraham to Moses. Poignantly, the congregation was requested "to be as still as possible" so the weakening voice could be heard.[129]

The end of the jubilee year found Orson prostrated with one fulminating shock after another. His portliness worked against him, but the diabetes soon wasted him to nothing; nevertheless he fought earnestly to survive.[130] A great family reunion was planned for autumn 1881, involving, at his request, all the descendants of Apostles Parley and Orson and brothers Anson and William Dickinson: he dearly wished to meet once again and bless his many children, wives, nephews, and nieces all together.[131] He gained sufficient strength to take the second seat among the apostles at general conference and once again at a service held on the first of July, the day word shook Salt Lake City that the president of the United States, James A. Garfield, had been shot.[132] The assassin, it was rumored, was a Mormon.[133]

The tales of mythical "Destroying Angels" who murdered enemies of the Saints revived again, and the nation turned its accusing eyes on the Mormon kingdom in the West. Although Charles Guiteau, the President's assailant, was later proved to have no connection whatever with Mormonism, popular opinion grew more and more strident in demanding the abolition of polygamy.

There would be no Fourth of July celebration that year,[134] and while the president of the United States lay slowly dying in the East, Orson Pratt sank from consciousness in the house on Third North and Third West. His wife Marian bathed his forehead and watched.

In the fall of that year a bizarre glow filled the sky; a bright orange haze came creeping like fire over the continent, and in the East it was dark at noon. Newspapers reported that the Millerites and Adventists were donning their "ascension robes,"[135] and many trembled that the day so long predicted by prophets, numerologists, pyramidologists, and crackpots was finally to break upon the world. The extraordinary clouds were probably volcanic dust or some other stagnant atmospheric condition and the heavens did not open after all. The nation was filled with fear, however, as the president slowly lapsed, and in his wakeful moments perhaps Orson Pratt looked with anticipation at the newspapers and at the lurid sky from his window. Perhaps he wondered if he would not indeed see Christ descend in glory over the Wasatch Mountains before he closed his eyes for good.

The day before Orson's birthday he got out of bed and rode to the Sunday services in the Tabernacle. As the Tabernacle Choir sang "While of these Emblems," the Saints watched with amazement to see the ghostly apostle stand to the pulpit. Only hours before, the city had despaired of him; and now he stood miraculously before them to deliver a message—his last—while the sacrament trays circulated:

> It has been almost one year since I have been able to stand up before a congregation . . . I am now blessed with the opportunity of occupying a few minutes, as long as my health would justify . . . I am just able to stand upon my feet, most of the time scarcely able to sit up . . . Notwithstanding the afflictions of my body and the long silence that I have kept, I have felt the same enduring love for the principles of truth and for the people of God . . . Fifty one years ago tomorrow . . . I entered this Church . . . then confined to a small district in the State of New York . . . Tomorrow—if I live till tomorrow—I shall be seventy years of age . . . They are the years appointed to man . . . so far as my mind is concerned, my understanding, that is at rest, that is at peace. I know what my hopes are. I know the plan of salvation.[136]

To the congregation he was like a figure from another world . . . still hoping for missions to come, still praying for the "humble privilege of lifting up my voice and testifying, before thousands of people." He left his apostolic benediction upon the "people of Zion . . . May He favor us before many years with a full and complete redemption according to the promises."

Melancholy congratulations came around to Orson on his seventieth birthday, but the effort of the Sabbath had finished him. After trying to work in the historian's office, he was seized with vomiting and sank to his bed. Infection and fever continued to weaken him, and he listened in half-sleep to the bells of the city tolling the death

Orson Pratt in his later years. *Courtesy, Utah State Historical Society.*

Orson Pratt in his later years. *Courtesy, Utah State Historical Society.*

of Garfield only a few days later.[137] The autumn days were dark with crepe flutters. Black pennants hung everywhere, from the scaffolding of the temple and the pinnacles of ZCMI right down to the Chinese washhouses.

On Sunday night, October 2, Orson awoke for the first time in two weeks and asked for his family. Slipping away again almost at once, he murmured to Joseph F. Smith, who was keeping vigil with him, the words for his epitaph: "My body sleeps for a moment, but my testimony lives and shall endure forever."[138] The family rallied quickly, waiting outside for news. When finally admitted, they saw only a peaceful old man slumbering gently and drifting gradually away. He died during the night.

12
The Legacy

Farewell, Brother Orson Pratt, until we meet you in the Paradise of God, or until the bright morning of the glorious day when they that are in Christ shall come forth to greet the Sun of Righteousness and enter into their dominions as Kings and Priests unto God for ever. Amen.—Apostle Wilford Woodruff[1]

The tenor of the eulogies was predictable—the legacy of Orson Pratt defied summation, at least from the Mormon perspective. The *Deseret News* published a long tribute: "No man in the Church was better known . . . his refined and intelligent countenance, silvery hair and beard, dignified manner and powerful public address, were familiar to all . . . He was the last of the original council of the Twelve Apostles . . . crossed the ocean sixteen times on missions . . . found time to study higher mathematics."[2]

Pratt's funeral services coincided with the convening of the Fifty-first Semiannual General Conference of the Church, on Thursday morning, October 6, 1881. Between conference sessions, seven or eight thousand people led by the First Presidency, the Twelve Apostles, and other authorities, filed two abreast past the flower-draped casket. Elder Wilford Woodruff stood for the eulogy:

President Wilford Woodruff said if he were to express his desire to the Lord it would be, O Lord, give us grace that we may be able to accomplish the work required of us. But oh, the chains that bind this immortal spirit? Sometimes he felt, oh that he could break the bands of mortality and open his eyes in the spirit world to receive that which Orson Pratt is now enjoying . . . It would be impossible to give the history

> of that great man, or to depict the glory that awaits him. It would take the trump of the sixth angel to do that . . . Brother Pratt had lived longer in this Church, traveled more miles and preached more sermons than any man in it. He had baptized thousands, and fulfilled the revelation given to him through the Prophet Joseph Smith, November 4th 1830. His garments were clear from the blood of this generation. He had studied and written more upon the Gospel and upon science than any man in the Church. He had now gone home. It was all right.[3]

President John Taylor was more cautious: "Let us try to imitate the examples of Brother Orson wherein they were good."[4] And Franklin D. Richards remarked that "his nature was so firm that it amounted almost to obstinacy, yet he always yielded to that which was declared by authority."[5] Richards also predicted that Orson Pratt's works would follow him "in his generations."

After the Tabernacle Choir had sung "Thou dost not weep, to weep alone" and "Mourn not the dead who peaceful lay/Their weary bodies down," an "exceedingly large cortege" moved up crepe-lined Brigham Street, where the muted spectators crowded to attention. The apostles served as pallbearers, and the other authorities of the Church followed the Pratt families, all in "excellent order."[6] Orson Pratt's remains were interred in the Salt Lake City Cemetery.[7]

The next Utah legislature resolved to eulogize its late speaker:

> The Honorable Orson Pratt has been called to a higher sphere . . . Gifted with remarkable powers, possessing a vigorous intellect and, until his later years, with great physical strength, his highly cultivated powers of mind and body were fully and freely given for the benefit of his fellows. As an astronomer he shone with stars of the first magnitude. As a mathematician he stood in the foremost rank. As a theologian he had few equals. As a writer he was forcible, logical, perspicuous, and convincing. As a public speaker he was bold, original, masterly and eloquent. As a legislator he was cautious, discreet, liberal, and progressive. As a gentleman he was courteous, sedate, affable, and considerate. His career was most remarkable, showing what may be achieved by self-culture and perseverance, in the face of the greatest obstacles. In his boyhood he devoted himself to the good of his race, and he never ceased his exertions until cut down by the scythe of the universal reaper. He was a successful explorer, a hardy pioneer, and one of the very first colonists of this arid mountain region . . . we rejoice in the incalculable good that has accrued from his noble works, and the benefits that will be derived from his library legacies and his illustrious example. He rests from his toil; he sleeps with the just; and no historic title, whether of plumed warrior, or learned sage, or crowned king, will shine more

> brightly in the eyes of Utah's people than the great and honored name of Orson Pratt.[8]

Even critics of Mormonism joined in praise of Orson Pratt. Utah's Methodist missionary bishop, Daniel S. Tuttle, wrote: "Mormon faith held such a man as Orson Pratt true to the service of the church all his life through, although many snubbings, and oppositions, and mortifications were visited upon him. He was a mathematician, a surveyor, an astronomer, a Greek and Hebrew linguist, and a very learned man."[9]

Hyperbole is only natural to such occasions, and the "great and honored name of Orson Pratt" seems today only an echo of more resonant names in Mormon history, like Joseph Smith or Brigham Young. Yet no one who has surveyed Pratt's accomplishments can deny the epic quality of his life and the magnitude of concentration that produced his sixteen theological and philosophical studies and hundreds of discourses and articles—the 320 pages of exposition in *The Seer* not the least of his accomplishments.

Out of what Leonard J. Arrington has called the intellectual ferment of early Mormonism, Orson Pratt has emerged as a symbol. He is perceived as "the foremost Mormon intellectual of the nineteenth century,"[10] who gave "philosophical meaning and depth to many of the theological teachings."[11] A 1968 survey of thirty-eight Mormon scholars listed Orson Pratt second (after B. H. Roberts) as one of the five most eminent intellectuals in Mormon history. John Henry Evans, a counselor in the First Presidency of the Church, spoke of Orson Pratt as a "quadrant among the plowshares," emphasizing his role as scientist and philosophical exponent of the faith in contrast to his more pragmatic associates. "In the first century of 'Mormonism' there is no leader of the intellectual stature of Orson Pratt," says Evans. The "New Christianity" boasts no one "more prolific in his written defense of the faith."[12]

"There is among the Mormons a pronounced intellectualism in matters pertaining to religion and a strong commitment to the capacities of human reason," Sterling M. McMurrin has written.[13] One irresistible attraction of Mormonism for men like the brothers Pratt was its grounding in free inquiry and a dynamic view of truth—the same sort of restless appeal others of their generation found in the new scientism of the nineteenth century. Orson Pratt's

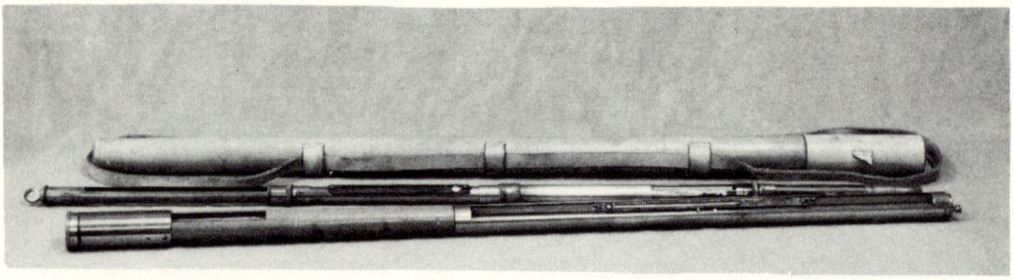

Orson Pratt's thermometer, barometer, and hygrometer. *Courtesy, Church Museum of History and Art, Church of Jesus Christ of Latter-day Saints.*

efforts at a Mormon cosmology are obviously extrapolated from the principles taught by the Prophet Joseph Smith and embellished by his brother Parley; but the general tenor of nineteenth-century physics and Newtonian natural theology, as developed particularly in the work of the Scottish realists, resounds as well in Pratt's writings. His vision of the Latter-day Saint as a philosopher in a kingdom of philosophers, a missionary and laborer for the truth in a celestial realm of truth-seekers, reflected the contagious idealism of the previous century in both British and American thought.

Orson first encountered the aging and failing "natural philosophy" movement during the last, declining period of the Scottish Enlightenment while working at Edinburgh in 1840. He became infected with the feverish attempt to reconcile Christianity with the mechanism of Newton's universe. Orson Pratt carried into Mormonism (with only partial success) the "insistence on mechanical models in science and life" that so thoroughly dominated British ways of thinking.[14] These views so colored Orson's religious perspective that he felt himself justified in calculating the number of spirits God created (105 billion) and even presented a mathematical proof of the existence of numberless gods! ("This may be exemplified, by conceiving the existence of endless straight lines in boundless space: conceive each of these lines to be divided . . . into an endless number of yards. All can at once see, that there would be a beginning to each of these yards, but there would be no beginning to the endless succession . . . each world and the inhabitants thereof would have a beginning; but . . . there could not be a first world in this endless succession, nor a first Father in the endless genealogy.")[15] Such an alliance between natural philosophy and mathematics was a hallmark of British (particularly Scottish) intellectual life.[16]

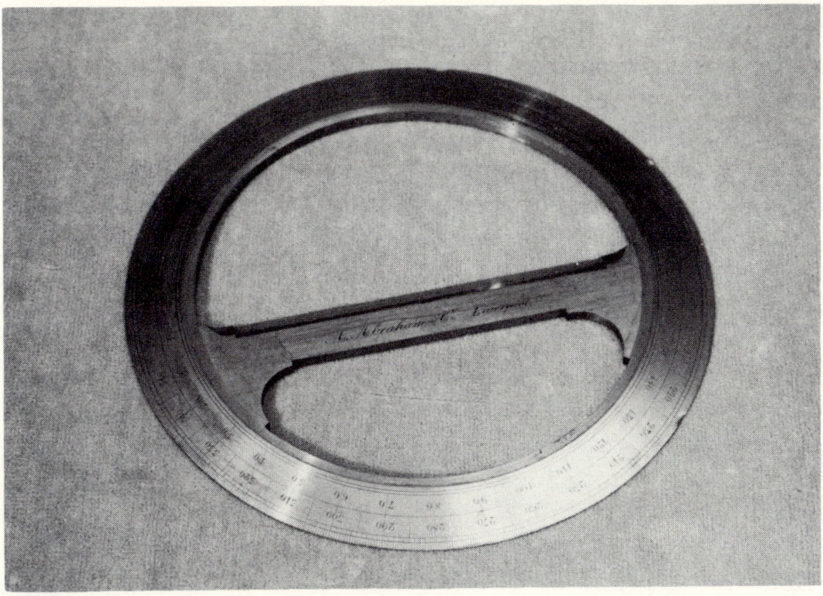

Orson Pratt's protractor. *Courtesy, Church Museum of History and Art, Church of Jesus Christ of Latter-day Saints.*

Pratt himself embodied in an admirable way the eighteenth-century "man of parts,"[17] an ideal derived from Scottish philosophy: "The highest tribute to an enlightened Scot was to be known as a 'man o'parts', meaning not only an extremely capable man in his field but also a man of wide-ranging interests and abilities. The primary aim and object of all education was thus, 'to cultivate *all* the various principles of our nature, both speculative and active, in such a manner as to bring them to the greatest perfection of which they are susceptible.' "[18] For Orson Pratt, this was an eternal ideal; in a way, it was his definition of God: the Father was first of all a man who had *attained* perfection in all the "various principles of our nature," in whom was found the fullness of truth ("Persons are only tabernacles or temples, and TRUTH is the God, that dwells in them.")[19] This idea, which Orson in his commitment to reason thought inescapable, was condemned by Brigham Young more roundly than any other—in McMurrin's words, it "cannot be regarded as conforming to Mormon orthodoxy because it appears to deny that, in the last analysis, God as God is a person."[20] There is some evidence that the other apostles were uneasy with Brigham's denunciation of Pratt's works,[21] but Brigham Young stoutly defended the primacy of revelation over the presumption of "learned ideas."[22]

From Brigham Young's perspective Pratt's greatest weakness was his insistence on preaching "philosophy," which to Brigham meant more of the same kind of scholasticist nonsense which the revelations of Joseph Smith had swept away. In *The Idea of the Holy* Rudolf Otto points out the danger to revelatory religion posed unwittingly by men like Orson Pratt: "the rationalization of religion, which often ends by constructing such a massive structure of theory and such a plausible fabric of interpretation" ends at last in the death of spiritual feeling. "Both imaginative 'myth', when developed into a system, and intellectualist Scholasticism, when worked out to its completion, are methods by which the fundamental fact of religious experience is, as it were, simply rolled out so thin and flat as to be finally eliminated altogether."[23] Brigham Young's uneasiness at Pratt's attempt to define the "Great First Cause" and systematize the workings of celestial worlds probably derived from his fear of the sterile effect of rationalism upon revelation.

In addition, the Pratt thesis to account for the ubiquity of God's influence sounds very much like a reversion to the same kind of mystic sophistry taught by Christian philosophers from the time of Augustine. Orson's theory of a "Supreme Being or Substance, whose dwelling place is nature, and whose tabernacle is the elements"[24] resembles very closely the orthodox God. While Orson preached the Mormon anthropomorphic God, he also insisted that there must be a higher, or perhaps prior, "Substance" which is the "great universal Spirit which pervades all things."[25] On the other hand he did not hold that this Spirit was, as most Christian mystics teach, "wholly other," unconnected from "Being itself and all that 'is'," called by some " 'that which is nothing.' "[26] On the contrary, nothing for Pratt exists outside of "Being itself." At the same time his doctrine came just close enough to a denial of the supremacy of the Father to threaten the revealed understanding of God laid down by Joseph Smith.

Many Mormons consider Brigham H. Roberts the inheritor of Orson Pratt's role as the leading intellectual of the Church. Roberts, who eventually presided over the First Council of the Seventy, continued to struggle in his work with many of the same problems that faced Pratt. He did not hesitate to refute Pratt whenever he found logical and doctrinal inconsistencies: He issued in 1907 a treatise entitled "The Immortality of Man," in which he emphasized that Mormonism does not teach the existence of a "First God," or "Great First Cause," and many of the arguments he used are similar to those of Brigham Young's 1865 statement on Orson Pratt's writings.[27] Yet elsewhere Roberts came close to expounding Pratt's theory of the "higher attributes" as constituting a kind of divine "essence": "*God-nature* is doubtless always the same, without reference to those who may attain unto it."[28] And Roberts did not hesitate to join Orson Pratt with his own eloquent denunciation of the mystic God of traditional Christianity; he criticized the theology of his time as a mere extension of the "philosophy of the orthodox creeds to its legitimate conclusion, [which] leaves us with the paradox . . . of regarding God at once as the most real existence, and as the most absolute nonexistence."[29]

As Orson's intellectual "successor," Roberts shared Pratt's eloquence and dogged writing talent; however, in the opinion of Professor McMurrin, "was somewhat less original in thought than Orson Pratt. Certainly he lacked Pratt's disposition for speculative metaphysics as well as his analytic and logical talent. There is nothing in Roberts' writings, for instance, comparable in character to Pratt's finest philosophical piece, 'The Absurdities of Immaterialism' . . . If less analytical and innovative than Pratt, Roberts had a better feel for relevance and a firmer grasp of the larger implications of the Mormon doctrine, and he had, I believe, more common sense in his treatment of religious issues."[30]

Another Mormon thinker, Nels L. Nelson, prominent English professor at Brigham Young University, shared Orson Pratt's belief in an ultimate "Holy Spirit": "all forces are but variously tensed forms of one final, supreme spiritual energy filling the universe," Nelson wrote in 1904. "The energy of the universe . . . is the Holy Ghost."[31] Reasoning as Pratt does, from a materialistic, scientific model, Nelson pictured the Holy Spirit as the dynamic principle of the cosmos whose workings bring to mind the action of sound, heat, and light. As with Pratt this was more than just a poetic analogy. The Holy Spirit is the ultimate "unified field" of energy, and all motion in the universe derives from it: it cannot be observed in laboratory tests, for "it responds only in the human soul."[32] Mormon commentator W. Cleon Skousen characterized the "light of truth" as a "collective term to designate the masses of organized intelligences in God's kingdom," and God's power as a result of "the voluntary cooperation and support of vast concourses of intelligences."[33] Mormon thinkers have clearly refused to abandon the Pratt thesis of a "Great First Cause" although these speculations "do not enjoy official acceptance by the Church."[34]

Outside the Mormon church, Orson Pratt's theory of "Holy Spirit" and "Great First Cause" bears an affinity to the views of various contemporary and modern philosophers. Schopenhauer, one notable example, believed like Orson Pratt in the oneness of the "Will," the governing energy of all things, which "knows no plurality, and consequently is *one*."[35] Pratt's notion of a universe made up of self-combining, intelligent particles has an interesting modern echo in the writings of Nobel laureate biologist George Wald of Harvard University. Wald suggests that the "universe wants to be known," that there must exist a kind of cosmic consciousness that "formed the material universe and brought out life and overt forms of consciousness," suggesting also that "matter and mind are a complementarity . . . two contradictory sides of the same reality."[36] Orson Pratt drew a similar conclusion in *Great First Cause*: "Unintelligent primary powers are not only inexplicable but inconceivable! . . . organization could not take place—anterior powers could not exist independently of intelligence, which must be the first moving cause, anterior to all other causes or effects."[37]

Evolution of intelligences toward or away from godhood is the teleology of Orson Pratt's Mormon cosmos. This process of divinization is, for Pratt, dependent upon the acquisition of knowledge, which he himself pursued as best he could. Furthermore, the process is as much earthly as heavenly: the business of man is to learn, and the highest purpose of society is the schooling of man in the fullness of truth. "We are now speaking of what ought to be, and what must be when Zion is built up according to the celestial law . . . As in temporal things, so in spiritual . . . when each Saint obtains the fullness of all the knowledge revealed, instead of being made an accountable steward over a small portion of the joint fund, he is accountable for the whole."[38] For Orson Pratt, Zion was built up of men and women who have reached perfection in knowledge. In this, the Mormon vision recalls once again the social idealism of the eighteenth century.

Condorcet, the great Enlightenment social philosopher, also "enshrines the idea of progress as a moral absolute," and looks forward to "the climax of man's progress, when reason and science would secure the natural rights of man in a world of peace, prosperity and equality." Condorcet preaches unlimited human potential ("Nature has set no term to the perfection of human faculties; . . . the perfectibility of man is truly indefinite") and envisions "an Elysium created by reason,"[39] very similar to the Utopia of Scottish natural philosophers such as Thomas Dick. "The soul of man," writes Dick, "appears to be capable of making a perpetual progress towards intellectual and moral perfection . . . without the possibility of ever arriving at a boundary to its excursions."[40] In this respect Orson Pratt's view of the "celestial order of Zion" reflects the Enlightenment concept of man's glorious "future state."[41] The modern Latter-day Saint still cherishes this dream as both an earthly and a heavenly possibility.

"Patriarchal matrimony" was Orson's term for the plural marriage principle which he saw as complementary to the celestial commonwealth envisioned by the Saints. "It is for this reason that God has ordained that the righteous shall have a plurality of wives; for they alone are prepared to beget and bring forth offspring whose bodies and spirits, partaking of the nature of the parents, are pure and lovely, and will manifest, as they increase in years, those heaven-born excellencies so necessary to lead them to happiness and eternal life."[42] To perpetuate the earthly Zion, God had ordained and Orson Pratt vigorously upheld the "principle." Although the outside world considered polygamy a consequence of the "crude materialism" of Mormon doctrine,[43] to Orson it was "one of the greatest blessings of this last dispensation."[44] Of course, Orson's defense of plural marriage has become purely academic to the Mormons. Because of continual harassment by the federal government, and despite the sympathetic pleas on their behalf of even so eminent a philosopher as John Stuart Mill ("It is difficult to see on what principles but those of tyranny they can be prevented from living there under what laws they please"),[45] the Mormons ultimately abandoned the practice after the famous "Manifesto" of 1890. But the vision of the family sealed together in an eternal bond of progress remained the foundation of happiness: "What can be more heavenly and God-like than to see a well regulated family, governed in wisdom and righteousness!" exclaimed Pratt. "It is the commencement of heaven on earth!—it is an organization destined to be eternal!"[46]

Orson's own enormous family testified to his zeal for this belief. At his death Orson left thirty living children, fourteen male and sixteen female. Of Sarah Marinda Pratt's twelve, six children survived to adulthood. Orson Pratt, Junior, lived out his life estranged from the Church to which his father had dedicated fifty-one years of labor and devotion; an obscure piano and organ teacher, he died in Ogden, Utah, in 1903.[47] Sarah's son Arthur, who had been excommunicated at the time of her property disputes with Brigham Young, remained actively hostile to Mormonism. He was a United States Marshal, then Warden of the territorial prison at the same time George Q. Cannon, Rudger Clawson, and other prominent Mormons were incarcerated for polygamy. His anti-Mormonism was clearly the result of Sarah's teaching: "I am the son of my father's first wife," he told an interviewer, "and had a mother who taught me the evils of the system."[48] He was chief of the Salt Lake City Police from 1894–97. Before his death in 1919 he served another thirteen years (1904–17) as warden of the Utah State Penitentiary and from 1916–17 as president of the American Prison Congress. His older brother Harmel was a lawyer who assisted him as chief clerk at the prison. Harmel died in 1907. Laron Pratt, the only one of Sarah's children who continued as an active Mormon, organized the first Mormon Sunday schools for the deaf in Salt Lake City and "for a nine-year duration he traveled to Ogden each Sunday to teach deaf children the gospel."[49] Deafened by fever before he was three years old, he spoke with difficulty but was highly adept at sign language. The *Deseret News* reported his first attempt at speaking to a Mormon congregation in 1894: "Mr. Pratt. . . bore a strong testimony of the truth of the Gospel and pointed out to his attentive audience the Divine providence in his behalf in placing him under what most people regarded as an affliction, but in which he realized a blessing."[50]

Sarah herself continued embittered against the Church, if her testimony in the 1886 anti-Mormon book *Mormon Portraits*[51] is to be believed. There is some indication that she softened in her feelings just before her death. Methodist Bishop Tuttle became closely acquainted with her in her last years and recalled that she "dearly loved" Orson Pratt. She was a "superior woman" from Tuttle's perspective, for she had "rebelled against the church and brought her children up in rebellion. I knew her well and esteemed her and her children. In pathetic bursts of outraged affection she would sometimes speak of the personal goodness and kindness of her husband."[52] Sarah died of a heart attack on Christmas Day 1888. According to her grandchildren by Laron, she remarked on her deathbed: "If Mormonism is not true then there is no truth on earth."[53] Nevertheless, a Protestant funeral was held at Arthur's home, and Sarah became the only one of Orson Pratt's wives to be buried beside her husband.

Adelia Ann's six children survived the poverty and famine they had suffered in Tooele Valley and grew to maturity. Lorus Pratt, her fourth child, became a well-known painter in Utah, having studied in Paris at the Académie Julien under Jean-Benjamin Constant and others; his work was exhibited in the Grand Salon of the Louvre.[54] Lorus returned to produce landscapes and murals for the Salt Lake Temple.[55] Adelia lived the longest of any of the Pratt wives, dying at 87 in 1913.[56] Mary Ann Merrill Pratt lived until 1903, nearly 85 years; her most prominent child was Milando Pratt, who contributed a short history of his father's life and was an accomplished genealogist.[57]

The devoted Marian Ross Pratt saw five children grown and married before her death at 71 in 1901. Juliaet, or Juliet, Phelps Pratt, mothered Orson's Fillmore household and raised all seven of her children to adulthood, surviving to her eightieth year in 1919. In 1877 she bore Orson's youngest child, Julius Phelps Pratt, who was four years old at the death of his father[58] and survived until 1947. His older sister, Neva Phelps Pratt Shiverick, died in 1957, the last child of Orson Pratt to die.[59] The family of Eliza Crooks Pratt suffered more than its share of pathos: She watched a four-year-old son, Lerius, die of a childhood disease in 1862 and two years later another boy, Onthew, lived only one day. Eliza herself passed away at age 40 leaving behind three children. Dora, the oldest, was only eight. Dora's two surviving brothers were both killed young in bizarre accidents: Jared died in a snowslide near Tooele at age fifteen, and Samuel tumbled into a boiling hot spring at Wadsworth, Nevada, in his nineteenth year.[60]

Margaret Graham Pratt, Orson's last plural wife, was a native of Edinburgh just three weeks shy of her seventeenth birthday when she married him (he was 57). Despite the forty years difference in their ages, Orson and Margaret had three children: Orlon, Pearl, and Royal, all of whom lived well into the twentieth century.

Many of the Pratt daughters married into prominent Mormon families such as Kimball, Snow, Eldredge, Nebeker, Morgan, and Beesley. One of Juliaet's daughters, Clomenia Phelps Pratt Low Bailey Ivins Larson, was married four times.[61]

By the year 1967, the last time a count was taken, Orson Pratt's descendants numbered 1,158.[62] This ample family is his most significant legacy—a living one.

Orson Pratt's world has, of course, disappeared. Both the Endowment House and the observatory on Temple Square were gone by 1900, and a new century brought vigorous, disturbing changes in spiritual and scientific realms. Orson Pratt's writings have been "pathetically neglected" in the Mormon church, despite the "unquestionably vital and relevant" themes of his work.[63] Ironically, fifty-seven years after his death, Orson Pratt was inducted into the Eugene Field Society, a prestigious association of literary Americans, in honor of his discourse "The Majesty of God."[64] His fame even among Mormons is a vague thing: he has left the shadowy impression of those who focus their attentions on things of the mind, as his son Milando explains:

> He was one of those peculiar spirits not liable to be too highly appreciated among their more practical fellow-men. He was a kind of world within himself, and was frequently oblivious to his grosser surroundings in this. Most of the time he dwelt in the world of thought, and being in mental pursuit of the profound, he was liable to be looked upon as a child comparatively in the material matters pertaining to every day life. His spirit did not delight in nibbling little bunches of grass in a limited pasture, nor slaking his thirst at a diminutive spring. He was in his element when he could drink copiously of the waters of the ocean of truth and appease his hunger upon the manna of eternity. Men of that stamp are not appreciated by those who hug closely the earth and have to twist their necks in order to catch a glimpse of those who have climbed to the summit of a majestic mountain.[65]

From the spiritual searches of a young farmhand in "the silent shades of night"[66] came a lasting synthesis of faith and reason which has helped to shape the modern Church of Jesus Christ of Latter-day Saints. T. Edgar Lyon wrote, "Orson Pratt did more to formulate the Mormon idea of God, the religious basis of polygamy, the pre-existence of spirits, the doctrine of the gathering, the resurrection, and eternal salvation than any other person in the Church, with the exception of Joseph Smith."[67] Although this assessment must be qualified—Oliver Cowdery, Brigham Young, Parley P. Pratt and others had significant impact on the Mormon way of seeing the world —Orson Pratt's contributions remain unequaled in volume and scope: his ingenious attempt to bring together a unified theory of nature, God, and humanity, his deeply affirmative vision of man as a noble truthseeker and son of God bring to mind a Mormon Aquinas; a Mormon Aristotle; a "philosopher apostle"—hence a Mormon Paul. Where Joseph Smith revealed the restoration of the gospel of the kindgom, Orson Pratt sought to restore Christianity to a legitimate rational grounding. Actually, Orson Pratt was less a philosopher than a missionary, who like all crusaders, sometimes found the quest troubled by doubt and wavering purpose. Nevertheless, the first Mormon in the Salt Lake Valley was not afraid of his own pioneering mind and, like his Prophet, dared to explore new worlds.

Notes

INTRODUCTION

1. Orson Pratt, "History of Orson Pratt," *Millennial Star* 27:33.

2. Journal History of the Church of Jesus Christ of Latter-day Saints, 3 October 1881, Library-Archives of the Historical Department of the Church of Jesus Christ of Latter-day Saints, Church Office Building, Salt Lake City, Utah (hereafter cited as Church Archives).

3. "Records of Early Church Families," *Utah Genealogical and Historical Magazine* 27:114–16.

4. Orson Pratt, *Great First Cause; or the Self-Moving Forces of the Universe* (Liverpool: R. James, 1851), 15.

CHAPTER 1

1. Orson Pratt to Parley P. Pratt, 10 March 1853, Parley P. Pratt Correspondence, Church Archives.

2. Orson Pratt, "History," 23.

3. Daniel J. Boorstin, *The Americans: The Colonial Experience* (New York: Random House, 1958), 19.

4. David Hawke, *The Colonial Experience* (Indianapolis: Bobbs Merrill, 1966), 70; Arthur D. Coleman, comp., *Pratt Pioneers of Utah* (Provo: J. Grant Stevenson, 1967), xiv.

5. Oliver Perry Chitwood, *A History of Colonial America* (New York: Harper & Brothers, 1961), 124.

6. Orson Pratt to Parley P. Pratt, 10 March 1853.

7. Vernon L. Parrington, *Main Currents in American Thought: The Colonial Mind* (New York: Harcourt, Brace & World, 1954), 55.

8. Hawke, *Colonial Experience*, 148.

9. Orson Pratt to Parley P. Pratt, 10 March 1853.

10. Parrington, *Colonial Mind*, 55.

11. Orson Pratt to Parley P. Pratt, 10 March 1853.

12. From the "Survey of the Summe of Church Discipline," cited in Parrington, *Colonial Mind*, 61.

13. Perry Miller, *The New England Mind: The Seventeenth Century* (Boston: Beacon Press, 1961), 415.

14. See Parrington, *Colonial Mind*, 71; Hawke, *Colonial Experience*, 428; Milando Pratt, "Life and Labors of Orson Pratt," *The Contributor* 12:1:4–5.

15. Miller, *Seventeenth Century*, 420.

16. Hawke, *Colonial Experience*, 150.

17. Parrington, *Colonial Mind*, 58.

18. Miller, *Seventeenth Century*, 409.

19. *Community Biographical Record of Middlesex County, Connecticut* (Chicago: J. H. Beers, 1903), 500.

20. Frederick W. Chapman to Orson Pratt, cited in Orson Pratt to Parley P. Pratt, 10 March 1853.

21. Frederick W. Chapman, *The Pratt Family, or the Descendants of Lt. William Pratt* (Hartford: Case, Lockwood & Co., 1864), 144–45.

22. Edward M. Chapman, ed., *The First Church of Christ in Saybrook* (New Haven: Yale University Press, 1947), 130.

23. Coleman, *Pratt Pioneers*, xix; Orson Pratt, "History," 23.

24. Richard L. Bushman, *From Puritan to Yankee: Character and the Social Order in Connecticut 1690–1765* (Cambridge: Harvard University Press, 1967), 21.

25. "A Lady's Travel in New England by Madam Sarah Kemble Knight" (1704), in Albert Bushnell Hart, ed., *American History Told by Contemporaries: Building of the Republic 1689–1783*, 2 vols. (New York: Macmillan, 1961), 2:228.

26. Bushman, *From Puritan to Yankee*, 150, 152.

27. Ibid., 208.

28. Milton V. Backman, Jr., *American Religions and the Rise of Mormonism* (Salt Lake City: Deseret Book, 1970), 263.

29. Boorstin, *The Americans*, 30.

30. Backman, *Rise of Mormonism*, 263–70.

31. Bushman, *From Puritan to Yankee*, 287.

32. Gilbert C. Fite and Jim E. Reese, *An Economic History of the United States* (Boston: Houghton Mifflin, 1973), 58.

33. Ibid., 114.

34. Orson Pratt, "History," 39.

35. Fite and Reese, *Economic History*, 58.

36. Stanley Coben and Forest G. Hill, *American Economic History: Essays in Interpretation* (Philadelphia, New York: J. B. Lippincott, 1966), 39.

37. Orson Pratt, "History," 39.

38. *Columbia County at the End of the Century*, 2 vols. (Hudson, New York: Hudson Gazette and Record Printing Co., 1900), 2:682–84.

39. Orson Pratt to Parley P. Pratt, 10 March 1853; Orson Pratt, "History," 23.

40. Orson Pratt, "History," 23.

41. Coleman, *Pratt Pioneers*, xviii.

42. Hawke, *Colonial Experience*, 146, 169.

43. Miller, *Seventeenth Century*, 389.

44. Parrington, *Colonial Mind*, 49; also "Report of the Trial of Mrs. Anne Hutchinson," in David D. Hall, ed., *The Antinomian Controversy, 1636–1638 A Documentary History* (Middletown, Conn.: Wesleyan University Press, 1968), 377.

45. Hawke, *Colonial Experience*, 146.

46. Coleman, *Pratt Pioneers*, xviii; Winnifred King Rugg, *Unafraid: A Life of Anne Hutchinson* (Boston: Houghton Mifflin, 1930), 252.
47. Orson Pratt, "History," 39.
48. Parley P. Pratt, *Autobiography of Parley P. Pratt*, 4th ed., ed. Parley P. Pratt, Jr., (Salt Lake City: Deseret Book, 1950), 19.
49. Orson Pratt, "History," 39.
50. *Columbia County* 1:128, 167.
51. Orson Pratt to Parley P. Pratt, 10 March 1853.
52. Ibid.
53. Parley P. Pratt, *Autobiography*, 19.
54. Isabella Brayton, *The Story of Hartford* (Glens Falls, New York: Bullard Press, 1929), 158.
55. Ibid., 3.
56. Ibid., 32, 42.
57. Junius F. Wells, "Three Orsons," *Improvement Era* 22:1:15–18.
58. Orson Pratt to Parley P. Pratt, 10 March 1853.
59. Orson Pratt, "History," 39.
60. Bushman, *From Puritan to Yankee*, 14.
61. Parley P. Pratt, *Autobiography*, 19, 20.
62. Brayton, *Story of Hartford*, 32.
63. Ibid., 40.
64. Orson Pratt, "History," 39.
65. Brayton, *Story of Hartford*, 39; also *Volcano: The Eruption of Mount St. Helens* (Longview, Wash.: Longview Publishing Co., 1980), 95.
66. F. W. Chapman, *The Pratt Family*, 145.
67. *Columbia County*, 2:682–90 passim.
68. Orson Pratt, "History," 39.
69. *Columbia County*, 2:690.
70. Parley P. Pratt, *Autobiography*, 25.
71. Orson Pratt, "History," 39.
72. Milando Pratt, "Life and Labors of Orson Pratt," *The Contributor* 12:2:41.
73. *Columbia County*, 2:692.
74. Marguerite F. Melcher, *The Shaker Adventure* (Princeton: Princeton University Press, 1941), 56.
75. Ibid.
76. See Edward Deming Andrews, *The People Called Shakers* (New York: Oxford University Press, 1953), 75.
77. Vernon Parrington, *Main Currents in American Thought: The Romantic Revolution in America 1800–1860* (New York: Harcourt, Brace & World, 1954), 321–23.
78. Ibid., 313–16.
79. Orson Pratt, "History," 39.
80. Fite and Reese, *Economic History*, 125.
81. Orson Pratt, "History," 39.
82. Ibid.
83. Ibid.
84. *History of Queens County, New York* (New York: W. W. Munsell Co., 1882), 266–67.
85. Orson Pratt, "History," 39.
86. Fite and Reese, *Economic History*, 194, 241.
87. Orson Pratt, "History," 40.

88. Ibid.

89. Harlan Hatcher, *The Western Reserve: The Story of New Connecticut in Ohio* (Indianapolis: Bobbs-Merrill, 1949), 181.

90. Parley P. Pratt, *Autobiography*, 27–30; Orson Pratt, "History," 40.

91. *History of Lorain County, Ohio* (Philadelphia: Williams Brothers, 1879), 332.

92. Ibid., 335; also Orson Pratt, "History," 40.

93. *1830 Census of Lorain County, Ohio*.

94. Orson Pratt, "History," 40.

95. *Cleveland and Its Environs*, 3 vols. (Chicago: Lewis Publishing Co., 1918), 3:169.

96. For information on the Ohio canal system, see Hatcher, *The Western Reserve*, 82–89.

97. A. S. Hayden, *Early History of the Disciples in the Western Reserve* (Cincinnati: Chase & Hall, 1875), 191–209.

98. Parley P. Pratt, *Autobiography*, 33–35.

99. Orson Pratt, "History," 40; Milando Pratt, "Life and Labors of Orson Pratt," *The Contributor* 12:12:464.

100. Bushman, *From Puritan to Yankee*, 287.

101. Orson Pratt, "History," 55.

102. Ibid.

103. Whitney Cross, *The Burned-Over District* (New York: Harper & Row, 1965), 163–64.

104. Klaus J. Hansen, *Mormonism and the American Experience* (Chicago: University of Chicago Press, 1981), 59.

105. *Columbia County*, 2:691–92.

106. Parley P. Pratt, *Autobiography*, 33.

107. *History of Ontario County*, 2 vols. (New York: Lewis Publishing Co., 1911), 2:183.

108. Parley P. Pratt, *Autobiography*, 36–43.

109. Orson Pratt, *Divine Authenticity of the Book of Mormon* (Liverpool, 1851), 83.

110. Orson Pratt, "History," 55; Parley P. Pratt, *Autobiography*, 43.

111. Journal History, 19 September 1880.

112. *Journal of Discourses*, 26 vols. (London: Latter-day Saints' Book Depot, 1854–86; reprint ed., 1967), 7:177.

113. Orson Pratt, "History," 55.

114. Hansen, *Mormonism*, 20.

CHAPTER 2

1. John Henry Evans, *The Heart of Mormonism* (Salt Lake City: Deseret Book Company, 1930), 416.

2. Reva Stanley, *The Archer of Paradise: A Biography of Parley P. Pratt* (Caxton Caldwell, Idaho, 1937), 36.

3. Parley P. Pratt, *Autobiography*, 79.

4. Ibid., 49.

5. Ibid., 44.

6. Ibid., 45.

7. Thomas Ford, *A History of Illinois from its Commencement as a State in 1818 to 1847*, ed. Milo Milton Quaife (Chicago: Lakeside Press, 1945), 214.

8. Orson Pratt, "History," 55.

9. Joseph Smith, Jr., *History of the Church of Jesus Christ of Latter-day Saints*, ed. B. H. Roberts, 7 vols., 2d ed. rev. (Salt Lake City, Deseret News, 1932–51), 1:104–5, 109–10; hereafter cited as *History of the Church*; James B. Allen and Glen M. Leonard, *The Story of the Latter-day Saints* (Salt Lake City: Deseret Book, 1976), 47–51.

10. *Doctrine and Covenants* (1971 ed.) 32–33.

11. *Book of Commandments* (Independence, Missouri, 1833) XXXVI. This passage is now published as *Doctrine and Covenants* 34.

12. Thomas Edgar Lyon, "Orson Pratt: Early Mormon Leader," Master's thesis, University of Chicago, 1932, 21.

13. *Doctrine and Covenants* (Kirtland, Ohio, 1835) 51:3 (hereafter cited as Kirtland *DC*), now 28:9.

14. Parley P. Pratt, *Autobiography*, 48.

15. Orson Pratt,"History," 55.

16. Ibid., 55.

17. *Book of Commandments* XXXVI:1.

18. William F. Seward, ed., *Binghamton and Broome County, New York*, 2 vols. (New York: Lewis Publishing Company, 1924), 2:529.

19. *History of the Church*, 1:47.

20. Ibid., 1:81.

21. Ibid., 1:82–83.

22. Ibid., 1:96.

23. H. P. Smith, ed., *History of Broome County* (Syracuse, New York: D. Mason & Company, 1885), 334, 337; also *History of the Church*, 1:87. Two churches had been built in the township: St. Luke's Episcopal and the Nineveh Presbyterian, which was under the pastorship of John Sherer, the man who had brought the complaint against the Prophet that summer. It is safe to conclude that these pulpits were not opened to the young Mormon, but it was nevertheless common for the missionaries to find audiences of the covertly curious in schoolhouses.

24. *History of the Church*, 1:173, 180–81.

25. Seward, *Binghamton and Broome County*, 529.

26. Orson Pratt, "History," 55.

27. *History of the Church*, 1:44–45.

28. Orson Pratt, "History," 55.

29. Journal History, 27 February 1831.

30. Hayden, *Early History of the Disciples*, 191–209 passim.

31. *History of the Church*, 1:146.

32. See Arthur Bestor, *Backwoods Utopias: the Sectarian Origins and the Owenite Phase of Communitarian Socialism in America: 1663–1829* (Philadelphia: University of Pennsylvania Press, 1970), 6.

33. Phillips Russell, *Emerson, the Wisest American* (New York: Brentano's, 1929), 193–94.

34. Leonard J. Arrington, Feramorz Y. Fox, Dean L. May, *Building the City of God: Community and Cooperation Among the Mormons* (Salt Lake City: Deseret Book, 1976), 4.

35. Hayden, *Early History of the Disciples*, 191–209 passim.

36. Arrington, Fox, May, *Building the City*, 19.

37. Kirtland *DC* 13:9–10, now 42:32–33.

38. Bestor, *Backwoods Utopias*, 266.
39. Ibid., 8–10, 13–15.
40. Arrington, Fox, May, *Building the City*, 4–5.
41. Orson Pratt, "History," 56.
42. *History of the Church*, 1:180–81.
43. Orson Pratt, "History," 55.
44. Andrew Jenson, *Latter-day Saint Biographical Encyclopedia*, 4 vols. (Salt Lake City: Deseret News Press, 1901–36), 1:93.
45. Orson Pratt, *The Seer* (Washington, D.C., 1853–54), 290.
46. Kirtland *DC* 28:9, now 54:7–8.
47. *Doctrine and Covenants* (1971 ed.) 57:4.
48. Kirtland *DC* 27:1, now 57:3.
49. Francis S. Philbrick, *The Rise of the West 1754–1830* (New York: Harper & Row, 1965), 287–89; Ronald N. Satz, *American Indian Policy in the Jacksonian Era* (Lincoln: University of Nebraska Press, 1975), 212; Clinton A. Weslager, *The Delaware Indians* (New Brunswick: Rutgers University Press, 1972), 371.
50. Max H. Parkin, "Missouri's Impact on the Church," *Ensign* 9:4:60.
51. Orson Pratt, "History," 56; Kirtland *DC* 66:6, now 52:26.
52. Orson Pratt, "History," 56; Parley P. Pratt, *Autobiography*, 68–69.
53. Philbrick, *Rise of the West*, 317.
54. *History of the Church*, 1:189–99.
55. Ibid., 1:96.
56. Parley P. Pratt, *Autobiography*, 72.
57. Orson Pratt, "History," 56.
58. *History of the Church*, 1:322.
59. Ibid., 1:242–43.
60. Orson Pratt, "History," 56.
61. Kirtland *DC* 87:3, now 75:14.
62. Orson Pratt Diaries (vol. 1, 2 February 1832–8 June 1833; vol. 2, 11 June 1833–6 May 1834; vol. 3, 7 July 1834–22 January 1835; vol. 4, 6 February 1835–6 November 1837), Church Archives, 2 February 1832.
63. Orson Pratt, "History," 56.
64. H. N. Muller, et al., "Jedidiah Burchard and Vermont's New Measure Revivals," *Vermont History* 46:1:5–20.
65. Orson Pratt, "History," 56.
66. *History of the Church*, 1:332.
67. Orson Pratt, "History," 56.
68. Milando Pratt entry, n.d., Orson Pratt Journal, 1 vol., Church Archives; Andrew Karl Larson, *Erastus Snow* (Salt Lake City: University of Utah Press, 1971), 15–16. The Erastus Snow family record indicates that the woman healed was the wife of Winslow Farr, Olive Farr, who had not walked for seven years.
69. Orson Pratt, "History," 56.
70. Orson Pratt, *The Kingdom of God Part IV* (Liverpool: R. James, 1849), 6.
71. Orson Pratt Diaries, 28 August 1832; Orson Pratt, "History," 57.
72. Orson Pratt Diaries, 20 December 1832; Orson Pratt, "History," 71.
73. See Ernest Sandeen, "Millennialism," in Edwin S. Gaustad, ed., *The Rise of Adventism* (New York: Harper & Row, 1974), 110–11.
74. Orson Pratt Diaries, 2 February 1833.
75. Orson Pratt, "History," 56; Larson, *Erastus Snow*, 17; Jenson, *Latter-day Saint Biographical Encyclopedia*, 1:186, 192, 196–99.

76. Kirtland *DC* 7:19–21, now 88:70, 74, 77.
77. *History of the Church*, 1:301.
78. *Doctrine and Covenants* (1971 ed.) 87:1–2, 8.
79. *History of the Church*, 1:322.
80. Orson Pratt Diaries, 18 February 1833.
81. Kirtland *DC* 7.
82. Kirtland *DC* 80, now 89.
83. Orson Pratt Diaries, 18 February, 8 June 1833.
84. Sandeen, "Millennialism," 114.
85. Orson Pratt Diaries, 15 June 1833.
86. Edward T. Fairbanks, *The Town of St. Johnsbury, Vermont*, (St. Johnsbury, Vermont: Cowles Press, 1914), 217–19.
87. Orson F. Whitney, *History of Utah*, 4 vols. Salt Lake City: Geo. Q. Cannon & Sons Co., 1898) 3:112.
88. *Millennial Star* 27:72; Orson Pratt Diaries, 18 September 1833.
89. Orson Pratt Diaries, 19 September 1833.
90. Ibid., 8 February 1834.
91. Ibid., 27 November 1833–13 February 1834.
92. Parkin, "Missouri's Impact on the Church," 60.
93. Orson Pratt Diaries, 24, 27 February 1834.
94. *History of the Church*, 2:34–35.
95. Ibid., 2:44.
96. Orson Pratt Diaries, 1, 4, 6 May 1834.
97. Ibid., 6 May 1834.
98. Parley P. Pratt, *Autobiography*, 115.
99. *History of the Church*, 2:79–80.
100. Ibid., 2:106, 115–16.
101. Ibid., 2:71, 100.
102. Ibid., 2:103–4.
103. Ibid., 2:121–23.
104. Ibid., 2:124.
105. Ibid., 2:136.
106. Orson Pratt Diaries, 31 July 1834.
107. Ibid., 21 August 1834; Milando Pratt, "Life and Labors of Orson Pratt," *The Contributor* 12:12:460.
108. Orson Pratt Diaries, 6 May 1834.
109. Ibid., 21 August 1834, 2 January 1835.
110. *Latter-day Saints' Messenger & Advocate* 1:5:77.
111. Lorenzo Dow Barnes Diary, 2 vols., Church Archives, 1:7–9.
112. Orson Pratt to Oliver Cowdery, *Messenger & Advocate* 1:6:89.
113. Journal History, 13 October 1834.
114. *The Bible & Polygamy. Does the Bible Sanction Polygamy? A Discussion Between Professor Orson Pratt and Rev. Doctor J. P. Newman* (Salt Lake City: Deseret News Steam Printing Establishment, 1874), 8.
115. Orson Pratt Diaries, 3 March 1835.
116. Postscript to Orson Pratt to Oliver Cowdery, *Messenger & Advocate* 1:6:89.
117. Orson Pratt Diaries, 20 April 1835.
118. *Journal of Discourses*, 12:85–87.
119. Lorenzo Dow Barnes Diary, 1:9.
120. *Messenger & Advocate* 1:6:90.

121. *Journal of Discourses*, 12:87.
122. *Millennial Star* 27:87.
123. *Journal of Discourses*, 12:87.
124. Orson Pratt Diaries, 24 April 1835.
125. Ibid., 24 April 1835.
126. Kirtland *DC* 43:5, now 18:27–28.
127. Kirtland *DC* 3:11, now 107:24.
128. *Journal of Discourses*, 12:87.
129. Ibid., 12:85.
130. Ibid.
131. Orson Pratt, "Family Record," Book A, Church Archives, 2.

CHAPTER 3

1. *History of the Church*, 2:197–98.
2. Ibid., 2:198n.
3. Ibid., 2:194.
4. D. Michael Quinn, "The Evolution of the Presiding Quorums of the LDS Church," *Journal of Mormon History* 1:28; *History of the Church*, 2:200.
5. Orson Pratt Diaries, 4 May 1835.
6. *History of the Church*, 2:219.
7. Joseph Fielding Smith, *Essentials in Church History* (Salt Lake City: Deseret News Press, 1922), 658–60.
8. Ibid., 193–94.
9. Ibid., 670.
10. Orson Pratt Diaries, 5 May–2 June 1835.
11. *History of the Church*, 2:225.
12. Orson Pratt Diaries, 13, 17, 18 June 1835.
13. Journal History, 26 September 1835; Orson Pratt Diaries, 19 June–14 September 1835.
14. Orson Pratt Diaries, 14–19 October 1835.
15. *Doctrine and Covenants* 93:39.
16. Ibid., 88:77–79.
17. *History of the Church*, 2:356.
18. Ibid., 2:368–97; Orson Pratt Diaries, 3 December 1835.
19. Orson Pratt Diaries, 2, 3 December 1835.
20. Louis C. Zucker, "Joseph Smith as a Student of Hebrew," *Dialogue: A Journal of Mormon Thought* 3:2:40–55.
21. *History of the Church*, 4:356.
22. Ibid., 2:309.
23. Orson Pratt Diaries, 3 December 1835.
24. Oliver Cowdery, "Sketch Book," postscript to entry for 16 January 1836, cited in Leonard J. Arrington, "Oliver Cowdery's Kirtland, Ohio, 'Sketch Book,' " *Brigham Young University Studies* 12:4:416.
25. John Whitmer, "History of the Church," John Whitmer Collection, Church Archives, chap. 3.
26. Truman O. Angell Journal, Special Collections, Harold B. Lee Library, Brigham Young University, 5.
27. *Messenger & Advocate* 2:6:281.

28. *Doctrine and Covenants* 109:22–23.
29. *History of the Church*, 2:430.
30. Orson Pratt Diaries, 3 December 1835.
31. Parley P. Pratt, *Autobiography*, 133.
32. Orson Pratt Diaries, 6 April 1836.
33. Parley P. Pratt, *Autobiography*, 134.
34. Orson Pratt Diaries, 6 April 1836.
35. *History of the Church*, 1:421.
36. Orson Pratt Diaries, 28 April 1836.
37. *Messenger & Advocate* 3:1:397.
38. Ibid.
39. Ibid.
40. Orson Pratt Diaries, 28 April 1836.
41. Parley P. Pratt, *Autobiography*, 152.
42. Ibid., 151–52.
43. Orson Pratt Diaries, 27 May 1836.
44. Parley P. Pratt, *Autobiography*, 151.
45. Orson Pratt Diaries, 6 June 1836.
46. *Messenger & Advocate* 3:439–40.
47. Orson Pratt Diaries, 4 July 1836.
48. Ibid., 12 July 1836.
49. *Messenger & Advocate* 3:396–97.
50. Orson Pratt Diaries, 4 September 1836.
51. Marvin S. Hill, et al., *The Kirtland Economy Revisited* (Provo: Brigham Young University Press, 1977), passim.
52. Orson Pratt Diaries, 4 September 1836.
53. Orson Pratt, "History," *Millennial Star* 27:88.
54. *History of the Church*, 2:467.
55. Boorstin, *The Colonial Experience*, 247; Orson Pratt Diaries, 4 September 1836.
56. *History of the Church*, 2:467.
57. Leonard J. Arrington, *Great Basin Kingdom: An Economic History of the Latter-day Saints 1830–1900* (Cambridge: Harvard University Press, 1958), 13.
58. *History of the Church*, 2:468; Allen and Leonard, *Story of the Latter-day Saints*, 111.
59. *Messenger & Advocate*, 3:477.
60. Heber C. Kimball Diary, Church Archives, 48.
61. Arrington, *Great Basin Kingdom*, 14.
62. Allen and Leonard, *Story of the Latter-day Saints*, 113; *History of the Church*, 2:487n.
63. *History of the Church*, 2:488.
64. Parley P. Pratt to Joseph Smith, Jr., 23 May 1837, quoted in Richard Livesey, *An Exposure of Mormonism, Being a Statement of Facts Relating to the Self-styled 'Latter Day Saints' and the Origin of the Book of Mormon* (Preston, England: J. Livesey, 1838), 9.
65. *History of the Church*, 2:485.
66. Ibid., 2:486.
67. Lyman E. Johnson and Orson Pratt, "To the Bishop & his council in Kirtland, the Stake of Zion," 29 May 1837, Newell K. Whitney Collection, Lee Library Special Collections, Brigham Young University.

68. Coleman, *Pratt Pioneers*, 309.
69. Hatcher, *The Western Reserve*, 127.
70. Orson Pratt, "History," *Millennial Star* 27:88; Orson Pratt Diaries, 2 October 1837.
71. *History of the Church*, 2:509–10.
72. Orson Pratt Diaries, 2 October 1837.
73. Ibid., 3 October 1837.
74. Parley P. Pratt, *Autobiography*, 169, 171.
75. Ibid., 169.
76. Whitney, *Life of Heber C. Kimball*, 202.
77. *History of the Church*, 3:47.
78. *Doctrine and Covenants* 118:4–5; *History of the Church*, 3:46.
79. *History of the Church*, 3:41, 42n.
80. Allen and Leonard, *Story of the Latter-day Saints*, 120–30.
81. *History of Caldwell and Livingston Counties, Missouri* (St. Louis: National Historical Co. 1886), 137; *History of the Church* 3:183–86.
82. *Elders' Journal* (Far West, Missouri, August 1838), 61–62.
83. Orson Pratt, "History," *Millennial Star* 27:88.
84. Coleman, *Pratt Pioneers*, 309.
85. *History of the Church*, 3:250.
86. See Stanley B. Kimball, "The Saints and St. Louis, 1831–1857: An Oasis of Tolerance and Security," *Brigham Young University Studies* (hereafter *BYU Studies*) 13:489–519.
87. Orson Pratt, "History," *Millennial Star* 27:88.
88. *History of the Church*, 3:178–81, 192, 209–10.
89. Joseph Smith to Heber C. Kimball and Brigham Young, Winslow W. Smith Collection, n.d., Church Archives.
90. *History of the Church*, 3:250.
91. Orson Pratt, "History," *Millennial Star* 27:88.
92. *History of the Church*, 3:261.
93. Elden J. Watson, ed., *Manuscript History of Brigham Young, 1801–1844* (Salt Lake City: Elden J. Watson, 1968), 34.
94. Brigham Young, "History of Brigham Young," *Millennial Star* 25:567.
95. Edward W. Tullidge, *The History of Salt Lake City and Its Founders* (Salt Lake City: Edward W. Tullidge, 1886), "Biographies," 5.
96. *History of the Church*, 3:175.
97. Whitney, *Life of Heber C. Kimball*, 252.
98. Ibid., 252.
99. Ibid., 253.
100. Brigham Young, "History," *Millennial Star* 567–68, 583–84.
101. Wilford Woodruff Journal, Church Archives, 26 April 1839.
102. *History of the Church*, 3:319–20.
103. Whitney, *Life of Heber C. Kimball*, 254.
104. Wilford Woodruff, *Leaves from My Journal* (Salt Lake City: Deseret News, 1909), 74–75.
105. Zucker, "Joseph Smith as a Student of Hebrew," 48.
106. *History of the Church*, 3:366.
107. Parley P. Pratt, *Autobiography*, 242.
108. Parley P. Pratt, *The Millennium and Other Poems: To Which Is Annexed a Treatise on the Regeneration and Eternal Duration of Matter* (New York: W. Molineaux, 1840), 105, 109–10, 111.

109. Parley P. Pratt, *Autobiography*, 238–39, 243.
110. *The Book of Mormon* (1969 ed.) Alma 20:3.
111. Parley P. Pratt, *Autobiography*, 243.
112. Ibid., 245–46.
113. Ibid., 245–53.
114. Ibid., 258.
115. Ibid., 263–80.
116. Whitney, *Life of Heber C. Kimball*, 262–63; Parley P. Pratt, *Autobiography*, 293–94.
117. Coleman, *Pratt Pioneers*, 309.
118. *History of the Church*, 4:7.
119. Parley P. Pratt, *Autobiography*, 294.

CHAPTER 4

1. Parley P. Pratt, *Autobiography*, 294–96.
2. *History of the Church*, 4:22.
3. Marshall B. Davidson, *The American Heritage History of the Writers' America* (New York: American Heritage Publishing Co., 1973), 126.
4. *History of the Church*, 4:22.
5. Orson Pratt to Sarah Pratt, *Times & Seasons* 1:61.
6. *History of the Church*, 4:40.
7. Parley P. Pratt, *Autobiography*, 297–98.
8. Orson Pratt to Sarah Pratt, *Times & Seasons* 1:61.
9. "Farewell Song," *Millennial Star* 1:48.
10. James B. Allen and Thomas G. Alexander, eds., *Manchester Mormons: The Journal of William Clayton 1840 to 1842* (Salt Lake City: Peregrine Smith, 1974), 137n.
11. *History of the Church*, 4:104.
12. "Brigham Young, Heber C. Kimball, Orson Pratt, and Parley P. Pratt, to the church," 19 February 1840, *Times & Seasons* 1:70.
13. Parley P. Pratt, *Autobiography*, 301.
14. *History of the Church*, 4:104.
15. Ibid., 4:114–19.
16. Allen and Alexander, *Manchester Mormons*, 141–42.
17. Ibid., 11–12.
18. James B. Allen and Malcolm R. Thorp, "The Mission of the Twelve to England 1840–41: Mormon Apostles and the Working Classes," *BYU Studies* 5:512.
19. John W. Dodds, *The Age of Paradox: A Biography of England 1841–1851* (London: Victor Gollancz, 1953), 24.
20. Ibid., 26, 27.
21. See *Journal of Discourses*, 21:303–16.
22. Allen and Alexander, *Manchester Mormons*, 11.
23. "Life Story of John Leishman," typescript in possession of Mrs. Leo C. Nielsen, Logan, Utah; also Orson Pratt, *Remarkable Visions* (Liverpool: R. James, 1848), 16.
24. Dodds, *Age of Paradox*, 29.
25. A. J. Youngson, *The Making of Classical Edinburgh* (Edinburgh: Edinburgh University Press, 1966), 1.

26. Richard L. Evans, *A Century of Mormonism in Great Britain* (Salt Lake City: Deseret News Press, 1937), 80–81.
27. Youngson, *Classical Edinburgh*, 284.
28. Ibid., 15, 265.
29. Orson Pratt, "History," *Millennial Star* 27:88.
30. Orson Pratt to Parley P. Pratt, 17 October 1840, *Millennial Star* 1:213.
31. *History of the Church*, 4:251.
32. Ibid., 4:332.
33. Reuben Hedlock to Parley P. Pratt, *Millennial Star* 1:92.
34. Henry Thomas Buckle, *On Scotland and the Scotch Intellect* (Chicago: University of Chicago Press, 1970), 385–86, 387.
35. James McCosh, *The Scottish Philosophy, Biographical, Expository, Critical, from Hutcheson to Hamilton* (New York: Robert Carter & Bros., 1874), 393–97.
36. Elizabeth Flower and Murray G. Murphey, *A History of Philosophy in America*, 2 vols. (New York: G. P. Putnam's Sons, 1977), 1:xiv.
37. Allen and Alexander, *Manchester Mormons*, 158.
38. Oliver Cowdery to *Messenger & Advocate* 1:1:14–16.
39. See James B. Allen, "Contemporary Accounts of Joseph Smith's First Vision," *Improvement Era* 73:4:12; also "Significance of Joseph Smith's First Vision in Mormon Thought," *Dialogue* 1:29–45.
40. See Orson Pratt, *A Interesting Account of Several Remarkable Visions, and of the Late Discovery of Ancient American Records* (Edinburgh: Ballantyne and Hughes), 1840.
41. Oliver Cowdery to *Messenger & Advocate* 1:1:2.
42. *History of the Church*, 4:540–41.
43. Orson Pratt, *Remarkable Visions*, 13.
44. All references are from Orson Pratt, *Remarkable Visions*, 12–16.
45. All references are from "Articles of Faith," *Pearl of Great Price* (1969 ed.) 60.
46. Orson Pratt to Parley P. Pratt, 16 April 1841, *Millennial Star* 2:12.
47. *Improvement Era* 15:198.
48. Marilyn Goodrich, "History of Marian Ross Pratt," manuscript in possession of author, 2; Milando Pratt, "Reminiscences of Sister Marian Ross Pratt," 7 March 1923, in possession of Sterling Beesley, Bountiful, Utah.
49. T. Edgar Lyon, "Nauvoo and the Council of the Twelve," in *The Restoration Movement: Essays in Mormon History*, ed. F. Mark McKiernan, et al. (Lawrence, Kansas: Coronado Press, 1973), 180.
50. Orson Pratt to Parley P. Pratt, 16 April 1841, *Millennial Star* 2:12.
51. Allen and Alexander, *Manchester Mormons*, 13.
52. Allen and Thorp, "The Mission of the Twelve," 499–500; Frederick S. Buchanan, "Scots Among the Mormons," *Utah Historical Quarterly* 36:4:329.
53. *History of the Church*, 4:348.
54. "History of Brigham Young," *Millennial Star* 26:139.
55. *History of the Church*, 4:382.
56. Heber C. Kimball to Parley P. Pratt, 15 July 1841, *Millennial Star* 2:77–78.
57. "BOOKS! BOOKS!! BOOKS!!!," *Times & Seasons* 2:502.
58. *History of the Church*, 4:400.
59. *Times & Seasons* 2:517.
60. *History of the Church*, 4:414.
61. *Times & Seasons* 3:631.
62. Ibid., 2:517.

63. Ibid., 3:631.

64. Boorstin, *The Colonial Experience*, 168.

65. Davidson, *The Writers' America*, 126–27. The most famous example of the scholar-laborer was Elihu Burritt, the "Learned Blacksmith," who aimed to "stand in the ranks of the workingmen of New England and beckon them onward and upward to the full stature of intellectual men." Burritt studied Greek, geology, French, Hebrew, Syriac, Danish, Bohemian, Polish and astronomy—all at the forge!

66. Eliza R. Snow, "The Transformation," Orson Pratt Collection, Church Archives.

67. *Times & Seasons* 3:630–31.

68. Junius F. Wells, "Three Orsons," *Improvement Era* 22:1:21.

69. *The Wasp* (published at Nauvoo by William Smith and John Taylor), 12 September 1842.

70. *Times & Seasons* 3:630.

71. *History of the Church*, 4:400.

72. Lyon, "Nauvoo and the Council of the Twelve," 187–89; *History of the Church*, 4:433–38.

73. *Times & Seasons* 3:638.

74. *History of the Church*, 4:169, 172.

75. John C. Bennett to the *Sangamo Journal*, 2 July 1842.

76. "The Workings of Mormonism related by Mrs. Orson Pratt, Salt Lake City, 1884," Church Archives.

77. *History of the Church*, 4:288.

78. See Hugh W. Nibley, *An Egyptian Endowment: The Message of the Joseph Smith Papyri* (Salt Lake City: Deseret Book, 1975); also Heber C. Kimball to Parley P. Pratt, 17 June 1842, Parley P. Pratt Collection, Church Archives, 80.

79. See *Doctrine and Covenants* 132:19.

80. "Orson Pratt's Testimony" in Andrew Jenson, *Historical Record*, 9 vols. (Salt Lake City, 1882–90), 6:280; Journal History, 17 September 1878.

81. Danel W. Bachman, "New Light on an Old Hypothesis: The Ohio Origins of the Revelation on Eternal Marriage," *Journal of Mormon History* 5:24.

82. See *Doctrine and Covenants* 132, preface.

83. Jenson, *Historical Record*, 6:219.

84. Ibid., 6:221.

85. *Doctrine and Covenants* 110:11–16.

86. Lyon, "Nauvoo and the Council of the Twelve," 177.

87. *History of the Church*, 5:18–19, 32.

88. Testimony of Catherine Fuller Warren, Nauvoo High Council Minutes, 20–25 May 1842, cited in Robert D. Hutchins, "Joseph Smith, III: Moderate Mormon," Master's thesis, Brigham Young University, 1977, 33. (I am indebted to Richard Van Wagoner for pointing this out to me.)

89. John C. Bennett to the *Sangamo Journal*, 15 July 1842.

90. Sarah Pratt, "Workings of Mormonism," Church Archives.

91. Wilhelm W. Wyl [Wymetal], *Mormon Portraits, Joseph Smith, the Prophet, His Family and His Friends* (Salt Lake City, 1886), 61.

92. John C. Bennett to the *Sangamo Journal*, 15 July 1842.

93. *Times & Seasons* 3:630.

94. Ibid., 3:830.

95. Lyon, "Nauvoo and the Council of the Twelve," 177.

96. *History of the Church*, 5:4, 22.

97. Heber C. Kimball to Parley P. Pratt, Parley P. Pratt Collection, Church Archives, 17 June 1842.

98. *Sangamo Journal*, 1 August 1842.

99. "Affidavit of J. B. Backenstos," Church Archives, 28 July 1842.

100. *The Wasp*, 23 July 1842, 3.

101. *Sangamo Journal*, 1 August 1842.

102. *History of the Church*, 5:60–61.

103. Alexander Neibaur, Journal, Church Archives, 15 July 1842.

104. Ebenezer Robinson, "Items of Personal History of the Editor; Including Some Items of Church History Not Generally Known," in *The Return* (Davis City, Iowa, 1889), 2:11:110, 111.

105. *History of the Church*, 5:138.

106. Sterling Beesley to the author, 10 March 1981, in author's possession.

107. *Sangamo Journal*, 1 August 1842.

108. *Times & Seasons* 3:869; Brigham Young Papers #103, Church Archives.

109. Brigham Young to Parley P. Pratt, Brigham Young Collection, Church Archives, 17 July 1842.

110. "History of Brigham Young," *Millennial Star* 26:151.

111. John Taylor, "Succession in the Priesthood, A Discourse by President John Taylor, delivered at the Priesthood Meeting, held in the Salt Lake Assembly Hall, Friday Evening, October 7th, 1881, Reported by Geo. F. Gibbs," Utah Historical Society Library, 18.

112. Robert Bruce Flanders, *Nauvoo: Kingdom on the Mississippi* (Urbana: University of Illinois Press, 1965), 270 n.

113. "History of Brigham Young," *Millennial Star* 26:151; also Taylor "Succession in the Priesthood," 19.

114. Manuscript History of the Church of Jesus Christ of Latter-day Saints, Church Archives, 29 August 1842.

115. Wilford Woodruff Journals, Church Archives, August 1842.

116. Manuscript History of the Church, 29 August 1842; see also Stephen H. Goddard to Orson Pratt, sworn to 23 July 1842, *Weekly Missouri Republican*, 3 July 1844, in John Taylor scrapbook, Special Collections, Marriott Library, University of Utah.

117. Manuscript History of the Church, 29 August 1842; see also "Testimony of Mrs. Zeruiah Goddard," John Taylor scrapbook.

118. *History of the Church*, 5:42.

119. Orson Pratt to *The Wasp*, 2 September 1842.

120. *History of the Church*, 5:74.

121. Orson Pratt to *The Wasp*, 1 October 1842.

122. Lyon, "Nauvoo and the Council of the Twelve," 178.

123. *The Wasp*, 1 October 1842, 4.

124. Ibid., 2.

125. Ibid., 24 September 1842, 2.

126. John C. Bennett to Sidney Rigdon and Orson Pratt, 10 January 1843, Sidney Rigdon Collection, Church Archives.

127. *History of the Church*, 5:251, 252.

128. Watson, Manuscript History of Brigham Young 1801–1844, 126.

129. "Minutes of the Council of Twelve," 20 January 1843, Church Archives,.

130. *Journal of Discourses*, 7:176–77.

131. Ibid., 17:224–25. Additional sources on the Sarah Pratt affair are: Mary

Elizabeth Rollins Lightner to Emmeline B. Wells, 21 November 1880, Church Archives (I am indebted to Richard Van Wagoner for this source); Jenson, *Historical Record* 6:232; D. Michael Quinn, "Latter-day Prayer Circles"; Robert D. Foster to *The Wasp*, 1 September 1842; Wyl, *Mormon Portraits*, 60–61; Allen and Leonard, *Story of the Latter-day Saints*, 151; Richard Van Wagoner, "Sarah M. Pratt: The Woman Behind the Controversy," unpublished ms. in possession of Richard Van Wagoner, Lehi, Utah; Lyon, "Nauvoo and the Council of the Twelve," 177; Memoirs of President Joseph Smith," *Saints Herald*, 22 January 1935, 109; Journal History, 22 January 1875, Church Archives; Taylor, "Succession in the Priesthood," 17–18.

132. Orson Pratt, "History," *Millennial Star* 27:88.

CHAPTER 5

1. *Times & Seasons* 3:9:704–6.
2. See *Pearl of Great Price*, Abraham 3:9.
3. Orson Pratt, *The Majesty of God*, comp. Nels B. Lundwall (Salt Lake City, 1950), 10.
4. *Times & Seasons* 4:152.
5. Pratt, *Majesty of God*, 12, 13.
6. *Times & Seasons* 4:204.
7. *Doctrine and Covenants* 27:11; 116.
8. *History of the Church*, 5:339.
9. See Truman G. Madsen, *Eternal Man* (Salt Lake City: Deseret Book, 1970), 47.
10. *History of the Church*, 5:289–90.
11. Ibid., 5:368.
12. Ibid., 5:367.
13. Ibid., 5:475.
14. Ibid., 5:368.
15. Ibid., 3:366.
16. Brigham Young, "History," *Millennial Star* 26:338.
17. *History of the Church*, 6:22.
18. Ibid.
19. Ibid., 6:22, 23; Theodore Dwight Bozeman, *Protestants in an Age of Science: The Baconian Ideal and Antebellum American Religious Thought* (Chapel Hill: University of North Carolina Press, 1977), 93.
20. Joseph Fielding Smith, *Essentials in Church History*, 318–19.
21. See James E. Talmage, *The House of the Lord*, rev. ed. (Salt Lake City: Deseret Book, 1968), 84.
22. Wilford Woodruff Journal, 23 December 1843.
23. Watson, *Manuscript History of Brigham Young 1801–1844*, 159.
24. See David John Buerger, " 'The Fulness of the Priesthood': The Second Anointing in Latter-day Saint Theology and Practice," *Dialogue* 16:1:21, 22.
25. D. Michael Quinn, "The Council of Fifty and Its Members, 1844 to 1945," *BYU Studies* 20:2:163–97.
26. Harold Schindler, *Orrin Porter Rockwell: Man of God, Son of Thunder* (Salt Lake City: University of Utah Press, 1983), 79–80, 81n; see also Wilhelm Wyl, *Mormon Portraits, Joseph Smith the Prophet, His Family and His Friends* (Salt Lake City,

1886), 33–34. The crime was generally attributed to Joseph's friend and bodyguard, Orrin Porter Rockwell. After forty years, Sarah Marinda Pratt maintained that she had refused to lend Rockwell Orson's prize rifle. John C. Bennett hinted to her that the rifle was wanted for "that job."

27. *History of the Church*, 6:124–30.

28. Donna Hill, *Joseph Smith*, 311.

29. *History of the Church*, 4:465 and 6:124, 262.

30. Orson Pratt, *Prophetic Almanac for 1845* (New York: The Prophet Office, 1844), 18.

31. *History of the Church*, 6:177.

32. Donna Hill, *Joseph Smith*, 390–99.

33. *History of the Church*, 6:279–80.

34. Ibid., 6:286.

35. Ibid., 6:260.

36. Ibid., 6:369–72.

37. Ibid., 6:372.

38. Ibid., 6:373–76.

39. Ibid., 6:386–97.

40. Orson Pratt, *Prophetic Almanac for 1845*, 5–10.

41. *The Prophet* 1:4:2.

42. Thomas Ford, *A History of Illinois from its Commencement as a State in 1818 to 1847*, ed. Milo Milton Quaife (Chicago: Lakeside Press, 1945), 160–61.

43. Donna Hill, *Joseph Smith*, 391–96.

44. *History of the Church*, 6:519.

45. Ford, *History of Illinois*, 184–85.

46. Ibid., 212.

47. Ibid., 212, 213; Allen and Leonard, *Story of the Latter-day Saints*, 194–96.

48. Parley P. Pratt, *Autobiography*, 331.

49. *History of the Church*, 7:175.

50. Brigham Young, "History," *Millennial Star* 26:359.

51. Ibid., 26:359.

52. *History of the Church*, 7:228–42.

53. Allen and Leonard, *Story of the Latter-day Saints*, 198–206.

54. Sidney Rigdon to *The Prophet*, 1:24:1.

55. *History of the Church*, 7:299.

56. T. Edgar Lyon, "Orson Pratt: Early Mormon Leader" (Master's thesis, University of Chicago, 1932), 171; Coleman, *Pratt Pioneers*, 309.

57. Lyon, "Orson Pratt," 171.

58. Allen and Leonard, *Story of the Latter-day Saints*, 202–6.

59. *History of the Church*, 7:344–45.

60. Ibid., 7:345, 349.

61. Ibid., 7:352.

62. B. H. Roberts, *A Comprehensive History of the Church of Jesus Christ of Latter-day Saints*, 6 vols. (Salt Lake City: Deseret News, 1930), 2:468.

63. *History of the Church*, 7:378.

64. *Doctrine and Covenants* 124:32.

65. *History of the Church*, 7:393.

66. *Times & Seasons* 6:919.

76. *History of the Church*, 7:428.

68. Ibid., 7:425.

69. Ibid., 7:435.

70. *New York Messenger*, 2 August 1845, 37, 40.

71. Ibid., 13 September 1845, 81–82.

72. "Mormon Philosophy," *New York Messenger*, 13 September 1845, 81–82.

73. See Sterling M. McMurrin, *The Theological Foundations of the Mormon Religion* (Salt Lake City: University of Utah Press, 1965), 45.

74. James McCosh, *The Scottish Philosophy, Biographical, Expository, Critical, from Hutcheson to Hamilton* (New York: Robert Carter & Bros., 1874), 327.

75. Flower and Murphey, *Philosophy in America*, 285.

76. Orson Pratt, *Absurdities of Immaterialism* (Liverpool: R. James, 1849), 7, 19.

77. *Doctrine and Covenants* 93:33–35.

78. Ibid., 130:22.

79. *History of the Church*, 6:302–17.

80. *Doctrine and Covenants* 93:29.

81. *History of the Church*, 6:311.

82. McMurrin, *Theological Foundations*, 3.

83. Fawn M. Brodie, *No Man Knows My History: The Life of Joseph Smith the Mormon Prophet* (New York: Alfred A. Knopf, 1978), 171.

84. See *Pearl of Great Price*, Abraham 3:18–22.

85. Thomas Dick, *The Philosophy of a Future State* (New York: R. Schoyer, 1831), 44, 156.

86. Rene Dubos, *The Dreams of Reason: Science and Utopias* (New York: Columbia University Press, 1961), 32.

87. Dick, *Philosophy of a Future State*, 255.

88. Ibid., 229.

89. Ibid., 106.

90. Ibid.

91. Edward T. Jones, "The Theology of Thomas Dick and its Possible Relationship to that of Joseph Smith," (Master's thesis, Brigham Young University, 1969), 14, 94, 95.

92. Brodie, *No Man Knows My History*, 171.

93. *Messenger & Advocate* 3:3:417–23.

94. Joseph Willard Tingey, "An Explication of Some Philosophical Aspects of the Thought of Orson Pratt," (Master's thesis, Brigham Young University, 1958), Abstract, 2.

95. *New York Messenger*, 6 September 1845, 76.

96. Ibid., 18 October 1845, 125.

97. Ibid.

98. Coleman, *Pratt Pioneers*, 309.

99. Orson Pratt, *Prophetic Almanac for 1846* (New York: New York Messenger Office, 1845), 17–18.

100. Vernon L. Parrington, *The Romantic Revolution in America* (New York: Harcourt, Brace, and World, 1954), 324, 382.

101. Ralph Waldo Emerson, *Essays and Lectures* (New York: Viking Press, 1983), 386.

102. Edward T. Jones, "Theology of Thomas Dick," 27, 28.

103. Orson Pratt, *Prophetic Almanac for 1846*, 20.

104. McMurrin, *Theological Foundations*, 42.

105. Allen and Leonard, *Story of the Latter-day Saints*, 209, 213–14.

106. *History of the Church*, 7:543.

107. Orson Pratt to Brigham Young, 21 October 1845, Brigham Young Papers, Church Archives; Thomas Jefferson Farnham, *Travels in the Great Western Prairies* (New York, 1841), 5–6.

108. *New York Messenger*, 15 November 1845, 153. As a result of this call to the Saints, Orson had his hand in the founding of an important American city, for Brannan's company did indeed double Cape Horn the following year making their landfall at the Golden Gate and joining the first settlers of the present city of San Francisco. Ironically, between the departure and arrival of Brannan's vessel, the *Brooklyn*, California became a territory of the "evil nation," the United States.

109. Allen and Leonard, *Story of the Latter-day Saints*, 211–12.

110. B. H. Roberts, *Comprehensive History*, 2:505.

111. *New York Messenger*, 15 November 1845, 153.

112. *History of the Church*, 7:543.

113. Ibid., 7:541–42.

114. Ibid., 7:544.

115. Ibid.

116. Ford, *History of Illinois*, 304–5.

117. Allen and Leonard, *Story of the Latter-day Saints*, 220.

118. *History of the Church*, 7:554.

119. Orson Pratt to Brigham Young, 12 January 1846, Brigham Young Papers, Church Archives.

120. Coleman, *Pratt Pioneers*, 60.

121. *History of the Church*, 7:573, 576.

122. Coleman, *Pratt Pioneers*, 309.

CHAPTER 6

1. Orson Pratt Journal (14 February–23 June 1846), Church Archives, 14 February 1846; see also published version, Orson Pratt, "History," *Millennial Star* 11:362–12:180. For a literate account of the Mormon trek, see Wallace Stegner, *The Gathering of Zion: The Story of the Mormon Trail* (New York: McGraw-Hill, 1964).

2. Orson Pratt Journal, 14 February 1846.

3. Richard D. Poll, Thomas G. Alexander, Eugene E. Campbell, David E. Miller, eds., *Utah's History* (Provo: Brigham Young University Press, 1978), 117.

4. *History of the Church*, 7:580.

5. Coleman, *Pratt Pioneers*, 310.

6. Orson Pratt, "History," 11:362.

7. Parley P. Pratt, *Autobiography*, 340.

8. *History of the Church*, 7:587–91.

9. William Clayton, *The Latter-day Saints' Emigrants' Guide*, ed. Stanley B. Kimball (Gerald, Mo.: The Patrice Press, 1983), 27.

10. Orson Pratt Journal, 18 February 1846.

11. Orson Pratt, "History," *Millennial Star* 11:362.

12. Orson Pratt Journal, 1 March 1846.

13. Ibid., 1 March 1846.

14. Ibid., 2 March 1846.

15. Ibid., 4 March 1846.

16. Ibid., 5, 6 March 1846.

17. Ibid., 23 March 1846.

18. Hosea Stout, *On the Mormon Frontier: The Diary of Hosea Stout 1844–1861*, ed. Juanita Brooks (Salt Lake City: University of Utah Press, 1964), 1:136, 143.

19. Milando Pratt, "The Life and Labors of Orson Pratt," *The Contributor* 12:4:131.

20. Orson Pratt Journal, 9, 10, 11 April 1846.

21. *History of the Church*, 7:608.

22. Orson Pratt Journal, 12 April 1846.

23. Brigham H. Roberts, "Manuscript History of Brigham Young," Church Archives, 26 April 1846.

24. Orson Pratt Journal, 27 April 1846.

25. William Clayton, *William Clayton's Journal* (Salt Lake City: Deseret News, 1921), 26.

26. Wilford Woodruff Journal, 30 April 1846.

27. Allen and Leonard, *Story of the Latter-day Saints*, 221.

28. Parley P. Pratt, *Autobiography*, 342; see Deuteronomy 3:27.

29. Orson Pratt, "History," *Millennial Star* 12:3.

30. Orson Pratt Journal, 22 May 1846.

31. Ibid., 22 May 1846.

32. Ibid., 22 May, 10 June 1846.

33. Ibid., 12, 13 June 1846.

34. Juanita Brooks, *John Doyle Lee, Zealot—Pioneer Builder—Scapegoat* (Glendale, Calif.: Arthur H. Clark, 1961), 94–95.

35. Orson Pratt, "History," *Millennial Star* 12:3.

36. Orson Pratt Journal, 14–17 June 1846.

37. Ibid., 19 June 1846.

38. Cited in Leonard J. Arrington, *Charles C. Rich: Mormon General and Western Frontiersman* (Provo: Brigham Young University Press, 1974), 98; also Orson Pratt, "History," *Millennial Star* 12:3.

39. Clayton, *Journal*, 44.

40. Roberts, "Brigham Young," 26, 30 June, 12 July 1846.

41. Ibid., 16 August 1846.

42. Stout, *On the Mormon Frontier*, 1:186.

43. Ibid., 1:193.

44. Clayton, *Journal*, 44–47, 60–63.

45. Roberts, "Brigham Young," 3 September 1846.

46. Ibid., 5 September 1846.

47. Ibid., 4 October, 1 November 1846.

48. Stout, *On the Mormon Frontier*, 1:203.

49. Roberts, "Brigham Young," 17 December 1846.

50. Stout, *On the Mormon Frontier*, 1:208–9.

51. Ibid., 1:230.

52. Roberts, "Brigham Young," 19 December 1846.

53. Stout, *On the Mormon Frontier*, 1:221.

54. Roberts, "Brigham Young," 14 January 1847.

55. Ibid., 15 January, 12 February 1847.

56. Allan Nevins, ed., *Polk: The Diary of a President 1845–1849* (New York: Longmans, Green and Co., 1952), 109.

57. Roberts, "Brigham Young," 17 December 1846, 26 April 1847.

58. Journal History, 9 April 1847.

59. Kate B. Carter, comp., *Heart Throbs of the West*, 3 vols. (Salt Lake City: Daughters of the Utah Pioneers, 1940), 2:278.

60. Stegner, *Gathering of Zion*, 113–14.

61. Guy E. Stringham, "The Pioneer Roadometer," *Utah Historical Quarterly* 42:3:258–72; also Clayton, *Journal*, 83, 136, 143; also Orson Pratt Journal, 12 May 1847.

62. Orson Pratt Journal, 4 May 1847.

63. Wilford Woodruff Journal, 23 April 1847; also Clayton, *Journal*, 92–93.

64. Clayton, *Journal*, 102.

65. Clayton, *Emigrants' Guide*, 15, 45.

66. Orson Pratt Journal, 7 May 1847.

67. Bernard DeVoto, *The Year of Decision 1846* (Boston: Houghton Mifflin, 1941), 146–86.

68. Orson Pratt Journal, 9 May 1847.

69. Ibid., 11 May 1847.

70. Ibid., 15 May 1847.

71. Ibid., 24 May 1847; Stegner, *Gathering of Zion*, 136.

72. Orson Pratt Journal, 14 May 1847.

73. Ibid., 22 May 1847.

74. Clayton, *Journal*, 172.

75. Washington Irving, *Astoria*, quoted in John Conron, *The American Landscape* (New York: Oxford University Press, 1974), 332.

76. Clayton, *Journal*, 175.

77. Orson Pratt Journal, 22 May 1847.

78. Clayton, *Journal*, 159.

79. Ibid., 199–200.

80. Ibid., 184.

81. Clayton, *Emigrants' Guide*, 57.

82. Orson Pratt Journal, 21, 18 May 1847.

83. Ibid., 29 May, 7 June 1847.

84. DeVoto, *Year of Decision*, 459.

85. Hubert Howe Bancroft, *History of Utah* (Salt Lake City: Bookcraft, 1964), 256.

86. Orson Pratt "History," *Millennial Star* 12:100; Stegner, *Gathering of Zion*, 141.

87. Wilford Woodruff Journal, 13 June 1847.

88. Orson Pratt Journal, 19–26 June 1847; Orson Pratt, "History," *Millennial Star* 12:130–31, 145–46.

89. Orson Pratt Journal, 26 June 1847.

90. Orson Pratt, "History," *Millennial Star* 12:140; also Clayton, *Journal*, 270–71.

91. Orson Pratt, "History," *Millennial Star* 12:147.

92. DeVoto, *Year of Decision*, 462; Clayton, *Journal*, 273–78.

93. Orson Pratt, "History," *Millennial Star* 12:161.

94. Clayton, *Emigrants' Guide*, 75.

95. Orson Pratt, "History," *Millennial Star* 12:163.

96. Orson Pratt Journal, 10 July 1847.

97. Orson Pratt, "History," *Millennial Star* 12:164–65.

98. Orson Pratt Journal, 13 July 1847.

99. Carter, *Heart Throbs*, 2:87.
100. Orson Pratt Journal, 14 July 1847.
101. Carter, *Heart Throbs*, 2:281; John Brown, *Autobiography of Pioneer John Brown, 1820–1896*, John Zimmerman Brown, ed. (Salt Lake City: 1941), 77; Orson Pratt, "History," *Millennial Star* 12:165.
102. Orson Pratt, "History," *Millennial Star* 12:165.
103. Ibid., 12:166.
104. Ibid.
105. Ibid., 12:177.
106. Brown, *Autobiography*, 78.
107. Clayton, *Journal*, 303.
108. Ibid., 301.
109. Clayton, *Emigrants' Guide*, 85.
110. Andrew Karl Larson, *Erastus Snow: The Life of a Missionary and Pioneer for the Early Mormon Church* (Salt Lake City: University of Utah Press, 1971), 17.
111. Orson Pratt, "History," *Millennial Star* 12:178.
112. Bancroft, *History of Utah*, 260.
113. Orson Pratt, "History," *Millennial Star* 12:178.
114. Brown, *Autobiography*, 78.
115. Clayton, *Journal*, 409.
116. Erastus Snow Journal, Church Archives, vol. 4, 23 July 1847.
117. Orson Pratt, "History," *Millennial Star* 12:178–79.
118. Brown, *Autobiography*, 78.
119. Bancroft, *History of Utah*, 261; Orson Pratt, "History," *Millennial Star* 12:179.
120. Orson Pratt Journal, 25 July 1847.
121. Ibid., 27 July 1847.
122. Ibid.
123. Ibid., 28 July 1847.
124. Orson Pratt, "History," *Millennial Star* 12:180.
125. Bancroft, *History of Utah*, 264.
126. Clayton, *Journal*, 331–32.

CHAPTER 7

1. Journal History, 2 August 1847; Clayton, *Journal*, 340.
2. Journal History, 3 August 1847.
3. Ibid., 5 August 1847.
4. Ibid., 6 August 1847; Clayton, *Journal*, 342.
5. Carter, *Heart Throbs of the West*, 2:269; Journal History, 7 August 1847.
6. Clayton, *Journal*, 345.
7. Coleman, *Pratt Pioneers* 309; Journal History, 12 August 1847.
8. Journal History, 30 August 1847.
9. See Clayton, *Emigrants' Guide*, 5.
10. Journal History, 5 September 1847.
11. Parley P. Pratt, *Autobiography*, 359–60.
12. Coleman, *Pratt Pioneers* 309.
13. Journal History, 25 September 1847.
14. Bancroft, *History of Utah*, 275.

15. Journal History, 9 September 1847.
16. Journal History, 7 November 1847.
17. Coleman, *Pratt Pioneers* 312.
18. Journal History, 3 February 1848.
19. "Incidents of the Battle of Nauvoo," Journal History, 30 September 1846.
20. See "Miscellaneous Minutes," 5 December 1847 and 12 February 1848, Brigham Young Papers, Church Archives.
21. Stout, *On the Mormon Frontier*, 1:292.
22. Orson Pratt to Brigham Young, 22 July 1847, Brigham Young Papers, Church Archives.
23. Journal History, 19 March 1848.
24. Ibid., 22 April 1848.
25. Journal History, 26 April 1848.
26. Ibid., 20 July 1848.
27. Goodrich, "Marian Ross Pratt," 2.
28. Journal History, 11 July 1848.
29. Ibid., 12 April 1849.
30. Full title: *Divine Authority, or The Question, Was Joseph Smith Sent of God*? (Liverpool: R. James, 1848).
31. Ibid., 1.
32. Ibid., 15.
33. Ibid., 16.
34. Journal History, 11 December 1848.
35. Ibid., 31 October 1848.
36. E. J. Hobsbawm, *The Age of Revolution 1789–1848* (New York: World Publishing Co., 1962), 140.
37. Parley P. Pratt, *Voice of Warning*, 49; Orson Pratt, *The Kingdom of God* (Liverpool: R. James, 1848–49), 1, 2.
38. Orson Pratt, *Kingdom of God*, 1.
39. Ibid., 3.
40. See Parley P. Pratt, *Mormonism Unveiled: Zion's Watchman Unmasked and its Editor, Mr. L. R. Sunderland, Exposed: Truth Vindicated: The Devil and Priestcraft in Danger!* (New York, 1838), 29.
41. Orson Pratt, *Kingdom of God*, 40.
42. Ibid., 5.
43. McMurrin, *Theological Foundations*, 45.
44. Orson Pratt, *Kingdom of God*, 6.
45. Ibid., 16.
46. Richard Olson, *Scottish Philosophy and British Physics 1750–1880: A Study in the Foundations of the Victorian Scientific Style* (Princeton: Princeton University Press, 1975), 28.
47. See Joseph Paton, *Remarks on Mormonism, with the Approbation of Clergymen of Different Denominations* (Glasgow, 1849).
48. Orson Pratt, *Reply to a Pamphlet Printed at Glasgow, with the "Approbation of Clerymen of Different Denominations," entitled "Remarks on Mormonism"* (Liverpool: R. James, 1849), 1.
49. Ibid., 3–4.
50. Joseph Willard Tingey, "An Explication of Some Philosophical Aspects of the Thought of Orson Pratt" (Master's thesis, Brigham Young University, 1958), 16.
51. Orson Pratt, *Absurdities of Immaterialism; or, A Reply to T. W. P. Taylder's*

Pamphlet, Entitled: "The Materialism of the Mormons or Latter-day Saints Examined Exposed (Liverpool: R. James, 1849), 3.

52. Ibid., 4–5.
53. Ibid., 5.
54. Ibid., 5–6.
55. Ibid., 8.
56. Ibid.
57. Ibid., 10–11.
58. Ibid., 3.
59. See Tingey, "The Thought of Orson Pratt," 18.
60. Orson Pratt, *Absurdities of Immaterialism*, 13.
61. Ibid., 6.
62. Ibid., 7.
63. See Tingey, "The Thought of Orson Pratt," 26–27; Orson Pratt, *Absurdities of Immaterialism*, 5.
64. See Tingey, "The Thought of Orson Pratt," 22–23.
65. Orson Pratt, *Absurdities of Immaterialism*, 17.
66. Ibid., 7.
67. Ibid., 15.
68. See Tingey, "The Thought of Orson Pratt," 25–26.
69. Olson, *Scottish Philosophy and British Physics*, 24.
70. George Elder Davie, *The Democratic Intellect: Scotland and Her Universities in the Nineteenth Century* (Edinburgh: University Press, 1961), 299.
71. Orson Pratt, *Absurdities of Immaterialism*, 14.
72. Ibid., 15.
73. See Tingey, "The Thought of Orson Pratt," 28.
74. Orson Pratt, *Absurdities of Immaterialism*, 15.
75. Ibid., 7.
76. Tingey, "The Thought of Orson Pratt," 21.
77. Orson Pratt, *Absurdities of Immaterialism*, 15.
78. Ibid., 6.
79. Theodore Dwight Bozeman, *Protestants in an Age of Science: The Baconian Ideal and Antebellum American Religious Thought* (Chapel Hill: University of North Carolina Press, 1977), 89.
80. Orson Pratt, *Great First Cause, or the Self-Moving Forces of the Universe* (Liverpool: R. James, 1851), 10.
81. Herbert Hovenkamp, *Science and Religion in America 1800–1860* (Philadelphia: University of Pennsylvania Press, 1978), 27.
82. Dick, *Philosophy of a Future State*, 229.
83. Ibid., 233.
84. Orson Pratt, *Absurdities of Immaterialism*, 11.
85. Brigham H. Roberts, *A Comprehensive History of the Church of Jesus Christ of Latter-day Saints*, 6 vols. (Salt Lake City: Deseret News Press, 1930), 2:410.
86. Orson Pratt, *Absurdities of Immaterialism*, 6.
87. Orson Pratt, *Great First Cause*, 3.
88. Orson Pratt, *Absurdities of Immaterialism*, 6.
89. Calder, *Key to the Universe*, 132.
90. Nels B. Lundwall, ed., *Masterful Discourses of Orson Pratt* (Salt Lake City: Bookcraft, 1981), 18.
91. Edward W. Tullidge, *History of Salt Lake City and Its Founders* (Salt Lake

City: Edward Tullidge, 1880), appendix, 33.

92. Ibid., 32.

93. Ibid., 33; see also George Jacob Holyoake, *Bygones Worth Remembering* (London: T. Fisher Unwin, 1905). Holyoake makes no mention of Pratt or the Mormons in his biography.

94. Journal History, 27 September 1850.

95. Ibid., 30 July 1849.

96. Ibid., 14 October 1849.

97. *Millennial Star* 12:40:41.

98. Tullidge, *History of Salt Lake*, appendix, 32–33.

99. Orson Pratt, *New Jerusalem; or, The Fulfilment of Modern Prophecy* (Liverpool: R. James, 1849), 3.

100. Ibid., 7.

101. Ibid., 9.

102. Journal History, 1 March 1849 and 26 January 1850.

103. Ibid., 8 July 1849.

104. Ibid.

105. Ibid., 17 April 1850.

106. *Utah Genealogical & Historical Magazine* 27:111.

107. Orson Pratt, *New Jerusalem*, 2.

108. Journal History, 1 April 1850.

CHAPTER 8

1. Journal History, 19 May 1850; see also Coleman, *Pratt Pioneers*, 310.

2. Orson F. Whitney, *History of Utah*, 4 vols. (George Q. Cannon & Sons: Salt Lake City, 1904), 4:28.

3. Sarah Pratt to Bathsheba Smith, 4 April 1850, Church Archives.

4. Journal History, 25, 27, September 1850.

5. Ibid., 8 May 1852.

6. Arrington, *Great Basin Kingdom*, 101–2.

7. Orson Pratt, *Divine Authenticity of the Book of Mormon* (Liverpool: R. James, 1850–52), 24.

8. Ibid., 35, 36, 48.

9. Ibid., 35.

10. Ibid., 36.

11. Ibid., 38, 39.

12. Ibid., 48.

13. Ibid., 1.

14. Ibid., 96.

15. Orson Pratt, *Great First Cause; or the Self-Moving Forces of the Universe* (Liverpool: R. James, 1851), 1; see also Tingey, "The Thought of Orson Pratt," 38.

16. Tingey, "The Thought of Orson Pratt," 111.

17. Ibid., 39–40.

18. Orson Pratt, *Great First Cause*, 2, 3.

19. Tingey, "The Thought of Orson Pratt," 41.

20. Orson Pratt, *Great First Cause*, 2.

21. Tingey, "The Thought of Orson Pratt," 42.

22. Orson Pratt, *Great First Cause*, 4.
23. Ibid., 5.
24. Ibid.
25. Tingey, "The Thought of Orson Pratt," 47.
26. Orson Pratt, *Great First Cause*, 8.
27. Ibid., 7.
28. Ibid., 8.
29. Tingey, "The Thought of Orson Pratt," 49.
30. Orson Pratt, *Great First Cause*, 9.
31. Ibid., 10.
32. Tingey, "The Thought of Orson Pratt," 52.
33. Bozeman, *Protestants in an Age of Science*, 28.
34. Orson Pratt, *Great First Cause*, 10.
35. Ibid.
36. Ibid., 11.
37. Tingey, "The Thought of Orson Pratt," 52.
38. Orson Pratt, *Great First Cause*, 11.
39. *The Philosophy of Aristotle* (New York: New American Library, 1963), 128.
40. Orson Pratt, *Great First Cause*, 10.
41. Ibid., 15; see Tingey, "The Thought of Orson Pratt," 60.
42. Orson Pratt, *Great First Cause*, 16.
43. Ibid.
44. Ibid., 6, 7, 13.
45. Davie, *The Democratic Intellect*, 181.
46. Paul Edwards, ed., *The Encyclopedia of Philosophy*, 10 vols. (New York: Macmillan, 1967), 6:22–31.
47. Olson, *Scottish Philosophy and British Physics*, 28.
48. Orson Pratt, *Great First Cause*, 1–2.
49. McMurrin, *Theological Foundations*, 45.
50. Davie, *The Democratic Intellect*, 141.
51. Jules Remy and Julius Brenchley, *A Journey to Great-Salt-Lake City* (London: W. Jeffs, 1861), 2:11–12.
52. Ibid., 2:9, 19.
53. Flower and Murphey, *Philosophy in America*, xiv.
54. *The Encyclopedia of Philosophy*, 1:247.
55. Stow Persons, *American Minds* (New York: Henry Holt & Co., 1958), 189.
56. Henry Warner Bowden, Review of Herbert Hovenkamp, *Science and Religion in America, 1800–1860*, *American Historical Review* 84:4:1155.
57. Orson Pratt, *Absurdities of Immaterialism*, 6.
58. Flowery and Murphey, *Philosophy in America*, 6.
59. Tingey, "The Thought of Orson Pratt," 86; see also *Doctrine and Covenants* 88:37.
60. Orson Pratt, *Absurdities of Immaterialism*, 15.
61. Remy and Brenchley, *Journey*, 2:19.
62. Tingey, "The Thought of Orson Pratt," 85.
63. John A. Nicholson, *Philosophy of Religion* (New York: Ronald Press Co., 1950), 143, 145.
64. DeVoto, *Year of Decision*, 82.
65. Flower and Murphey, *Philosophy in America*, 285.
66. See Orson Pratt, *Absurdities of Immaterialism*, 7.

67. McMurrin, *Theological Foundations*, 7.
68. *Journal of Discourses*, 1:93.
69. Thomas Brown Holmes Stenhouse, *The Rocky Mountain Saints: A Full and Complete History of the Mormons from the First Vision of Joseph Smith* (New York: D. Appleton and Co., 1873), 9–10.
70. Orson Pratt, "History," *Millennial Star* 27:23.
71. Goodrich, "Marian Ross Pratt," 3.
72. Journal History, 28 June 1851.
73. See Arrington, *Great Basin Kingdom*, 64–71.
74. Carter, *Heart Throbs*, 2:245, 490.
75. Journal History, 5 October 1851.
76. Ibid., 13 October 1851.
77. Ibid., 7 April 1851.
78. Everett L. Cooley, "Report of an Expedition to Locate Utah's First Capitol," *Utah Historical Quarterly* 23:330–31.
79. See Poll, et al., *Utah's History*, 141, 731.
80. Cooley, "Report," 334.
81. Journal History, 18, 19, 22, 23, 28 October 1851.
82. Ralph V. Chamberlin, *The University of Utah: A History of Its First Hundred Years 1850 to 1950* (Salt Lake City: University of Utah Press, 1960), 25.
83. Journal History, 15 December 1851.
84. *Deseret News*, 27 December 1851.
85. Journal History, 20 January 1852.
86. Ibid., 25 January 1852.
87. Ibid., 8 February 1852.
88. Ibid., 22, 23 February 1852.
89. Ibid., 12 April 1852.
90. Ibid., 22 April 1852; see also Arrington, *Great Basin Kingdom*, 86–87.
91. Allen and Leonard, *Story of the Latter-day Saints*, 260.
92. Journal History, 23 May 1852.
93. Ibid., 21 June 1852.
94. Ibid., 28 August 1852.
95. Ibid., 29 August 1852.
96. *Journal of Discourses*, 1:53–66.
97. Kimball Young, *Isn't One Wife Enough?* (New York: Henry Holt, 1954), 36.
98. Journal History, 29 August 1852.
99. Stout, *On the Mormon Frontier*, 2:449, 450.
100. Stanley S. Ivins, "Notes on Mormon Polygamy," *Utah Historical Quarterly* 35:4:311, 313.
101. *Deseret News*, 30 August 1852.
102. Journal History, 21 September 1852.
103. William Clayton to Brigham Young, 4 October 1852, Church Archives.
104. Ibid.
105. *Journal of Discourses*, 1:50–51.
106. Ibid., 6:275.
107. William Clayton to Brigham Young, 4 October 1852.
108. Ibid.
109. Thomas Evans Jeremy Journal, Church Archives, 30 September 1852.
110. Journal History, 5 August 1854.
111. Ibid., 22 November 1852.

112. Orson Pratt to Brigham Young, 20 November 1852, Brigham Young Collection, Church Archives.

113. Roy F. Nichols, *Franklin Pierce: Young Hickory of the Granite Hills* (Philadelphia: University of Pennsylvania Press, 1931), 236.

114. Journal History, 4 March 1853.

115. Orson Pratt to Brigham Young, 31 December 1852, Brigham Young Collection, Church Archives.

116. Journal History, 29 October 1852.

117. Orson Pratt, *The Seer* (Washington, D.C.: 1853–54), 1:1.

118. Ibid., 1:1:11–16.

119. *Journal of Discourses*, 3:28–43.

120. Orson Pratt, *The Seer* 1:12:176–81.

121. Ibid., 1:5:76.

122. Ibid., 1:8:127.

123. Journal History, 4 March 1853.

124. Ibid., 14 May 1853.

125. "Records of Early Church Families," *Utah Genealogical & Historical Magazine* 27:81–82.

126. Parley P. Pratt to Orson Pratt, 25 May 1853, Orson Pratt Papers, Church Archives.

127. Parley P. Pratt to Orson Pratt, 23 August 1853, Orson Pratt Papers.

128. Nelson Pratt to Orson Pratt, 27 March 1853, Orson Pratt Papers.

129. Asenath Pratt Gorsline to Orson Pratt, April 1854, Orson Pratt Papers.

130. Seth Pratt to Orson Pratt, ca. 1853, Orson Pratt Papers.

131. David Pratt to Orson Pratt, ca. 1853, Orson Pratt Papers.

132. Parley P. Pratt, *Autobiography*, 457.

133. See Chapman, *The Pratt Family*.

134. Journal History, 29 May 1853.

135. Orson Pratt to Lucy Mack Smith, 28 October 1853, Church Archives.

136. Coleman, *Pratt Pioneers*, 310.

137. Journal History, 16 June 1854.

138. Ibid., 8 August 1854.

139. Carter, *Heart Throbs*, 2:245.

140. Eliza R. Snow, "Lines for Mrs. Marian R. Pratt on the Death of her little child," Orson Pratt Papers, Church Archives.

CHAPTER 9

1. *Journal of Discourses*, 3:101.

2. Journal History, 5, 22 October 1854.

3. Ibid., 11, 20 December 1854.

4. Ibid., 16 November 1854.

5. *Deseret News*, 28 December 1854.

6. Journal History, 7 April 1855.

7. "Minutes, November 16, 1847," Brigham Young Papers, Church Archives.

8. *Journal of Discourses*, 3:80.

9. See Wilford Woodruff Journal, 4 March 1860. See also Gary James Bergera, "The Orson Pratt–Brigham Young Controversies: Conflict Within the Quorums, 1853–1868," *Dialogue* 13:2:7–49, for an excellent account of the episode of conflict over *The Seer* and other teachings.

10. Brigham Young to Orson Pratt, 1 September 1853, cited in Orson Pratt to Brigham Young, 4 November 1853, Brigham Young Papers, Church Archives.

11. Orson Pratt, *The Seer* 1:24.

12. Orson Pratt to Brigham Young, 4 November 1853.

13. Orson Pratt, *The Seer* 1:131.

14. Orson Pratt to Brigham Young, 4 November 1853; see also *Journal of Discourses*, 7:285–86.

15. Wilford Woodruff Journal, 17 September 1854.

16. Parley P. Pratt, *Key to the Science of Theology*, 10th ed. (Salt Lake City: Deseret Book, 1948), 55.

17. *Journal of Discourses*, 13:187.

18. Brigham Young discourse, 25 April 1855, Church Archives.

19. Wilford Woodruff Journal, 11 March 1856.

20. *Millennial Star* 17:19:298.

21. *Deseret News*, 21 March 1855.

22. Journal History, 27 June 1855.

23. Ibid., 8 July 1855.

24. *Journal of Discourses*, 3:116.

25. Journal History, 4 August 1855.

26. William J. Christensen, "Critical Review of Orson Pratt Sr.'s Published Scientific Books" (Master's thesis, University of Utah, 1929), 46.

27. Donald Skabelund, "Cosmology on the American Frontier: Orson Pratt's Key to the Universe," *Centaurus* 11:3:193.

28. *Deseret News*, 1 August 1855.

29. Ibid., 4 August 1855.

30. Journal History, 18 June 1855.

31. Ibid., 30 September 1855.

32. Ibid., 18, 31 October 1855.

33. Coleman, *Pratt Pioneers*, 310.

34. Journal History, 11 December 1855; Allen and Leonard, *Story of the Latter-day Saints*, 162–63, 197.

35. Journal History, 29 November 1855.

36. Ibid., 13 April 1856.

37. Parley P. Pratt, *Autobiography*, 432.

38. Journal History, 15 May 1856.

39. Ibid., 15 May 1856.

40. Orson Pratt to Parley P. Pratt, 2 November 1853, Church Archives,.

41. Orson Pratt, *True Repentance* (London: L.D.S. Book and Star Depot, 1856), 21–23.

42. Orson Pratt, *The Holy Spirit* (London: L.D.S. Book and Star Depot, 1856), 50.

43. Ibid.

44. Ibid., 51.

45. Ibid., 53.

46. See Ralph Waldo Emerson, "The Oversoul," in *Essays and Lectures* (New York: Literary Classics of the United States, Inc., 1983), 385–86; also Will Durant, *The Story of Philosophy* (New York: Simon and Schuster, 1961), 131–32.

47. Orson Pratt, *Holy Spirit*, 54.

48. Journal History, 26 October 1856.

49. Jedediah M. Grant, discourse of 12 March 1854, *Deseret News*, 27 July 1854.

50. *History of the Church*, 6:311.
51. Journal History, 1 November 1856.
52. Orson Pratt to Juliaet Pratt, 3 April 1857, Orson Pratt Papers, Church Archives.
53. Orson Pratt to Juliaet Pratt, 31 October 1856, Pratt Papers.
54. Nathaniel Hawthorne, *English Notebooks* (New York: Modern Language Association, 1941), 442. See also Richard H. Cracroft, "Liverpool 1856: Nathaniel Hawthorne Meets Orson Pratt," *Brigham Young University Studies* 8:3:270–72.
55. See Orson Pratt to Brigham Young, 4 November 1853.
56. *Journal of Discourses*, 4:267.
57. Journal History, 31 January 1857.
58. Ibid., 6 September 1857.
59. *Journal of Discourses*, 6:47.
60. Journal History, 6 September 1857.
61. Orson Pratt, *Latter-day Kingdom, or, The Preparations for the Second Advent* (London: L.D.S. Book and Star Depot, 1857), 125.
62. Orson Pratt to Juliaet Pratt, 3 April 1857, Pratt Papers.
63. Parley P. Pratt to Orson Pratt, 2 January 1857.
64. Quoted in Steven Pratt, "Eleanor McLean and the Murder of Parley P. Pratt," *Brigham Young University Studies* 15:2:248.
65. Journal History, 30 June 1857.
66. Coleman, *Pratt Pioneers*, 310.
67. Norman F. Furniss, *The Mormon Conflict, 1850–1859* (New Haven: Yale University Press, 1960), 56–57.
68. Ibid., 96–97.
69. Ibid., 129; Journal History, 14 October 1857.
70. Furniss, *Mormon Conflict*, 101–14.
71. Ibid., 18–19.
72. Journal History, 23 December 1857.
73. See Juanita Brooks, *The Mountain Meadows Massacre* (Norman, Okla: University of Oklahoma Press, 1970).
74. *Journal of Discourses*, 7:199–203.
75. Furniss, *Mormon Conflict*, 126.
76. Wilford Woodruff Journal, 24 March 1858.
77. *Journal of Discourses*, 4:267.
78. Wilford Woodruff Journal, 24 March 1858.
79. Furniss, *Mormon Conflict*, 184.
80. Journal History, 24 May 1858.
81. Furniss, *Mormon Conflict*, 196, 205.
82. Journal History, 6 October 1858.
83. Ibid., 1 November 1858.
84. *Journal of Discourses*, 6:200.
85. Journal History, 8 May 1859.
86. Ibid., 9 July 1859.
87. Quoted in Warren S. Tryon, ed., *A Mirror for Americans* (Chicago: University of Chicago Press, 1952), 3:735–36.
88. Journal History, 10 June 1860.
89. Ibid., 9 July 1859.
90. *Diary of Brigham Young*, Everett L. Cooley, ed. (Salt Lake City: University of Utah Library–Tanner Trust Fund, 1980), 8 July 1857.

91. Journal History, 23 October 1859.
92. Wilford Woodruff Journal, 27 January 1860.
93. Orson Pratt, *The Seer* 1:24.
94. Ibid., 131, 133.
95. Wilford Woodruff Journal, 27 January 1860.
96. See Orson Pratt, *Great First Cause*, 15–16.
97. Orson Pratt, *The Seer* 1:117.
98. Ibid., 116–17.
99. Wilford Woodruff Journal, 27 January 1860.
100. "Journal of President B. Young's Office," Brigham Young Papers, 28 January 1860.
101. *Journal of Discourses*, 7:374–75.
102. Journal History, 29 January 1860.
103. Ibid., 20 February 1860; "Young Office Journal," 31 January 1860.
104. Journal History, 1 March 1860.
105. Wilford Woodruff Journal, 4 March 1860.
106. Journal History, 2 March 1860.
107. "Minutes of a meeting in the Historian's Office," 4 April 1860, Brigham Young Papers.
108. Journal History, 4 April 1860.
109. "Historian's Office Minutes," 4 April 1860.
110. Ibid., 5 April 1860.
111. Richard F. Burton, *The City of the Saints, and Across the Rocky Mountains to California*, ed. Fawn M. Brodie (New York: Alfred A. Knopf, 1963), 393–94.
112. See Bruce R. McConkie, *Mormon Doctrine*, 2d. ed. rev. (Salt Lake City: Bookcraft, 1966), 239.
113. *Improvement Era* 15:417.
114. *Journal of Discourses*, 3:277.
115. McMurrin, *Theological Foundations*, 45.
116. *Improvement Era* 13:570. See also Joseph Fielding Smith, *Doctrines of Salvation*, 3 vols., Bruce R. McConkie, ed. (Salt Lake City: Bookcraft, 1954), 1:96–106.
117. "Young Office Journal," 1 October 1860.

CHAPTER 10

1. Journal History, 13 September 1860.
2. Erastus Snow to Elizabeth Snow, 18 November 1860, Erastus Snow Papers, Church Archives.
3. Journal History, 24 May 1861.
4. Orson Pratt, *The Seer* 1:241.
5. Orson Pratt to Juliaet Pratt, 17 April 1861, Orson Pratt Papers, Church Archives.
6. Journal History, 24 May 1861.
7. Orson Pratt to Juliaet Pratt, 17 April 1861.
8. Andrew Karl Larson, *I Was Called to Dixie* (Salt Lake City: Deseret News Press, 1961), 102.
9. Juanita Brooks to Joseph K. Nicholes, 16 April 1946, Juanita Brooks Papers, Lee Library Special Collections, Brigham Young University.

10. Larson, *I Was Called*, 114.

11. Brigham Young to Orson Pratt, 26 February 1862, Brigham Young Collection, Church Archives.

12. Orson Pratt to Brigham Young, 11 March 1862, Brigham Young Collection, Church Archives.

13. Andrew Karl Larson, *Erastus Snow: The Life of a Missionary and Pioneer for the Early Mormon Church* (Salt Lake City: University of Utah Press, 1971), 342; Journal History, 26 October 1862.

14. Juanita Brooks to Joseph K. Nicholes, 16 April 1946, Brooks Papers.

15. Larson, *Erastus Snow*, 333.

16. Juanita Brooks to Joseph K. Nicholes, 16 April 1946.

17. Larson, *Erastus Snow*, 338–39, 370.

18. Journal History, 4 March 1863.

19. Ibid., 22 January 1863.

20. Ibid., 1 January, 1 April 1863, 2 March 1864.

21. Larson, *I Was Called*, 424–25.

22. Ibid., 425, 546.

23. James Godson Bleak, "Annals of the Southern Utah Mission," Book A, 142–59, Church Archives.

24. Larson, *I Was Called*, 425.

25. "Orson Pratt's Harem," *New York Herald*, 18 May 1877, 2.

26. Goodrich, "Marian Ross Pratt," 2.

27. Orson Pratt to Juliaet Pratt, 17 April 1861.

28. Orson Pratt to Sarah M. Pratt, 18 September 1878, Orson Pratt Papers.

29. "Orson Pratt's Harem," 3.

30. See Sarah Pratt, "Workings of Mormonism," Church Archives.

31. Wyl, *Mormon Portraits*, 191–92. See also Quinn, "The Council of Fifty," *Brigham Young University Studies* 20:2:169.

32. George Alfred Townsend to the *Cincinnati Commercial*, cited in Harold Schindler, *Orrin Porter Rockwell*, 354.

33. Orson Pratt to Sarah M. Pratt, 18 September 1878.

34. Journal History, 7, 14 May 1864.

35. See "Statement by Solomon F. Kimball, January 4, 1919," Solomon F. Kimball Papers, Church Archives.

36. "List of articles of Merchandise," n.d., Orson Pratt Papers.

37. Orson Pratt to Juliaet Pratt, 5 January 1865, Orson Pratt Papers.

38. Orson Pratt to Juliaet Pratt, 2 February 1865, Orson Pratt Papers.

39. *Millennial Star* 28:410; Orson F. Whitney, *History of Utah* (Salt Lake City: George Q. Cannon & Sons, 1904), 4:322.

40. Journal History, 15 September 1865.

41. "Journal of the Historian's Office," 13 June 1865, Church Archives.

42. Journal History, 18 June 1865.

43. Wilford Woodruff Journal, 24 September 1865.

44. *Millennial Star* 27:657–63.

45. Orson Pratt to Brigham Young, 12 December 1865, Brigham Young Papers, Church Archives.

46. *Millennial Star* 27:698.

47. Journal History, 23 August 1865; *Millennial Star* 27:663.

48. *Millennial Star* 28:776–77.

49. Journal History, 6 June 1866.

50. William J. Christensen, "Critical Review of Orson Pratt Sr.'s Published Scientific Books" (Master's thesis, University of Utah, 1929), 14, 23, 26.
51. Joel E. Hendricks to Orson Pratt, 6 September 1876, Orson Pratt Papers.
52. Edward R. Hogan, "Orson Pratt as a Mathematician," *Utah Historical Quarterly* 41:1:61–62, 67.
53. Levi Edgar Young, *The Founding of Utah* (New York: Charles Scribner's Sons, 1924), 320.
54. Christensen, "Critical Review," 27.
55. Whitney, *History of Utah*, 4:27.
56. See Richard Anthony Proctor, *Myths and Marvels* (New York: Longmans, Green, & Co., 1896).
57. Hogan, "Orson Pratt as a Mathematician," 66–67.
58. Benjamin Moran, *Journal of Benjamin Moran 1857–1865*, 2 vols. (Chicago: University of Chicago Press, 1949) 2:1365.
59. Journal History, 27 April, 6 May 1867.
60. Roberts, *A Comprehensive History*, 5:269–70.
61. See *Journal of Discourses*, 13:266.
62. Orson Pratt to Juliaet Pratt, 28 June 1867, Orson Pratt Papers.
63. Ibid.; Journal History, 2 December 1867.
64. Orson Pratt to Juliaet Pratt, 31 August 1867, Orson Pratt Papers.
65. Journal History, 15 October 1867.
66. Ibid., 23 February 1859.
67. Ibid., 9 February, 23 March, 7 April 1868.
68. Orson Pratt to Juliaet Pratt, 29 March 1868, Orson Pratt Papers.
69. Orson Pratt to Juliaet Pratt, 28 May 1868, Orson Pratt Papers.
70. Carter, *Heart Throbs of the West*, 2:245.
71. Orson Pratt to Juliaet Pratt, 12 November 1868, Orson Pratt Papers.
72. Journal History, 26 September 1869.
73. Ralph V. Chamberlin, *The University of Utah: A History of Its First Hundred Years 1850 to 1950* (Salt Lake City: University of Utah Press, 1960), 44.
74. Ibid., 90.
75. Journal History, 4 July 1868.
76. Ibid., 30 June 1868.
77. Robert J. Matthews, *"A Plainer Translation" Joseph Smith's Translation of the Bible: A History and Commentary* (Provo: Brigham Young University Press, 1975), 228.
78. Daniel S. Tuttle, *Reminiscences of a Missionary Bishop* (New York: Whittaker, 1906), 344.
79. Ibid., 345.
80. Ibid., 345–46.
81. Arrington, *Great Basin Kingdom*, 295, 297.
82. Roberts, *A Comprehensive History*, 5:259, 268–69.
83. Ibid., 5:269.
84. Journal History, 19 December 1869.
85. Ibid., 10 April 1870.
86. Ibid., 12 February 1870.
87. Ibid., 4 July 1871.
88. Ibid., 31 March 1870.
89. Stanley S. Ivins, "Notes on Mormon Polygamy," *Utah Historical Quarterly* 35:4:311.

90. Coleman, *Pratt Pioneers*, 310.

91. Orson Pratt to Sarah M. Pratt, 18 September 1878, Orson Pratt Papers.

92. *The Bible and Polygamy: Does the Bible Sanction Polygamy? A Discussion* (Salt Lake City: Deseret News Steam Printing Establishment, 1874), 1.

93. *Deseret Evening News*, 10 August 1870.

94. See Roberts, *A Comprehensive History*, 5:301–4.

95. Robert D. Hatch, "The Pratt–Newman Debate" (Master's thesis, Brigham Young University, 1960), passim.

96. *Deseret Evening News*, 13 August 1870.

97. *The Bible and Polygamy*, 97.

98. Ibid., 36, 39.

99. Ibid., 49–51.

100. *Deseret Evening News*, 15 August 1870.

101. Louis C. Zucker, "Joseph Smith as a Student of Hebrew," *Dialogue* 3:2:54.

102. Cited in Lundwall, *Masterful Discourses*, 16.

103. Robert Joseph Dwyer, *The Gentile Comes to Utah: A Study in Religious and Social Conflict 1862–1890* (Salt Lake City: Western Epics, 1971), 161–62.

104. *Deseret Evening News*, 26 August 1870.

105. Zucker, "Joseph Smith as a Student of Hebrew," 53–55.

106. *Millennial Star* 20 September 1870.

107. Whitney, *History of Utah*, 4:29.

CHAPTER 11

1. Archibald F. Bennett, "Orson Pratt as a Genealogist," *Deseret News*, 25 April 1936.

2. Carter, *Heart Throbs of the West*, 2:282, 283.

3. Orson Pratt, *Wonders of the Universe*, Nels B. Lundwall, comp. (Salt Lake City, 1937), plate between 328–29.

4. *Pearl of Great Price*, Book of Abraham, Facsimile 2, "Explanation of the Foregoing Cut," p. 35.

5. *Deseret Evening News*, 14 January 1871.

6. Ibid., 11 February 1871.

7. Truman G. Madsen, *Defender of the Faith: The B. H. Roberts Story* (Salt Lake City: Bookcraft, 1980), 97.

8. Chamberlin, *The University of Utah*, 25.

9. Journal History, 20 August 1871.

10. Young, *Founding of Utah*, 324.

11. Chamberlin, *The University of Utah*, 89.

12. *Journal of Discourses*, 7:155–57.

13. Journal History, 20 January 1872.

14. Orson Pratt to Joseph R. Porter, 4 January 1877, Pratt Papers, Church Archives.

15. "Orson Pratt's Harem," *New York Herald*, 18 May 1877, 4.

16. Amasa Lyman, Journal, 9 March 1871, Church Archives.

17. Andrew Jenson, *Church Chronology*, 2d. ed. (Salt Lake City: Deseret News, 1914), 92.

18. *Deseret News*, 1 December 1875.

19. Journal History, 26 November 1875, 8 July 1876.

20. "Orson Pratt's Harem," 3–4.

21. Jeffrey R. Holland, "Analysis of Selected Changes in Major Editions of the Book of Mormon, 1830–1920" (Master's thesis: Brigham Young University, 1966), 37.

22. Matthews, *A Plainer Translation*, 227.

23. Arrington, *Great Basin Kingdom*, 324.

24. For discussion of the United Order movement, see Arrington, Fox, and May, *Building the City of God*; see also Arrington, *Great Basin Kingdom*, 323–41.

25. Journal History, 28 May, 4 June 1874.

26. Ibid., 31 March 1876.

27. *Pearl of Great Price*, Moses 7:18.

28. *Journal of Discourses*, 17:34.

29. Orson Pratt, *The Seer* 1:264.

30. Ibid., 290; see also *Doctrine and Covenants* 65:3.

31. Orson Pratt, *The Seer* 1:291–92.

32. See Ibid., 293–94; *Journal of Discourses*, 2:98, 17:104.

33. *Journal of Discourses*, 17:34–35.

34. Ibid., 17:110–11.

35. Orson Pratt, *The Seer* 1:293.

36. Ibid., 1:115.

37. Ibid., 1:116.

38. Henry David Thoreau, *Walden, or Life in the Woods* (New York: New American Library, 1960), 67.

39. Dubos, *Dreams of Reason*, 28.

40. *Journal of Discourses*, 2:96.

41. Ibid., 17:57.

42. Ibid., 17:75.

43. Arrington, *Great Basin Kingdom*, 338.

44. Matthew Josephson, *The Politicos 1865–1896* (New York: Harcourt, Brace & World, 1938), 226–36.

45. Orson Pratt, *The Kingdom of God*, 1.

46. Klaus J. Hansen, *Quest for Empire: The Political Kingdom of God and the Council of Fifty in Mormon History* (Ann Arbor: Michigan State University Press, 1967), 185.

47. Journal History, 8 November 1875; Hansen, *Quest for Empire*, 122–23. Although the "Council of Fifty" had years before organized to bring in the kingdom of God as both a "spiritual and a political reality," a kind of "Mormon commonwealth," Orson now emphasized the purely spiritual "celestial order" he had envisioned in his pamphlet.

48. Journal History, 12, 13 October 1874.

49. Ibid., 7, 25 October 1874.

50. Ibid., 23 March 1878.

51. Ibid., 20 January 1872.

52. Ibid., 11 March 1876.

53. Ibid., 17 February 1875.

54. Ibid., 8 June 1876.

55. Ibid., 7 October 1861.

56. John Taylor, "Succession in the Priesthood," 17.

57. Chad J. Flake, "The Newel K. Whitney Collection," *Brigham Young University Studies* 11:4:327–28.

58. Journal History, 1 April 1877.
59. See report of Brigham Young's sermons at St. George Temple dedication, April 1877, in Leonard John Nuttall Journal, Lee Library Special Collections, Brigham Young University.
60. Journal History, 18 March 1877.
61. Milando Pratt, "Brief Sketch of My Life and Ancestry," Church Archives, 29.
62. Ibid., 29–31.
63. Ibid., 31.
64. Journal History, 27 August 1877.
65. Ibid., 22 September 1877.
66. Eugene England, *Brother Brigham* (Salt Lake City: Deseret Book, 1980), 87.
67. Stanley P. Hirshson, *The Lion of the Lord: A Biography of Brigham Young* (New York: Alfred A. Knopf, 1969), 323.
68. "Orson Pratt's Harem," 4–5.
69. Goodrich, "Marian Ross Pratt," 3; see also "Minutes, 16 November 1847," Brigham Young Collection, Church Archives.
70. Lyon, "Orson Pratt–Early Mormon Leader," 74.
71. *Deseret News*, 1 October 1877.
72. Journal History, 5 October 1877.
73. Roberts, *Comprehensive History*, 5:523–24.
74. *Pearl of Great Price*, Book of Abraham, Facsimile 2.
75. Pratt and Lundwall, *Wonders of the Universe*, 18.
76. "Orson Pratt's Harem," 4–5.
77. Roberts, *Comprehensive History*, 5:563–65.
78. Orson Pratt to Marian Ross Pratt, 23 December 1878, Orson Pratt Papers.
79. Account of Orson Pratt's tour of Church history sites, along with all quoted material, taken from *Millennial Star* 40:49–50.
80. Orson Pratt to Marian Ross Pratt, 23 December 1878.
81. Orson Pratt to Sarah Marinda Pratt, 18 September 1878, Orson Pratt Papers.
82. Journal History, 21 December 1878.
83. Orson Pratt to Marian Ross Pratt, 23 December 1878.
84. Ibid.
85. *Doctrine and Covenants* 88:45.
86. Orson Pratt, *Key to the Universe, or a New Theory of its Mechanism*, 2d. ed. (Salt Lake City, 1879), v–vi.
87. Ibid., vii.
88. Ibid., 31.
89. Herbert Butterfield, *The Origins of Modern Science 1300–1800* (New York: Macmillan, 1958), 157: see also Davie, *The Democratic Intellect*, 179–80.
90. Olson, *Scottish Philosophy and British Physics*, 28.
91. Butterfield, *Origins of Modern Science*, 157.
92. Orson Pratt, *Key to the Universe*, 92.
93. Ibid., 95–96.
94. Skabelund, *Cosmology on the American Frontier*, 202.
95. *Doctrine and Covenants* 130:15.
96. Orson Pratt, *Key to the Universe*, 97.
97. *Pearl of Great Price*, Book of Abraham, Facsimile 2, "Explanation of Forego-ing Cut," 35.
98. H. T. Pledge, *Science Since 1500: A Short History of Mathematics, Physics, Chemistry, Biology* (New York: Harper & Row, 1959), 283.

99. John H. Gardner, "Science and the Mormon Quest for Truth," in *One Hundred and Fifty Years: Sesquicentennial Lectures on Mormon Arts, Letters and Sciences* (Provo: Harold B. Lee Library Forum Committee, 1980), 58.

100. Orson Pratt, *Key to the Universe*, 30.

101. Skabelund, *Cosmology on the American Frontier*, 194.

102. Orson Pratt, *Key to the Universe*, 14.

103. Ibid., 45.

104. Ronald L. Numbers, *Creation by Natural Law: Laplace's Nebular Hypothesis in American Thought* (Seattle: University of Washington Press, 1977), vii.

105. Butterfield, *Origins of Modern Science*, 157–58.

106. Skabelund, *Cosmology on the American Frontier*, 194.

107. Ibid., 197.

108. Ibid., 198.

109. Christensen, "Critical Review of Orson Pratt Sr.'s Published Scientific Books," 43.

110. Skabelund, *Cosmology on the American Frontier*, 198.

111. *Pearl of Great Price*, Book of Abraham, Facsimile 2.

112. See Charles Piazzi Smyth, *Our Inheritance in the Great Pyramid* (London: C. Burnet, 1890).

113. *Millennial Star* 41:280–83.

114. *Doctrine and Covenants* 130:15.

115. *Pearl of Great Price*, Book of Abraham 3.

116. See Hugh Nibley, "A New Look at the Pearl of Great Price," *Improvement Era* 72:9:89; see also Book of Abraham, Facsimile 2, Figure 6. Orson thought the four-sided monument part of a grand pattern of revelation dealing with the heavens, which had once been available to ancient dispensations and then renewed through Joseph Smith. Mormon scholarship has drawn a possible connection between the Great Pyramid and the papyri which play such an important part in the story of the Book of Abraham. Journal History, 27 July 1879.

117. Milando Pratt, "Life and Labors of Orson Pratt," *The Contributor* 12:12:464.

118. Journal History, 12 August 1879.

119. Ibid., 12 August 1879.

120. Ibid., 5 February 1880.

121. Ibid., 6 April 1880.

122. *Deseret Evening News*, 8 August 1880.

123. *Journal of Discourses*, 17:324; discourse also published as *The Majesty of God*, Nels B. Lundwall, comp. (Salt Lake City: privately published, 1950).

124. *Journal of Discourses*, 17:326.

125. Ibid., 17:332.

126. *Doctrine and Covenants* 88:17.

127. *Journal of Discourses*, 21:303.

128. Journal History, 19 September 1880.

129. Ibid., 8 October 1880.

130. Ibid., 3 April 1881.

131. Ibid., 7 July 1881.

132. Ibid., 1 July 1881.

133. Ibid., 14 October 1881.

134. Ibid., 3 July 1881.

135. *Deseret Evening News*, 12 September 1881.
136. Journal History, 18 September 1881.
137. Ibid., 20 September 1881.
138. Whitney, *History of Utah*, 4:29.

CHAPTER 12

1. Journal History, 6 October 1881.
2. *Deseret Evening News*, 4 October 1881.
3. Milando Pratt, "Life and Labors of Orson Pratt," *The Contributor* 12:12:460.
4. Ibid., 462.
5. Ibid., 461.
6. Journal History, 6 October 1881.
7. Milando Pratt, "Life and Labors," 462.
8. Ibid., 463.
9. Tuttle, *Reminiscences of a Missionary Bishop*, 354.
10. Leonard J. Arrington, "Charles MacKay and His 'True and Impartial History' of the Mormons," *Utah Historical Quarterly* 36:1:26.
11. Leonard J. Arrington, "The Intellectual Tradition of the Latter-day Saints," *Dialogue: A Journal of Mormon Thought* 4:1:17, 22.
12. John Henry Evans, *The Heart of Mormonism* (Salt Lake City: Deseret Book, 1930), 415–16.
13. McMurrin, *Theological Foundations*, 47.
14. Pledge, *Science Since 1500*, 150.
15. Orson Pratt, *The Seer* 1:38, 131–32.
16. Davie, *The Democratic Intellect*, 147.
17. Carl Becker, *The Heavenly City of the Eighteenth-century Philosophers* (New Haven: Yale University Press, 1932), 48.
18. Olson, *Scottish Philosophy and British Physics*, 17.
19. Orson Pratt, *The Seer* 1:24.
20. McMurrin, *Theological Foundations*, 16.
21. See Joseph J. Cannon, "George Q. Cannon: Relations with Brigham Young," *The Instructor* 80:259.
22. See *Journal of Discourses*, 1:51.
23. Rudolf Otto, *The Idea of the Holy: An Inquiry into the Non-Rational Factor in the Idea of the Divine and its Relation to the Rational* (New York: Oxford University Press, 1958), 27.
24. Orson Pratt, *The Seer* 1:227.
25. Orson Pratt, *Holy Spirit*, 54.
26. Otto, *The Idea of the Holy*, 29.
27. See *Millennial Star* 27:659–63.
28. Brigham H. Roberts, *The Mormon Doctrine of Deity* (Salt Lake City: Deseret News, 1903), 94; cf. Orson Pratt, *The Seer* 1:132–33.
29. Roberts, *The Mormon Doctrine of Deity*, 104; cf. Orson Pratt, *Absurdities of Immaterialism*, 11.
30. Sterling M. McMurrin, Introduction to Brigham H. Roberts, *Joseph Smith the Prophet-Teacher* (Princeton: Deseret Club of Princeton University, 1967), ii.
31. Nels L. Nelson, *Scientific Aspects of Mormonism, or Religion in Terms of Life* (New York: G. P. Putnam's Sons, 1904) 199, 203.

32. Ibid., 204.
33. W. Cleon Skousen, *The First 2000 Years* (Salt Lake City: Bookcraft, 1953), 356, 355.
34. McMurrin, *Theological Foundations*, 7.
35. Arthur Schopenhauer, *The World as Will and Representation*, trans. E. F. J. Payne, 2 vols. (New York: Dover Publications, 1969), 1:128.
36. Dietrick E. Thomsen, "A Knowing Universe Seeking to be Known," *Science News* 123:124.
37. Orson Pratt, *Great First Cause*, 11.
38. Orson Pratt, *The Seer* 1:293, 297–98.
39. Antoine Nicholas de Condorcet, "The Progress of the Human Mind," in *Classics of Western Thought: The Modern World*, ed. Charles Hirschfeld, 3 vols. (New York: Harcourt, Brace & World, 1968), 3:209–10, 232.
40. Dick, *Philosophy of a Future State*, 44.
41. Becker, *The Heavenly City*, 48.
42. Orson Pratt, *The Seer* 1:157.
43. Kimball Young, *Isn't One Wife Enough?*, 39.
44. Orson Pratt, *The Seer* 1:155.
45. John Stuart Mill, *On Liberty* (London: Oxford University Press, 1969), 113.
46. Orson Pratt, *The Seer* 1:154.
47. "Records of Early Church Families," *Utah Genealogical and Historical Magazine* 27:114.
48. *Anti-Polygamy Standard*, 20 vols. (Salt Lake City, 1882), 11:81.
49. I am indebted to Richard Van Wagoner for this information. It is drawn from his unpublished manuscript, "Sarah M. Pratt: The Woman Behind the Controversy," 59, 60, 61.
50. *Deseret Evening News*, 10 September 1894.
51. See Wyl, *Mormon Portraits*, 60–61.
52. Tuttle, *Reminiscences of a Missionary Bishop*, 354.
53. Lyon, "Orson Pratt—Early Mormon Leader," 155.
54. Coleman, *Pratt Pioneers*, 341.
55. Carter, *Heart Throbs of the West*, 2:468–69.
56. "Records of Early Church Families," 113.
57. See Milando Pratt, "Life and Labors of Orson Pratt," 460–65.
58. "Records of Early Church Families," 116.
59. Coleman, *Pratt Pioneers*, 311.
60. "Records of Early Church Families," 116.
61. Ibid.
62. Coleman, *Pratt Pioneers*, 309–93.
63. Tingey, "The Thought of Orson Pratt," 3.
64. Copy of notification letter in author's possession.
65. Milando Pratt, "Life and Labots of Orson Pratt," 464.
66. Orson Pratt, "History," *Millennial Star* 27:55.
67. Lyon, "Orson Pratt—Early Mormon Leader," 104.

Bibliography

The published work of Orson Pratt amounts to some two dozen titles, ranging from mathematics texts to sermons to detailed philosophical tracts. Many of his sermons are recorded in the twenty-six volumes of *Journal of Discourses, by Brigham Young, President of the Church of Jesus Christ of Latter-day Saints, His Two Counselors, the Twelve Apostles, and Others* (Liverpool, 1854–1886). Essays and pamphlets Pratt published himself are listed below. Many of his tracts were translated into Danish, Dutch, Spanish, Swedish, and Welsh during his lifetime: for a detailed list see Chad J. Flake, ed., *A Mormon Bibliography 1830–1930* (Salt Lake City: University of Utah Press, 1978), 512–20.

1. *PUBLISHED WORKS BY ORSON PRATT*

Absurdities of Immaterialism; or, A Reply to T. W. P. Taylder's Pamphlet, Entitled: "The Materialism of the Mormons or Latter-day Saints Examined and Exposed." Liverpool: R. James, 1849.

The Bible and Polygamy. Salt Lake City: Deseret News Steam Printing Establishment, 1877.

Discourses on Celestial Marriage, Delivered in the New Tabernacle, Salt Lake City, October 7th, 8th, and 9th, 1869, by Elder Orson Pratt, President George A. Smith, and Elder George Q. Cannon. Salt Lake City: Deseret News, 1869.

Divine Authenticity of the Book of Mormon. Liverpool: R. James, 1850.

Divine Authority, or the Question, Was Joseph Smith Sent of God? Liverpool: R. James, 1848.

Great Discussion! Does the Bible Sanction Polygamy? Held in the New Tabernacle at Salt Lake City, August 12, 1870. Variant edition under title *The Bible & Polygamy. Does the Bible Sanction Polygamy? A discussion between Professor Orson Pratt, One of the Twelve Apostles of the Church of Jesus Christ of Latter-day Saints, and Rev. Doctor J. P. Newman, Chaplain of the United States Senate, in the New Tabernacle, Salt Lake City, August 12, 13, and 14, 1870*. Salt Lake City: Deseret News Steam Printing Establishment, 1874.

Great First Cause; or the Self-Moving Forces of the Universe. Liverpool: R. James, 1851.

The Holy Spirit. Liverpool: Latter-day Saints Book and Millennial Star Depot, 1856.
A [sic] Interesting Account of Several Remarkable Visions, and of the Late Discovery of Ancient American Records. Edinburgh: Ballantyne and Hughes, 1840. Also published as *Remarkable Visions*. Liverpool: R. James, 1848.
Key to the Universe, or a New Theory of its Mechanism. Liverpool, 1879. Also privately published as *Key to the Universe, or a New Theory of its Mechanism*. Second Edition, from the First European Edition. Salt Lake City, 1879.
The Kingdom of God. [four parts]. Liverpool: R. James, 1848–1849.
Latter-day Kingdom, or the Preparations for the Second Advent. Liverpool, London: Latter-day Saints Book and Millennial Star Depot, 1857.
Listen to the Voice of Truth. New York: S. Brannan & Co., 1844.
Necessity for Miracles. Liverpool, London: Latter-day Saints Book and Millennial Star Depot, 1857.
New and Easy Method of Solution of the Cubic and Biquadratic Equations. London: Longmans, Green, Reader and Dyer, 1866.
New Jerusalem; or, The Fulfilment of Modern Prophecy. Liverpool: R. James, 1849. (Later reprinted in Salt Lake City by Parker P. Robison as *New Jerusalem, and Equality and Oneness of the Saints; a Forecast of Events to be Established by a Chosen and Dedicated People. The World's Answer to Communism* [n.d.].
Prophetic Almanac for 1845. New York: The Prophet Office, 1844.
Prophetic Almanac for 1846. New York: New York Messenger Office, 1845.
Reply to a Pamphlet Printed at Glasgow, with the "Approbation of Clergymen of Different Denominations," Entitled "Remarks on Mormonism." Liverpool: R. James, 1849.
The Seer. Washington, D.C., and Liverpool, 1853–1854.
A Series of Pamphlets by Orson Pratt. Liverpool: Franklin D. Richards, 1851.
Spiritual Gifts. Liverpool, London: Latter-day Saints Book and Millennial Star Depot, 1856.
Tracts by Orson Pratt. Contents: 1. The True Faith; 2. True Repentance; 3. Water Baptism; 4. The Holy Spirit; 5. Spiritual Gifts; 6. Necessity for Miracles; 7. Universal Apostacy [sic] in the Seventeen Centuries of Darkness; 8. Latter-day Kingdom, or, The Preparations for the Second Advent. London: Latter-day Saints Book and Millennial Star Depot, 1856.
Water Baptism. Liverpool, London: Latter-day Saints Book and Millennial Star Depot, 1856.

2. *COMPILATIONS OF ORSON PRATT'S WORKS*

Exodus of Modern Israel, by Orson Pratt and Others. Comp. by Nels B. Lundwall. Independence, Mo.: Zion's Printing and Publishing Company, n.d.
How to Live Acceptably, A Discourse by Elder Orson Pratt. Comp. by Nels B. Lundwall. (Copied from *Deseret Evening News*, October 2, 1875.) Salt Lake City, n.d.
The Majesty of God. A Discourse by Elder Orson Pratt, Delivered in the 16th Ward Assembly Rooms, Salt Lake City, March 14, 1875, Reported by David W. Evans. Comp. by Nels B. Lundwall. Salt Lake City, 1950.
Masterful Discourses and Writings of Orson Pratt. Comp. by Nels B. Lundwall. Salt Lake City, Bookcraft, 1981.
Orson Pratt's Works on the Doctrines of the Gospel. Comp. by Parker Pratt Robison. Salt Lake City, 1965.
Redemption of Zion, by Orson Pratt. Comp. by Clyde Neilson and Alonzo Cole. Holladay, Utah, 1940.

Wonders of the Universe; or, A Compilation of the Astronomical Writings of Orson Pratt. Comp. by Nels B. Lundwall. Salt Lake City, 1937.

Writings of an Apostle. Comp. by Jerry Burnett and Charles Pope. Salt Lake City: Mormon Heritage Publishers, 1976.

3. *MANUSCRIPTS AND DOCUMENTS*

Angell, Truman O. Journal. Special Collections, Brigham Young University Library, Provo, Utah.

Backenstos, J[acob] B. Affidavit. *Weekly Missouri Republican*, St. Louis, Mo., July 3, 1844. Copy in John Taylor Scrapbook, Special Collections, University of Utah Library, Salt Lake City.

Barnes, Lorenzo Dow. Journal. Archives of The Church of Jesus Christ of Latter-day Saints, Salt Lake City, Utah. Hereinafter Church Archives.

Beesley, Sterling E. to Breck England, March 10, 1981. In possession of author.

Bennett, John C. Letter to Sidney Rigdon and Orson Pratt, January 10, 1843. Sidney Rigdon Collection, Church Archives.

Bleak, James G. "Annals of the Southern Utah Mission," Book *A*. Church Archives.

Brooks, Juanita to Joseph K. Nicholes, April 16, 1946. Juanita Brooks Collection, Brigham Young University Library, Provo, Utah.

Brown, John. Journal, 1847. Church Archives.

Clayton, William. Diaries. Church Archives.

______. Letter to Brigham Young, October 4, 1852. Church Archives.

Cowdery, Oliver. Sketch Book. Church Archives.

Goddard, Stephen H. Affidavit. *Weekly Missouri Republican*, St. Louis, Mo., July 3, 1844. Copy in John Taylor Scrapbook, Special Collections, University of Utah Library, Salt Lake City.

Goddard, Zeruiah N. Affidavit. *Weekly Missouri Republican*, St. Louis, Mo., July 3, 1844. Copy in John Taylor Scrapbook, Special Collections, University of Utah Library, Salt Lake City.

Goodrich, Marilyn. "History of Marian Ross Pratt." Typescript in possession of author.

"High Council Meetings, etc., Conference and Public Meetings of the Church Historian's Office." Church Archives.

Historian's Office Journal. Church Archives.

"Historian's Office Minutes, 4 April 1860." Brigham Young Collection, Church Archives.

Jeremy, Thomas Evans. Journal. Church Archives.

"Journal History of the Church of Jesus Christ of Latter-day Saints." Film. Church Archives.

Kimball, Heber C. Diary. Church Archives.

Kimball, Solomon F. "Statement by Solomon F. Kimball, January 4, 1919," Solomon F. Kimball Collection, Church Archives.

"Life Story of John Leishman." Typescript in possession of Mrs. Leo C. Nielsen, Hyrum, Utah.

Lyman, Amasa. Journal. Church Archives.

"Manuscript History of Brigham Young." Comp. by B. H. Roberts. Church Archives.

Neibaur, Alexander. Journal. Church Archives.

Nuttall, Leonard John. Journal. Special Collections, Brigham Young University Library, Provo, Utah.

Pratt, Milando. "Brief Sketch of my Life and Ancestry." Church Archives.
______. "Reminiscences of Sister Marian Ross Pratt." Manuscript in possession of Sterling E. Beesley, Bountiful, Utah.
Pratt, Orson. "Autobiography." (Brief sketch of his life from birth to baptism into the Mormon church; includes financial accounts for 1836–37.) Church Archives.
______. "Brief Abstract of My Genealogy and Ancestry." Orson Pratt Collection, Church Archives.
______. Correspondence File. Orson Pratt Collection, Church Archives.
______. Diaries, 1833–1837. 4 vols. Church Archives.
______. Diary. January–December 1868. Orson Pratt Collection, Church Archives.
______. "Family Record." 2 vols. Church Archives.
______. Journal. February 23–June 23, 1846; May 4–July 31, 1847. Church Archives.
Pratt, Orson and Lyman E. Johnson, "To the Bishop & his council in Kirtland, the Stake of Zion." Newel K. Whitney Collection, Brigham Young University Library, Provo, Utah.
Pratt, Sarah M. Letter to Bathsheba Smith, April 4, 1850. Church Archives.
______. " 'Workings of Mormonism,' related by Mrs. Orson Pratt, Salt Lake City, 1884." Church Archives.
Smith, Joseph. Letter to Heber C. Kimball and Brigham Young. (No date.) Winslow W. Smith Collection, Church Archives.
Snow, Erastus. Journals. Church Archives.
______. Correspondence File. Erastus Snow Collection, Church Archives.
Snow, Eliza R. "Lines for Mrs. Marian R. Pratt on the Death of her Little Child." Orson Pratt Collection, Church Archives.
______. "The Transformation." Orson Pratt Collection, Church Archives.
Taylor, John. "Succession in the Priesthood, a Discourse by President John Taylor, delivered at the Priesthood Meeting, held in the Salt Lake Assembly Hall, Friday Evening, October 7th, 1881. Reported by George F. Gibbs." Utah State Historical Society, Salt Lake City.
Whitmer, John. "History of the Church." John Whitmer Collection, Church Archives.
Woodruff, Wilford. Journals. Church Archives.
Young, Brigham. Correspondence File. Brigham Young Collection, Church Ar chives.
Young, Brigham. "Office Journal, 1860." Brigham Young Collection, Church Archives.

4. *BOOKS AND ARTICLES*

Ahlstrom, Sidney. "The Scottish Philosophy and American Theology." *Church History* 24 (September 1955): 257–72.
Allen, James B., and Alexander, Thomas G., eds. *Manchester Mormons: The Journal of William Clayton, 1840 to 1842*. Santa Barbara and Salt Lake City: Peregrine Smith, Inc., 1974.
Allen, James B., and Leonard, Glen M. *The Story of the Latter-day Saints*. Salt Lake City: Deseret Book, 1976.
Allen, James B., and Thorp, Malcolm R. "The Mission of the Twelve to England 1840–41: Mormon Apostles and the Working Classes." *Brigham Young University Studies*, 15 (Summer 1975): 499–526.
Andrews, Edward Deming. *The People Called Shakers*. New York: Oxford University Press, 1953.

Arrington, Leonard J. *Great Basin Kingdom: An Economic History of the Latter-day Saints, 1830–1900*. Cambridge, Mass.: Harvard University Press, 1958.

______. "Charles MacKay and His 'True and Impartial History' of the Mormons." *Utah Historical Quarterly* 36 (Winter 1968):26–39.

______. "The Intellectual Tradition of the Latter-day Saints." *Dialogue: A Journal of Mormon Thought* 4 (Spring 1969):16–22.

Arrington, Leonard J., and Bitton, Davis. *The Mormon Experience: A History of the Latter-day Saints*. New York: Alfred A. Knopf, 1979.

Arrington, Leonard J.; Fox, Feramorz Y.; and May, Dean L. *Building the City of God: Community and Cooperation Among the Mormons*. Salt Lake City: Deseret Book Company, 1976.

Backman, Milton V., Jr. *American Religions and the Rise of Mormonism*. Salt Lake City: Deseret Book Company, 1965.

Bancroft, Hubert Howe. *History of Utah 1540–1886*. San Francisco: The History Company, 1889.

Becker, Carl. *The Heavenly City of the Eighteenth Century Philosophers*. New Haven: Yale University Press, 1932.

Bell, Alan, ed. *Lord Cockburn: A Bicentenary Commemoration 1779–1979*. Edinburgh: Scottish Academic Press, 1979.

Bennett, John C. *The History of the Saints: Or an Expose of Joe Smith and Mormonism*. Boston: Leland and Whiting, 1842.

Bergera, Gary James. "The Orson Pratt–Brigham Young Controversies: Conflict Within the Quorums, 1853–1868." *Dialogue: A Journal of Mormon Thought* 13 (Summer 1980): 7–58.

Bestor, Arthur E., Jr. *Backwoods Utopias: The Sectarian Origins and the Owenite Phase of Communitarian Socialism in America, 1663–1829*. Philadelphia: University of Pennsylvania Press, 1950.

Bitton, Davis. "Kirtland as a Center of Missionary Activity, 1830–1838." *Brigham Young University Studies* 9 (Autumn 1969): 512–15.

Book of Commandments. Independence, Mo.: [Church of Jesus Christ of Latter-day Saints], 1833.

Boorstin, Daniel J. *The Americans: The Colonial Experience*. New York: Random House, 1958.

Bowden, Henry Warner. Review of *Science and Religion in America, 1800–1860*, by Herbert Hovenkamp. *American Historical Review* 84 (October 1979) :1155.

Bozeman, Theodore Dwight. *Protestants in an Age of Science: The Baconian Ideal and Antebellum American Religious Thought*. Chapel Hill: University of North Carolina Press, 1977.

Brayton, Isabella. *The Story of Hartford*. 3 vols. Glen Falls, N.Y.: Bullard Press, 1929.

Brodie, Fawn M. *No Man Knows My History: The Life of Joseph Smith, the Mormon Prophet*. 2nd ed. New York: Alfred A. Knopf, 1978.

Brooks, Juanita. *The Mountain Meadows Massacre*. 2nd ed. Norman, Okla.: University of Oklahoma Press, 1974.

Buchanan, Frederick S. "Scots Among the Mormons." *Utah Historical Quarterly* 36 (Autumn 1968): 329–35.

Burton, Richard F. *The City of the Saints, and Across the Rocky Mountains to California*. Edited by Fawn M. Brodie. New York: Alfred A. Knopf, 1963.

Buerger, David John. " 'The Fulness of the Priesthood': The Second Anointing in Latter-day Saint Theology and Practice." *Dialogue: A Journal of Mormon Thought* 16 (Spring 1981): 10–44.

Bushman, Richard. *From Puritan to Yankee: Character and Social Order in Connecticut, 1690–1765*. Cambridge, Mass.: Harvard University Press, 1967.

Butterfield, Herbert. *The Origins of Modern Science, 1300–1800*. New York: Macmillan, 1958.

Carter, Kate B., comp. *Heart Throbs of the West*. 3 vols. Salt Lake City: Daughters of the Utah Pioneers, 1940. Vol. 2.

Chamberlin, Ralph V. *The University of Utah: A History of Its First Hundred Years, 1850 to 1950*. Salt Lake City: University of Utah Press, 1960.

Chapman, Frederick W. *The Pratt Family, or the Descendants of Lieutenant William Pratt*. Hartford: Case, Lockwood and Company, 1864.

Clayton, William. *The Latter-day Saints' Emigrants' Guide*. Edited by Stanley B. Kimball. Gerald, Missouri: The Patrice Press, 1983.

______. *William Clayton's Journal*. Edited by Lawrence Clayton. Salt Lake City, 1921.

Coben, Stanley, and Hill, Forest G. *American Economic History: Essays in Interpretation*. Philadelphia, New York: J. B. Lippincott, 1966.

Coleman, Arthur D. *Pratt Pioneers of Utah*. Provo, Utah: By J. Grant Stevenson, 1967.

Columbia County at the End of the Century. 2 vols. Hudson, N.Y.: Hudson Gazette and Record Printing Company, 1900.

Cooley, Everett L. "Report of an Expedition to Locate Utah's First Capitol." *Utah Historical Quarterly* 23 (Autumn 1955): 329–36.

Condorcet, Antoine Nicholas de. "The Progress of the Human Mind." In *Classics of Western Thought: The Modern World*. Edited by Charles Hirschfeld. 4 vols. New York: Harcourt, Brace and World, 1968. Vol. 3.

Cracroft, Richard H. "Liverpool 1856: Nathaniel Hawthorne Meets Orson Pratt." *Brigham Young University Studies* 8 (Spring 1968): 270–72.

Crawley, Peter. "Parley P. Pratt: Father of Mormon Pamphleteering." *Dialogue: A Journal of Mormon Thought* 15 (Autumn 1982): 13–26.

Creer, Leland H. *The Founding of an Empire: The Exploration and Colonization of Utah, 1776–1856*. Salt Lake City: Bookcraft, 1947.

Cross, Whitney. *The Burned-Over District*. New York: Harper & Row, 1965.

Davidson, Marshall B. *The American Heritage History of the Writers' America*. New York: American Heritage Publishing Company, 1973.

Davie, George Elder. *The Democratic Intellect: Scotland and Her Universities in the Nineteenth Century*. Edinburgh: University Press, 1961.

DeVoto, Bernard. *The Year of Decision: 1846*. Boston: Little, Brown, 1943.

Dick, Thomas. *The Philosophy of a Future State*. New York: R. Schoyer, 1831.

The Doctrine and Covenants of the Church of Jesus Christ of Latter-day Saints. Salt Lake City: The Church of Jesus Christ of Latter-day Saints, 1981.

Dodds, John W. *The Age of Paradox: Biography of England, 1841–1851*. London: Victor Gollancz, Ltd., 1953.

Dubos, René. *The Dreams of Reason: Science and Utopias*. New York: Columbia University Press, 1961.

Dwyer, Robert Joseph. *The Gentile Comes to Utah: A Study in Religious and Social Conflict, 1862–1890*. 2nd ed. rev. Salt Lake City: Western Epics, 1971.

Emerson, Ralph Waldo. "The Oversoul." In *Essays and Lectures*, pp. 385–86. New York: Literary Classics of the United States, Inc., 1983.

England, Eugene. *Brother Brigham*. Salt Lake City: Deseret Book, 1980.

Evans, John Henry. *The Heart of Mormonism*. Salt Lake City: Deseret Book Company, 1930.

Fairbanks, Edward T. *The Town of St. Johnsbury, Vermont.* St. Johnsbury, Vermont: Cowles Press, 1914.

Farnham, Thomas Jefferson. *Travels in the Great Western Prairies*. New York, 1841.

Fite, Gilbert C., and Reese, Jim E. *An Economic History of the United States*. Boston: Houghton Mifflin, 1973.

Flake, Chad J. "The Newel K. Whitney Collection." *Brigham Young University Studies* 11 (Autumn 1971): 327–28.

Flanders, Robert Bruce. *Nauvoo: Kingdom on the Mississippi.* Urbana: University of Illinois Press, 1965.

Flower, Elizabeth, and Murphey, Murray G. *A History of Philosophy in America*. 2 vols. New York: G. P. Putnam's Sons, 1977.

Ford, Thomas. *History of Illinois from its Commencement as a State in 1818 to 1847*. Edited by Milo Milton Quaife. Chicago: Lakeside Press, 1945.

Foulke, William Dudley. *A Random Record of Travel During Fifty Years*. New York: Oxford University Press, 1925.

Furniss, Norman F. *The Mormon Conflict, 1850–1859*. New Haven: Yale University Press, 1960.

Gardner, John H. "Science and the Mormon Quest for Truth." In *One Hundred and Fifty Years: Sesquicentennial Lectures on Mormon Arts, Letters, and Sciences*. Provo, Utah: Harold B. Lee Library Forum Committee, 1980.

Greeley, Horace. *An Overland Journey*. New York, 1860.

Hansen, Klaus J. *Mormonism and the American Experience*. Chicago, London: University of Chicago Press, 1981.

Hatcher, Harlan. *The Western Reserve: The Story of New Connecticut in Ohio*. Indianapolis: Bobbs-Merrill Company, 1949.

Hawthorne, Nathaniel. *Our Old Home and English Notebooks*. New York: Modern Language Association, 1941.

Hayden, A. S. *Early History of the Disciples in the Western Reserve*. Cincinnati: Chase and Hall, 1875.

Hill, Donna. *Joseph Smith, the First Mormon*. Garden City, N.Y.: Doubleday and Company, 1977.

Hill, Marvin S. "Cultural Crisis in the Mormon Kingdom: A Reconsideration of the Causes of Kirtland Dissent." *Church History* 49 (March 1980): 286–97.

______. "The Shaping of the Mormon Mind in New England and New York." *Brigham Young University Studies* 9 (Spring 1969): 351–72.

Hill, Marvin S. et al. *The Kirtland Economy Revisited*. Provo, Utah: Brigham Young University Press, 1977.

Hill, Marvin S.; Rooker, C. Keith; and Wimmer, Larry T. "The Kirtland Economy Revisited: A Market Critique of Sectarian Economics." *Brigham Young University Studies* 17 (Autumn 1977): 394.

Hirshson, Stanley P. *The Lion of the Lord: A Biography of Brigham Young*. New York: Alfred A. Knopf, 1969.

History of Caldwell and Livingston Counties, Missouri. St. Louis: National Historical Company, 1886.

History of Lorain County, Ohio. Philadelphia: Williams Brothers, 1879.

History of Queens County, New York. New York: W. W. Munsell Company, 1882.

Hobsbawm, E. J. *The Age of Revolution 1789–1848*. New York: The New American Library, 1962.

Hogan, Edward R. "Orson Pratt as a Mathematician." *Utah Historical Quarterly* 41 (Winter 1973): 59–68.

Hovenkamp, Herbert. *Science and Religion in America 1800–1860*. Philadelphia: University of Pennsylvania Press, 1978.

Jenson, Andrew. *Church Chronology—A Record of Important Events Pertaining to the History of the Church of Jesus Christ of Latter-day Saints*. 2nd ed. Salt Lake City: Deseret News, 1914.

______. *Latter-day Saint Biographical Encyclopedia: A Compilation of Biographical Sketches of Prominent Men and Women in the Church*. 4 vols. Salt Lake City: Andrew Jenson History Company, 1901–1936.

Josephson, Matthew. *The Politicos 1865.1896*. New York: Harcourt, Brace, and World, 1938.

Kimball, Stanley B. "The Saints and St. Louis, 1831–1857: An Oasis of Tolerance and Security." *Brigham Young University Studies* 13 (Summer 1964): 489–519.

Knight, Sarah Kemble. "A Lady's Travel in New England." In *American History Told by Contemporaries*. 4 vols. Edited by Albert Bushnell Hart, Vol. 2, *Building of the Republic 1689–1783*, p. 228. New York: Macmillan, 1961.

Larson, Andrew Karl. *Erastus Snow: The Life of a Missionary and Pioneer for the Early Mormon Church*. Provo, Utah: Brigham Young University Press, 1971.

______. *I Was Called to Dixie*. Salt Lake City: Deseret News Press, 1961.

Lee, John D. *A Mormon Chronicle: The Diaries of John D. Lee, 1848–1876*. Edited by Robert G. Cleland and Juanita Brooks. San Marino, California: Huntington Library, 1955.

Lyon, T. Edgar. "Nauvoo and the Council of the Twelve." In *The Restoration Movement: Essays in Mormon History*. Edited by F. Mark McKiernan, et al. Lawrence, Kansas: Coronado Press, 1973.

Madsen, Truman G. *Defender of the Faith: The B. H. Roberts Story*. Salt Lake City: Bookcraft, 1980.

Matthews, Robert J. *"A Plainer Translation": Joseph Smith's Translation of the Bible: A History and Commentary*. Provo, Utah: Brigham Young University Press, 1975.

McConkie, Bruce R. *Mormon Doctrine* 2d. ed. rev. Salt Lake City: Bookcraft, 1966.

McCosh, James. *The Scottish Philosophy, Biographical, Expository, Critical, from Hutcheson to Hamilton*. New York: Robert Carter and Brothers, 1874.

McMurrin, Sterling M. *The Theological Foundations of the Mormon Religion*. Salt Lake City: University of Utah Press, 1965.

______. Foreword to *Joseph Smith, the Prophet-Teacher*, by B. H. Roberts. Princeton: Deseret Club of Princeton University, 1967.

Mill, John Stuart. *On Liberty*. London: Oxford University Press, 1969.

Moran, Benjamin. *Journal of Benjamin Moran 1857–1865*. 2 vols. Edited by Sarah Agnes Wallace and Frances Elma Gillespie. Chicago: University of Chicago Press, 1949. Vol. 2.

Muller, H. N. et al. "Jedidiah Burchard and Vermont's New Measure Revivals," *Vermont History* 46 (Winter 1978): 1.

Nelson, Nels. *Scientific Aspects of Mormonism*. New York: G. P. Putnam's Sons, 1904.

Nichols, Roy F. *Franklin Pierce: Young Hickory of the Granite Hills*. Philadelphia. University of Pennsylvania Press, 1931.

Numbers, Ronald L. *Creation by Natural Law: Laplace's Nebular Hypothesis in American Thought*. Seattle: University of Washington Press, 1977.

O'Dea, Thomas F. *The Mormons*. Chicago: University of Chicago Press, 1957.

Olson, Earl E. "The Chronology of the Ohio Revelations." *Brigham Young University Studies* 11 (Autumn 1971): 333.

Olson, Richard. *Scottish and British Physics 1750–1880: A Study in the Foundations of the Victorian Scientific Style*. Princeton: Princeton University Press, 1975.

"Orson Pratt's Harem." *New York Herald*, 18 May 1877. Typescript in possession of author.

Otto, Rudolf. *The Idea of the Holy: An Inquiry into the Non-Rational Factor in the Idea of the Divine and its Relation to the Rational*. Translated by John W. Harvey, New York: Oxford University Press, 1958.

Parkin, Max H. "Missouri's Impact on the Church." *Ensign* 9 (April 1979): 60.

Parrington, Vernon L. *Main Currents in American Thought: The Colonial Mind*. New York: Harcourt, Brace and World, 1954.

Parrington, Vernon L. *Main Currents in American Thought: The Romantic Revolution in America 1800–1860*. New York: Harcourt, Brace and World, 1954.

Paul, E. Robert. "Early Mormon Intellectuals: Parley P. and Orson Pratt, A Response." *Dialogue: A Journal of Mormon Thought* 15 (Autumn 1982): 42–48.

The Pearl of Great Price. Salt Lake City: The Church of Jesus Christ of Latter-day Saints, 1981.

Philbrick, Francis S. *The Rise of the West 1754–1830*. New York: Harper and Row, 1966.

Piercy, Frederick Hawkins. *Route from Liverpool to Great Salt Lake Valley*. Edited by Fawn M. Brodie, Cambridge, Mass.: Harvard University Press, 1962.

Pledge, H. T. *Science Since 1500: A Short History of Mathematics, Physics, Chemistry, and Biology*. New York: Harper and Row, 1959.

Pratt, Milando. "Life and Labors of Orson Pratt." In *The Contributor*. Salt Lake City: Deseret News Company, 12 (November 1890–October 1891): 1–12.

Pratt, Orson. "History of Orson Pratt." *Deseret News Weekly* 8 (1858); reprinted in *Millennial Star* 27 (21 October 1865).

______. "How to Warn the Whole British Nation in One Year." *Millennial Star* 12 (1 February 1850), 40–41.

Pratt, Parley P. *Autobiography of Parley P. Pratt*. 4th ed., edited by Parley P. Pratt, Jr. Salt Lake City: Deseret Book, 1950.

______. *Key to the Science of Theology*. Liverpool: F. D. Richards, 1855.

______. *The Millennium and Other Poems: To Which is Annexed a Treatise on the Regeneration and Eternal Duration of Matter*. New York: W. Molineaux, 1840.

______. *Mormonism Unveiled: Zion's Watchman Unmasked, and its Editor, Mr. L. R. Sunderland, Exposed: Truth Vindicated: The Devil and Priestcraft in Danger!* New York, 1838.

Pratt, Parley P. to Joseph Smith, Jr., 23 May 1837. Quoted in Richard Livesey, *An Exposure of Mormonism, Being a Statement of Facts Relating to the Self-styled 'Latter Day Saints' and the Origin of the Book of Mormon*, p. 9. Preston, England: J. Livesey, 1838.

Pratt, Steven. "Eleanor McLean and the Murder of Parley P. Pratt." *Brigham Young University Studies* 15 (Winter 1975): 225–56.

Quinn, D. Michael. "The Council of Fifty and Its Members, 1844–1945." *Brigham Young University Studies* 20 (Spring 1980): 163–97.

______. "The Evolution of the Presiding Quorums of the LDS Church." *Journal of Mormon History* 1 (1974): 21–38.

______. "Latter-day Prayer Circles." *Brigham Young University Studies* 19 (Fall 1978): 82–96.

"Records of Early Church Families." *Utah Genealogical and Historical Magazine* 27 (July 1936): 110–24.

Remy, Jules, and Brenchley, Julius. *A Journey to Great-Salt-Lake City*. 2 vols. London: W. Jeffs, 1861.
Roberts, B. H. *A Comprehensive History of the Church of Jesus Christ of Latter-day Saints*. 6 vols. Salt Lake City: Deseret News Press, 1930.
______. *The Mormon Doctrine of Deity*. Salt Lake City: Deseret News, 1903.
Russell, Phillips. *Emerson, the Wisest American*. New York: Brentano's, 1929.
Sandeen, Ernest R. "Millennialism." In *The Rise of Adventism*, pp. 104–18. Edited by Edwin S. Gaustad. New York: Harper & Row, 1974.
Satz, Ronald N. *American Indian Policy in the Jacksonian Era*. Lincoln: University of Nebraska Press, 1975.
Schindler, Harold. *Orrin Porter Rockwell: Man of God, Son of Thunder*. 2nd ed. Salt Lake City: University of Utah Press, 1983.
Schopenhauer, Arthur. *The World as Will and Representation*. Translated by E. F. J. Payne, 2 vols. New York: Dover Publications, 1969.
Seward, William F., ed. *Binghamton and Broome County, New York*. 2 vols. New York: Lewis Publishing Company, 1924. Vol. 2, p. 529.
Skabelund, Donald. "Cosmology on the American Frontier: Orson Pratt's Key to the Universe." *Centaurus* 11 (March 1965): 190–204.
Smith, H. P., ed. *History of Broome County*. Syracuse, New York: D. Mason & Company, 1885.
Smith, Joseph. *History of the Church of Jesus Christ of Latter-day Saints*. 7 vols. Edited by B. H. Roberts. Salt Lake City: Deseret Book Company, 1974.
Smith, Joseph Fielding. *Essentials in Church History*. Salt Lake City: Deseret News Press, 1922.
Stanley, Reva. *The Archer of Paradise: A Biography of Parley P. Pratt*. Caldwell, Idaho: Caxton, 1937.
Stegner, Wallace. *The Gathering of Zion: The Story of the Mormon Trail*. New York: McGraw-Hill, 1964.
Stenhouse, T. B. H. *The Rocky Mountain Saints: A Full and Complete History of the Mormons*. New York: D. Appleton and Company, 1873.
Stringham, Guy E. "The Pioneer Roadometer." *Utah Historical Quarterly* 42 (Summer 1974): 258–72.
Stout, Hosea. *On the Mormon Frontier: The Diary of Hosea Stout*. 2 vols. Edited by Juanita Brooks. Salt Lake City: University of Utah Press, 1964.
Thomsen, Dietrick E. "A Knowing Universe Seeking to be Known." *Science News*, February 19, 1983, pp. 124–25.
Tullidge, Edward W. *The History of Salt Lake City and Its Founders*. Salt Lake City: Edward W. Tullidge, 1886.
Tuttle, Daniel S. *Reminiscences of a Missionary Bishop*. New York: Thomas Whittaker, 1906.
Watson, Elden J., ed. *Manuscript History of Brigham Young, 1801–1844*. Salt Lake City: Elden J. Watson, 1968.
Watson, Elden J., ed. *The Orson Pratt Journals*. Salt Lake City: By the editor, 1975.
Wells, Junius F. "Three Orsons." *Improvement Era* 22 (November 1918): 15–18.
Weslager, Clinton A. *The Delaware Indians*. New Brunswick: Rutgers University Press, 1972.
Whitney, Orson F. *History of Utah*. 4 vols. Salt Lake City: George Q. Cannon and Company, 1904.
______. *Life of Heber C. Kimball*. 3rd ed. Salt Lake City: Deseret Book, 1967.
Whittaker, David J. "Orson Pratt: Prolific Pamphleteer." *Dialogue: A Journal of Mormon Thought* 15 (Autumn 1982): 27–41.

Woodruff, Wilford. *Leaves from My Journal.* Salt Lake City: Juvenile Instructor Office, 1881.

Wyl [Wymetal], Wilhelm. *Mormon Portraits, Joseph Smith, the Prophet, His Family and His Friends.* Salt Lake City: Tribune Printing and Publishing Company, 1886.

Young, Brigham. *Diary of Brigham Young, 1857.* Edited by Everett L. Cooley. Salt Lake City: Tanner Trust Fund, University of Utah Library, 1980.

Young, Kimball. *Isn't One Wife Enough?* New York: Henry Holt, 1954.

Young, Levi Edgar. *The Founding of Utah.* New York: Charles Scribner's Sons, 1924.

Youngson, A. J. *The Making of Classical Edinburgh.* Edinburgh: University Press, 1966.

Zucker, Louis C. "Joseph Smith as a Student of Hebrew." *Dialogue: A Journal of Mormon Thought* 3 (Summer 1968): 40–55.

4. *Periodicals*

The Contributor. Salt Lake City: Deseret News Press. 1879–96.

Deseret News. Salt Lake City. 1850–94.

Elders' Journal. Far West, Missouri. 1837–38.

The Ensign of the Church of Jesus Christ of Latter-day Saints. Salt Lake City. 1971–81.

Evening and Morning Star. Independence, Missouri. 1832–34.

Historical Record. Salt Lake City: Andrew Jenson. 1882–90.

Improvement Era. Salt Lake City. 1898–1970.

Latter-day Saints' Messenger and Advocate. Kirtland, Ohio. 1834–37.

Latter-day Saints Millennial Star. Liverpool, London. 1840–91.

New York Messenger. New York. 1845–46.

The Prophet. New York, Boston. 1844–45.

The Return. Davis City, Iowa. 1888–90.

The Salt Lake Tribune. Salt Lake City. 1870–81.

Sangamo Journal. Quincy, Illinois, 1842–43.

Times and Seasons. Nauvoo, Illinois, 1839–46.

Utah Genealogical and Historical Magazine. Salt Lake City. 1910–40.

The Wasp. Nauvoo, Illinois, 1842–43.

5. *Unpublished Studies*

Beesley, Kenneth Reid. "The Dialect of Orson Pratt." Typescript in Church Archives, 1976.

Christensen, William J. "Critical Review of Orson Pratt Senior's Published Scientific Books." M.A. thesis, University of Utah, 1929.

Flake, Joel Alva. "Orson Pratt's Early Life." M.A. thesis, Brigham Young University, 1970.

Hatch, Robert Duane. "The Pratt-Newman Debate." M.A. thesis, Brigham Young University, 1960.

Holland, Jeffrey R. "Analysis of Selected Changes in Major Editions of the Book of Mormon, 1830–1920." M.A. thesis, Brigham Young University, 1966.

Jacob, Edward Grant. "A Bibliography of Orson Pratt Containing Works of and about Orson Pratt." M.A. thesis, Brigham Young University, 1970.

Jones, Edward T. "The Theology of Thomas Dick and its Possible Relationship to that of Joseph Smith." M.A. thesis, Brigham Young University, 1969.

Lyon, T. Edgar. "Orson Pratt—Early Mormon Leader." M.A. thesis, University of Chicago, 1932.

Mendenhall, Bayard. "The Philosophical and Scientific Works of Orson Pratt." Typescript in Church Archives, 1943.

Pond, Diane Burgoyne. "Science, Religion, and Orson Pratt: The Religion of Benjamin Franklin." M.A. thesis, Utah State University, 1967.

Tabone, Paul Robert. "Orson Pratt." M.A. thesis, Brigham Young University, 1969.

Tingey, Joseph Willard. "An Explication of Some Philosophical Aspects of the Thought of Orson Pratt." M.S. thesis, Brigham Young University, 1958.

Van Wagoner, Richard S. "Sarah M. Pratt: The Woman Behind the Controversy." Typescript in possession of Richard S. Van Wagoner, Lehi, Utah, 1984.

Index